D0189935

THE WRITING LIFE

The Writing Life

Writers on How They Think and Work

A COLLECTION

FROM THE

Washington Post Book World

EDITED AND

WITH AN INTRODUCTION

AND COMMENTARY BY

Marie Arana

PUBLICAFFAIRS
New York

Published in the United States by PublicAffairs™,
a member of the Perseus Books Group.

Printed in the United States of America.

BOOK DESIGN AND COMPOSITION BY JENNY DOSSIN.

SET IN ITC STONE SERIF AND ITC STONE SANS.

Library of Congress Cataloging-in-Publication data
The writing life: writers on how they think and work:
a collection from the Washington post book world / edited and with
an introduction and commentary by Marie Arana.— 1st ed.
p. cm.
ISBN 1-58648-149-5
1. Authors, American—20th century—Biography.
2. American literature—20th century—History and criticism—Theory, etc.
3. English literature—20th century—History and criticism—Theory, etc.
4. Authors, English—20th century—Biography.
5. Authorship.
I. Arana, Marie. II. Washington post (Washington, D.C.:1974)
PS225 .W734 2003
810.9'0054—dc21
2002036744

FIRST EDITION

1 3 5 7 9 10 8 6 4 2

For Donald E. Graham,

A LOVER OF BOOKS

CONTENTS

INTRODUCTION BY MARIE ARANA xiii

PART ONE: ON BECOMING A WRITER

The Seduction of the Text 3
Francine Du Plessix Gray

The Importance of Childhood 11
Joyce Carol Oates

Looking for the Spark 19
Joanna Trollope

How to Identify and Nurture Young Writers 25
James Michener

Touched by an Angel 33
Mary Higgins Clark

The Leap from Necessity to Invention 39
John Keegan

A Real-Life Education 46
Susan Minot

Emerging from Under Your Rejection Slips 52
Muriel Spark

Being a Product of Your Dwelling Place 58
Nadine Gordimer

Doing It for Love 64
Erica Jong

Part Two: Raw Material

Too Happy for Words 73
Alice McDermott

Using My Father's Story 78
Craig Nova

Between Origins and Art 84
George P. Pelecanos

The Writer As Outlaw 90
Jayne Anne Phillips

From Memory to the Imagination 95
Ntozake Shange

Can Whites Write About Blacks? 103
Scott Turow

In Praise of Silence 111
John Edgar Wideman

Bicultural, Adrift, and Wandering 118
Anita Desai

On Finding a Latino Voice 126
Julia Alvarez

Living in Irish, Writing in English 134
John Banville

Part Three: Hunkering Down

Holidays at the Keyboard Inn 143
Wendy Wasserstein

The Passionate Researcher 150
Patricia Cornwell

From Packrat to Historian 156
Stanley Karnow

Climbing Into Another Head 162
David McCullough

Hunter of Metaphors 168
Ray Bradbury

Following the Script 178
Edmund Morris

Headbirths: Bookish Midwifery 184
Michael Korda

Guided by Voices: The Work of a Ghostwriter 194
David Chanoff

Part Four: Old Bottle, New Wine

From Will-of-the-Wisp to Full-Blown Novel 205
E. L. Doctorow

Reincarnation, Translation and Adventure 212
Umberto Eco

Master of My Universe 221
Stanley Elkin

Sounds and Sensibilities 228
Ned Rorem

Writer with Scalpel 235
Richard Selzer

A Chronicle of the Plague Years 242
Reynolds Price

On Being a Novice Playwright 250
Cynthia Ozick

Acting Out, Letting Go 258
Gloria Naylor

Pen Names Galore 264
Donald E. Westlake

Summer Lite 270
Barbara Mertz

Part Five: Facing the Facts

History Is Their Beat: The New Journalist Historians 279
David Halberstam

A Novel Approach to Reality: Basing a Story in Facts 289
Dominick Dunne

Making the Truth Believable 297
Tracy Kidder

Describing the World As It Is, Not As It Would Be 304
Carl Sagan

The Political Memoir: Taking Note of History 312
George P. Shultz

President in Search of a Publisher 322
Jimmy Carter

Biographer, Get a Life 330
Stacy Schiff

From the Clinic 338
Kay Redfield Jamison

Notes from the Road 344
Jonathan Raban

Natural Selections 351
E. O. Wilson

Speaking Up for the Environment 359
Bill McKibben

Part Six: Looking Back

The Trouble with Finishing 367
Frances FitzGerald

The Hardest Critics 373
Carol Shields

Literary Executions 380
Julian Barnes

Taking It All Back 387
Jane Smiley

Writer, Be Afraid 393
Michael Chabon

In Search of the Next Idea 399
Ward Just

INTRODUCTION

BY MARIE ARANA

"A poem," Robert Frost once wrote in a letter to a friend, "begins as a lump in the throat . . . a homesickness." So it was for this series, The Writing Life, which began for me—quite simply—as a bout of nostalgia. It was 1993, a few months after I had joined *The Washington Post's Book World*, and despite being in the company of 2 of the best critics in the country—Michael Dirda and Jonathan Yardley—I genuinely missed working as I had before with authors, "real" writers, individuals who for one reason or another choose to work in solitude, struggling against oblivion, spilling their hearts and minds onto endlessly blank pages, often for meager recognition and pay.

Before joining *The Post*, I had spent 15 years as a book editor for Harcourt Brace Jovanovich and Simon & Schuster, and the crossover from creative to critical, from publishing to reviewing, was—in its own small way—nothing short of defection. An editor in a publishing house toils behind closed doors in intimate contact with no one so much as the author she is publishing; because the process from acquisition to finished volume can take as long as 5 years or more, her gross annual product is scant—10 to 15 books, perhaps. An editor at a major newspaper's book review, on the other hand, works with legions of reviewers, surveys a broad rush of forthcoming books, publishes almost every day, and accomplishes all amid the busy collegiality of a newsroom. There is a natural opposition here: The editor who makes books feels the critic is her natural enemy, that the critic is very possibly a cretin, doesn't read books properly, and only rarely understands them. The book review editor feels that people who work for publishers are gluttons, far more interested in profits than excellence—that there are far too many books published, and that not many of them are very good.

My notion was to find some way to continue to function in both worlds—an impossible hope, really, given the remove at which an honest book critic must labor. But that hope, nevertheless, ended up bearing the fruit of an idea: Why not invite seasoned writers to mull about their craft, address the singular ways they approach the challenges of writing and thereby give *Book World* readers some insights into the creative process? Why not accompany those essays with short profiles, sidebars that characterized the writers' personalities and briefly listed their works? The utterly selfish motive on my part was to keep a foot on the other side of the fence, to remind myself as often as possible that the writing of books is an excruciatingly difficult enterprise. It is not easy to focus one's intelligence and go about the business of stringing words together, one by one, thousands at a time, until a full-fledged, well-executed book emerges. I asked my colleagues in *Book World* whether such a series about the *writing* of books would interest them. Their immediate willingness to let me give it a try resulted in the launching of The Writing Life, the first ongoing series of its kind in any major American newspaper.

At the heart of this exercise were some important convictions about how good writing—no matter what its category—gets learned and done. What you are about to discover, in this impressive cavalcade of confessionals, is that everyone does it a different way. There is no one way to approach the writing of a book, unless, of course, you are producing pulp—cookie-cutter versions of the same thing. If you strive to become a real writer, an original, you need to be told clearly: There is no magic formula. Someone can teach you to formulate a good sentence; someone can teach you to do the legwork, build evidence, fashion persuasive arguments, connect the dots. But if readers carry away one lesson from this book it should be that writers learn their craft, above all, from the work of other writers. From reading. They learn it from immersing themselves in books. They do not learn it from classrooms, or workshops, or manuals—they cannot be programmed to perform. It is, in essence, lonely work; isolation is what they must learn to savor. Perhaps they will have been encouraged along the way by a single, pivotal person; perhaps they will have learned perseverance after much rejection; perhaps they will get the recognition of readers and peers. Come what may, they must go to their desks alone.

For all the experience I had had with writers, first at publishing houses and then at *Book World*, I could not appreciate the full contours of a writing life until I had gone into my study, closed the door, sat down and tried to write a book myself. Editing books and judging them do not necessarily qualify one for the task. If anything, the critical professions emphatically do not prepare you to write a book of your own. I found that out a few years ago when I decided to give it a try. Initially I was unable to take off my editorial hat and surrender myself to the creative business of writing. I was hesitant, intensely critical, clogged up by the analytical. How can that be? you say. How can an editor who guides writers and helps them shape ideas—not to mention a book review editor whose job is to decide how well they've done it—how can that person *not* be capable of putting together a book? The answer reveals something about the process: You cannot write books with a critical head. You cannot produce good prose if you are the skeptic, scouring every line for the false note, the exaggeration, the argument that doesn't persuade.

It was during this preparatory period that the essays in this series assumed particular importance to me. I recalled the similar insecurities of so many writers represented here and the strategies that enabled them to write. There was Wendy Wasserstein's counsel: Go to a far, secluded place; live in pajamas. Edmund Morris's advice: Find a good pen, get physical with words. Cynthia Ozick's warning: Reading and writing are like "getting born or dying, you are obliged to do it alone." So there I sat—in a room, as far away as I could get—in my pajamas, with a pen in hand. The editor's hat was gone, the critic's sneer in a drawer; I was ready to be the fool.

The hat and sneer came in handy later—once I'd written the first draft. It was then I needed to slap myself around, give the manuscript a hard time, and I was glad to have been a former editor. But I had learned something I'd never known: No amount of study, or work in the field, could prepare me for facing the page alone.

Of course, that is the point of this book. Writers create themselves. They are pulled from potential to realization, discovered not taught. To educate—*educere* in the root Latin—means quite literally "to bring out." The process of being brought out, of developing an innate capacity, of realizing that you harbor an overwhelming impulse to write things down, is touched on again and again by writers in this book. If you are willing to be led from within—if you are willing to allow your most rigorous teacher to be a clear, well-written page—perhaps you will discover the spark of a talent that was there all along.

Does everybody have that same spark? Of course not. What do crime novelist George Pelecanos and historian David McCullough—both contributors here—have in common? They cannot write except in their own way. It is precisely because everyone does it differently that good writing is difficult to teach. You cannot capture it, manufacture it, pass it on. The good news is that there are so many ways to be a writer. In this collection, 55 writers impart something about the very particular ways they think and work.

The first essay in the Writing Life series, published in April 1993, was written by the inimitable Stanley Elkin, one of the most original and underappreciated American writers of the 20th century. Elkin argued that a novelist may be incapable of being political, but he will make up for it by ruling his characters with all the relish of a tin-pot dictator. For 10 years after Elkin's premiere, different writers were invited to explore a great variety of subjects. E. L. Doctorow described how a novel could spring from a mere phrase: The words "loon lake," glimpsed on a road sign, were so mesmerizing to him that he built a 300-page story around them. Umberto Eco confessed that his translator's versions were, very possibly, improvements on his own. Carl Sagan reflected on the demands of nonfiction, laying down a strict imperative: Science writers must record the world as it is, not as they would have it be. In this collection, you will encounter novelists, biographers, historians—yes—but you will also find an American president, a secretary of state, a celebrated entomologist, a psychiatrist, a surgeon, a classical composer, a lawyer, an astrophysicist, a ghostwriter of the famous—each telling how he or she relates to the craft. Suffice it to say, this volume accommodates a dizzying variety of styles and straddles a great many subjects. To better explain the perspectives, I've prefaced each essay with a brief profile of the writer's career.

As impressively populated as this book is, it would not have come to pass if it weren't for a good many more people behind the scenes. I want to thank the staff of *Book World* for sponsoring the series month in, month out, for a decade and running. They are, in alphabetical order: Jabari Asim, Michael Dirda, Dennis Drabelle, Jay Fernandez, Jennifer Howard, Nina King, Chris Lehmann, Mary Morris, David Nicholson, Christopher Schoppa, Zofia Smardz, Ednamae Storti, Kunio Francis Tanabe and Jonathan Yardley. Mary Morris deserves particular thanks for doggedly tracking down each participant to get the necessary permissions. Kelly Doe gave us a beautiful cover design.

I am grateful to *The Washington Post*'s managing editor, Steve Coll, for his direct involvement in facilitating the publication of this book; to legal counsel Megan Rupp for ironing out the permissions conundrums; to executive editor Len Downie, for his hearty support at all times; and to our publisher, Boisfeuillet Jones Jr., and corporate president, Donald E. Graham, for their very evident love of books.

At PublicAffairs, our editor, Kate Darnton, was gracious and unflaggingly enthusiastic; our publisher, the tireless, admirable Peter Osnos, has been a rock.

Here, then, is the writing life in all its diversity. Culled from hundreds of essays, it represents a 10-year effort to bridge the divide between doing and judging—between creativity and criticism. May it be as instructive to you as it has been for me.

Washington, D.C., May 2003

THE WRITING LIFE

I

On Becoming a Writer

Francine Du Plessix Gray

Joyce Carol Oates

Joanna Trollope

James Michener

Mary Higgins Clark

John Keegan

Susan Minot

Muriel Spark

Nadine Gordimer

Erica Jong

Francine du Plessix Gray

The name itself does much to describe her: the contrapuntal sounds that suggest her far-flung provenance. Then there is her expression—strong, yet filled with enough wonder to betray a finely tuned femininity. But it is her voice that says the most about her: deep, earthy and so in love with words that her syllables roll up against one another like Vouvray on a vintner's tongue.

She was born in Warsaw in 1930, the daughter of French diplomat Bertrand du Plessix and famed Russian beauty Tatiana Iacovleva. Raised in a genteel but impoverished home, Tatiana, as a child, recited poetry on the street corners of Penza, reeling off Pushkin and Lermontov in exchange for bread and potatoes. In 1926, as the result of a bout with tuberculosis, Tatiana emigrated to Paris with her family, and it was there that the legendary Mayakovsky, Russia's poet of the revolution, fell in love with her. When she married du Plessix, it is said that she broke Mayakovsky's heart.

Shortly before Francine's 10th birthday in 1940, Bertrand du Plessix answered de Gaulle's appeal for a Free France. He boarded a French airplane in Casablanca to join the resistance, but was shot down over Gibraltar and killed.

Two years later Tatiana married a Kiev-born childhood friend, Alexander Liberman, and with young Francine in tow, they headed for a new life in New York. Tatiana was soon sewing hats at Bendel's to make ends meet. Liberman embarked on an artistic career that would catapult him from unknown painter to executive at Vogue and finally to editorial director of Conde Nast.

Fluent in Russian and French, du Plessix Gray did not begin to learn English until the age of 12, when she was accepted at the Spence School on full scholarship. Within a year she had won the school's spelling bee. A solitary, sickly child—even partially deaf at one point—she spent much of her time reading: Dostoevsky by 14; Kierkegaard by 15. Before long she was editing the school paper. She did so well in English, in fact, that her family was accused of faking their refugee status in order to win her the scholarship to Spence.

Du Plessix enrolled at Bryn Mawr, but finished college at Barnard. Upon her graduation in 1952, she passionately wanted to study theology but decided she needed to free herself from her "powerful and seductive parents." She got herself a room and work as a writer on the night shift of UPI's radio desk.

She attributes her decision to write to two summer sessions she spent at Black Mountain College in North Carolina. And indeed the group congregated there in 1952 would have been a powerful inducement to the arts: John Cage, Merce Cunningham, Robert Rauschenberg, Robert Motherwell, Ben Shahn and du Plessix's mentor, Charles Olson, among others. "I worked in the fields with them, I did dishes with them, I got to know them, and they taught me rebellion," she says. Since then, her writerly life has been "a tension—a dialectic—between rebellion and community." Balancing herself between a fierce sense of feminism and a "deeply entwined" devotion to family, she began writing seriously.

In 1956 she met the artist Cleve Gray, to whom she was married one year later and by whom she has two sons. Throughout their marriage they have lived in the same house in Cornwall Bridge, Conn.

Du Plessix Gray is the author of three novels: *Lovers and Tyrants*, 1976; *World Without End*, 1981; and *October Blood*, 1985. But she is most recognized for her nonfiction books: *Divine Disobedience: Profiles in Catholic Radicalism*, 1970; *Hawaii: The Sugar-Coated Fortress*, 1972; *Adam and Eve in the City*, 1987; *Soviet Women*, 1990. *Rage and Fire*, a biography of Flaubert's mistress Louise Colet, was published in 1994, when this essay was written. "Flaubert burned Colet's letters," she says intensely, "2,000 pages of them. Guy de Maupassant was called to Flaubert's house to help him do it, get rid of them—fulfill his sense of propriety." It was her outrage over that effacement, says du Plessix Gray, that drove her to reconstruct the life of Colet.

So impassioned is du Plessix Gray about "what abject depths love can push us to" that her next book, *At Home with the Marquise de Sade*, was on a variation of that theme—a biography of the Marquise de Sade, an extraordinary woman whose love for the revolutionary de Sade eventually engulfed her own notions of decency and decorum. Rebellion and family. Grit and grace. Women and the lengths they will go for men. Du Plessix Gray's obsessions are as eclectic and beguiling as her name.

M. A.

The Seduction of the Text

BY FRANCINE DU PLESSIX GRAY

For some years now, whenever I've been asked to teach the craft of writing, I've told my prospective hosts that I would consider their invitation, on one condition: that the term "creative"—a word so stagnated by overuse that it should be confined to naming goldfish—be excluded from the title of my course. By way of clarification, I state my belief that the phrase "Creative Writing" and the very institution of "Creative Writing" departments uphold a myth that may have done more harm to young Americans than all the marijuana in Mexico: the illusion that there are certain genres of writing that are more "creative" than others and that fiction is the most "creative" of prose genres.

If the host institution accedes to my cranky request—splendid! Be it a three-day seminar or a semester's, I give my course a stark little title such as "The Writing of the Text" and proceed to organize my remarks around four central principles:

- Keep Your Sentences Erotic
- Create a Pact of Trust
- Strive for Muscle
- Rebel Against the Tyranny of Genre.

I'm a nuts-and-bolts teacher, and long before tackling narrative line or character development, I focus on the sound-bytes of diction, on the crafting of euphonious and pellucid phrases. So before my apprentices have even come into the classroom I've written several sentences on the blackboard to illustrate my points. One of them is always taken from Nabokov's memoir of his youth in pre-Revolutionary Russia, *Speak Memory*, and goes as follows:

"She turned on the steps to look back at me before descending into a jasmine-scented, cricket-mad dusk of a small train station."

The other—from Agee's *Let Us Now Praise Famous Men*—is a portrait of two young Appalachian sharecroppers during the depression years of the 1930s:

"The young man's eyes had the opal lightings of dark oil and . . . fed too strongly inward to draw to a focus: whereas those of the young woman had each the splendor of a monstrance, and were brass."

Axiom One: What do these two sentences have in common? I ask my class, hoping to elicit the following answers: They each have that central attribute of great prose—a tonality and rhythm so flawless that no one syllable can be altered without radically upsetting the dynamics of the phrase. They each communicate, with eerie immediacy, the pitch of the author's central theme—Nabokov's, the pain of severance from a society irretrievably doomed; Agee's, the tragic isolation of the dispossessed. But above all they captivate us by their vigor and freshness, by their never-before-seenness ("cricket-mad dusk," "opal lightings"). And compare their erotic impact, dear class, their sheer sexiness, to the clichés of pulp fiction ("trembling mouth," "glittering eyes")—banalities that act like saltpeter on the lust of any intelligent reader because of their tyrannical staleness, their violent predictability. So think of each word as a potential spouse or lover, I tell my recruits: We can only avoid bromides and platitudes by combating the embrace of all words that are too long married, by struggling against any form of verbal missionary positions.

Axiom Two: The Pact of Trust. Erotic strategies, I next tell my novices, remain central to the covenant of trust that must be forged between reader and author, for it is very similar to the relationship evolved by happy lovers. These two kinds of pacts share the same trait: In order not to become tediously predictable, a good writer, like a good lover, must create a pact of trust with the object of his/her seduction that remains qualified, paradoxically, by a good measure of uncertainty, mystery and surprise.

At no moment in the writing of prose are these tactics more crucial than in the beginnings of our writings, for it is in our very first phrases, that I, potentially all-powerful author, must convince you—potentially captive reader—that I am a worthy object of your attention, trust and literary lust. And as in all skillful acts of seduction, my challenge is to create a tension, in my initial approach to you, between the promise of gratification and the refined delay of that gratification—to intimate how much information I shall offer and how much I shall withhold. In sum, writers must practice, with impeccable craft, the techniques of verbal foreplay.

Take, for instance, the first lines of Flannery O'Connor's story "The Geranium:"

> Old Dudley folded into the chair he was gradually molding to his own shape and looked out the window fifteen feet away into another window framed by blackened red brick. He was waiting for the geranium.

How much is offered, and how much is withheld! We're instantly led to infer the entire mood of the community Old Dudley lives in—

hemmed in, claustrophobic and most clearly south of the Mason-Dixon Line. And yet we're urgently pressed to read on because of the eerie ominousness of that staccato phrase—"He was waiting for the geranium"—which follows the mellifluous, long-limbed rhythm of the first sentence. O'Connor has set up a wealth of appetites in us that we yearn to fulfill, and she lures us all the more by her intimation of uncertainty. Like an ideal lover—like that archetypal storyteller Scheherazade—the author has immediately let us know that she will offer us just as much sensory information as she needs to seduce us without offering us enough ever to sate us.

Axiom Three: Strive for Muscle. Few writers seem to avoid the erotic nature of their craft. I am struck by how the masters tend to describe their working process through scatological or sexual metaphors: Avoid "pissless" prose, William Gass warns us, phrases that are cautious, voiceless, timid; do not civilize your requests too much; it is the energy of our reprisal against reality that will give our sentences the muscle, physicality, gait they need to come to life. "Thoroughbred horses and thoroughbred styles have plenty of blood in their veins," Flaubert writes, "and it can be seen pulsing everywhere in them, under the skin and the words—Life, Life, to have erections! Nothing else matters!"

So I go again to the blackboard to illustrate the potential gait, piss, pulse of a good prose sentence—this from George Orwell's *Down and Out in Paris and London*:

> By seven I was in the desolation of the cold, filthy kitchen, with the potato skins and bones and fishtails stuck together in their grease waiting littered on the floor, and a pile of plates, stuck together in their grease, waiting from overnight.

How much we learn from the ruthless repetition of "waiting" and "stuck together in their grease"—the olfactory, tactile, visual precision of the desolate scene! On to my last precept:

Axiom Four: Rebel Against the Tyranny of Genre. I hope we've had some good times, I tell my novices on our last days together, but I shall end on a pugnacious note: I wish to state my great unease toward the very nature of classes such as the one we've just shared. For I have met too many students who can glibly discuss Voice, Mimetic Strategy or Narrative Dislocation but are tone-deaf to the euphonies of prose and are incapable of lucidly communicating a smell, or a texture, or even the lineaments of a face or place. And I fear that too many of the writing programs currently thriving at our universities might be shooting out, with the speed of tennis-ball machines, a new breed of fiction-scribblers who are groveling for the glitz of being labeled "creative writers" but have never glanced at Homer or Sir Thomas Browne or Agee's *Let Us Now Praise Famous Men*. And I despair that instead of learning to be admirable readers—the first step in becoming a decent writer—these misguided souls might merely be mastering the technical tricks of the narrative trade, and barking them out like contestants at a dog show, with a sole eye to marketability. This is a trend that Flannery O'Connor already detected in the last year of her life—the late 1960s—when, reflecting on the growing vogue for writing workshops, she stated: "Any idiot with a nickel's worth of talent can emerge from a writing class able to write a competent story. In fact so many people can now write competent stories that the short story as a medium is dying of competence."

Furthermore: I remind all my students that, like the majority of the prose samples I have drummed into them during our days together—Agee's and Orwell's journalism, Nabokov's memoir—some of the greatest American prose, in past years, is found in nonfiction works seldom taught in creative writing programs, or in hybrid forms that defy all classifications: Norman Mailer's *The Executioner's Song*, Elizabeth Hardwick's *Sleepless Nights*, Philip Roth's *Patrimony*, Susan Sontag's meditations on illness, Janet Malcolm's reflections on Sylvia Plath. I convey to my young colleagues my own excessive passion for the reading and practice of fiction, which has kindled my life's most elating moments, and my rueful acceptance of the fact that we cannot choose fiction, for it can only choose us. And in case they, too, might suffer from the inconstancy of the Fictional Muse, I comfort them with the prospect that in the best examples of nonfiction, there occurs some fertile act of the imagination, some alchemy upon the phonemes of our diction, some subtle handling of ellipses, metaphors and particularly sound values that can transform our texts into far greater art than 99 percent of the fiction titles published in the past years. Or as Yeats put it best, "Only the singer matters, not the song."

So good-bye, dear class, and Godspeed. Read voraciously, keep the reader seduced and never worry about what "category" your texts might fall into. The world, alas, will pigeonhole you before you know it, griping and caviling when you stray from the niche into which they've glued you. For the time being each of you is free to gambol and frolic in the delectable, Lord-given fields of human language. How we envy you.

February 13, 1994

Joyce Carol Oates

How foolish to attempt a description of one of the most prolific writers alive today in a space as diminutive as this.

Joyce Carol Oates is an engine of the word: By 59, when she wrote the following essay, she was the author of almost 70 published books, not to mention hundreds of short stories, poems and essays scattered through a wide range of publications. Her archive at Syracuse University then boasted a gargantuan "4,000 pages of journal, 5,000 letters, 50,000 pages of manuscripts and typescripts, and 920 volumes of published books and periodicals." And it only housed materials gathered after 1973, when she already had 18 books to her name.

She is the daughter of middle-school dropouts. Her father was a tool and die maker in a General Motors factory, her mother the child of a murdered man, her sister institutionalized with autism. Growing up in rural New York, she never expected to become a literary giant. But all that changed when she was handed a rickety typewriter at the age of 14.

She is often asked why her work is so explicit, a question she finds ignorant and insulting. "It's so sexist . . . I can scarcely reply."

And she is endlessly asked why she writes so much. "Well, I think that's sexist too," she chirps. Henry James wrote close to 100 volumes, Balzac more than 90, Trollope 130. A woman attempts that scale, and "it is made to seem wrong."

Her writing is not effortless. "I work hard," she says. She writes by hand, starting stories countless times, making comments as she goes, often producing as many as 1,000 pages of notes for every 250 printed pages. *Bellefleur* (1980), which has been characterized as springing from a dream, "took lots of work," with charts and graphs and heavy engineering. "When people accuse me of writing easily, I can't imagine what they mean."

Her novel *American Appetites* had 3,000 pages of worksheets. *You*

Must Remember This had 3,500 pages of side notes. *My Heart Laid Bare*, 5,000 pages. "If I knew how hard I'd have to work each time, I couldn't do it," she says in her small, tentative voice.

In 1995 she published *Zombie*. In 1996: *We Were the Mulvaneys*.

But most recently, she produced a highly acclaimed novel based on the life of Marilyn Monroe, *Blonde* (2001), and another about a predatory college professor in an apparently idyllic college town, *Beasts* (2002). In 1997, just before she wrote this essay, she had issued *Man Crazy*, a novel about women who find comfort in abuse. ("A bit like me," says Oates. "I get nervous when I'm treated well.") Ah, well then, maybe we can cut this introductory tribute down to size.

M. A.

The Importance of Childhood

BY JOYCE CAROL OATES

It is easy to work when the soul is at play.

EMILY DICKINSON

We begin as children by imagining and fearing ghosts. By degrees, through our long lives, we come to be the very ghosts haunting the lost landscapes of our childhood.

My love of writing grew out of my love of reading, with which my very life is identified. I can't imagine a mental life, a spiritual existence, not inextricably bound up with language of a formal, mediated nature. Telling stories, choosing an appropriate language with which to express each story: This seems to me quintessentially human, one of the great adventures of our species. For me, reading and writing were developed when I was between the ages of 5 and 10, attending a one-room schoolhouse in rural Niagara County, about

25 miles north of Buffalo, N.Y., in the years 1943–1948. I took for granted what seems wonderful to me now, that this was the school that my mother, Carolina Bush, had attended 20 years before, and that, apart from the introduction of electricity and a few minor improvements, not including indoor plumbing, the school had hardly changed in the intervening years. It was a rough-hewn, weather-worn, uninsulated clapwood building on a crude stone foundation, across the Tonawanda Creek from the tiny crossroads called Millersport, where my family lived (and still lives). I loved my first school!—so I've many times said, and so perhaps it was.

How vividly I see Rural District School #7, Niagara County, N.Y., in my memory. It was set back in a field off an unpaved road called the Tonawanda Creek Road, which became impassable after snowstorms. It had disproportionately high windows, a steep-slanted shingled roof, and a shed-like space at the front called the "entry," where our coats and boots were kept. There was nothing so romantic as a cupola with a ringing bell to summon us inside: Our teacher rang a bell vigorously by hand, and I can remember the grim and determined set of Mrs. Dietz's face as she stood, a stocky, big-boned woman, in the entry doorway ringing this bell, this visible symbol of her precarious authority. (Some of her older male pupils were as tall and big-boned as she.) Behind the school was the deep, swift-running Tonawanda Creek; on either side of the school were wild, uncultivated fields. "Out back" was our euphemism for the crudely built wooden outhouses (boys' to the left, girls' to the right) with their drainage, raw sewage, into the creek. (To be dragged terrified, desperately resisting, in the direction of the boys' outhouse, to the accompaniment of collective jeering and laughter, was a nightmare experience for younger girls unprotected by older brothers and sisters.)

Inside was a single room that seemed, when I was in first grade, cavernous. In fact, it was modest: There were only about 35 desks arranged in five rows, attached at their bottoms by runners, like toboggans; the smaller desks were at the front. My memory of several desks that were assigned to me is both visual and tactile: The wood was of the smoothness and burnished-stained hue of horse chestnuts, but covered in scars made by jackknives and the sharp points of compasses, every sort of inked initial and design. Generations of schoolchildren must have left their marks on these desks. Across the front of the room was a blackboard at one end of which an American flag hung dispirited with dust and above which were cardboard squares displaying the alphabet in both printed letters and graceful Palmer script that we were to emulate. The floor was made of untreated planks through whose cracks cold air steadily sifted upward.

A special set of talents and temperament must have been required to be a teacher in a one-room country schoolhouse in those days. Not only was it Mrs. Dietz's task to lead eight very disparate grades through their lessons each day, but to maintain a modicum of discipline in the classroom, where many, perhaps most, of the older boys attended school grudgingly and had to be prevented from brutally "teasing" (the harsher term "harassing" hadn't yet been invented) those weaker than themselves. Mrs. Dietz was also required to heroically maintain the wood-burning stove, the school's sole source of heat in that pitiless upstate New York climate in which below-zero (Fahrenheit) temperatures were common on winter mornings. Some of us had to wear mittens through the day and stamp our booted feet to keep our toes from freezing. Yet I remember loving school hours: reading aloud, spelling aloud, diagramming sentences and doing arithmetic problems on the blackboard, being allowed to read books from the several shelves that constituted the school's "library"—these were, for me, privileged moments. (In our farmhouse in Millersport there were few books; both my parents, growing up in the Depression, had had to quit school at about eighth grade to go to work. But one memorable Christmas my grandmother gave me an illustrated edition of Lewis Carroll's *Alice in Wonderland* and *Through the Looking-Glass*, which made an enormous impression on me at the age of 8.)

As a younger child, pre-dating school, when I couldn't yet read or write, I'd composed "books" in tablet form, dealing with the adventures of awkwardly drawn chickens and cats with captions in flamboyant scrawls in mimicry of adult handwriting. (Maybe I'd imagined this was handwriting.) The earliest stories I wrote must have been imitations of stories out of our school readers and library books; I recall being intrigued by Edgar Allan Poe's "The Tell-Tale Heart," which I could not have known was a masterpiece of 19th-century American Gothic literature, and stumbling through the far less accessible "The Gold Bug"; I was an avid, uncritical and impractical reader, struggling long hours over the obdurate prose of Washington Irving, Nathaniel Hawthorne, Ralph Waldo Emerson and Henry David Thoreau. If *Huckleberry Finn* was available, or the poetry of Emily Dickinson, Walt Whitman or Robert Frost, I don't recall encountering it. We were made to memorize poems of a pious, didactic, discouragingly "feminine" nature, and 50 years later I'm still haunted by the reproachful lines of a Charles Kingsley poem:

Be good, sweet maid,
And let those who will, be clever.
Do lovely things, not dream them all day long.
And so make Life, Death, and that For Ever
One grand, sweet song.

I still feel a vague tinge of guilt knowing that I probably did grow up more clever than good; as a "sweet maid," I've been a disappointment.

Franz Kafka has famously said that a book is an ax for the frozen sea within. How more accurate to see any artwork as a portal of a kind through which we step, like Alice through the looking-glass, into worlds not our own and unimaginable by us, conjoining ourselves with persons not known to us. In the cramped, finite space of the one-room schoolhouse what an infinite space was evoked: Each book, its cover opened, led miraculously inward and downward, tunneling away from the mere surface of things.

How fascinating to a child are words: the shapes, sounds, textures and mysterious meanings of words; the way words link together into elastic patterns called "sentences." And these sentences into paragraphs, and beyond. Until I was 22 and married I had in my keeping my first, battered, beloved Webster's dictionary with its thrilling bookplate "Joyce Carol Oates, Buffalo Evening News Spelling Bee Winner 1948." (I think there must have been numerous "winners.") The simplest definition of a writer is one who is in love with the language into which he or she has been born; this love predates the uses we make of language, as a toddler's excited, ecstatic chatter, accompanied by windmill arm motions, predates content. The wish to tell stories predates the stories told. Despite the quality of the poetry we were made to memorize, I loved memorizing poems and reciting them. And my earliest memories of writing have to do with being made to replicate "perfect" Palmer penmanship; I still write out in longhand the early sketches and drafts of my manuscripts, and would be lost, probably incapable of writing at all, if I couldn't write in this way. We were also drilled in grammar and the diagramming of sentences, which must have seemed a perverse waste of time for students eager to quit school and work on their fathers' farms; for me, it was a kind of puzzle-solving, therefore pleasurable. Most important, Mrs. Dietz drilled us in spelling. Spelling was sacrosanct. We were forever memorizing and spelling vocabulary words; one of my favorite activities was the "spelling bee"—a competitive ritual that involved standing beside your desk when called upon by the teacher, repeating words after her by enunciating each syllable, spelling the words slowly, repeating them again and, if you were given the nod of approval, sitting down again. Spelling correctly seemed as much a moral activity as something merely academic and intellectual.

Surely, in the confined little universe of District School #7, it was next to godliness.

My lifelong love of words, and my predilection for browsing through the dictionary for long, dreamy minutes, spring from these drills of Mrs. Dietz's that to others were onerous, wasteful of time and frustrating.

The one-room schoolhouse, now almost totally vanished from the American countryside, was of course a rough-hewn educational experience, and I don't want to romanticize it. In all honesty I would not wish any child of my own to have been educated in this way, in such a context. Until I was in fifth grade the school contained eight grades, and few of the pupils, like their farmer parents, many of them German immigrants, had any interest in schooling. They resented being made to attend and would quit when legally freed at the age of 16, to work at home. Not only the near-grown boys but some of the more aggressive girls routinely harassed and molested younger children. My knees still bear the faint scars from my having been knocked down repeatedly on the schoolyard cinders, and my heart quickens with memories of being tormented, usually on the way home from school, with nowhere to run and no way of protecting myself. None of this abuse was particularly personal; if you hadn't older brothers or sisters to protect you, you were fair game. Some of what was done to us was sexual, though never so extreme as rape or "assault"; rather more poking, prodding, pummeling, punching, causing pain. One vividly recalled schoolyard humiliation that occurred when I was in fourth grade left me with so profound a sense of helplessness and estrangement that I seem to accept the ill-will of others as a natural fact of life; deeply imprinted in my soul is the melancholy wisdom, no one will help you, finally—not even your friends. I learned young not to expect mercy from the hands of bullies of either sex. I still don't. It's the generous gesture, the gratuitous kindness, that leaves me disoriented and at a loss for words. (I was never able to tell my parents fully what happened to me, but I did tell them some things, and they did complain to Mrs. Dietz, who was powerless to do much about it. She assured my parents that the boys were only "teasing Joyce because they like her." Perhaps she believed this.)

It would not occur to me until years later, when I was an adult and involved in writing, that the world of my beleaguered childhood replicated a more universal experience than simply my own. *Tragedy breaks down the dykes between human beings,* William Butler Yeats has said. One might argue that any hurt, any insult or humiliation, any horror can have an illuminating and not merely a debilitating effect upon the sufferer. One of the compelling facts of the world of my childhood, which might be defined as working-class, farm society in which most men and women hadn't gone beyond eighth grade, is that the division between acceptable male and female behavior was absolute. Men and boys, even very young grade-school boys, like my own cousins, commonly used profane, vulgar and obscene language; women and girls, never. Men and boys commonly expressed anger, hostility, derision, mockery; women and girls, rarely. Such behavior, in men and boys, was the very sign of "maleness"—"masculinity." To stone small animals and birds, to gouge out the eyes of fish with sticks, to pursue and torment younger children—to be contemptuous of the life of the mind—this was male behavior, though it was not the behavior, of course, of all males. When in later years critics would severely castigate me for the "violence" of my work (in fact, I've usually focused upon victims of violence who are likely to be women and children), they could not have guessed what a transgressive act writing itself was for me: to take on the language of men, to write about men from the inside, and even with sympathy, as freely as if I weren't limited by birth to the perspective of "female." For is biology destiny? Not for the writer or artist, it isn't.

March 16, 1997

Joanna Trollope

The Roman poet Horace once said that the exceptional writer was one who could wield ordinary words so skillfully that, in his hands, the ordinary was made new. But for the fact that Horace said it more than two thousand years ago, he might have been speaking of Joanna Trollope. Here is a writer who marshals simple prose and constructs stories around everyday people, but in her hands the humdrum is made strikingly fresh.

Trollope was born in Gloucestershire, England, during World War II. Her father, an infantryman at Dunkirk, disappeared into India after the war, abandoning his little family; when she was almost 4, he reappeared, begging to be taken in. The Trollopes were poor, lived "Bohemian, unorthodox" lives, "shivered with chilblains in various suburbs of London," but there were always books around the house. At the age of 14, rescued from a mediocre education by a teacher who plied her with Wordsworth, Trollope produced her first novel.

But it would take more than 20 years before she would call herself a writer. She won "a tiny scholarship" to Oxford to study drama. She worked at the Foreign Office, researching Maoist China. She was a teacher for 12 years, "a sensible profession," she says, for a woman managing marriage and children. While her first husband, "a young Turk of a banker," went off on business, she wrote on a wobbly table in the bedroom at night, and before long began producing historical novels, which she published at first as Trollope, then under the pseudonym of Caroline Harvey. At 57, when she wrote the following essay, and in the full flower of her writing career, she had numerous novels to her names. As Joanna Trollope, she has written *Next of Kin, Marrying the Mistress* and *Other People's Children*, among others; as the more operatic Caroline Harvey, she has given us *Legacy of Love, The Brass Dolphin, A Second Legacy*.

Her prolificacy alone calls to mind the other Trollope—"the real Trollope," as she refers to that "collateral relative"—author of many great Victorian novels (*Phineas Finn*, *The Way We Live Now*, along with 45 others). Like him, the contemporary Trollope tells stories that mirror the times.

She does not achieve this by imagination alone. She researches her novels deeply. For *The Men and the Girls* she worked in a hostel for battered women. For *The Rector's Wife* she checked groceries in a supermarket. *The Spanish Lover* required extensive travel in Spain. *Girl From the South* (2002) was the product of time in Charleston, S.C., a community that is, according to her, "surprisingly English in its courtesy, charm and hypocrisy."

"But mostly," she says, "my life is dull and orderly. I try to have the dog walked, the wash in the machine, and the post opened before I sit down to work. I'm not good at writing with disorder all about." At 9 a.m., these pesky demands behind her, she finally puts pen to paper. At 1:30 in the afternoon, she stops.

Trollope refuses to glamorize her profession, much as she refuses to glamorize the characters in her books. "I love the moment when ordinary people turn protagonist, when they realize they can take the steering wheel for themselves. . . . The older I get, the more I believe in the absolute value of those stories. If someone is passionate to hear them, there comes an enormous desire to communicate what one has learned." That quality, she insists, is what makes a good writer. "Stories are the secret," she says, and she does so with so much conviction that one feels even Horace would agree.

M. A.

Looking for the Spark

BY JOANNA TROLLOPE

I am always faintly fussed by the idea of creative writing courses. I completely accept that you can teach the craft, that you can give instruction on how to structure a book, how to vary pace and tension, how to write dialogue. But what you can't teach, it seems to me, is the right kind of observation or the right kind of interpretation of what has been observed. It worries me to think of all those earnest pupils who have diligently mastered the mechanics, wondering with varying degrees of misery and rage why the finished recipe just hasn't somehow worked.

Coleridge explained it, really. He said, in his *Biographia Literaria*, that there are two kinds of imagination, the Primary and the Secondary. We all, he said, possess the Primary Imagination, we all have the capacity to perceive, to notice. But what only poets—loosely translated as all truly creative people, I suppose—have, the Secondary Imagination, is the capacity to select, and then translate and illuminate, everything that has been observed so that it seems to the audience something entirely new, something entirely true, something excitingly wonderful or terrible.

There is, after all, nothing new to say about the human condition. There's nothing to say that Shakespeare or Sophocles hasn't already inimitably, brilliantly, said. Codes of conduct, fashions in morality and ethics, all may come and go, but what the human heart has desired—and feared—down the ages goes on being very much the same. The novelist's task is not—easier said than done—to shrink from the well-trodden, time-worn path of human hopes and terrors but to re-interpret those old hopes and terrors for his or her own times. Never forget: Sexual betrayal may be as old as time, it may happen every nanosecond of every minute there's ever been, but the first time it happens to you is the first time in the history of the world. A cliché is a cliché only if it is comfortably taking place in someone else's life.

This sympathy—or do I mean empathy?—is vital in the writing of fiction. Coleridge's view of the poet as prophet to the hungry hordes is in truth a bit grand for me. I admire it, but I am not, personally, quite up to it. I am happier seeing the novelist, sleeves rolled up, in the thick of things alongside the reader, bleeding when pricked, just as the reader does. The only capacity I would claim—and heaven knows how it works or where it comes from—is that I do seem to have an instinct to select, from everything I have noticed in half a century's beady-eyed people-watching, the telling detail, the apt phrase. I seem to be quite good at the rhythms of dialogue. I seem to know how not to overwrite. But that is it, really. Except—well, except that the older I get, the more prepared I am to surrender and trust to the power of the unconscious mind. Maybe this is a modest form of the Secondary Imagination, maybe not. Whatever it is, it produces a level and intensity of communication that causes people to buy my books and to write to me about them in numbers that I still can't get over. As a friend said to me, "You'd believe it, wouldn't you, if it was happening to somebody else?"

What I do believe, fervently, is that we are all in this boat together—writer, reader, critic. I have a couple of tattered little quotations that lie about my desk and that become only more valuable to me as time goes on. One is from the English critic Philip Toynbee: "The definition of moral progress is the realization that other human beings are fully as human as oneself." Quite. The other is something from Trollope—the real Trollope. It comes from his autobiography, that peculiar, cantankerous book, published posthumously, which did his reputation such acute damage because the late Victorians could not bear his refusal to be high-minded about his art. He said many remarkable things in this book—including the accurate observation that "nobody gets in closer to a reader than a novelist, not even his mother"—but my own particular favorite is on the subject of the novelist's central preoccupation. Trollope was not so much concerned, he said, with the landscape of the grand passions (was he thinking of Tolstoy, whom he much admired and who admired him in return?) as with something else, something less glamorous perhaps, but just as intense and certainly more universal: "My task," he wrote, "is to chronicle those little daily lacerations upon the spirit."

I feel a thrill of recognition every time I read that, or even think about it. Yes. Yes. Speaking absolutely personally, that is what the writer's life is all about, for me. The point of it is to emphasize that we are none of us immune to longing, or disappointment (much underrated, in my view, as a force for distress), or frustration, or idiotic hope or bad behavior. What fiction does, in this difficult world, is reassure us that we are not alone, nor are we (most of us) lost causes. There is a theory—Puritan in origin, no doubt—that suffering strengthens and elevates us in a way that joy can never somehow do. I'm not so sure about that. Isn't it just that we have, on the whole, so much more suffering than joy that we have resolved, out of our great surviving instinct, to insist that something worthwhile must be made of it? And isn't fiction a handrail, of a kind, which we can all grasp while we blunder about in the dark? Isn't fiction written by people for people about people? And is there a subject more fascinating or more important?

I'm getting quite heated. I also get heated when journalists—mostly English journalists, I must admit—ask me how much of my life is in my work. I don't get heated because I think the question is discourteous, but because it seems to me ignorant, because it shows a blithe disregard of the workings, or even the presence, of that great observing and interpreting tool, the imagination. Of course my life goes into my work. Not literally, naturally, not childbirth here, and school exams there, and divorce somewhere else (we don't want anything wasted, do we?). But everything I write is, must be, informed by my experience, by everything I've learned, and failed to learn. Experience, the basic business of having life just shunt you about carelessly for several decades, is as vital a part of the mix as is the factor X that makes me a writer and you a musician or a cook or an engineer or a lawyer. I sometimes wish people wouldn't try to write fiction before they are 35—or at least, to realize that they will write infinitely better fiction after they are 35. Back to suffering, I suppose. Oh, bother.

Writing is admired these days, isn't it? Admired and envied. Even people who have cast-iron careers in other fields—politicians, movie stars, tennis players—seem to need to write a book, seem to feel driven to leave behind this particular little monument, this testament to the way they thought and spoke—or wish to have been seen to think and speak. But what they forget (Coleridge forgot it too, but, being a near-genius, receives immediate pardon) is that the writers who last, the writers whose writing is indeed their monument, not only have an essential benevolence, a fundamental affection for the human race, but also, more uncomfortably, possess a hefty dose of humility. Most writers—all but a very few in fact—are translators, not inventors, of language, and of life. It's all in a Jewish saying, really: "Truth rests with God alone. And a little bit, with me."

September 30, 2001

James Michener

"I never applied for a job in my life," said James Michener—no mean feat for a man who didn't write his first book until 40 and then went on to publish 48 books in the 46 years since. "Never asked for a raise. Never asked for a promotion. It's just that I've had this great good fortune all my life—older people spotted me, singled me out and gave me a helping hand." He was speaking to me in the fall of 1993, four years before his death.

But looking back on Michener's eight decades as a teacher, historian, researcher, world traveler, best-selling writer, art collector and philanthropist, one thing is very clear: This was not a man who just got by. He was hard at work all the time. And like all obsessive workaholics, he was the last to see the treadmill whirling below. He juggled work with the intensity of a general, the glee of a mad scientist and the wonder of a 10-year-old boy. What was most remarkable, perhaps, for this writer who did so much was that he came from so little.

Michener was probably born in New York City in 1907. For all the research he has done in his lifetime, he never was able to pin that down for sure. He did not know his parents' names. What he knew for certain was that he was abandoned on Mabel Michener's doorstep in Doylestown, Pa., before he reached the age of 2. There was no letter, no artifact—nothing to identify him.

Mrs. Michener, a Quaker widow, was known to take foundlings into her home and raise them as her own. "There were always 4 or 5 other children around," recalls Michener. "We were a good unit. Good citizens." That was until times got hard and money short: Michener would often shuttle back and forth from the state-run poorhouse, returning when Mrs. Michener had collected enough money to feed him again.

"It may not sound that way, but life was organized," he told me.

"There were times we went to bed hungry. Bleak times. But more often I remember Mrs. Michener reading to us. Dickens when I was 5 or 6. Then Thackeray. And Sienkiewicz—*Quo Vadis*, as I recall. She and her 2 sisters, a nurse and a schoolteacher, brought me up. They were strong women. I never had a father figure, but I wouldn't have traded those women for anything."

Michener excelled in the local schools. By 14 he had seen most of the Eastern states, hitchhiking in the summer for adventure. One alert and farsighted teacher guided him to an athletic scholarship at Swarthmore College. He graduated from there summa cum laude in 1929 just in time to greet the Great Depression.

For the next 10 years he traveled and taught, attending 9 universities "always at public expense," but teaching as he went along. "Even as a teacher, I always felt I was learning far more than I taught," he says. It was hard to see this as work. With his voracious hunger for books and near-photographic memory, he began to hoard away the information that would later furnish his novels. By the time he was offered a faculty position at Harvard University, he had switched from English to history.

Macmillan Publishers then hired him as a history textbook editor, but World War II intervened and he joined the Navy "as a paper-pusher." Within a few years he had attained the rank of lieutenant commander, served on 49 islands in the South Pacific, and honed his knowledge of aviation. It was on one of the islands, Espiritu Santo, that Michener sat down "in an inspired spurt" and strung together a number of stories that had intrigued him about the war in that far-off place. The result was *Tales of the South Pacific*. Macmillan published it in 1947 and the book won Michener the Pulitzer Prize. "Well, that was because it had no competition," he says with characteristic modesty. Not so. It was up against hefty names, among them two Steinbeck books, one Sinclair Lewis and A. B. Guthrie's *Big Sky*.

Eventually, Michener's book was refashioned as Rodgers and Hammerstein's musical *South Pacific*. And Michener went on to become a font of big, whopping best-sellers: *Sayonara* (Japan); *The Source* (Israel); *Iberia* (his favorite); *Caravans* (Afghanistan); *The Covenant* (South Africa); *Poland; Mexico; Centennial* (the West); *Chesapeake* (the Eastern Shore); *Texas; Hawaii; Space*. His books have sold close to 100 million copies and been translated into over 50 languages. In their writing he lived in more than 100 countries.

Contrary to assertions that he had a factory of researchers to do his work for him, Michener had one research assistant, John Kings, an English editor he met in Wyoming and hired in 1971. "Michener is an insatiable reader, taking in 2–300 books for each of his novels," said Kings, when I interviewed him for this piece. "My work is to get those books for him, but he always knows what he wants. He travels to do his own interviews. For *Centennial* alone, he traveled 26,000 miles. I know. I was at his side."

And if Faulkner was right, that "No man can write who is not first a humanitarian," Michener's concern for the less fortunate may be why his old Hermes typewriter was so prolific. Although he never had children of his own, he put over 150 young people through college. He and his third wife, Japanese-American Mari Sabusawa—an editor-librarian he met after the war and after her internment in U.S. concentration camps—brought bright, underprivileged youngsters to live in their various homes from time to time. "I would love to be a black boy today," Michener said to me, "about 14 years old and with the native intelligence God gave me. I would play society like a violin. I would make everyone want me." According to some sources, the Micheners have given $50 million away to educational institutions, including 2 impressive American and Japanese art collections.

After Michener told me about his then passion, *Recessional*—the Fall 1994 novel he had just completed about a group of elderly characters in a Florida retirement home—we talked a bit about places we'd lived in our lives. Eventually, we hit upon Malaysia. "Ah, Malaysia," he said. "It must be decades now, but I vividly remember. One of the most remarkable human beings I ever saw in my life: He was a boy in the Chinese circus there in Kuala Lumpur—riding a bicycle, balancing one thing with one foot, one thing with another, juggling balls, playing the bugle at the same time. Doing it all. Everything but turning the tigers! Now there's a kid with his whole life on show."

Indeed.

M. A.

How To Identify and Nurture Young Writers

BY JAMES MICHENER

As I head toward my 87th birthday, I have the good fortune to serve as assistant to two distinguished professors of creative writing: Fall term I will be in a high-caliber small religious college in Florida, Eckerd in St. Petersburg; spring term at the enormous University of Texas in Austin, which has 48,000 students on campus and 23 highly specialized libraries in which to work.

It is a thrilling and rejuvenating experience to work with young people who range from 17-year-old undergraduates to postgraduates of various ages. But as I read their papers and contemplate their increasingly difficult next steps in the writing profession, I am awed by the memory of how relatively easy it was for a young writer to make his or her way in the 1930s as opposed to how frustrating it is now.

In those days the rule was simple: Place 4 really good short stories in the popular magazines or 3 in the literary journals, and New York publishers will come knocking on your door, asking you to try a novel. And back then there were almost a dozen monthly and weekly magazines that published three or four short stories in every issue: the *Saturday Evening Post, Colliers, Redbook, Ladies' Home Journal, Liberty* and a journal that I peddled door-to-door when I was a boy, but whose name I cannot now recall.

If a young aspirant had a modicum of skill and a busy typewriter she or he would sooner or later get a foothold in one of the magazines and a leaping start on the ladder upward. After I sold 2 short stories to the *Post* in 1946, 2 book publishers expressed an interest in my future writing and one of the magazines mentioned above offered me a most enticing editorial job. I decided to stick with writing.

How different the publishing scene is today; how infinitely more difficult for the beginning writer. Most of the magazines that nurtured new talent in my day no longer exist, and those that have survived publish little fiction. A recent copy I saw of the *New Yorker* had no fiction at all.

To gain a foothold today requires not only skill but also fortitude, the ability to accept temporary rejection, and in some cases, a liberal amount of sheer brass. What do I tell my young students about this?

First, learn to master the English sentence in all its richness of expression and variation in structure.

Second, acquire an individualized vocabulary on at least three social levels, including modern street lingo.

Third, familiarize yourself with the fine books that have already been published so that you can acquire a sense of where fiction or nonfiction is heading. Because I was classically trained I used to believe that one had to know Chaucer, Dante, Balzac, Dickens, Dostoyevski, George Eliot and Thomas Hardy. I no longer believe that. A young person with a good education can learn the secrets of good writing by reading the best contemporary writers: Albert Camus, Günter Grass, John Updike, Toni Morrison and Joyce Carol Oates, for example. But a wide historical knowledge of books is still a tremendous asset.

Fourth, use every device in the repertory to get to know people in the publishing business who might be of help later on. Editors, publicists and agents circulate looking for talent and are approachable. Go to where they are likely to be. Introduce yourself, get to know them or, more important, enable them to know you. This leads to my fifth and last suggestion.

Consider applying to one of the writing programs sponsored by a good university. The one at the State University of Iowa has a solid reputation, but I also have high regard for the University of Houston's. The new multidisciplinary Master of Fine Arts program in writing at the University of Texas at Austin has high hopes but no track record as yet. Programs at such universities as Princeton, Columbia, Northwestern, Missouri and Stanford have produced professional writers. One of the virtues of such institutions is that in them the student will meet professionals who might be of help later on, among both the professors and the visiting lecturers.

Here are 4 examples of what can happen in student-teacher relationships in such places, all taken from my work at the graduate level with young people who have already made a serious commitment to writing. I asked my students to compose an imaginary letter to a real publishing house, asking permission to submit an outline and three sample chapters of either a fiction or nonfiction book.

One student, a gifted and highly sensitive black woman, turned in such a brilliant outline for a book on the experiences of black people in conservative Texas that, when she finished reading her proposal, I said, "You write that book, you'll find a publisher."

Another, a young California writer, had several appealing ideas for her next effort, but in the middle of the term she received assurances that if she hurried over to Bosnia, officials there would help her research an account of how Muslim women were treated by the Serbs in their brutal crusade of ethnic cleansing. When she asked me what she should do, I said, "Catch the next plane to Sarajevo. The other subjects can wait."

An interesting pair were extremely gifted students who could never seem to come to grips with the realities of publishing. They ran the risk of becoming the idle drifters who wander from one graduate school to another. They happened to come to my office at the same time, with nothing done on the assignment.

One I will call Martin, a dreamy-eyed lad from the bilingual society along the Rio Grande, who has a foot in both the Mexican and Texas worlds. He went off after our conversation and returned with an exciting draft of a short story illustrating the values of the two societies, their friction points, and their hopes for the future. I was ecstatic: "Martin, you get this written, I know you'll find a publisher. This subject will be on the front burner for the next half century. Make your statement now."

His partner in apathy, whom I will here call Vanessa, is a bright woman from Maine of whom teachers say: "She's got to be better than whatever she's showing us in this class. Let's give her another shot." Well, her second attempt was a short story with a brilliant solution to the writer's constant problem: How does the girl meet the boy? She wrote about a reclusive nerd who haunts a library to eye an extremely shy girl whom he does not know how to approach, unaware that she sits in her isolated carrel just as eager to meet him. I couldn't see that the story was going to accomplish much until the girl secretly scans the books he is reading in an orderly fashion and slips into the pages of his next probable choice the following message: "The Chinese Circus is coming to the fair field on Friday. I have tickets."

It was so perfect, so cleverly contrived and accurately phrased that I said it straight out in class: "Vanessa, for 2 years you've bewildered me. Endless promise but no execution. But this is the most exciting solution to the boy-meets-girl requirement I've come upon in years. You can be a writer. Now get to it."

We have our failures, too, people who have no skill with words, no vision, no realistic likelihood of ever telling a story well. They are what one of my colleagues describe as "People who want to have written a book." They don't fantasize about the hard work of actually writing it. They're the ones who, in the question-and-answer period always ask more questions about finding an agent than about the actual process of writing.

At my age I can't afford to waste my time on such dawdlers. I seek the young person trying to master her or his craft, who dares to grapple with new subject matter and who, perchance, may have a burning vision of how to express old truths in new forms.

October 30, 1993

Mary Higgins Clark

For more than a quarter-century now, Mary Higgins Clark has made a very good living keeping readers on the edge of their chairs, wondering what will become of ordinary heroes in extraordinary circumstances. But there is little suspenseful about her writing life. Her career hums along like clockwork: Clark's publisher (the same one that released her first mystery 27 years ago) pays her a cool $12 million per story; hands her contracts for 3 novels at a time; and, every year at about this time, she responds with a new best-seller.

In the spring of 1999, when she wrote this essay, the book was *We'll Meet Again*, a story about 2 friends, 1 crime and half a life in prison. In the well-oiled machinery of her publishing schedule, the paperback edition of her last novel, *You Belong to Me*, hit the stores at precisely the same time.

There is little in Clark's life, save the guiding angel she credits in the following piece and a good dose of Irish determination, that would have predicted this kind of success. She was raised in the Bronx during the Depression, a plucky girl in a family of 5. It was a childhood defined by straitened finances, singed with tragedy. "We were broke, not poor," she insists. "There's a difference." But there were 2 brothers killed—1 in war, another by accident—and a father whose heart simply stopped when she was 11.

She learned determination from her mother, a former bridal buyer for B. Altman's who was married at 40, widowed at 50, and singlehandedly responsible thereafter for her daughter. Clark and her mother babysat, did odd jobs—at 15, Clark was a telephone operator in a local hotel—but she never saw herself as less than lucky. "I'd walk down the street, look in shop windows, and pick out the clothes I'd have some day," she says.

She went to secretarial school on scholarship at 17, became a secretary at an ad agency, wrote stories in her spare time. Inspired by Pearl Buck's *The Good Earth* at 9, she had been scribbling these and mailing them to magazine slush piles since she could remember.

By 20, she was a Pan Am stewardess. "It was like becoming a star," she says. You had to be petite, pretty, slender. She traveled throughout Europe, to the Middle East and Africa, keeping her eyes open, gathering color for future books. When she married and left stewardessing behind, her writing career began.

Although she had 5 children in 8 years, she enrolled in New York University. She wrote her first suspense story that sold, "Stowaway," while attending a course there; it earned her a tidy $100. There was many a rejection slip after that, however, and then the sudden death of her husband. She persevered, started a "ladies' writing circle" that carried on for 40 years. She put herself through college. She made a salary writing scripts for radio shows. She sold what short stories she could to *Saturday Evening Post, McCall's, Redbook*. But life changed for her irrevocably when her 3-year-old disappeared for a few hours, gave her a good scare, and inspired her to produce a full-length book manuscript she called *Die a Little Death*. It was bought by Simon & Schuster and published as *Where Are the Children*? That, of course, is where the clockwork kicks in. Every year, come spring, another Mary Higgins Clark mystery pushes out as surely as the crocuses, and fans from here to Japan line up to buy.

The books are too numerous to list but a few titles stand out: *Aspire to the Heavens*; *All Around the Town*; *A Cry in the Night*. A Clark story often begins with nothing more than a title. The book she would go to work on after this essay, she already knew, would be called *If Ever I Would Leave You* and would be based on the craze for psychics. "First I go to dinner with Michael Korda [her editor at S & S] and we talk ideas," says Clark. "The other day, I told him about a teenager I knew who ran up a $400 bill in one night with a telephone psychic. We kicked that around for a while, and by the end of the evening, I had my next book." She sends Korda 30 pages at a time. He edits, she writes the next chapter, they talk the plot through. By the time the last sentence is written, S & S will have whirred into production. Within two months the final copy is in the stores.

Her novels are often tied to social issues (her European readers are far more attuned to this than we are). The subjects are in vitro fertilization, capital punishment, gender equity. But mainly, a Mary Higgins Clark mystery is sheer entertainment—a quick slip of a story. Here and gone like springtime. Back again next year.

M. A.

Touched by an Angel

BY MARY HIGGINS CLARK

It is just 25 years since the magical telephone call informed me that Simon & Schuster wanted to buy my first suspense novel. What's most shocking to me is that it seems as though that call came yesterday. I was amazed to realize that the years have gone so quickly; that although time isn't running out exactly, it is finite, and there are so many stories I want to tell.

A common question asked of writers is "When did you decide to become a writer?" The answer, of course, is that we didn't decide anything. It was decided for us. I firmly believe that mythical godmothers make appearances at our cradles, and bestow their gifts. The godmother who might have blessed me with a singing voice did not show up; the goddess of dance was nowhere in sight; the chef-to-the-angels was otherwise engaged.

Only one made the journey to my cradle, and she whispered, "You will be a storyteller."

I began telling stories to my friends when we took breathers from tag or follow-the-leader or our favorite game, giant-steps. I wrote plays and made my long-suffering brothers perform in them for visiting relatives at dinnertime. Reflecting on those theatrical events, I doubt the relatives considered the dinner worth the price of admission.

Throughout my school years, I was always tuning out in math and chemistry classes and writing stories in notebooks that were supposed to be reserved for equations and formulas. Forty years after I graduated from Villa Maria Academy, I stopped there for a visit. Mother St. Thomas of Canterbury, the mathematics and science teacher of those high school years, was then nearly 90—old and confined to a wheelchair. Over the vista of 4 decades, she looked at me with wise gray eyes and said severely, "Miss Higgins, you were a dreadful math student."

I immediately swept into the curtsy that was de rigueur in our time and said, "God bless your memory, Reverend Mother."

My first attempt to sell a short story was when I was 16. I submitted it to the magazine *True Confessions*. I felt as the author of *Please Don't Eat the Daisies*, Jean Kerr, did, when she wrote about her first submission to *Liberty Magazine*: Anything *Liberty* published was so bad they probably would accept her offering. But she was rejected by *Liberty*; and my story, "I, With My Guilt," came back by return post from *True Confessions.*

I married two days after my 22nd birthday, which meant quitting my job as a Pan American flight hostess, and signed up for writing courses at New York University. I knew that if I really wanted to be a writer, I needed to learn the craft, the structure of a good short story.

The first one I wrote in that class eventually sold, but it had the distinction of opening the file for the dozens of rejection slips that I accumulated in my short story writing career. A word about rejection slips: They only whetted my appetite, produced a "just wait and see, pal" response in my soul.

Some of the editors wrote rejection slips that were more creative than anything I had written. On my 10th submission to *Redbook*, the printed rejection slip included a handwritten sentence: "Mrs. Clark, your stories are light, slight, and trite." My first novella was returned with the succinct note: "We found the heroine as boring as her husband had."

My first book, *Aspire to the Heavens*, a historical novel about George Washington, was remaindered as it came off the press and published as a whispering campaign. It virtually slithered into a bookstore near the Madison Avenue office where I worked writing radio scripts. A group of us went to lunch, and I proudly pointed it out in the bookstore window. When we returned from lunch it was missing and I opined that it had been snapped up.

The same group and I passed the bookstore at 5 o'clock, and a copy of my novel was once again in the window. One of the guys said, "Whoever bought it returned it." But *Aspire to the Heavens* did prove I could get a book published. That was when it occurred to me that if I loved to read suspense novels, maybe I could write one.

One of the many joys of writing is that everything is grist for the mill. When I plan a new novel, I press a mental "search and retrieve" button and find in memory the people or the events that will help me tell the tale. The horror of my 3-year-old going briefly missing near a deep lake helped to trigger that first suspense novel, *Where Are the Children?*

Now, 25 years, 17 novels and 3 short story collections later, I'm still in love with what I do. Writing is essentially a solitary profession. It is: the idea that won't go away, the characters who start out as silhouettes and then take on flesh, the place, the season, the time span. It is: the excitement of setting out on a journey that will have unexpected twists and turns, unexpected land mines, a good dose of self-doubt, and a final sense of fulfillment.

Having 5 children makes it easy to compare finishing a novel to birthing a baby. When I was pregnant, I did my best to see that insofar as it was within my control the baby would be healthy. I ate the right foods, faithfully scheduled doctor visits, shunned wine and exercised.

In the same way, when I turn in a manuscript, I know it is the story I wanted to tell and it isn't within my power to tell it a better way. If it is praised, I am grateful. If it is roundly criticized, I console myself by saying I did the best I could do.

Letters from readers can be gratifying and heartwarming. But I think my all-time favorite came from a 13-year-old who wrote:

Dear Mrs. Clark:
I have read the first half of *Where Are the Children*.
You are a wonderful writer.
Someday I hope to read the second half.
Your friend,
Jack

April 18, 1999

John Keegan

On Oct. 8, 2001, just as our warplanes pierced the Afghan ether to rain bombs on Osama bin Laden and his Taliban guard, Sir John Keegan—war historian par excellence—manned a column out of the defense desk of London's *Daily Telegraph* and launched his own major offensive. Harvard's Samuel Huntington had been right, Keegan proclaimed: Now that the Cold War was over, a new violence would sharpen; we would see a clash of civilizations unlike any other—a war between East and West.

But Huntington hadn't gone far enough, wrote Keegan. "The crucial ingredient" in any Western-Islamic conflict could be found in a simple distinction: "Westerners fight face to face . . . they choose the crudest weapons and use them with appalling violence. . . . Orientals, by contrast, shrink from pitched battle . . . preferring ambush, surprise, treachery and deceit." On Sept. 11, "the Oriental tradition . . . returned in an absolutely traditional form. Arabs, appearing suddenly out of empty space like their desert raider ancestors, assaulted the heartlands in a terrifying surprise raid and did appalling damage." The proper response to these "predatory, destructive Orientals," he said, was a classic Western show of force: a relentless, massive, crushing retaliation.

What was the reaction to Keegan's column? "Outrage," he responds. "They didn't want to hear that the attacks were classically Arab, distinctive of raids in the 6th, 7th and 8th centuries. People said I didn't know my history. I was scorned, told I had crossed the bounds of political correctness; that I had implied Asians were inferior. I was told my views on war were ethically unacceptable."

Keegan remains unabashed. "I've read more than 10,000 works on war," he says. He has taught at the Royal Military Academy for 25 years and has written or edited many celebrated books, among them *The Face of Battle* (1976) and *The Mask of Command* (1989). "If my opinion isn't worth something, what is?"

Hampered by a severe limp, Keegan was never able to serve in the military himself but was an early convert to war-watching when, as a 10-year-old boy, he witnessed thousands of American soldiers descend on England's West Country to prepare for D-Day. That, and a healthy penchant for reading, led him to pursue war on the page.

A graduate of Oxford, Keegan first came to the United States on scholarship in the '50s; he taught at Princeton in 1984 and at Vassar in 1997. Today, in a manor house in Wiltshire from which he can survey the "hardway" where Alfred the Great battled the Danes, he is finishing a history of intelligence operations. His longterm strategy, however, is to write not about clashes between East and West, but about those between brother and brother. Toward this end, in 2002, he published *The American Civil War and the Wars of the Nineteenth Century*.

M. A.

The Leap from Necessity to Invention

BY JOHN KEEGAN

Tuition. That's the answer. Whenever people ask me why I became a writer, I just say "tuition." Only, in England, what Americans call "tuition," we call "school fees."

There is an important difference. Tuition, to most American parents, starts to loom over their lives only when their children's college approaches. School, for the majority, has not hit their pockets. In

Britain, it is the other way around. College is free, not as free as it used to be, but still an affordable cost. School, on the other hand, is expensive, for those parents who choose not to educate their children in state-run public schools. It is a choice that the middle class almost always makes, though financial prudence and common sense argue against it. Some fall by the wayside; some carry the debt into retirement. We all know the penalties. We still struggle on. It really is a struggle, for school fees begin when parents are at the beginning of their careers, before they have had a chance to accumulate savings, build up insurance policies or, indeed, to start earning very much.

Why do we do it? Many state schools, particularly in country districts and the outer suburbs, are excellent. Some fee-paying, private schools are not all that good. Private education does not bring any guaranteed advantage, since the best universities—at least in Britain—bend their admission policies to favor the state-educated. The middle class nevertheless seems to regard the fee-paying ordeal as a test of character. If you want to remain where you are in the social order, if you want to be seen to be doing what is still deemed to be the best by your offspring, you pay school fees. Keep going and the Devil take the hindmost. End of story.

The story of my life as a writer began in my early thirties. I had 4 children and an academic salary. School fees loomed fast round the corner. How, I began to wonder, could I begin to educate them, "educating your children" having, among the British middle class, a sense quite different from "sending them to school"? It was not possible to take a second job. My wife, immersed in childcare, could not take a job herself. The answer, I concluded, was to become a writer.

Looking back over 30 years of a literary career, I still laugh at my naiveté. Most writers, I now know, can scarcely earn enough to pay for paper clips. Of the 100,000 books published in Britain every year, 90,000 barely cover their printing costs, some are subsidized by their authors, and, even among those that do pay, few sell enough to support a writer in an independent way of life. If I were beginning again, I would think of some other way of raising $100,000 a year, which is what it costs today to keep 4 children at private schools at the same time.

So what sustained my wildly unrealistic optimism that I could make up the difference between what an academic salary paid and what private schools cost? Most of all, I think, blind self-confidence. Not self-esteem; I constantly wonder why the difference between the two is not more widely recognized. I had no opinion of myself, indeed rather the opposite. I did, on the other hand, think I could do certain things rather better than other people, and one was to manipulate the English language. I thought that because I had noticed that my essays were better, as pieces of writing, than other people's had been, at school and university. I also noticed that such small things as I had written were, occasionally, not inferior to the sort of writing I admired in books and literary magazines. If they can do it, I can do it, I thought. So I set off.

How did I get going? Very haphazardly. I was teaching history in the 1960s at the Royal Military Academy Sandhurst, Britain's West Point, a time when a renewed interest in the history of the Second World War had alerted some fringe publishers to the existence of a market among readers who did not buy hardback books. Part-works—weekly magazines, which, if collected and stored in loose-leaf folders, became books—were selling well. A fringe publisher, who had made money in part-works on antiques, gardening and pets, thought he would make some more in military history. He wondered where to find authors and decided Sandhurst might supply some. It was a bad idea. The academic old guard at the academy strongly disapproved of authorship, an intellectual activity in a fiercely anti-intellectual establishment. The young guard were more susceptible to inducement. Much to the disapproval of their seniors, they accepted commissions and began to write. I was one of those who broke out.

Part-work articles, which brought in $200 per thousand words, paid a lot of school fees. Even better was the part-work publisher's next enterprise—short, so-called original paperbacks on Second World War episodes. They paid $1,500 for 30,000 words. No royalties, no foreign rights, but cash on the barrel. I wrote six, straight off. They paid the school fees for several years, and several other now well-known authors succumbed to the same temptation, including the historian Paul M. Kennedy. I don't think a single one of us regrets it for a moment.

On the contrary. I am extremely grateful to the series' mastermind, Barrie Pitt, who for a moment oversaw the futures of a whole stable of promising young writers. What we all learned—I certainly did—was how to write to length and to deadline, inestimably valuable lessons. None of that doctoral thesis agony, satisfying by endless rewriting the neuroses of a Doktorvater, intent on revisiting the torture chamber of his own past. Barrie Pitt wanted short, clear, well-written, accurate historical narratives, which satisfied the appetite of television-watching readers for a good story and the critical eye of the self-taught for truth. He got what he wanted, and his young scribblers learned their trade in the process.

Part-works and paperbacks, besides paying the school fees, also financed, if one wrote hard enough, the excursion into serious literature. In 1972, I proposed to an Oxford friend, who had set up as a literary agent, an idea for a hardback book. There were lots of books about battles, I wrote in my outline, but no book about what it was actually like, for an individual, to take part. He took my proposal away, came back with an offer from Jonathan Cape, and transferred a small advance. I kept taking the paperback money but started hardback writing—paperback in the morning, hardback in the afternoon, both in teaching intervals. By 1975, *The Face of Battle*, as I called that hardback, was finished. In 1976 it was published in England and, by Viking, in America.

I began shortly afterward to experience the pleasure of favorable reviews, eventually very favorable. Sir Michael Howard, colossus of military historians, decided that *The Face of Battle* was "one of the half-dozen best books about war" published since 1945. My self-confidence increased. I even allowed myself a flicker of self-esteem. Then, one evening, during family supper, I got a telephone call from Alan Williams at the Viking Press. He told me that *The Face of Battle* had been chosen as its main selection by the Book-of-the-Month Club. I returned to the supper table, looked round the assembled faces, and said, "I think it's all right. The school fees are safe for a few years yet."

That wasn't quite true. Over the next few years I discovered a truth about the writing life I hadn't perceived: that a writer has to keep going. In the early 1980s, I fell behind with a manuscript, ran out of money and had an unpleasant year or two. The episode wasn't disastrous because the children were then in college, for which the British state largely then paid, but it taught me a lesson. I resolved thereafter never to let anything get in the way of long-distance composition and, on the whole, have stuck to my resolve.

Since *The Face of Battle*, I have written a dozen books, some less good than others, none unsuccessful. Insofar as I can estimate their quality, I would put it down to two things. The first is eavesdropping. As a young academic at Sandhurst, I had the extraordinary good fortune to be able to listen to the conversations of soldiers who had fought in the Second World War; since they were among themselves, none spun yarns, while the truths they told were quite unlike official military history. From the clues they supplied, I learned to read the records in a new and discerning way. All soldiers, my private knowledge told me, were afraid, except for a tiny, admired minority who were the people who made battles work. The other factors that made battles work were practical arrangements, not grandiose strategic ideas. War is a very workaday business.

As to writing itself, what helped? I have an ear for the rhythm of prose, which I think essential to readability. The other great help was foreign languages. I had been taught Latin and Greek until I was 16 and had learned French very well. Knowledge of foreign languages is the best of guides to the structure and subtleties of one's own. It is, alas, dying out in the English-speaking world, which all foreigners now want to join. The result is that English-speaking writers don't write as well as those even of the last generation did, while strange varieties of English are taking form outside its historic heartland. The absolute certainty of touch that came so naturally to Rudyard Kipling and Evelyn Waugh is probably gone forever. I deeply regret its disappearance.

October 28, 2001

Susan Minot

Susan Minot's career began with a best-seller, *Monkeys* (1986), the story of a girl's painful coming of age in the shadow of her mother's death and father's alcoholism. It was followed by a collection called *Lust and Other Stories* (1989) and by *Folly* (1992), a novel about an unconventional young woman in 1920s Boston, trying to make her way in a society ruled emphatically by convention.

Her novel, *Evening* (1998), describes a woman on her deathbed as family and friends gather to accompany her in the waning hours. What rushes to her mind as they stand about gloomily awaiting the end is not the pathos of her situation, but a remarkable screening of the most passionate weekend of her life, a memory so powerful that it dwarfs her timid past—and bleak future. Here is an excerpt:

> She knew the room. It had been her room for some time. She had known other rooms and lived in other houses and been in other countries but this was the last room and she knew what was coming to her in it. It was coming to her slowly and the room remained indifferent. The bedposts rose up with notched pine cones at the end and the narrow desk stood there shut with the key in the keyhole and on the bureau were the silver frames with her children. . . . She wanted it to speed up but whenever she urged it forward the effort only bound her faster to life. So she pretended she wasn't trying, pretended she was being borne along at whatever speed the wheels wanted to take her, pretended indifference. She ought to be good at pretending, she thought, she'd had a lifetime of doing it.

In 2002, Minot published *Rapture*, a very piquant novella about how a single sexual act transforms the lives of two jaded New Yorkers.

Minot's story-world is set in upper middle-class New England, and generally involves women who yearn for something beyond the staid parameters of their lives. Her work has been likened to Virginia Woolf's and Edith Wharton's—inept comparisons ultimately, for Minot's craft is nothing if not contemporary.

M. A.

A Real-Life Education

BY SUSAN MINOT

I never wanted to be a writer. That is, I never had the notion I want to be a writer. I started the way other people did, writing compositions in school. I liked doing that; it pulled at my imagination with a sort of elastic tension I enjoyed. The same thing happened when I made up games with friends or put on plays with my brothers and sisters. There was something about elaborating on the world that gave great pleasure.

But I also liked art class—art wasn't even like a class it was so good; you got to make things with your hands—and I liked science. Who wouldn't? We got to go outside and collect polliwogs in the pond. We got to dissect frogs and see the secret goings-on inside. If I had thought about it, which I didn't because I was not practical, I would have pictured myself as an artist. I could picture painting in a studio with easels and brushes or, even better, out in a landscape with a box of paints.

But a writer? I had no picture in my mind of what being a writer was. How could one aspire to that? I'd never met a writer. What did a writer actually do? What did a writer have? Words? I did not come from a literary family, despite the fact that 2 siblings and 1 step-sister became writers, too. (And I would not be surprised if there were more to come.) My youngest sister, Eliza, who is a novelist, believes that part of it was our having to relay information among the siblings—there were 7 of us and a lot going on—which encouraged our putting things into words.

At home the room where we spent the most time had books in bookshelves, but it was not called the library; it was called the TV room, and it was on the TV that our attention centered. As for our parents, my mother had written her college thesis on Christopher Marlowe, but I never heard more about it than that, and though my father was given to quoting Shakespeare or Tennyson as we dug sand castles or chipped ice off the driveway, his taste in books ran from Sidney Sheldon paperbacks to books on astronomy to historical biographies. What my parents did provide us with was an attitude of appreciation—we, despite being children, were little beings capable of creating interesting things, whether they were thoughts or drawings or a good pass in a field hockey game. And there's no question that getting attention from a parent when you are 1 of 7 was an incentive for doing something to get more.

My mother had a particular talent for celebrating life. She was a buoyant person. My father was decidedly more wry. Her enthusiasm for life and his skepticism about humanity presented 2 conflicting world views—the sorting out of which has provided me with enough material for a lifetime. That and a restless imagination. In our large family there was a lot of make-believe. Our favorite game was called Let's Pretend. The plays we put on often had no audience; we would imagine one.

I mention these things because they were, along with the episodes of *Twilight Zone*, *Dobie Gillis* and *Gilligan's Island*, and later with the black-and-white movies from the '40s and '50s on the odd television channels, just as important developmentally as the first moments of reading *The Catcher in the Rye*. Comic books, too. I preferred the ones about normal people, like the Archie comics, which to a young reader were fascinating explorations into human behavior. Their short, episodic form, echoing the form of TV episodes, surely was influential in my choice of the short story as my initial and still most beloved form. Just as fascinating were the romance comics—"Brad had changed since our first kiss . . . "—with their pat morality amid delvings into human desire. Later came the racier *True Confessions* with the added heat of real sex—and my first encounter with the confessional form, particularly piquant to a girl raised as a Catholic.

You often hear stories of the incubating writer who never took her nose out of a book; you couldn't drag her out of the library. I wasn't like that. That burrowing came long after. I was not a particularly precocious reader, though I remember the power with which certain books struck me. *The Secret Garden*, by Frances Hodgson Burnett, read to me by my mother, was about a little girl discovering a walled-in garden where she makes a friend. It was like the experience of reading! One went into a hushed and private place, put oneself there and learned about other people. I didn't really like fairy tales—my mind was probably too much of a fairy already—but preferred stories of real life.

What went on out there in the world? As an 11-year-old I particularly liked biographies—Calamity Jane, Dorothea Dix, Geronimo, Helen Keller, Davey Crockett. It turned out there were more interesting men and women than one usually heard about in history class. Harriet the Spy left an indelible impression with her note-taking in her little book and her spying, both important qualities for a writer.

When I left home for boarding school I began to write on my own—prose poetry, journal writing. It was the first time I had a room of my own, and I found that writing was a way both of being alone and of finding out what was going on inside of my self. Instead of doing homework, I wrote pages of stream-of-consciousness long into the night.

The novelist Jim Harrison has said that he is suspicious of any budding writer who is not drunk with words. I was completely inebriated. I was compelled to write; it became a compulsion. I wrote out of desperation. In the great turmoil and gloom and euphoria of adolescence, I found there was nowhere to express the chaos of emotions I was feeling, nowhere but in words. I began to rely so much on writing that I was living a double life—one in the world and one on the page. The one on the page was more intense, more satisfying and for a long time much more real.

It was then that I was also beginning to be overwhelmed by the power of books. There was one moment I do remember when ambition entered into my feelings about writing. It was a spring day, and I was lying on the grass in front of the library in Concord, Mass., where I attended high school, reading William Faulkner's *The Sound and the Fury*. It was a book I had not been assigned but which had intrigued me when I heard some friends, boys from a nearby school, quote the line "Caddy. She smelled like leaves." Suddenly in the middle of a passage, the power of the words rose up and whacked me on the forehead. I felt the earth move as if a huge safe were being swiveled open and afterwards felt flushed and stunned as you are after sex. I'd had this reaction before—to other books, and to music and painting, but this time as I stared at the light-green blades of grass in front of me, vibrating, I was aware that it was the writer who had done something to me. And I thought, I'd like to do that to someone back.

When I started to publish stories and then books, in a strange way these events seemed like flukes, moments of luck or fortuity when my compulsion to write just happened to intersect with real activities in the world. Being a writer was never what drove me; writing did. In fact, though it's odd to say, I don't think of myself as a writer. I agree with Chekhov, who hated labels and said he wanted simply to be a free artist. "Free artist"—now, that's a label I wouldn't mind.

Everyone in my family now makes things—books, paintings, sculptures, movies, photographs, decoupage. After I'd published a couple of books, my father, who wasn't one for commenting too much on the lives of his children, obliquely observed that writing was doing what you want and that it was a wondrous thing. "Imagine being able to do what you want all day," he said. It was a suggestion his children took.

I am very fortunate to make my living by writing, though I feel I got to this point through no more design than having followed an often bewildered instinct and by simply always writing. I believe that what an artist needs most, more than inspiration or financial consolation or encouragement or talent or love or luck, is endurance. Often the abstraction of using only words frustrates me—I write on paper with a dipped pen and ink, and type on a manual typewriter in order to have some three-dimensional activities with my hands—but again and again I discover how far words are capable of going, both in the world and on the page. The fact is, this side of the mind, nothing goes farther than words. With words I am able to do those things that first intrigued me when I was young, those things that made me feel most alive—I am able to paint pictures, collect things from muddy ponds, dissect insides, make things up, put on costumes, direct the lights, inspect hearts, entertain, dream. And, if it goes well, I might convey some of that vitality to others, and so give back a drop into that huge pool of what other artists have, as strangers, given me: reasons to live.

January 16, 2000

Muriel Spark

"I could write before I could speak," says Dame Muriel Spark in a sonorous contralto that makes her sound far younger than her 83 years, which is how old she was when she wrote this essay. Family legend has it that she was forming words out of toy blocks long before she could say them. Poet, biographer, editor, literary eminence, Spark is best known for her novels, notably *Memento Mori* (1959), *The Ballad of Peckham Rye* (1960) and, especially, *The Prime of Miss Jean Brodie* (1961).

She was born in Edinburgh in 1918. Although she is known as a "Catholic novelist," her father was Jewish, a technician with the North British Rubber Company; her mother, the daughter of a Hertfordshire shopkeeper, taught music. "My parents were young, lighthearted. They liked to go to the movies, dance. My mother thought I was wasting my time reading books. My father only read the racing papers." She attended the James Gillespie School in Edinburgh, a girls' school where she was encouraged to read, borrow library books, write. "It was a progressive place, now that I look back on it," Spark says. "We were a mixed group, but there was no racism. Teachers taught simple morals, tolerance."

When she finished school, she traveled to Zimbabwe, looking for adventure. There she met her future husband, Oswald Spark—"rather a mental case, really," she says. "We were married only three years."

Returning to England with her infant son after the war, she became involved in London's literary circles, serving briefly as the editor of the *Poetry Review*. She was expelled for being "too adventurous"—a story she tells in her memoir *Curriculum Vitae* (1992). During the 1950s, she wrote poetry and short stories and struggled to get published, as she recounts below. Her unnamed "literary companion" was Derek Stanford, with whom she co-authored a life of Emily Brontë. With the publication of *The Comforters*, however, in 1956, her reputation was established. She went on to publish 20 more novels.

To her great dismay, much of her personal collection—early manuscripts, correspondence, juvenilia—was stolen, she claims, from her house and sold through London dealers. "At least the thieves sent me copies," she reports. The dealers had bought them in good faith. There was little she could do.

Perhaps that is why crime has been on her mind lately. Her most recent novel, *Aiding and Abetting* (2001), is based on the real story of an earl who reputedly killed the house nanny, stuffed her into a mail sack and then disappeared, never to be seen again. The novel she is working on now is set in a finishing school in Switzerland, and there may be skulduggery in it, too.

Spark now lives in Italy with artist and sculptor Penelope Jardine. Spark's work—lapidary in *Memento Mori*, whimsical in *A Far Cry From Kensington* (1988)—is difficult to categorize. Each novel is different from the one before. She is ever, one could say, in her prime.

M. A.

Emerging from Under Your Rejection Slips

BY MURIEL SPARK

"The Editor thanks you for your kind contribution but regrets he is unable to publish it." My mail was full of such messages in those early days in the 1950s, when I "commenced author," as the phrase went.

What came with the rejection slips were poems and essays. I hadn't yet got around to the stories.

At the time I was sharing part of my meager life with a man my own age, a literary critic; he possessed lots of literary information, which I found fascinating, even useful. (But I suspected he had no idea what to do with his knowledge, and so it proved.)

We sent out our productions always accompanied by a stamped and addressed envelope; otherwise we wouldn't see our pieces of work again. (I must interpose a memory of the then-poet laureate John Masefield, already old and famous and honored, whose exquisite manners were expressed even to the point of sending that stamped, addressed envelope every time he sent a poem to, say, the *Times Literary Supplement*, although of course he knew full well that the grateful editor would receive his poem with joy.)

I must say that my rejection slips, if they fell out of the envelopes at a rate of more than two in one day, depressed me greatly. However, I had a list of possible weeklies and little magazines to hand, and immediately I put the poem or article into a new envelope with a new letter to the editor and a new S.A.S.E. If the work I was offering looked shopworn, I would type it out again. The money for these stamps for my outgoing mail was a pressing part of my budget in those days.

Thinking back, it is surprising how many—almost all, in fact—of my once-rejected pieces were subsequently published, as I began to make my name. Among the rejects, of course, I found some which, on reflection, I was not quite happy with. Those I set aside. But the majority of those one-time rejects have become a part of my oeuvre, studied in universities.

I started writing stories after my first story, "The Seraph and the Zambesi," won first place in a competition run by the *London Observer*. My companion blew up when he heard that I had "wasted my time" writing the story for the competition, and was quite put out when I won the prize, although he didn't mind sharing it.

At that time I found it really good to have a literary companion. Sharing the same profession, though in conditions of considerable poverty, gave me the courage to resist any other course of action. Occasionally I took office jobs to help out, but I was always drawn back to freelance writing, especially when eventually I obtained some advance money for books from various publishers. I was given 50 pounds to write my book on Mary Shelley. Somehow I managed to do it well and thoroughly. I revised it a few years ago, and it is in print today; I can honestly say I am proud of this work.

Sharing my writing life with the man in question in the early '50s was, however, a great problem. Severe rationing of food was still in force, and as he was mainly living at home with his parents, they kept his ration book. Roughly three days a week he stayed and worked with me, and he shared my food rations. I was really hungry and undernourished in those days and had to pay the price in a few years' time in the mid '50s, when my health broke down.

Some good emerged from that, however. I broke with the man I had shared with, and felt the wonderful breath of freedom. Soon I recovered from my illness, wrote stories and started a novel. It was commissioned by Macmillan, London—an act that brought a great deal of criticism down on their heads: In those days publishers did not commission first novels. They gave me 100 pounds. Graham Greene, who admired my stories, heard of my difficulties; he voluntarily sent me a monthly check with some bottles of wine for two years to enable me to write without economic stress. My first novel, *The Comforters*, was a success. I was suddenly "the new young thing." Graham was delighted, and of course from that time on I was able to fend for myself. I shall never forget Graham's sweet thoughtfulness.

The success of my creative work was a great relief to me. I am reminded of the great Italian author Leonardo Sciascia's advice to writers: "Want as much money as you like, but be careful not to need it."

I was now, also, Evelyn Waugh's favorite author, since *The Com-*

forters touched on a subject, hallucinations, which he himself was working on in his novel, *The Ordeal of Gilbert Pinfold*; he was generous enough to write a review of my novel in which he said that I had handled the subject better than he had done. Imagine the effect this had on a first-novel author.

I find it difficult to re-read the 21 novels and abundant stories I have written in the past 40 years. Each one represents the convictions and humors of the writing personality I was at the time. I read them as I would another writer's work. Did I write that? I suppose I did. Well, anyway, it has some thought behind it.

Thought is the main ingredient of a creative work, and thought goes with intention of some sort. I remember visiting Auden at his house in Austria some years before he died. He was rewriting some of his poems at the time. He said to me, "I'm not changing my first intentions, but getting closer to what I really meant."

What a writer really means can come to light in a great many mysterious ways. On that same visit Auden told me that a typist had rendered the words "foreign ports" in a poem in his handwriting as "foreign poets." "I realized that 'poets' was the word I really meant," Auden said.

I have found that once I've started on a work, the subject acts as a magnet, almost as if I were consciously surfing the Internet for information. I suppose this has to do with a functioning of our powers of observance. So many facts and phenomena that would normally go unnoticed in the course of a day simply present themselves, as if they positively wanted to be in the book. On occasion this selective process can even influence a book. As an example I can cite one of my novels, *The Only Problem*.

It deals with the problem of good and evil as it is expressed in the biblical Book of Job. The main character in the book is studying the biblical text and the mysterious problems involved in God's relation to humankind depicted by the patriarch Job. I had come to a part of the book where nothing seemed to square. I had, for some reason quite unknown to myself, placed the scene of action near Épinal in France. Then I went there en route to England with my artist friend Penelope Jardine.

Soon after our arrival at Epinal, my friend was looking at one of the numerous tourist brochures littered about the hotel room. Suddenly she said, "There is a museum here at Épinal containing a famous painting of Job and his wife by Georges de la Tour." It was the turning point of my book. We went to look at the painting, and I could see that it would give me all the impetus and logic I needed for continuing with my story. But why had I already chosen Épinal? I know I had never before heard of this painting. And why did Penelope happen to look at that brochure?

Creativity is mysterious. I have been writing since the age of 9, when, on a corner of the kitchen table I wrote an "improved" version of Robert Browning's *The Pied Piper*. (I called him "the Piper Pied" to rhyme with "he cried.") I gave my poem a happy ending, not being at all satisfied with the children of Hamelin disappearing into a mountainside forever, as Browning made them do.

Since then I have learned that happiness or unhappiness in endings is irrelevant. The main thing about a book is that it should end well, and perhaps it is not too much to say that a book's ending casts its voice, color, tone and shade over the whole work.

March 11, 2001

Nadine Gordimer

Few citizens of the republic of letters have as complicated a relationship with the word as Nadine Gordimer does. She is a novelist of considerable subtlety and skill. But she is also an activist, a human Geiger counter, a moral force for South Africa, not only during its most oppressive hour, but now, as it steps from the rubble of apartheid to try its fortunes as a fledgling democracy. Gordimer has lived through her country's fractious history and forged from it novels that do more than mirror a landscape—they dig down like weapons and strike elemental rock.

She is not an easygoing person; she has none of the affable approachability you might expect from a woman who once had dancing and acting ambitions. She is intensely private, prickles at interviews, rejects amiable preambles, cuts questions to the quick. "Artists often try many things before they settle down to do what they do well," she says when asked about the dancing. "It's a kind of showing off, that's all. . . . Eventually they develop one thing. In my case I developed the writing."

Gordimer was born in 1923, the daughter of Jewish immigrants, and grew up in the South African mining town of Springs. Her father had come from Latvia at the age of 13, "a premature man," and went into the jewelry business. Her maternal grandparents moved from London when her mother was 6, to pursue a life in the diamond trade. "My roots are effectively South African," she says, for she had little or no contact with her European relations.

She began to write children's stories at the age of 9 and gathered them up in a newspaper she fashioned daily for herself. She attended a Catholic convent until she was "taken out" at the age of 11, an event she will not discuss. At 15, she published her first short story in a South African magazine. For a brief time in her twenties, she studied at the University of Witwatersrand. But that is the extent of Gordimer's formal education. "I am an autodidact," she says crisply. "The library was my education. I was taught by the literary imaginations of others. It's impossible to learn any other way."

First published in the *New Yorker* in 1949, she now has more than 200 short stories and 13 novels to her name, including her latest, *The Pickup* (2001), a novel about the love between the daughter of a white South African banker and an illegal immigrant from a poor Arab country. Among her many works (once banned in South Africa) are *A Guest of Honour, The Conservationist, July's People* and *A Sport of Nature*. Ten years ago, she was awarded the Nobel Prize.

Seamus Heaney has called her "one of the guerrillas of the imagination," in reference, surely, to her stubborn insistence on focusing her literature tightly on racism, even during the perilous days when friends were in prison, Soweto was a powder keg, and censorship reigned. But when asked if she is a political writer with a mission at hand, she replies, "Not at all. Writing is an exploration of life. If you happen to live in the milieu of conflict, that obviously is what life means to you, and that is what you will explore. . . . I'm actually looking forward to the next few years in my country, after the censorship and oppression. There will be extraordinary stories out of the present. This is the exciting time."

M. A.

Being a Product of Your Dwelling Place

BY NADINE GORDIMER

People always want to know when and where you write. As if there's a secret methodology to be followed. It has never seemed to me to matter to the work—which is the writer's "essential gesture" (I quote Roland Barthes), the hand held out for society to grasp—whether the creator writes at noon or midnight, in a cork-lined room as Proust did or a shed as Amoz Oz did in his early days.

Perhaps the questioner is more than just curious, yearning for a jealously kept prescription on how to be a writer. There is none. Writing is the one "profession" for which there is no professional training: "Creative" writing courses can teach the aspirant only to look at her or his writing critically, not how to create. The only school for a writer is the library—reading, reading. A journey through realms of how far, wide and deep writing can venture in the endless perspectives of human life. Learning from other writers' perceptions that you have to find your way to yours, at the urge of the most powerful sense of yourself—creativity. Apart from that, you're on your own.

Ours is the most solitary of occupations; the only comparison I can think of is the keeper of a lighthouse. But the analogy mustn't go too far; we do not cast the beam of light that will save the individual, or the world, from coming to grief on the rocks.

Another standard inquiry put to fiction writers: What is your message? Milan Kundera has provided the response: "A novel searches and poses questions. . . . The wisdom of the novel comes from having a question for everything. It does not prescribe or proscribe answers." We have the right and the obligation of honesty to imply moral judgments we know that people have, as exemplified in our fictional characters, because—I paraphrase Goethe—wherever the writer thrusts a hand deep into society, the world, something of the truth will come up. The writer stands before what has been dredged to light just as the reader will; what either makes of it will be individual moral judgment: her or his, the writer's or reader's, self-message.

That is the low-wattage beam I would claim for my own writings cast from my lighthouse, and for those of the great writers who have illuminated my life. For me, writing has been and is an exploration of life. That is why my novels and stories are what I call open-ended:

I've taken up an invention of human beings at some point in their lives, and set them down again living at some other point. My novel written in the 1980s, *July's People*, ends with a central character, a woman, wading through a shallow river, running from a situation. To what? I am often asked. The answer is I don't know.

The only clues I have, and pass on for the reader in the text of the novel, are the social and historical context, the conflicting threats and pressures, personal and aleatory, of a time and place that would make up her options—what she could or might attempt next. The sole conclusion was one that I myself could come to, after I had reread the novel (for a writer becomes a reader when the publisher's proofs arrive): Crossing through the water was some kind of baptism into a new situation, new life, however uncertain, hazardous, even unimaginable in the light of how she had lived thus far.

One can't even say that an individual death is the end of a story. What about the consequences the absence is going to have for others?

What about the aftermath of a political and societal conflict apparently resolved, in a novel whose final page leaves the men and women, the country, the cities, the children born to these, at that point? Again, the reader has the narrative and text that have gone before, to waken his or her own awareness, his or her own questioning of self and society.

If the writer does not provide answers, is he or she absolved from the ordinary human responsibility of engagement with society (apart from the "essential gesture," extended through literature)?

Does the writer serve the raison d'être that every human being must decide for the self, by asserting the exploration of the word as the end and not the means of the writer's being? "Words became my dwelling place." The great Mexican poet and writer Octavio Paz wrote this; but in his superb life's work, on his intellectual journey, he invaded that place. He also wrote, "I learnt that politics is not only action but participation, it is not a matter of changing men but accompanying them, being one of them." The reason-to-be was a bringing together of the dwelling place of the artist and the clamorous world that surrounded it.

The great Günter Grass told me: "My professional life, my writing, all the things that interest me, have taught me that I cannot freely choose my subjects. For the most part, my subjects were assigned to me by German history, by the war that was criminally started and conducted, and by the never-ending consequences of that era. Thus my books are fatally linked to these subjects, and I am not the only one who has had this experience."

He certainly is not the only one.

In Europe, the United States, Latin America, China, Japan, Africa—where in the world could this not be so? None of us can "choose our subjects" free of the contexts that contain our lives, shape our thoughts, influence every aspect of our existence. (Even the fantasy of space fiction is an alternative to the known, the writer's imaginative reaction to it.) Could Philip Roth erase the tattoo of the Nazi camps from under the skin of his characters? Can Israeli writers, Palestinian writers, now "choose" not to feel the tragic conflict between their people burning the dwelling place of words? Could Kenzaburo Oe create characters that do not bear the gene of consciousness implanted by Hiroshima and Nagasaki? Could Czeslaw Milosz, living through revolution and exile, not have to ask himself in his poem "Dedication," "What is poetry, which does not save/ Nations or people?" Could Chinua Achebe's characters not have in their bloodstream the strain of a civil war in Nigeria? In Africa, the experiences of colonialism, its apogee, apartheid, post-colonialism and new-nation conflicts have been a powerful collective consciousness in African writers, black and white. And the increasing interconsciousness, the realization that what happens somewhere in the world is just one manifestation of what is happening subliminally, everywhere—the epic of emigration, immigration, the world-wanderings of new refugees and exiles, political and economic, for example—is a fatal linkage. Not "fatal" in the deathly sense, but in that of inescapable awareness in the writer.

However, when a country has come through long conflict and its resolution, its writers are assumed to have lost their "subject." We in South Africa are challenged—top of the list in journalists' interviews—"So what are you going to write about now that apartheid has gone?"

Apartheid was a plan of social engineering, and its novels, stories, poetry and plays were an exploration of how people thought and lived, their ultimate humanity out of reach of extinction. Life did not end with apartheid; it began, from that human base. "The new situation must bring new subjects"—Czech writer Ivan Klima wrote this, in exile, and out of the breakup of his country. In South Africa there is not breakup and its violent consequences, but rather a difficult and extraordinary bringing together of what was divided. The new subjects, some wonderful, some dismaying, have scarcely had time to choose us.

"What do we know / But that we face / One another in this place"—William Butler Yeats. That is surely the subject that in the dwelling place of words, everywhere, chooses the writer.

August 5, 2001

Erica Jong

There are books that mark genius and books that shift gears. There are writers who plumb hearts and those who find doors. Erica Jong will long be remembered by baby boomers as the woman who shifted the gears and threw open the door to a full frontal view of contemporary female sexuality in fiction. When Jong's edgy Isadora Wing (*Fear of Flying*) burst onto the sex-crazed, drug-hazed culture of the early '70s, she led the way to a new kind of American heroine—the carnal obsessive. The queen of "zipless" sex.

Jong grew up in New York City, the second daughter of a painter and a musician. Her mother was a portrait artist whose parents had emigrated from Russia; her father, a songwriter who turned businessman in order to support the various generations that inhabited their West Side apartment.

"We had all the problems of a New York Jewish intellectual family," she recalls, referring to that singular mix of Manhattan neurosis and fizz. "It was hard to get a word in at the dinner table. When I first saw Woody Allen's *Hannah and Her Sisters*, I thought he was writing about me."

She attended New York's public High School of Music and Art in the '50s, filling her notebooks with sketches and poetry, and reading her work out loud to anyone at home who would listen. Her favorite childhood book at 12 was Frances Hodgson Burnett's *The Little Princess*, a Victorian novel about a little girl shut in a garret. "After that, a rush of Russian novels, with no particular emotional equipment in place to understand them."

She studied writing at Barnard and 18th-century English literature at Columbia, "reading novels like bonbons" and combing poetry with Robert Pack, Stanley Kunitz and Mark Strand. By the time she was working on her Ph.D., she had produced two books of poetry, *Fruits and Vegetables* and *Halflives*. "I was such an academic, I don't recognize myself when I look back. I knew exactly how to write tedious, footnoted tomes, and never suspected I would do anything else."

But in the late '60s she tried her hand at a novel. "It was after I'd read some Nabokov. My story was about a male poet who sets out to kill his döppelganger."

Aaron Asher, an editor at Holt, read it and offered his advice. "Someone will probably publish this," he said. "I don't want to. Some day you'll thank me for it."

"And then he said another thing: 'That female voice in your poems. Why isn't it in this novel?'

"It was my Aha moment, as if a wind had come in behind me, pushing. I began to think—John Updike had written *Couples*, Henry Miller had published *Tropic of Cancer*, Roth had done *Portnoy's Complaint*—males were writing about the bedroom. Why not women? Why not me? But we were still undiscovered country—no one had written about what goes on in a woman's head with any nakedness, and by the time I shelved the first manuscript and went off and finished the new one, I had decided no one would want to publish it."

Asher did. At first, *Fear of Flying* was received as a literary feat. Updike reviewed it in the *New Yorker*. Henry Miller wrote about it elsewhere. And then, when it was published in paperback, the book's dynamic changed entirely. "There was a media frenzy. A scandal. Here was this young woman coming out of nowhere to talk about sex. And she had blond hair . . . The book became a bestseller for extraliterary reasons. I felt exposed, traumatized."

Jong has produced numerous books since, but none with the impact of *Fear of Flying*. The two Isadora sequels—*How to Save Your Own Life* (1977) and *Parachutes and Kisses* (1984)—never quite reached the greater public's consciousness. But Jong has been tireless in production: To date she has published 6 volumes of poetry and 7 novels, among them, *Fanny*,

Being the True History of the Adventures of Fanny Hackabout-Jones (1980), *Any Woman's Blues* (1990) and *Inventing Memory* (1997). She has written nonfiction as well: *The Devil at Large*, about her friendship with Henry Miller, and *Fear of Fifty*, her mid-life memoir about what she calls the Whiplash Generation—women raised to be Doris Day, wanting to be Gloria Steinem, and raising their daughters in the retrograde age of Princess Di and Madonna.

"I'm always asked in seminars to stand for contemporary womanhood," she says. "And I'm glad to do it. I like being a mentor." She marvels at bestsellers like *The Rules*, which counsels young women to lure marriage partners by appearing demure and naive. "It's as if they've just discovered flirting. Here's a generation that grew up on Oprah—describing every aspect of their lives on national TV—and then they have to be told not to give their secrets away on the first date. Pretty amusing, eh?"

M. A.

Doing It for Love

BY ERICA JONG

Despite all the cynical things writers have said about writing for money, the truth is we write for love. That is why it is so easy to exploit us. That is also why we pretend to be hard-boiled, saying things like "No man but a blockhead ever wrote except for money" (Samuel Johnson). Not true. No one but a blockhead ever wrote except for love.

There are plenty of easier ways to make money. Almost anything is less labor-intensive and better paid than writing. Almost anything is safer. Reveal yourself on the page repeatedly, and you are likely to be rewarded with exile, prison or neglect. Ask Dante or Oscar Wilde or Emily Dickinson. Scheme and betray, and you are likely to be rewarded with wealth, publicity and homage. Tell the truth, and you are likely to be a pariah within your family, a semi-criminal to authorities and damned with faint praise by your peers. So why do we do it? Because saying what you think is the only freedom. "Liberty" said Camus, "is the right not to lie."

In a society in which everything is for sale, in which deals and auctions make the biggest news, doing it for love is the only remaining liberty. Do it for love and you cannot be censored. Do it for love and you cannot be stopped. Do it for love and the rich will envy no one more than you. In a world of tuxedos the naked man is king. In a world of bookkeepers with spreadsheets, the one who gives it away without counting the cost is God.

I seem to have known this from my earliest years. I never remember a time when I didn't write. Notebooks, stories, journals, poems—the act of writing always made me feel centered and whole. It still does. It is my meditation, my medicine, my prayer, my solace. I was lucky enough to learn early (with my first 2 books of poetry and my first novel) that if you are relentlessly honest about what you feel and fear, you can become a mouthpiece for something more than your own feelings. People are remarkably similar at the heart level—where it counts. Writers are born to voice what we all feel. That is the gift. And we keep it alive by giving it away.

It is a sacred calling. The writers I am most drawn to understand it as such: Thomas Merton, Pablo Neruda, Emily Dickinson.

But one doesn't always see the calling clearly as one labors in the fields of love. I often find myself puzzling over the choices a writer is given. When I am most perplexed, I return to my roots: poetry. The novel is elastic: It allows for social satire, cooking, toothbrushes, the way we live now. Poetry, on the contrary, boils things down to essences. I feel privileged to have done both.

And I am grateful to have found my vocation early. I was also blessed to encounter criticism early. It forced me to listen to my inner voice, not the roar of the crowd. This is the most useful lesson a writer can learn.

Lately, we keep hearing dire warnings about the impending death of the novel. As one who has written frankly autobiographical fiction (*Fear of Flying*), historical fiction (*Fanny, Serenissima* or *Shylock's Daughter*) and memoir (*Fear of Fifty* and *The Devil at Large*), I think I've begun to understand how the process of making fiction differs from that of making memoir. A memoir is tethered to one's own experience in a particularly limiting way: The observing consciousness of the book is rooted in a real person. That person may be fascinating, but he or she can never be as rich and subtle as the characters that grow out of aspects of the author. In the memoir the "I" dominates. In the novel the "I" is made up of many "I's". More richness is possible, more points of view, deeper imitation of life.

When I finished *Fear of Fifty*, I felt I had quite exhausted my own life and might never write another book. What I eventually discovered was that the process had actually liberated me. Having shed my own autobiography, I now felt ready to invent in a new way. I wanted to write a novel about the 20th century and how it affected the lives of women. I wanted to write a novel about a Jewish family in the century that nearly saw the destruction of the Jewish people.

I began by reading history and literature for a year. And when I started to write again, it was in the voice of a woman who might have been my great-grandmother. Liberated from my place and time, I found myself inventing a woman's voice quite different from my own. But as I began to fashion this alternate family history, I found myself at play in the fields of my imagination. Characters sprang up like mushrooms after rain. I couldn't wait to get to work in the morning to see what I thought and who was going to embody it.

Eventually I found I had four heroines, born in different decades, and that they were all mothers and daughters. Each had a distinctive voice and way of looking at the world. Each was me and not-me.

Graham Greene once said: "The main characters in a novel must necessarily have some kinship to the author, they come out of his body as a child comes out of the womb, then the umbilical cord is cut and they grow into independence. The more the author knows of his own character the more he can distance himself from his invented characters and the more room they have to grow in."

That seems to me precisely right. A novelist's identity is fixed. Her character, however, can fly.

A character may even access some deep memory in the writer's brain that seemed lost forever. Fictional characters excavate real memories. Flaubert, after all, claimed to be Emma Bovary and gave her his restlessness and discontent. In some ways an author may be freer to expose himself in a character unlike himself. There is liberty behind a mask. The mask may become the condition for speaking the truth.

The line between novel and autobiography has never been as blurry as it is in our century. And this is probably a good thing. The novel endures because it mimics truth. So if we find truths in autobiography in our age, even fiction will come to mimic that genre. And genres themselves matter less and less. The most enduring books of the modern era are, like *Ulysses,* full of exposition, narrative, dramatic writing and even poetry.

As a reader, I want a book to kidnap me into its world. Its world must make the so-called real world seem flimsy. Its world must lure me to return. When I close the book, I should feel bereft.

How rare this is and how grateful I am to find it. The utter trust that exists between reader and author is like the trust between lovers. If I feel betrayed by the author, I will never surrender to him or her again.

That trust is why it is so hard to start a new book. You must find the right voice (or voices) for the timbre that can convince a reader to give himself up to you. Sometimes it takes years to find the tone of voice that unlocks the story.

The books we love best kidnap us with the first line. "Whether I shall turn out to be the hero of my own life, or whether that station will be held by anybody else, these pages must show" (David Copperfield). "You don't know about me, without you have read a book by the name of *The Adventures of Tom Sawyer,* but that ain't no matter" (Huckleberry Finn). It's not only the question of an arresting opening—the writer's best trick—but of letting the main character's quirks show too. I tried it myself in *Fear of Flying*: "There were 117 analysts on the Pan Am flight to Vienna and I'd been treated by at least six of them." And it's easier to do in first person than in third.

But, as I said in the beginning, you must do it for love. If you do it for money, no money will ever be enough, and eventually you will start imitating your first successes, straining hot water through the same old tea-bag. It doesn't work with tea, and it doesn't work with writing. You must give all you have and never count the cost. ("Sit down at the typewriter and open a vein," as Red Smith said).

Every book I have written has subsumed all the struggles of the years in which I wrote it. I don't know how to hold back. Editing comes only after the rush of initial feeling. I end up by cutting hundreds of pages sometimes. But in the writing process, I let it all hang out. Later I and my editor chop.

Generosity is the soul of writing. You write to give something. To yourself. To your reader. To God. You give thanks for having been given the words. You pray to be given words another day.

Laurence Sterne knew this: "I begin with the first sentence and trust to Almighty God for the second." Amen.

February 9, 1997

II

Raw Material

Alice McDermott

Craig Nova

George Pelecanos

Jayne Anne Phillips

Ntozake Shange

Scott Turow

John Edgar Wideman

Anita Desai

Julia Alvarez

John Banville

Alice McDermott

By 1993, when Alice McDermott wrote this piece, things seemed to come in threes in her life: three children, three novels, three universities in which she's taught, even three cross-country moves since the launching of her remarkable career. Her son Willie came after her first novel, *A Bigamist's Daughter*. The birth of Eames followed the publication of *That Night*, which was nominated for the National Book Award and made into a movie. Patrick, the child to follow her third book, *At Weddings and Wakes*, arrived a mere six weeks before the publication of this piece. Her children come as easily as her novels—both products of the fascination childhood and family hold for this quietly dazzling writer.

She was born in 1953, the third child of an Irish Catholic marriage, and spent her childhood in the little Long Island community of Elmont, just across the border from Queens. Her fiction mirrors those origins, evoking smalltown life with elegiac power and sadness.

From parochial schools, McDermott went on to study English at Oswego State College. She worked in New York City for one year as a typist at a vanity press, wresting from that quirky milieu the setting for her first novel. She then did graduate work at the University of New Hampshire, returning to New York to write freelance for women's magazines and read the slush pile for *Redbook* and *Esquire*—earning $40 for every manuscript she evaluated. Celebrating the sale of her first short story to *Ms.* in a bar named The Mad Hatter, McDermott met her future husband, David Armstrong, now a research scientist. Within a year, a publisher had bought her first novel on the basis of its first 50 pages alone.

Most striking about McDermott, apart from her memorable books, is her modesty. Emerging from the birth of her third child to do a reading marking the paperback release of *At Weddings* and Wakes, she was asked to talk a bit about her life. "About my life?" she mused as she looked out into the packed bookstore. "Well, let's see. All I can remember about my life right now is the furnace that gave out this morning. That and the leaky pipes. Oh, yes . . . and the very long line of plumbers."

In 2000, seven years after she wrote this "Writing Life," McDermott won the National Book Award for her novel, *Charming Billy*.

M. A.

Too Happy for Words

BY ALICE McDERMOTT

While in graduate school in the late '70s, I took a course in contemporary fiction by women and read, at a time when it still seemed radical and ground-breaking, *The Women's Room* by Marilyn French. I recall that the book inspired a great deal of discussion but none quite so passionate as what ensued when one of the members of the class, a middle-aged woman who, like the novel's heroine, had raised her children and now returned to school, objected to French's depiction of motherhood as "an unending mound of dirty dishes" and an endless stream of urine in the eye. An outrageous distortion, the woman said. She claimed that the time she herself had spent at home with her young children was the most glorious time of her life.

We single twentysomethings in the class responded with pitying smiles. Clearly childbirth had addled the woman's brain. Of course you were meant to believe it was the most glorious time of your life, one of us explained, but look at it for what it really was: lost time, time you're trying to make up for now. Look at what even the fiercest motherly love becomes for each of the women in the novel: another pair of emotional shackles, golden handcuffs.

A decade later, those of us who had so rationally disabused our older friend of any romantic notions about reproduction were sending birth announcements and gushing letters to one another across the country. The letters read like book jacket blurbs for some Vatican marriage manual: "Becoming a mother is the best thing I've ever done." "It's like floating in warm milk." "I could fill a stadium with babies."

Now the fiction we were reading and writing depicted motherhood as something more than a burden or a biological happenstance, now there were happy, loving mothers appearing as heroines in our novels and stories. And yet some sense of those emotional shackles lingered, for it seemed time and again that these happy mothers who loved their children did so at their own risk.

The novels we were now reading and recommending to one another (Sue Miller's *The Good Mother* comes to mind, Mary Gordon's *Men and Angels,* Toni Morrison's *Beloved*) all contained mothers who loved their children fiercely, who even celebrated that love, but who were nevertheless brought by it not to exalted and contented old age, but to the edge of the abyss, to some version of Sophie's choice.

The happy mother in fiction began to seem like the sweet-faced soldier in old war movies, the one who shows his young wife's photo or befriends a puppy in the first reel—the one most clearly marked for catastrophe.

As a writer I recognize that much of this can be accounted for by the demands of plot—no doubt all happy mothers are like happy families: alike. And as Tolstoy warned us, sustained joy doesn't make much of a story. But these days, as I lift myself out of the delighted fog that accompanied the birth of my third child and find myself once again in conversation with other mothers, trying to define what it is we feel as we progress through this whole experience of labor and delivery and watching our children grow—and grow away from us—I can't help but wonder if there is something else that keeps fiction writers, especially those of us who are mothers ourselves, from making the complexity, the challenge, the joy of our experience the full subject of our work.

I wonder if it's superstition: if we feel that to admit to such contentment in life would compromise our status as artists—perhaps recalling the poor actress in *The Portrait of Dorian Gray* who fell in love and lost her talent. Perhaps we fear alienating our male colleagues who would no doubt respond to such a work with the cry that fatherhood, too, is wonderful. (And we, the mothers of sons, would be obliged to tell them, soothingly, Of course, dear. Of course it is. Even better.)

More and more, I find myself recalling the story of Niobe, Queen of Thebes, who appeared before her people as they worshipped the goddess Leto and pointed out that she, Niobe, mother of seven sons and seven daughters, was far more worthy of their praise than Leto who was mother of only two. Her people, remarkably enough, saw the wisdom in this, put an end to their rituals and went home.

I sometimes suspect that had her story ended there, with Niobe's triumph, the motherhood novel might now be a genre all to itself, as common as the coming-of-age novel, the war novel, the novel that begins or ends with, or turns on, murder, but Leto calls on her twins to avenge her and one by one Niobe's 14 children are slain. She is left bereft, weeping and finally turned to silent stone.

I know plenty of women who understand Niobe's pride, I've read the essays they've written for women's magazines and baby books, I know of some poets who have captured it, but I've yet to hear her voice, undiminished by Leto's retribution, in fiction. It may simply be that such happiness doesn't make for much of a story. It may be that some of us see Leto as book critic and take Niobe's story as a cautionary tale to keep our mouths shut. It may be that there is some abiding sense that society and biology have indeed conspired to delude us and we only think that the days we spend with our children are the most glorious of our lives.

But at this stage in my own career as a mother, as I beam over my own brood, the writer in me begins to suspect something else: I begin to suspect that what we feel for our children is perhaps too satisfying, too marvelous to be carried fully into fiction. Fiction requires the attendant threat, the dramatic reversal, not only because these are the things that make for plot and tension and a sense of story, but because without them any depiction of our joy might appear overstated. We hesitate to include in our fiction what so often strikes us in life as something too good to be true.

May 9, 1993

Craig Nova

There was a time when Craig Nova worked as a Manhattan cabbie, hitting the road before dawn, trawling the streets bleary-eyed, hacking fares until dusk, then pulling over to scribble stories late into the night—bits he would later cobble together for his second novel, *The Geek* (1975). His first was *Turkey Hash*, written when he was in his 20s and published in 1972. *Incandescence* (1979) was the last product of what he now calls a callow youth. Thereafter, Nova left the big city for the woodlands of Vermont, moving into a maturity that would produce such novels as *The Good Son (1982), The Congressman's Daughter* (1986), *Tornado Alley* (1989) and *Trombone* (1992)—hailed in *Book World*'s pages as "among the best American fiction of the past two decades." In 2002, he published the remarkably original *Wetware*.

Fatherhood, says Nova, was what forged that maturity: "It was as if an invisible but palpable rope from my chest went to the chest of my child. The further away she got, the more I felt the tug. It was then I began to think about my own father—about how he always had been—always would be—a tug on my life."

The father-son conflict is a recurring theme in Nova's novels, endowing his dark, powerful storylines with a universality that is rare in this age of self-referential fiction. His characters are hungering souls, indomitable in the grim worlds they inhabit, familiar in their flaws. *Trombone*, for example, is the story of a young boy and his arsonist father—a failed, bitter mob pawn whose only pleasure is in defiance and whose only power is in a torch. The boy, a decent, moral sort, must find his way in the shadow of such a man.

Nova's own father was a Polish immigrant (Nowotarski was his name before he changed it), who worked as an engineer in a California aerospace company. Nova spent his childhood in Hollywood and, as a teenager, raced alongside Steve McQueen's AC Cobra on Mulholland Drive. He went to U.C. Berkeley, then on to Columbia, where he learned his craft under the wing of Jean Stafford.

He writes, as his piece here suggests, far more than he ever incorporates into his final novels. The 500-page Hollywood novel *The Book of Dreams* (1994) was 4,000 pages in first draft before he "sweated it down like a steambox" to the ideal combination of pace and texture that is his goal. "There's something comforting in watching those stories pile up day by day," he says in his gentle, pensive manner. "That's the nice-guy-good-cop part of me at work. The bad cop always comes through in the end, though—that's the guy with the anger, the one who cuts it all to the bone and makes it right."

M. A.

Using My Father's Story

BY CRAIG NOVA

While writing has its own charms, as Dickens pointed out some years ago, it has some of its own terrors, too. Perhaps terrors is too strong a word for the difficulty I have in mind, but I can tell you this: It keeps me awake at night. Every novelist I have ever known, and I have known a lot of them over the years, all had a story he or she would try again and again to use in a book, only to find, after considerable effort, that the story simply wouldn't work. In my case, there are five or six of these, and in some circumstances I have written thousands of pages in an attempt to hammer one into a book, and yet, in the end, I admitted, as I have admitted many times before, that it would have to be dropped after all. The worst part of this business is being midway through a new book and feeling that forbidden impulse toward writing the story again, which impulse I give in to with all the sweetness of delusion, just like anyone who is seduced by momentary pleasure without a thought as to its consequences.

For instance, for some time now I have been trying to work a story about the death of my father into a novel. I often think about his dying and his death. This doesn't come from a morbid state of mind, since mostly I am pretty cheerful and have long made a habit of counting the blessings I have. I suppose I think about my father for a number of reasons, not the least of which is that beneath the other things that attended his death (grief, awkwardness, relief, disorientation) there was a sure, distinct whiff of chaos.

My father died of cancer. He had a great ability to stand up to things, and it was something I always admired about him: He seemed to have an infinite capacity to endure almost anything that takes will and stamina (qualities, I might add, that come in handy in the life of a novelist, which is how I make my living). It was typical of my father that he made dying into a variety of contest, and he did so with a flat, unemphatic imperative that left me thinking, even near the end, that death had gotten itself into more than it had bargained for. When I went to visit my father, he pulled up his pant legs and showed me his ankles. Then he looked at me and said, "Do you see any swelling? If my ankles swell, I'm supposed to call the doctor." This question was always put to me with defiance in his eyes, the substance unstated but still clear, "Do you dare tell me there's swelling? Have you got what it takes to say that to me?" The possibility of calling the doctor was always presented in a tone he would have used if he had said, "When money grows on trees, I'll start planting a garden."

I didn't get to see my father that often when he was sick. I was living in New York and he was in the house where I had grown up, which was in Hollywood. The house was in the hills, north of Mulholland, and from the backyard you could see the Universal back lot. The studios always had a presence in my youth.

In the hills in Hollywood, or at least on the street where my parents lived, the slope was so steep that one house was built a little above the next one. The roof of my parents house was at about the height of the lawn of the house next door.

I had never met the man who lived next door, since he had arrived long after my departure. But one day, when my father was dying, the neighbor stopped my mother in the street and said to her, "What's wrong with that lazy husband of yours? Why is he always lying around?" My mother told the neighbor that my father was sick.

The neighbor had a habit of watering his lawn and letting the sprinklers go all night, and this made a flood that ran down into my parents' drive and then down into the garage, which was at the end of the drive. The garage was my father's "hooch," a place where he kept his tools and where he built a workbench and where he kept a 1955 Thunderbird, a car he stopped driving as soon as he learned he was sick.

My mother called the neighbor and asked him to turn off the water. He would not. My father got out of bed, unable to stand up straight, and built a dike to keep the water away from his tools and the car.

The neighbor seemed to delight in this business of the water. Perhaps it was a way he had of confronting the mysteries of someone dying. Or, perhaps, he was a man who enjoyed this kind of behavior. But this business of the flood continued. My father got out of bed to rebuild the dam when it gave way.

After my father died, I went to California to visit my mother. There was one afternoon when she had gone out to shop, and I realized I had been waiting for the right moment to visit the man who lived next door. It was the silence of my parents' house that made me realize how I had been waiting to settle old scores with him.

It is not more than 100 yards from the front door of my parents' house to the neighbor's door, but I remember that it took some time to get there: It was a fall California day, smoky, the sky pale, the air yellow, the shadows indistinct, just the kind of weather one would pick as appropriate for such a visit. It's the kind of weather for an unpleasant surprise.

It was a large Spanish house, three stories, with terra-cotta tile, pinkish stucco and an enormous, dark wood front door. The door had wrought iron hinges and an enormous wrought iron knocker. I remember standing there for a moment before I began to knock. So, it all comes down to this, is what I thought.

The man wasn't home. I had always assumed he would be, as though he knew that we had an appointment to keep. Or, if he was there on this afternoon, he had the good sense to leave the knock unanswered, although there can be no doubt that he heard it if he was there. After the first few unanswered knocks, I found myself hitting the door, banging on it, hearing the doom doom doom of it in that enormous, gaudy and empty house. The sound itself had a kind of maddening quality, as though the booming was a grossly amplified last beating of a heart, or the cadence of a special chaos we hardly ever get close to. In the midst of it, I stood there, knowing it was time to end my grieving and to get on with the things I had to, and to do it with the same defiance as that my father used to give death second thoughts about the entire business.

The question is, why won't such a story work, or why couldn't it be the point of departure for a section of a novel? Well, after some thought, it seems to me that the problem isn't in the story itself, so much as in the novelist's perception of it. As nearly as I can tell, the stories one writes again and again without success are usually part of a writer's personal experience, and somehow they are too "real," too tied to the details with which they took place. This doesn't seem like a great difficulty, but for the novelist, or so it seems to me, it is crucial. The truth for a novelist isn't the same as the facts, and for a story that is drawn from life to work in a book, a novelist needs to have a sense of the story's adjustability, or its "lightness" (if such a word can be used). If the story is mired in its own imperatives, the novelist is doomed to a simple, uninspired retelling of it, and, as such, is forbidden to do what should be done. It seems to me that when a writer is successful in using a story taken from experience, it is not told exactly the way it happened, but in the way that reveals, through all one's beliefs, hopes and fears, how the event should have happened.

Knowing this, however, doesn't make the problem go away. As Seneca wrote 2,000 years ago, "For what vice, pray, has ever lacked its defender?" Well, yes. After all, there's the story I know about that film director who moved a house from France to Malibu. Didn't they number the stones so they could put the house back together once it got to California? Well, sure. Maybe this time I could tell it in another voice. Just give the whole thing one good shake.

June 20, 1993

George P. Pelecanos

Crime, like virtue, has its rewards. Especially if your name is George Pelecanos and you've dedicated a whole life to crime.

Crime fiction, that is.

Pelecanos is not the typical "Washington writer." Not for him the alabaster monuments, congressional corridors, blue-blazered agents of influence. You will not find his kind of people on the pages of Allen Drury's *Advise and Consent*, or Joe Klein's *Primary Colors*, or Jeffrey Frank's *Columnist*, or even Margaret Truman's *Murder in Foggy Bottom*. Pelecanos's heroes strut their stuff in a capital city few politicians and tourists see: a greasy back alley of Chinatown, a coke-dusted tenement in Southeast, a broken-down bar in Anacostia. *Hell to Pay*, published just after he wrote this essay, was his 10th novel set in the District's underside.

Now this is not exactly like putting on the noir in L.A., where a long line of scribblers have shooed dicks down boulevards, chasing after bad guys while sultry dolls combed Pacific sand from their hair. Pelecanos has no real predecessor in gritty D.C. crime fiction. He invented the form.

He is Greek, from a family that is "100 percent Spartan." His grandfather sold fruit from a stand in Southeast Market; and after World War II, when his father returned from military duty in the Philippines, he opened a little carry-out kitchen on 14th and R. A ravenous reader, Pelecanos made his way through Silver Spring High School and the University of Maryland. When he looked around for something to write about, he saw a working-class Washington few writers had noticed before.

His first book was *A Firing Offense* (1992), a fairly formulaic yarn of the hard-boiled school, starring Nick Stefanos, an alcoholic salesman with a weakness for heavy-metal, naughty femmes and a fast chase. In the four years that followed, Pelecanos published four more crime novels, all with the drink-sodden Stefanos as gumshoe. "My turning point came in '96 with *The Big Blowdown*," he says. "It was a big, thick, research-driven epic that spanned 20 years. I'd always been proud to be a crime writer, but I wanted more honesty from my writing, more fearlessness. I wanted to write about this town the way it really is." His novels since—*King Suckerman* (1997), *The Sweet Forever* (1998), *Shame the Devil* (2000), and *Right As Rain* (2001)—are violent and troubling works that explore larger themes of urban decay, poverty and race.

When he's not writing, he's sitting in on trials, riding with D.C. cops, working midnight shifts, hanging out at a seedy bar, elbows pinned to the rails, listening to people talk. "There's that moment when you start to write: You've only produced one page all week and you're sitting there in the dark thinking you're a fraud." But if it's worked before, he keeps telling himself, it very likely will work again. For Pelecanos at least, crime seems to pay.

M. A.

Between Origins and Art

BY GEORGE P. PELECANOS

Most of us, it seems, end up where we are supposed to be. In the summer of 1968, two months after the riots, I went to work for my father at his lunch counter and carryout, the Jefferson Coffee Shop, on 19th St. between M and N. Every morning I took a D.C. Transit bus down Georgia Ave., passing by charred storefronts on 7th St., continuing on to F where I transferred to the crosstown line. The fires of April had crippled the city, but there had been a cleansing, too. It was obvious in the chin-high attitude, straight-up posture, and proud style of hair and dress of Washington's working class; obvious, even, to an 11-year-old boy. I found myself looking at these people on the bus, wanting to know more about their inner lives.

My father employed a skeletal, long-time staff. Through them I learned about struggle, friendship, hard triumphs, depression, alcoholism, loyalty and trust. Through our interaction with the suit-and-tie customers, I learned about race and class. We worked to the sounds of gospel and soul stations WOOK ("K comes before L") and WOL. The old-school jams of that era, and the voice of deejay Bobby "The Mighty Burner" Bennett, will be with me forever.

My job was to deliver food, on foot, to the offices in the Dupont Circle area. I listened closely to the rhythms of the speech and the unique slang of the street. I became familiar with every alley. On my runs I made up stories, serial-style, complete with music, to pass the time. I would space the stories out so that they would climax at the end of the week. I thought I was making movies, but I was writing my first books.

My teen years consisted of Rec Department baseball, beer and fortified wine, girls, marijuana, pick-up basketball, muscle cars, Marlboros, rock and funk concerts at Fort Reno and Carter Barron, and stock-boy positions at now-shuttered retailers like Sun Radio at Connecticut and Albemarle. Occasionally, I found trouble. When things threatened to spin out of control, I remained grounded by my family and a martial, Greek-American work ethic I had absorbed, by example, from my parents. It would be hypocritical now to rewrite my history or deny the elements of my former life. Yes, I wasted a lot of time. And yes, it was a whole lot of fun.

Meanwhile, my imagination continued to be ignited at the movies: *The Dirty Dozen* at the Town, *The Wild Bunch* at the Allen, spaghetti westerns and Bond at the RKO Keith's and the Loew's Palace, anything at the Circle, and blaxploitation and kung-fu wherever I could find them, from U Street to Hyattsville's Queens Chapel Drive-in.

And then, finally, in my last year of college at the University of Maryland, books. A teacher, Charles C. Misch, turned me on to the wonders of hardboiled crime fiction and its masters: Chandler, Hammett, Ross Macdonald and the rest. Peripherally, the stories were about crime; specifically, they dissected American society and human politics from the level of the street. In a reversal of the plot trajectory of most popular fiction, the protagonists in these novels rarely won. Noirists like David Goodis presented characters who stumbled and often fell, reaching for and sometimes grabbing a kind of tarnished, unbeautiful redemption. For the first time I knew, with the shock of recognition that only the most fortunate experience, what I wanted to "do."

How to get there was the question. Teachers had told me that I had a natural talent for writing, but I was clueless as to the mechanics. I had never taken a writing class. I wasn't connected. Novelists were other kinds of people, like pro athletes or movie stars. Writers had a certain pedigree and, as I had read many times on the back flaps of their books, "divided their time between Manhattan and Martha's Vineyard." How could any of this be for a guy like me?

Ten years passed. I fell in love with Emily Hawk and we were married. I continued to toil away at blue- and gray-collar jobs. It was not that I was putting on a literary pith helmet, going undercover among the masses to gather material for the books I was "someday" going to write. I was simply working to pay my bills. I sold women's shoes. I hustled other kinds of sales floors, washed dishes in kitchens and poured drinks in bars. All the while I read voraciously, amped by writers like James Crumley, Newton Thornburg and James Lee Burke, who were bringing a literary pedigree to the genre table and turning crime fiction on its head.

In 1989, inspired by the punk rock movement, in which untrained musicians picked up guitars and played, I decided that I was ready to write a novel. I spent the next year in a dark room, writing in longhand, filling notebook after notebook, not knowing if I was writing for anyone other than myself. My manuscript, *A Firing Offense*, was bought by the first publisher who looked at it. I was on my way. I took a job working in the local film industry, and in the next decade co-produced several independent features. I wrote a book a year, at night, as my family grew to five.

On an extended stay in Brazil, in the fall of 1993, I saw hungry children too weak to go on and children with murder in their eyes; it rocked my world and worldview. I began to write with more ambition. I chronicled the societal changes in Washington from 1933 to the present in four novels that have come to be known as the "D.C. Quartet." Those books and my most recent novels (*Right as Rain* and the forthcoming *Hell to Pay*) deal with local issues facing the working class: the endangerment of the city's youth, sub-par schools, racism, drugs, corruption, illegal guns, the importance of family, the responsibility of parenthood and the struggle to find some kind of spirituality in a violent world.

All of the novels, to some degree, attempt to humanize and illuminate the lives of people who are typically underrepresented in American fiction. I mean to leave a record of this town, to entertain and to provoke discussion. My method is simple: to present the world as it is, rather than the way readers want it to be.

It is an unusual way to make a living. The work itself can be intense, solitary and socially retarding. When I'm writing a novel, I write 7 days a week. On serious jags, I rarely leave the house. There are also long periods of inactivity, just sitting around thinking, bouncing a rubber ball on the hearth, listening to music, mind-navigating intricacies of plot and characters, dreaming. I've learned that this is part of my job, too. When I speak to groups of students in public schools, I tell them that, 25 years ago, I was exactly where they are today. I want to demystify all of this, make them see that whatever they want in life is within their grasp. But they have to take the first steps. They have to try.

My life has accelerated to a different level these past couple of years. I travel extensively, both nationally and abroad, to promote the books. I've done readings in rowdy London pubs, drunk Guinness and Irish whiskey in Dublin, eaten like a king in Athens, walked through Paris at Christmas time, and appeared on prime-time television shows overseas. I've been flown to foreign arts festivals to introduce and discuss my beloved westerns and film noirs. I ride in limousines, stay in first-class hotels, meet with rappers and actors on film projects, hear my voice on NPR, and routinely see my face in magazines and newspapers.

And, honestly, I just laugh. I laugh because I know where I came from, and that's not me. In the end, nothing has really changed. I'm still watching the people on the bus. I'm still walking the alleys, making up stories in my head. I'm where I'm supposed to be.

January 27, 2002

Jayne Anne Phillips

"Scratch the surface of any family," says Jayne Anne Phillips, "and you'll find that it has its secrets." The children may be unaware of them—"closed out," as she puts it—"but they sense the weight" and will spend the rest of their days tracking the elusive, underground history that marks their lives.

Secrecy is not a subject she reserves for the pages of her books. Phillips shrouds herself in it, making it clear to her interviewers that the most rudimentary facts of her life are strictly private. She will not reveal the name of her husband, for instance, or what their life is like in the suburbs of Boston. She will only say that she has two sons.

This much about her is known: She was raised in Buckhannon, West Va., a backwater locale that informs the tenor and texture of everything she has ever written. The only daughter of a construction worker and an elementary school reading teacher, she says she was an impressionable child who found refuge in books and in stringing words together.

She began by writing poetry; her three novels—*Machine Dreams, Shelter* and *Motherkind*—are testimony to an inclination to carefully crafted, lapidary prose. But Phillips quickly understood that her poems were "too narrative to be much good." By the time she was 14 or 15, she was teaching herself to write short stories.

The first of her stories to be published appeared in a small North Carolina magazine called *Truck*, in the mid–1970s. They were fragmented works—"brittle episodes" one critic called them, "of despair, violence and sex." Even today, Phillips concedes, her stories "Lecher" and "Slave" would not be welcome in the pages of a more mainstream literary journal. She was writing at "the outer margins of things." In 1979 she gathered a collection of those stories in one volume, *Black Tickets*. The book won an award from the prestigious American Academy of Arts and Letters. She was all of 26.

Phillips next wrote her first novel, *Machine Dreams* (1985), a sprawling, generational epic of a small-town family caught up in the engine of the Vietnam War. "I meant it as a kind of warning," she says now, "that ordinary people could be the brunt of the most remote actions . . . . Critics assumed that I had some direct experience with Vietnam, but neither of my brothers were involved. All the same, when I am asked if I had a personal experience with the war, I always say yes." The book got her a National Book Critics Circle Award nomination and entry into a group known in the mid-'80s as "the girls of Knopf"—a literary brat pack of women in their 20s and 30s (among them Tama Janowitz, Amy Hempel, Lorrie Moore, Mona Simpson and Louise Erdrich) destined for quick fame.

Her next collection of short stories, *Fast Lane*, appeared that same year. But it took Phillips 10 years to produce her second novel, *Shelter*. In the process she left behind her roving life as waitress, pre-school aide, home improvement worker (bathroom makeovers, with an emphasis on windows and panelling) and world wanderer (Nepal and India, looking for truths about faith and surrender) to get married, raise a family and see both of her parents through difficult deaths. Now Phillips is a mellower writer, a deliberate wordsmith intent on chronicling America's darkest preoccupations.

M. A.

The Writer As Outlaw

BY JAYNE ANNE PHILLIPS

The writing life is a secret life, whether we admit it or not. Writers focus perpetually on the half-seen, and we live in the dim or glorious shadows of partially apprehended shapes. We could bill ourselves as perceptually challenged—given that we live two lives at once, segueing from one to the other with some distress—but we accept, long before we publish, the outlaw's mantle. We occupy a kind of border country, focused on the details that speak to us. Ask those who marry us, or those who don't: We're too intensely involved, yet never quite present. Perhaps we're difficult to live with as adults, but often we were precocious, overly responsible children—not in what we accomplish, necessarily, but in what we remember, in the emotional burdens we take on.

Many of us were our mother's confidantes, the special children with whom hopes and betrayals were discussed. Our mothers were often women who lived alone, in reality or in spirit, women whose passionate beliefs and perceptions knew little outlet but this blood tie, this receptive listener who would take it all to heart. We listened out of love, and because we felt in ourselves a reservoir of longing: We were unfailingly attracted to the secrets of others, and to secrets shrouded in the phenomenon of the world. We knew too much: In this we were outlaws. Early on, we were awarded possession of a set of truths, enlisted to protect someone's version, yet we lived in the context of those stories and we understood the truth to shift. The truth was agile as a dream. Only language could match its permutations or approach its complexity.

So it is that we children who become writers evolve into a particular genus of angelic spy, absorbing information, bargaining with ourselves, banking on the possibility that we might one day intervene in the dynamics of loss, insist that sorrow not be meaningless. In this way we might speak, yet not betray a trust. Those whose voices first blessed us with an ambivalent power still stride through our heads, their luminous forms breaking down. They are lost, finally, as we know ourselves to be lost. Yet literature insists on history—the story of a life, intimately known—and writers gamble with redemption. Surely our hope in holding a world still between the covers of a book is to make that world known, to save it from vanishing. We may be agnostics or furious atheists, but we are all religious, and we practice a faith. We probably don't pray: Prayer is always a veiled request, and writers avoid asking for directions. Writing as practice is more similar to meditation, which requests nothing. There is the same silence and the waiting, but writers are notoriously failed seekers. We watch our thoughts arise and practice attachment, fascinated by the dance of the flames. There's a mystery to penetrate within that heat, one that defies boundaries. Writers grow up with permeable selves, and the very process of secrecy feels familiar.

Writers begin as readers, and words become a means of survival. At some juncture deep within family life, the child sees in written language a way to embrace her own burden. When I was young, words themselves seemed secret because I read them in my mind and no one else could hear. Knowledge was often secret; the most interesting things were repeated in low tones. And late at night the life of the house was magnified. My father was an insomniac who walked the long hallway; he'd camp out in the bathroom while everyone else was asleep, smoking and reading. What did he read? Those books were stacked on the top shelf of the bathroom cabinet, behind closed doors, out of reach. They were all paperbacks, detective stories with guns on their covers, or couples, half-undressed, or maybe a woman in defiant high-heels and clothes that clung.

We kids weren't allowed to lock doors, but we got around that rule in the bathroom by shutting the door and pulling out a drawer that in effect barred any entrance. I had to climb up on the counter and hang perilously to the shelves themselves in order to look at my father's books, to page through them looking for the most secret, forbidden lines, and so it was that I discovered at age 8 or 9, Updike's *Rabbit, Run*. I opened the book to find Janice on her knees beside the bathtub, drunk and panic-stricken, trying to find her baby in the deep water. I read the scene once, I read it twice: I felt myself flung inside Janice and I couldn't get out. I couldn't stop reading, maintaining my cramped balance by holding to the frame of the narrow window, only letting go to turn pages. Outside a drowsy bank of lilacs nodded in the heat, bulbous and densely fragrant, shaded in foliage, and suddenly it really was night, I was in my bed, seeing the image of the book, its cover illustration so like the others, shut away. There were layers of secrets. Adults failed miserably, parents killed their children: I knew this already, having heard the women talk about a 14-year-old girl out our road who gave birth alone in a field and left the baby there. That girl was a stranger. But I recognized Janice from my own nightmares; she was like me in dreams I couldn't stop having that summer; partially blind, on her knees in a room that tilted, and she'd done something that could never be undone; it was too late.

I woke from the dreams terrified, relieved to discover nothing was wrong—nothing visible, nothing real. I said the word in the dark, banishing last fears after every startled awakening: nothing. Janice was nothing like Marlo Thomas or Mary Tyler Moore, plucky icons of my childhood sitcoms, and nothing like my own mother, who would never, never lose her baby in a bathtub.

Who was Janice then, and why did I know her? I saw that the trick within the world of the book was like the trick in dreams: It had been too late always, even before the book began. The water in the tub was too deep, the baby was slippery, she was blind drunk and lost her grip, then forgot for an instant she'd lost it. Everything beyond that moment was drenched with shadow; everything before it was lit up. Now when I woke at night and saw a sliver of light cast across the dark hallway, spilled out from under the closed bathroom door, I knew Janice was in there. All my dark dreams had flown to her: I didn't have them anymore.

This, then, was how language worked. And if it could save me, it could save us all.

October 16, 1994

Ntozake Shange

Don't count on what feels real today, a Pirandello character warns, for by tomorrow all reality will slip into illusion. Ntozake Shange seems to work the other way around: She pulls illusions from her grab bag one by one to build a time and place that feels as certain as a childhood memory. She may not think she is a linear person, but as an African-American fiction writer, she has engineered worlds.

She was born Paulette Williams in Trenton, N.J., in 1948. Her father was a doctor in the Air Force; her mother a social worker. She spent her early years in a segregated military base in upstate New York. When the Korean War was over, her father moved the family to St. Louis, where he studied surgery at one of the few hospitals that would train black physicians.

At the mostly white Dewey School in St. Louis, Shange grew up in the late '50s and early '60s understanding that she was coming of age in a turbulent time. "There was a war going on, and I felt I would disappoint my parents if I didn't represent the race without faltering. It would have been cowardly to admit that I was tormented, scared. But if they could survive racism, so could I. I was obligated to perform."

And perform she did. At school she read Sartre, Molière, Chaucer, and got top grades. But she would come home and share her misgivings about that European canon with her mother. "I learned quickly that school would reprimand me for my views. Home was where all the interesting people congregated and the interesting things were said. When I got up my courage to tell my high school English teacher that I wanted to write a eulogy for Malcolm X, his response was "Oh, come on now. Stop beating that dead horse."

By 1966, when she enrolled at Barnard College, she was the quintessential good girl headed for the life of a scholar. She spent a summer at

New York's Lycée Français, determined to enter Barnard's French classes second to no one. And even though it was the decade of rebellion, she pretty much did as she was told: Her parents told her to put aside her jazz violin, and so she did. Her professors told her she had talent, and so she wrote. Her family told her she'd be a good teacher, and so she was.

Shange spent the next decade doing graduate work and teaching at a string of colleges around the country: the University of Southern California, California State at Long Beach, Trenton State, Sonoma State, City College, Rutgers. She published her poetry anywhere she could: *Black Maria*, *Kin Kan*, the *American Poetry Review*.

But in 1974 she got her big break. Her play *For Colored Girls Who Have Considered Suicide When the Rainbow Is Enuf* was produced by Joseph Papp, and performances sold out. "There was a frenzy about me that I couldn't explain. People began coming to my readings as if I had something they wanted. It wasn't altogether friendly."

In 1978, she published a poetry book, *Nappy Edges*. Then came *Sassafrass, Cypress and Indigo* (1982), *A Daughter's Geography* (1983), *Betsey Brown* (1985), *The Love Space Demands* (1992) and *Liliane* (1994).

Her personal life, she claims, "is confusing." She doesn't like to talk about it. "Let's just say that there were relationships," she says, and then there was a daughter, Savannah.

In 1996, when she wrote this piece, Shange was working on *How I Come by This Cryin' Song*, a novel that spans seven generations of women and chronicles the evolution of rock music. "I am a cultural worker," she says. "Just making sure that my history isn't erased and appropriated as my people once were . . . One of the writers I most admire is Jose Marti—a man who wrote about liberty with a laser-like passion and clarity. Give me a stick, some dirt to write in, and a writer like that, and I'll be all right."

M. A.

From Memory to the Imagination

BY NTOZAKE SHANGE

I am making up something. I make up things for a living, you know. So where do these things come from? Is this autobiographical, Ms. Shange? Did you throw your babies out of the window? How do you know what cornbread and molasses taste like? Did your Grandma make that for you? Weren't you raised a doctor's daughter? How can you know about hominy grits and potted meat on Friday? Are you a real colored person? Can you feel what I feel is what all these intrusive inquiries boil down to: a molten, pre-paleolithic mess of an unconscious I've grown to learn to live with, to depend upon.

Which memories are mine, as a writer, and which become part of the public domain through the gestures or thoughts of a character I come across, need to explore, want to share, is not exactly an easy space for me. Where I begin and the characters become whole is not an arena I purposely open to others. That is, perhaps, why I find literary interviews so painful. If someone needs to discover where I got a joy that touched them through fiction, they threaten not only to demystify my created world, but to concretize a part of me that I gave away. Gave away and maybe do not want back. Like children found in trashbins or on the doorsteps of churches, their umbilical cords placenta-damp, bloody.

I always say I'm from Charleston because that's what I heard my grandmother say. I sat in kitchens in Queens and Harlem with relatives whose voices lilt as a Geechee's would wherever we were. So, yes I remember Carolina—

> Coming down Chad Street or running thru the Yards, the Jr. G.C.'s served notice that the colored children were manifestations of the twentieth century. No mythology in the Old Slave Mart approached their realities. Nothing in the Calhoun House reminded them of themselves. Catfish Row was so old-fashioned, dusted pastel frame houses where hominy-grits, oysters & okra steamed each evening. Crap games went on as usual in the tiny alleyways, edged by worn porches where grandmas made believe they didn't have any idea all that was goin' on. Yet they'd smile if somebody had a high streak of luck, sending yelps & bass guffaws over the roofs. (*Sassafrass, Cypress and Indigo*, 1982)

—though I was never there till I turned 28. I had explored the Little Geechee River and the Old Slave Mart long before I really could see the Citadel in three dimensions. So yes, what I write is autobiographical.

> Sister Mary Louise put Indigo & her violin behind the shed where she kept her gardening tools—shovels, vitamins for roses & violets, peat moss, watering cans, heavy gloves, rakes, & strings. Too much of the Holy Ghost came out of Indigo & that fiddle. Sister Mary Louise swore even she couldn't stand that much spirit every day. (*Sassafrass, Cypress and Indigo*)

In fact, I did study the violin as a child, but I never practiced in a shed, nor was I privy to the fact that slave fiddlers in the colonies were able to hire themselves out, to travel, to improvise. I did not know as a child that it was the fiddle—not the saxophone or drum—that seduced early African American musicians to articulate what they were forbidden even to think. I may have felt the power of the instrument through "blood memory" or in the driving rhythms of charangas my parents danced to with abandon. Can I prove it? No.

Nor do I need to. I only feel a need to verify my emotional terrains when a stranger asks: the feelings that end up as Liliane's installation, Cypress's dance class, Betsey Brown's trolley rides. Otherwise, I am content with the character's ease there, with what I could pull together.

For me, a sweep of Texas plains can become Moroccan hills . . .

> The sunlight hit Jean-Rene. The sepia half-moon of a mole by his right cheekbone glistened, steaming coal in a fast car gliding through the hills of Morocco. We stopped to have a very French picnic: kisses. Shadows of lips and teeth against luxurious auburn soil. The sun always slipping in and out of the bends of limbs, wine from Lisbon dancing mouth to mouth, tongues tracing patterns of clouds, scents of goats, sheep, and the last of my Opium, somewhere near Meknes. I wanted to stay in Paris I'd thought, but no. He said he'd have to have me somewhere I'd never been. I'd laughed. I woke in Casablanca to morning prayers and croissants. (*Liliane*, 1994)

On a drive to San Antonio on a desperately hot afternoon, Texas simply disappeared for me. I was for all I knew in Rabat or Casablanca. This is when I became the character, Liliane, for the instant that she needed something I had access to. Liliane took my day trip and turned it into a month-long escapade with a Guadalupan "velvet spur of a man." There are men like that in Texas, but they are closer to Port Arthur, which is not on the way to San Antonio.

And then in the evanescent mist of a Nicaraguan volcano is the moist touch . . .

> Idrina knew some things Cypress didn't know: where to eat in the City; which piers to visit in the wee hours of the night and watch the waves and sunrise. How to love a woman like Cypress—something Cypress hadn't known; that she could be

> loved, because she'd never let anyone close enough. Yet Idrina seemed to move right in and slay the dragons Cypress had spouting "don't touch me," simply by looking at her. Holding her. Finding little things for her, going to hear music with her. Walking with her. Kissing her scalp, rubbing her legs, making her breakfast, taking her picture. Being there when Cypress came into the room. Idrina knew some things Cypress didn't know: loving is not always the same as having. And Idrina loved Cypress, but not to have . . . and Cypress didn't know that. (*Sassafrass, Cypress and Indigo*)

These two blithe creatures were not Sandinistas. They weren't among the collections of lovers Somoza had thrown into a volcano outside Managua where small, delicate blue-green birds fly helter-skelter in the rushes of steam, seeking heat. Seeking heat as lovers do. Lovers who are torn apart abruptly, cruelly. This was Cypress's version of her parting from Idrina. But I remembered stories of lovers falling, one after the other, into molten lava.

My grandma's kitchen at dawn, as I remember it, transforms into the blues spirits at Sassafrass's beck and call. It still is true. I am not literal or linear. Many stories of mine seep out of the chords of Cecil Taylor's solos. I met Cecil years ago at an upscale soul food restaurant in Greenwich Village with a college chum of mine, Thulani Davis. Over chicken and gravy, white wine and black coffee, the cadence of his voice approximated the thundering chords, unexpected harmonies and rhythms I'd found in his music. The piano as battering ram, rebel shout, the fresh cicatrix of fast life in a black space. When I need to feel whole, competent, daring, intricately evolving, I play Cecil Taylor. As Liliane reminds us: "The music of my body is deliberate. There's nothing I can do about how I sound."

Another memory: Running into Gary Bartz on a cold Paris night, while looking for a pack of Kools. It is/was a perfect re-conjured ambiance for an invented rendezvous that offered much more than a Negro's escape into menthol paradise:

the air in Paris warped my visions/gave
distance & psychosis clearance
sometimes there is too much poison
to attend to beauty
i had five nose rings
a gold circle
a silver circle
a star nefertiti
& a half moon
they have fallen away
(*Nappy Edges*, 1978)

I was trying to find some American cigarettes in late night Montmartre and came across a longtime horn-playing friend from the States, Gary Bartz, with his red-brown goatee and sparking eyes. He had found his brand of smokes and that was that.

I stand by my multiple realities with all my breath and heart. I have no choice. I always say I'm from St. Louis. When I remember my life that way, that is also how I write. Like a St. Louis girl.

> The street grew still, cept for the slurring oaks and jays in the winds. Everybody who had somewhere to go had gone. Brick houses, ranging from sun-yellow to night maroon, etched the walks and the maids swept the stairs as if dirt were a sin. Soon the housewives would saunter back and forth cross fences, sharing gossip and recipes or the plain old doldrums of living in the roses as they did. Haitians, East Indians, Ricans, and prize-fighters' wives went on bout their business: being beautiful and fertile. Weren't many places the likes of them could live

> in St. Louis and know the nooks and covies of fifteen- and twenty-room houses. Weren't many places the likes of them could be themselves and raise their children to own the world, which was the plan never spoken. (*Betsey Brown*, 1985)

My childhood friends are from St. Louis, but sometimes I will say I spent all my winter Saturdays at Ben's Chili Bowl downing half-smokes. Sometimes I actually did. If the richness of my memories bleeds into others, then my job as a writer is to use those memories well. If I hear Albert Ayler saying "My name is Albert Ayler" every time I think about my graduate school days in Los Angeles, hey, then that's what L.A. circa 1970 is to me. Albert Ayler, alto-saxophonist, defying known preconditions for what music is, where a solo goes, what a solo is. Ayler giving himself the right to speak was L.A. to me. His chiaroscuro silhouette my Hollywood.

This is where I come from, I want to say. This is how I manage to write what I write. As I say this, I feel Jean Toomer's words, something from *Cane*: "Oh, can't you see it? Oh, can't you see it?" That is why I pummel my memories, reveries and haunts relentlessly. I think, I'm asking too, "Oh, can't you see it? Oh, can't you see it?"

(This was written in rhythmic tandem to *Remembrance* by Cecil Taylor and Louis Moholo, FMP, 1989.—NS)

March 31, 1996

Scott Turow

If you've ever thought about taking a little time from your law office obligations, penning a legal thriller and becoming an overnight sensation like Scott Turow, think again. True, Turow is a working lawyer. And yes, he produced one nonfiction jewel (*One L*) and two fiction bestsellers (*Presumed Innocent* and *The Burden of Proof*) even as he held down full-time jobs (first at the Chicago U.S. Attorney's Office, then at Sonnenschein Nath & Rosenthal). But there is nothing overnight about him. He's been working at writing all his life.

Turow was born in 1949 in a Jewish enclave of Chicago so insular that he and his sister assumed the rest of the world was Jewish too, including the African Americans who came and went from other parts of town. When his family moved to the exclusive suburb of Winnetka, he learned that life was not so simple. By the time he was a high school sophomore, he was a passionate civil rights activist.

Turow's father was an obstetrician—a "taciturn, deeply depressed" former U.S. Army soldier who had helped liberate Bergen Belsen and witnessed its atrocities firsthand. His mother was a former teacher, an active socialist and amateur writer who produced short stories and novels for no other reason than to entertain her two children. "My first impulse to write came out of an admiring emulation of my mother," says Turow. "Then, when I read *The Count of Monte Cristo* at the age of 11, I decided I wanted to write stories that were as involving for another human being as that book was for me."

At Amherst he studied with the novelist Tillie Olsen, who became his literary mentor. Upon graduation, he won a fellowship at Stanford University, where he eventually was hired to teach creative writing.

But by 1975 he worried about living out his days in college English departments. "It never seemed enough to just teach students to think and read and write carefully. People came to those posts wanting to establish beachheads for world revolution, gay liberation or some obscure linguistic theory. I felt I was losing touch with reality."

He decided to look for the real world at Harvard Law School instead. "My big ambition was to practice law and write too. The great irony is that that pipe dream actually became my life." He makes it sound easier than it really was. *One L*—a book about his experiences as a first-year law student—was put together at night and on the commuter train. He quit his Asst. U.S. Attorney job to finish *Presumed Innocent*, only because his painter-wife, Annette, urged him to. By 1989, with two young children, a new fiction-writing career and a demanding private practice, he realized he had lost all sense of proportion about work and time. By the time he started work on *The Laws of Our Fathers*, his 1996 novel, he found he had to limit his law office visits to one day a week.

Now a staple on the thriller shelves, Turow produces a novel every three years or so. In 1999, it was *Personal Injuries*; in 2002, *Reversible Errors*.

On the phenomenal popularity of legal thrillers he has this to say: "We're in a phase when traditional institutions—schools, churches, the family—have lost their authority. The only institution we seem to respect is the court of law. It's where people feel the deeper questions about values get settled. Today's fiction reflects that the way any era's fiction reflects its preoccupations. I guess I just got lucky." His timing may be serendipitous, but the writing has been nothing less than late-night, long-term, wee-hour hard labor. A cut and dried case, one might say, of a self-imposed sentence.

M. A.

CAN WHITES WRITE ABOUT BLACKS?

BY SCOTT TUROW

One night a few weeks ago, while I was on a golf weekend with a group of men, conversation turned to the novel I'm publishing this fall.

"You got any black folks in this novel?" a friend asked me. "You never have any black folks in your books."

I do this time, I told him. There are poor black people and middle-class blacks and one major character a little like him, an enormously talented African-American attorney.

"Right," my friend said at once. "And what do you know about black folks?" This was largely badinage, characteristic of a 20-year friendship and part of a day-long repartee that began in the same golf cart and included observations about my spending habits, his marriages and the failings of our mutual golf games. But this back-and-forth struck me, since it illustrated what's confronted white American writers since the 1960s: a choice between appearing, on the one hand, blinkered or even bigoted in books that deal only with the white world or, on the other hand, presumptuous in books that address the black world we are not supposed to know.

As the decade of the '60s proceeded with its advances and tumult, as Stokely Carmichael's cry for Black Power resonated, as the movement for black progress came to be viewed as something the black community would have to undertake without a dependence on the largesse or participation of whites, notions of white exclusion also took hold in the arts. Whites, it was charged with considerable basis, had provided buffoonish images of blacks—*Amos 'N Andy* was the prototypical example—and thereby institutionalized America's most damaging racial stereotypes. Black folks knew black experience best and should be the sole custodians of artistic renditions. White portrayals of black life were unnecessary, unwelcome and fundamentally inaccurate. As the former LeRoi Jones put it in a typically pungent phrase, they were, "Albino doo doo in a dark auditorium."

Again and again, as the '60s moved to a close, writing intimately about black characters proved to be the Bermuda Triangle for many of the most acclaimed white novelists. William Styron (*The Confessions of Nat Turner*), Saul Bellow (*Mr. Sammler's Planet*) and John Updike (*Rabbit Redux*) were all thrashed for portrayals that were labeled as racist or clangingly inaccurate.

Chastened by these examples and the notion of political correctness that became galvanized in the '70s and '80s, white writers began to treat race as the aboriginal Touchy Subject. The popular media filled the void with their usual Happy Talk creations—lovable Clint Huxtable or the salt-and-pepper buddies of, say, the *Lethal Weapon* movies—figures whose popularity suggests that an America less divided remains a persistent national fantasy but who we all know reflect little of the reality of our streets. As for white novelists of decent impulse and serious intent, they, with rare exceptions, have decided to adopt a ban of silence, attempting few prolonged observations of black experience.

No matter how well-motivated, that kind of restraint on the imagination is preposterous. It defies the fundamental act of imaginative translation—of taking to heart what it's like to stand in someone else's shoes—that gives fiction its majestic moral power. Moreover, this self-censorship by white novelists meant that they avoided discussing what has clearly been the single most divisive public issue in America for the last 30 years. Furthermore, because the most hailed work of black novelists, writers like Alice Walker or Toni Morrison, has generally concerned the atrocities of the past, our literary silence about our contemporary racial situation has avoided informing an earnest, well-intentioned white audience about some unpleasant and desperately important facts that all of us would be just as happy not to know.

I had a largely privileged childhood. I grew up in a middle-class city neighborhood where gentiles, let alone Negroes, were only visitors. And yet somehow, by the time I reached my teens, I'd become consumed with anguish over the brutal oppression of African-descended Americans. In high school in the suburbs, I was the youth chairman of the Evanston, Ill., Urban League and an occasional member of the Young People's Board of the Evanston NAACP, relatively daring undertakings for a 15-year-old white suburbanite in 1963. I marched for open housing, agitated for passage of the Civil Rights Act and led a forum on the largely ignored subject of Negro history. When I headed off for college, I regarded myself as so advanced that I requested a black roommate. (I got one, but he was a prep-school graduate and the child of two Ph.D.s, and we did not really get along.)

After whites were ejected from the black liberation movements, I felt snubbed, but I also understood. Besides, by then, my attention, like that of most white activists, was on the war in Vietnam. In time I, like other white progressives, accepted the advice of Daniel Patrick Moynihan that a period of "benign neglect" was appropriate, in which, as its leaders then demanded, the black community could arrive at its own solutions, free of the unwelcome interference of white liberals.

Living in cities like San Francisco, Boston and Chicago, I thought about race a lot. I experienced the anger and the hostility that whites and blacks often feel as they deal with one another. But my impression was that with many fits and starts things were getting better, as indeed they have for millions of black Americans. Given the suburbanization of America, housing and education in this country remain largely segregated. But the American urban workplace is far more integrated, even if it's occasionally rent by the sullen controversies generated by affirmative action. To me the growth of a black middle class, the daily evidence of black people prospering in positions they would have been historically denied, made the legacy of the '60s an unambiguously happy one.

Then, in 1989, I was one of a number of lawyers from big law firms who became part of a new pro bono program representing defendants in the state criminal courts in Chicago. As a former federal prosecutor, I'd had only limited experience with street crimes. I was not prepared for this new vantage on the black poor who make up the overwhelming majority of defendants and victims in these courts, whose growing numbers were not evident in the workplace, and whose life was seldom written about in any popular news organs because of the politically correct fear that even the most balanced account would feed ugly stereotypes. Now I saw routine and often unspeakable violence committed by the poor against the poor, particularly against children; a relentless, necessary, but often unprincipled intrusion by the police into this community; and a justice system so determined to meet the political demand to warehouse the offenders that the presumption of innocence often disappeared.

Since 1989—especially since the L.A. riots in 1992—some of the nation's attention has returned to these places. And yet a crust of political correctness remains. No one seems willing to address the sense of utter differentness that pervades the confrontation between the black poor and the rest of us. Theirs is an existence of relentless deprivation, alienation, violence, dependency, ill health and nearly constant anxiety, in which the middle-class pieties of work and family, education and home—and any sense of building for the future—are filmy, elusive concepts. Lacking the most basic common experiences, our lives grow more divided. Figuratively—at times, literally—we barely speak the same language. For these millions of black Americans, by every objective measure, life has clearly gone backward since I exited the civil rights scene in the late '60s.

The '60s have always been my obsession. For young people of my age and social experience—the folks who make up what political pundit Michael Lind has referred to as the American overclass—it was a shaping period, in some ways as consequential as World War II and the Depression had been to our parents. Throughout my writing life, I've made halting approaches to this subject and in 1989, when I finished *The Burden of Proof*, I decided I had to try it again. As this effort came to form, I realized that I would have to damn the devils of political correctness. I couldn't write about the '60s and their aftermath without talking about race; and even though the perspectives of the book are predominantly white, I couldn't allow that to be the only viewpoint. I wanted to talk about the poor black world that's been shattered as the result of ideologies of the '60s, both Black Power and benign neglect, and to portray the different languages that have grown up—the haunted, separate terms of address.

Although the voice of the poor echoes through no more than a fifth of my novel, I knew that I couldn't approach a topic so volatile without trying to get the details right. My life as a lawyer gave me a measure of direct exposure: courtrooms, crime scenes, the jailhouse; the heroin-raddled mom whose moments of concern about her arrested son are both painfully genuine and frustratingly episodic. But that is hardly the whole picture. I've walked through Robert Taylor Homes—the world's largest housing project—and talked with the managers there, spoken to teachers and case workers, clients and residents. As my entire effort presumed, reading was also an invaluable window. The literature about the poor is sparse but some books are outstanding—Alex Kotlowitz's *There Are No Children Here*, Sanyika Shakur's *Monster*, the fiction of Jess Mowry. I also read studies by Chicago's Erikson Institute, monographs provided by my friend the criminologist Norval Morris, court records of the Chicago El Rukn prosecutions, and the random newspaper accounts that the *Chicago Tribune, The Washington Post* and the *New York Times* began to conscientiously offer their readers in the 1990s. I learned what I could from any source, whether it was rides on public transportation, rap music or movies.

If somebody else's version might reflect a different or more complex understanding, then so be it. But I hope I honored my basic compact with readers. I paid attention. I did my best. And I attempted what we haven't done enough of in recent decades: I tried to imagine.

September 15, 1996

John Edgar Wideman

Months after John Edgar Wideman first saw light in Washington, D.C., his father impulsively quit a post with the U.S. Treasury and drove his little family back to Pittsburgh, where they were from. His supervisor had been verbally abusive, a racist, and the humiliation had been more than he could take. Wideman remembers his father donning his tuxedo every night after that—tall, impressive, heading out to restaurants to wait on tables.

The family house was on a tree-lined street in a vibrant, racially mixed corner of Homewood. The eldest of 5 children, Wideman was known for two things: his ability to put a ball through a hoop and his gift for impromptu storytelling. When Helen DeFrance, his 9th grade English teacher, told him he could be somebody if he stopped using clichés, he decided he had a future in prose.

He attended the University of Pennsylvania, where he was a star basketball player and one of 11 African Americans in a student body of 3,000. "It was culture shock," he says. "The blacks there were as different from me as whites. They dressed differently, spoke differently." Within days he was at the bus terminal, headed for home. A professor talked him into staying.

That may have been the only time Wideman's career hung in the balance. He slipped comfortably into the milieu of Philadelphia, a city "full of African-American enticements." He played All-Ivy, won numerous awards, graduated Phi Beta Kappa, was made a Rhodes Scholar. He was doted on by poet Richard Eberhardt, encouraged by novelist Christopher Davis, and, when he realized that his basketball career had probably reached its climax with an induction into the Big Five Basketball Hall of Fame, he turned confidently to his other skill: writing.

Wideman took a job teaching at the University of Pennsylvania in 1967, the year he published his first novel, *A Glance Away*, a story based on his uncle, a self-cured drug addict. "It was, in many ways, a story about me—about being caught up in an alien culture and wending my way back to reality. I hadn't thought much about racism. I was too busy trying to swallow the world in one gulp. I was struggling to make sense of a world that was far away from the world I'd grown up in—Penn, Oxford, the writing workshop at the University of Iowa. I was the living exception in these places. There was something charmed and wrong about that. I felt at any moment a bell would ring, fingers would snap, all of it would fall apart and I would stumble, leaving an ugly handprint in the nice white cake."

His writing became a way to reclaim his roots. *Sent For You Yesterday*, a novel for which he won the PEN/Faulkner Award, was set in his old Homewood neighborhood. *Brothers and Keepers*, a memoir, was about his younger brother, convicted and sentenced to life in a robbery and murder case. How could a brother be so different? The younger ended up behind bars, the elder caged in his own bafflement.

Time eventually brought him another tragedy to ponder. His 16-year-old son was tried and convicted for the murder of a young man in an Arizona motel. "There was an illness there," Wideman says. "Something we didn't know, couldn't talk about." When he did talk about it, it was in *Philadelphia Fire*, a raging, jagged novel based on the 1985 police bombing of a black neighborhood in the City of Brotherly Love. The book won him another PEN/Faulkner prize.

Today, Wideman lives and teaches in Amherst, Mass. His most recent novel is *Two Cities*, a multilayered story that takes place in Pittsburgh and Philadelphia. His latest work is *Hoop Roots*, a book about basketball, race and national identity. You can bet Homewood is there, and Philadelphia, as well as a tamped-down, simmering rage. You can also bet that some form of shock rattles the story's heart.

It's as if Wideman were waiting for life to shift and turn, for powers beyond his control to alter the landscape forever: a father's sudden frustration, a brother's plunge into the streets; a son's inexplicable violence in a faraway motel. And in the course of that waiting, his stories will come.

M. A.

In Praise of Silence

BY JOHN EDGAR WIDEMAN

On a roomsize dock beside a Maine lake where for 30-some summers I've gone each morning to write, I often find myself thinking about silence. When I'm writing or, more likely, in the spaces between writing that are also writing—the spaces when words aren't being scratched on the page, either because one thought is finished or another won't come or because I'm having thoughts for which no words exist, no words I know yet anyway—when I'm pausing, looking out at water, trees and sky, the silence of my hideaway in the woods meets the silence inside me and forms a horizon as tangible and razor-sharp as the shoreline across the lake, dividing trees from their upside-down reflections on days when water and wind are calm.

Perhaps words lie behind this horizon, but for the moment they are utterly inaccessible and can remain so for what seems like minutes, hours, days, on and off the dock. Some mornings I'm frustrated by the pause, disquieted by a foreboding that no words exist, that even if there are words, they will always fail, that this pause might go on and on, but more often I find myself growing calmer, relaxing, spreading out, breathing deeper because I'm aware of time's motion, its capaciousness, aware of being inside it, bundled, dragged, gliding along. I never get closer to understanding time than in these moments when inner and outer silence meet: silence, a medium I enter and feel around and inside me, an affirming vital presence always, whether or not I'm conscious of it.

The more I write, the more I realize how deeply I'm indebted to a communal experience of time and silence, an African-American language evolving from that experience, a language vernacular, visceral, sensuous, depending on the entire body's expressive repertoire, subversive, liberating, freighted with laughter, song and sigh, burdened and energized by opposition. African-rooted, culturally descended ways and means of speaking that emerged from the dungeon and dance of silence.

For a people who have endured a long, long history of waiting—waiting at the Jordan river, waiting chained in stone forts on the west coast of Africa, waiting for slavery and discrimination to end, waiting for justice and respect as first-class citizens, waiting for prison gates to open, waiting eternities in emergency wards and clinic lines of sorry urban hospitals—silence is an old, familiar companion. Time and silence, silence and time. The silence attending waiting, waiting through times of enforced silence. Silence the ground upon which wishes are inscribed while the endless waiting continues. Silence a dreaming space where what's awaited is imagined and, when it doesn't come, the space where dreams are dismantled, dissolving again into silence. Dreams born and dying and born again in the deep womb of silence, and silence, tainted though it is by disappointment and waiting, also a reservoir of hope.

Imagine yourself disembarked on an alien shore after a long, painful voyage so harrowing you're not certain you survived it. You're sick, weak, profoundly disoriented. You fear you haven't actually arrived anywhere but are just slipping into another fold of a nightmare.

You are naked and chained to others who look like you, under the merciless control of brutal strangers who look and act nothing like you and, much worse, do not speak your language. To you their language is gibberish, the ba-ba-baaing of barbarians. They communicate their orders with blows, screams, shoves, crude pantomime. You are compelled at the peril of life and limb to make sense of verbal assault, physical abuse. You realize you're learning a new language even as you swallow the bitterness, the humiliation of learning the uselessness of your own. Much of this learning and unlearning occurs in silence inside your skull, in the sanctuary where you're simultaneously struggling to retain traces of who you are, what you were before this terrible, scouring ordeal began. In order to save your life, when you attempt to utter the first word of a new tongue, are you also violating your identity and dignity? When you break your silence, are you surrendering, acknowledging the strangers' power to own you, rule you? Are you forfeiting your chance to tell your story in your own words some day?

Silence in this context is a measure of resistance and tension. A drastic expression of difference that maintains the distinction between using a language and allowing it to use you.

That was yesterday. Yet much has not changed. Centuries have not erased the archetypal differences between people of African descent brought to the new world as slaves, and the people who claimed this new world, claimed our African bodies and minds. Tension and resistance characterize the practices African-descended peoples have employed to keep their distance from imposed tongues, imposed disciplines. Generation after generation has been compelled to negotiate—for better or worse, and with self-determination and self-realization at stake—the quicksand of a foreign language that continues by its structure, vocabulary, its deployment in social interactions, its retention of racist assumptions, expressions and attitudes, its contamination by theories of racial hierarchy to recreate the scenario of master and slave.

Uneasiness and a kind of disbelief of this incriminating language we've been forced to adopt never go away. Some of us choose to speak very, very little or not at all. Let our actions, other parts of our bodies besides the mouth, speak for us. Lots of us refuse to change speech habits that distinguish us as southern or urban or rural or hip or poor and lacking formal education. Some glory in these habits, others can switch when convenient, necessary or enjoyable. Plenty of us have mastered the master and always wear the mask. Many, whether proficient or not in standard dialects, despise them. Mangle, distort, satirize the would-be master's tongue. Reject most of it, stigmatize the so-called mainstream language, seal it in a ghetto, a barrio, separate and unequal. Some strategies are defensive, reactionary, destructive, others outrageously healthy and creative, and the totality of these strategies make up the African-American culture.

Silence marks time, saturates and shapes African-American art. Silences structure our music, fill the spaces—point, counterpoint—of rhythm, cadence, phrasing. Think of the eloquent silences of Thelonious Monk, sometimes comic, sometimes manic and threatening. Recall gospel's wordless choruses hummed, moaned, keened, words left far behind as singers strive to reach what's unsayable, the silent pulse of Great Time abiding within the song.

Silence times our habits of speech and non-speech, choreographs the intricate dance of oral tradition, marks who speaks first, last, how long and with what authority. Silence indicates who is accorded respect, deference, modulates call-and-response, draws out the music in words and phrases. Silence a species of argument, logical and emotionally persuading, heightening what's at stake. Silence like Amen at the end of a prayer invokes the presence of invisible ancestors whose voices, though quiet now, permeate the stillness, quicken the ancient wisdom silence holds.

The sign of silence presides over my work. Characters who can't speak, won't speak, choose never to speak until this world changes. Stories and essays whose explicit subject or theme is silence. My impulse to give voice to the dead, the unborn, to outlaws and outcasts whose voices have been stolen or muted by violence. Characters who talk in tongues, riddles, prophecies, at the margins, unintelligible until it's too late. Alternate forms of speech, in my fiction, which celebrate the body's ingenuity, how it compensates the loss of one expressive sense with eloquence in another. My ongoing attempt to define African-American culture, explicate its heavy debt, its intimacy with silence. My journey back to lost African cultures, to the stories of Homewood, the Pittsburgh community where I was raised. My struggle to emulate the achievement of African-American artists in song, dance, sport; invent a language that doesn't feel secondhand, borrowed, a language rich with time and silence that animate the written word.

And thinking about that struggle takes me back to those mornings on the dock in Maine. The silence I experience there is not really silence. It's an illusion. If we hear nothing, if one ever can hear nothing, it only means we aren't listening hard enough. At a minimum, we can hear ourselves listening. The total absence of sound is never a possibility for a hearing person, is it? Unless we pretend to have God's ear and can stand aside, outside being, outside self, and listen. So silence is a metaphor. A way of thinking about how it might feel to be both creature and creator, able to experience whatever there might be to hear or not hear if the earth stopped spinning. Silence is a way of imagining such a moment outside time, imagining the possibility of pausing at ground zero and examining our lives before the buzz of the world overtakes us. Nice work if we could get it, and even though we can't, we have the power to see ourselves other than we are. Silence is proof that the decision to listen or not is ours. Proof that we are called to pay attention.

November 29, 1998

Anita Desai

In Anita Desai's reckoning, one and one do not make two. They make three, four even. In her logic, if you are a compound of two cultures, you are more likely fractured in myriad ways, launched on a lifetime of shapeshifts and in-betweens. It is a theme she has explored in numerous quietly lyrical, profoundly moving works, among them the short story collection *Diamond Dust* and the novels *Clear Light of Day*, *Baumgartner's Bombay* and, most recently, *Fasting, Feasting*. She is, to other hybrids like her, an enlightened voice in an increasingly variegated world.

Desai is the daughter of a Bengali and a German. Her mother and father met in the late '20s while he was studying in Berlin, doing graduate work in engineering. She, in turn, was a nursery schoolteacher, musical, independent-minded. When they married and returned to his native Bombay, it was quickly evident that she could not live in her husband's ancestral home as an Indian bride. "They all adored her, worshiped the ground she stepped on," says Desai, "but it was simply too different a life from anything she'd known in Germany." She needed space of her own.

They made their home in Old Delhi, neutral ground, just as India was entering a difficult phase of history. Desai's uncle, who was involved in the Freedom movement, was imprisoned by the English for his anti-colonial views. He died there, but not before he wove a rug with the family name—Mazumdar—emblazoned on it. Desai remembers it hanging in her family's drawing room as a silent, defiant banner against the British raj.

She was born in Mussoorie in 1937, the year Hitler was scheming to expand the Rome-Berlin axis by invading Austria. For the Mazumdar children, a German background became something to be ashamed of, something deliberately "subdued and invisible." It was a bad time to be a

German. She remembers her four older brothers and sisters being embarrassed by their mother's foreignness, her essential oddness. "They made her promise never to speak her own language in public. They insisted she dress in a sari. I think we were all adults before we truly acknowledged she was German." Even so, Desai was the only one of her siblings to eventually read and research German history.

She started writing when she was 6—stories, diary entries. "I became known as 'the writer in the family.' It was in writing that I felt intense and alive. I don't think I ever planned or wanted to do anything else." Although the family spoke Hindi, Desai was raised in British schools, and so her creations, even at that young age, were mostly in English.

It may be hard to imagine, what with the current boom of Indian writers who choose to write in English—Salman Rushdie, Bharati Mukherjee, Arundhati Roy, Jhumpa Lahiri, Pankaj Mishra—but when Desai first decided to pursue publication after her graduation from Delhi University, there was not one Indian publisher willing to take the leap with her. She was forced to send her work to England, where, even as she raised a family of her own, she began to publish her stories.

In 1980, at 43, Desai published two novels, *Clear Light of Day* (about an Old Delhi family divided by its history and petty bitterness) and *In Custody* (about a teacher who sets out to interview a famous Urdu poet and learns that the man is nothing like the sage he imagined). Both were shortlisted for Britain's Booker Prize. Two years later, her book *The Village by the Sea* won the Guardian Award for children's fiction. In 1984, she left India for England to take up a visiting fellowship at Cambridge University. She has never returned. While in England, she wrote *Baumgartner's Bombay* (1988), a novel that allowed her to plumb Germany's past through its protagonist Hugo Baumgartner, a Jew who flees Nazi Germany for India, only to be imprisoned there.

In 1993, she took a position at the Massachusetts Institute of Technology, where she continues to teach writing. There she has produced two more novels, *Journey to Ithaca*, which allowed her to see India through

European eyes, and *Fasting, Feasting* (another Booker nominee), which allowed her to see America through Indian eyes. "But I could never really write about the United States," she says. "America has its own spokesmen." More to the point she feels adrift here, and returns often to Europe and India. "I've become one of those people who don't feel they belong anywhere," she adds. "I find myself traveling to Mexico now to write. Its clash of indigenous and Spanish cultures feels Indian in a way. It feels colonial, familiar, ancient. Not being a Spanish speaker, I'm thrown in with other misfits and stragglers." In other words: For the moment, for the particular novel she has in mind, and for entirely unexpected reasons, the place will anchor her awhile.

M. A.

Bicultural, Adrift, and Wandering

BY ANITA DESAI

For the sake of simplicity, I like to say that I was born in India at a time when it was a meeting place for two cultures, Indian and British. But the truth is that "Indian" and "British" are merely umbrella terms, for these were split into an infinitely larger number of spokes and panels that came together to form not an elegant object but a conveniently usable one.

In my home in Old Delhi, a rambling old bungalow weighed down with bougainvillea, of the kind the British built all across their empire in Asia, we listened to my mother sing us German lullabies and play Schubert on her piano (always out of tune because warped by Delhi's ferocious temperatures) while my siblings and I spoke

Hindi to each other and our neighbors, a Hindi that was actually mixed with Urdu to form—conveniently, usably—the hybrid Hindustani. We bicycled to school past the Nicholson Gardens and the British cemetery, where many stalwarts of the British Empire—and their more frail offspring—were buried.

At Queen Mary's High School for Girls, we sang hymns (curious, when one thinks of it, that the mild English missionaries who taught us so enjoyed hearing assemblies of a hundred or more girls, Hindu and Muslim every one of them, lustily and unthinkingly bellow *Onward Christian Soldiers*) and played rounders and badminton. In the evening we went for walks to the Quidsia Gardens, where at twilight we played hide-and-seek amid the tombs of emperors and empresses of the Moghul Empire moldering among the palm trees, or to the Jumuna river, where at twilight the bells of the temples along the river bank clanged and banged while we played in the sands till dark. We came home and read for the hundredth time old comic books like *Beano*, *Superman* and *Captain Marvel* that we had bought with our pocket money in the arcades of Connaught Circus, or listened to my mother tell us one of Grimm's fairly tales or heard my father talk of his childhood among the rivers and rice fields of Bengal, so far to the east and in the past as to be quite mythical.

So for me the European section of the umbrella had panels made up of both colonial Britain and the more distant, less physical world of my mother's prewar Germany while the Indian section had stripes that were Hindu—festivals, dress, food—and also Muslim—other festivals, other foods and dress. Was this ridiculous, this object we held over our head, fashioned by our motley ancestors? Was it schizophrenic?

We gave it little thought and got on with our lives. Its pied, patchwork structure seemed to us quite commonplace, normal. Turned upside down, we could use it to sail into wider seas, experience different worlds. And England, when I first visited it, did seem almost like an extension of that colonial outpost. One knew what to expect—daffodils blowing on a hill, red letterboxes and double-decker omnibuses, fish and chips shops, small dark pubs and bowler hats—and there they all were. I realized to what an extent English literature had prepared me for the English section of the Empire. Its familiarity was comforting and made the passage to the West seem easy.

Surely, I thought, to travel farther West, to the United States, would not prove any more difficult. But this is where I was brought up short, made to stop and reconsider. I had read and loved its literature, too; I had read as much Faulkner and Steinbeck and Hemingway as I had Dickens and Wordsworth and D. H. Lawrence. True, but I had not heard them—and the sounds of the American language proved foreign. I found it hard to understand what was said to me and, equally disconcerting, people seemed to find it hard to understand me. Also, I found that I laughed at things others considered serious and that they spoke at length of matters I would not think of divulging in company. I was a foreigner. I observed other foreigners—of a younger generation, brought up not on literature but on the current currency of movies and pop music, who on arrival jumped in feet first, laughing with confidence, and bobbed up fully baptized, first-generation Americans.

But I was too old, my joints too stiff, my jaw too stubborn. It was a chastening experience to find oneself, at my age, a beginner, a callow student (if a "mature" one). I studied once again Mark Twain's *Huckleberry Finn*, Nabokov's *Lolita*, DeLillo's *White Noise*, Updike's classics of suburbia. I prowled the streets, looking through big picture windows at lighted interiors. The sounds of lawn mowers, of boom boxes in passing cars, the smoke and smells of summer barbecues were items I studied anxiously for clues. But a glass pane separated us; I found myself trying to lip-read, puzzled.

Every few months I returned to India. It was comforting to put my feet into slippers again, dress in old soft cotton clothes, know what everyone was saying, or leaving unsaid, or thinking. But I could also see that that American experience had interposed between us, created an unease. Here too I was on the outside now and looking in. So much had happened while I was away, so much that I had not experienced or participated in, and I no longer had the right to comment. And while some things remain unchanged, stood still—the family, the circle of friends, the way of life—so much else had changed or was in flux—the economy, the media, digital technology and, above all, the politics of the time. Fluid, volatile, powerful—they were carrying everyone in their tide, except me. I was not a part of it and did not understand it.

How can one write of a scene one does not know and does not understand? One may write of one's bewilderment, but that has its limitations. And there was a new generation there to describe the scene, whose material it rightfully was. So I retreated—but where to? Having grown up in a cradle, a hammock woven out of the worlds my parents made, I found I had outgrown it, it no longer fit. I withdrew, feeling like a turtle that had shed its shell, or a crab without its carapace.

Hardly a subject for melodrama, let alone tragedy. I had no disaster to display. I was not a boat person struggling through the oceans to wade onto inhospitable shores. Far from it: I could go and come as I pleased. But even a traveler needs a shelter, and a writer a subject.

At times, one tends to think of one's experience as unique; at others, one looks to those who have gone before one, for their tracks, the maps they drew. There are writers, after all, who have found the new worlds they explored more rich, more complex, more challenging than the ones they fled from or abandoned. E. M. Forster's greatest book was the one he wrote about India, Henry James's greatest books were his European ones, Nabokov's masterpiece was American. I needed to learn, but their power was impossibly distant from my abilities; America made me feel incapable, incompetent. If I tried to make a call from a public phone booth or handled a tray in a cafeteria or attempted to fill my car with gas, all my fingers turned to thumbs, I dropped coins and forks, felt foolish and apologetic.

For some years I had had Joseph Brodsky as a neighbor and been struck by how he had recreated for himself, under New England's firs and spruces, the kind of dacha he might have acquired had he remained in Russia, down to the low beams, the sagging bookshelves, the smoky cobwebs. Next door I never even made an attempt at recreating an Indian bungalow. (As a child, when I was asked what I wanted "to be," I would reply, "a gypsy.") It is interesting that Brodsky chose as his final resting place Venice, that island in a lagoon where continents wash into each other, creating a confluence that belongs more to poetry, to art, than humdrum reality. I understand that wish—to have the wash and flow of waters as one's final home.

Place had been of an importance as basic to me as soil is to a plant, but once you have torn up your roots, you become a piece of driftwood. It is tides, and currents, that become your fluid, uncertain home. Every once in a while you find a shelf to pull yourself onto, a shore on which to catch your breath. Perhaps only momentarily, but these intervals take on a certain brilliant vividness, like a scene lit up by a flash of lightning. As a foreigner, you cannot participate, you only contemplate. Not knowing the language, you cannot converse, only listen. What appears to be a most passive phase of existence becomes one of intense and heightened response—although that may not make itself apparent till long after, when you find yourself turning it into words on paper.

How much isolation, even if willful isolation, can a writer bear? But one is rarely alone, even in so lonely an endeavor. Inevitably one comes across fellow misfits, and learns of the complicated lives of other professional strangers and foreigners. Some may become friends, others most certainly not. But all have stories to tell, and through them one lives many lives. What does a writer do, after all, but sing, with Brodsky: "So if only in our lifetime, let us be various!" ("Anno Domini" from *A Part of Speech*, 1980).

One meets this company of travelers not only in the flesh but just as often on the printed page, which is what I did when I read, in a German translation, the lines of the Czech writer Jiri Kratochvil in his *Inmitten der Nacht Gesang* (Berlin: Rowohlt, 1996. Original: *Uprostered Nocai Zpe'ev*, Brno: Atlantis, 1992):

> *Alle sind wir Emigranten. . . . Emigranten aus dem Reich Gottes, und alle laufen wir weiss der Teufel wohin, während Gott die Schäferhunde Seiner Gottlichen Absichten hinter uns herjagt, uns die Stacheldraht-Barrikaden Seiner Gnade in den Weg stellt und aus der Maschinenpistole Seiner Gottlichen Liebe auf uns schiesst.**

May 28, 2000

*Translation from the German: "We are all emigrants. . . . Emigrants from the Kingdom of Heaven, and we all run the devil knows where, while God sets the hounds of His Godly will on us, blocks our way with the barbed wire barricades of His grace, and shoots at us with the machine guns of His Godly love."

Julia Alvarez

Sometimes real life makes for the best material. So it was when a certain Dr. Alvarez was exiled from the Dominican Republic in the 1940s for his work against the military dictatorship of Rafael Trujillo. In New York, he met a young Dominican woman; they married, had a baby girl, returned to their country during the 1950 liberalization and had three more daughters before they emigrated to the United States a decade later. Their story is memorialized by their eldest daughter, Julia Alvarez, in a family saga that is considered among the finest of Latino American novels, *How the Garcia Girls Lost Their Accent* (1991).

"There were no books in my early life," Alvarez remembers. "It was an oral culture. We children were raised communally—like a pack of wolves. If we went off by ourselves to read, to think, it was because we were sick. Stories were for the dinner table; and everybody had them." When, at 10, she came to live in the United States, she began to have an inkling of what solitude was. "I instinctively retreated to books and the imagination," she says. "They became my portable homeland."

She went to New York's Abbot Academy, a Catholic school where the only other Hispanics were her own sisters. There she fell in love with the English language and with the range of color she could evoke in a single word. To this day, she speaks to her father in Spanish, the language of her childhood; her mother, however, she addresses in English, her language of "art and argument."

After graduation from Middlebury College in 1971, she became an "itinerant poet," hired by the state of Kentucky to travel from town to town teaching creative writing in schools, prisons and convents. A string of teaching posts in community colleges around the country finally landed her a job teaching English at the Andover School. She then worked at the University of Vermont, where she wrote her first book of poems, *Homecoming* (1984), and at George Washington University, where she spent a year as the Jenny McKean Moore Fellow.

The University of Illinois hired her away with a full professorship, but three years later she was lured back to Vermont with an offer from Middlebury College. Sometimes life has a way of circling back: At Middlebury she was referred to an eye doctor, an Anglo who had practiced in the Dominican Republic and knew her cousin. They were married in 1988.

In 1994, Alvarez published *In the Time of the Butterflies*, a novel based on a real-life story about the three Mirabal sisters who were active in the anti-Trujillo underground movement throughout the 1950s and were found murdered on a desolate mountain road in 1960. In 1994, Algonquin Press also published *The Second Side* (*El Otro Lado*), her second collection of poetry. Three years later came her novel *Yo!*

In 2000, she returned to the historical novel with *In the Name of Salome*, based on the life of the poet Salome Ureña, whose poems became inspirational lodestones for the 19th century revolution in the Dominican Republic.

Alvarez visits the Dominican Republic every summer. A committed community worker there, she has undertaken the care and raising of a deaf street-girl whom she found roaming the barrios of Santo Domingo some years ago. "It is a way to pay back, to do something real," she says. When you've achieved your dreams as I have, you have to find a way to return some of the riches." Hers is, after all, a life of circling back. And sometimes that, too, makes for the best material.

M. A.

On Finding a Latino Voice

BY JULIA ALVAREZ

I remember discovering William Carlos Williams's poetry over 25 years ago in my anthology of American literature. It was love at first sight:

So much depends
upon
a red wheel
barrow
glazed with rain
water
beside the white
chickens.

What a curious syntactic structure, our teacher noted: "So much depends . . ." So much what is depending on the wheelbarrow and the chickens? But the syntax seemed familiar to me. *Todo depende.* I had heard it all my life. Everything depended on, well, something else. It was our Spanish form of "maybe."

Scanning a collection of his poetry in the library, I found a half-dozen Spanish titles—even a volume named *Al Que Quiere!* But there was no mention in my anthology of the why of these Hispanicisms. It was only later that I came to find out that William Carlos Williams was—as he would be termed today—"a Hispanic-American writer."

His mother was Puerto Rican—upper-class Puerto Rican with a Paris education, but still . . . She married an Englishman who seems to have lived everywhere, including some years in the Dominican Republic, my homeland. The two moved to Rutherford, N.J., where they raised their two sons. Growing up, William Carlos never had a close association with Puerto Rico: In fact, he did not see the islands until he was almost 60 and had a deep longing to try to understand what his own roots really were. His was an American boyhood indeed, but with the powerful and sometimes baffling presence of his mother, who spoke Spanish in the home and who terrified and embarrassed her sons by going into trances and speaking to her Caribbean dead, especially during Unitarian church services as she was playing the organ. Williams did not phrase or even seem to understand his divided loyalties in terms of ethnicity. Still, as a first-generation American, he often felt "the islandness in him, his separateness," as his biographer Reed Whittemore has described it.

His friend Pound didn't help things. "What the hell do you a blooming foreigner know about the place?" Pound taunted. "My dear boy, you have never felt the swoop of the PEEraries." But it was Pound who jumped ship and fled to Europe. Williams stayed in New Jersey and struggled to set down on paper "the good old U.S.A."

As an adolescent immigrant, I too, like Williams, wanted to be an American, period. I was embarrassed by my ethnicity, which rendered me colorful and an object of derision to those who would not have me be a part of this culture, at least not without paying the dues of becoming like them. And I was encouraged in this by my parents and teachers, by the media and the texts I studied in school that never addressed the issues I was facing in my secret soul. Many of the ways of being, speaking, living I had once cherished seemed to have no place in this world and culture—and so I started to have a secret life, which perhaps is what started me on the road to being a writer.

In my effort to keep some of my old culture in this new world, I was at a disadvantage because my family did not move into a *comunidad* in this country, where a concentration of Dominicans or Latinos would have kept alive and affirmed the values and customs, the traditions and language that were an important though increasingly hidden part of me. We lived in Jamaica Estates, a pretentious—back then, anyway—area in Queens for solidly middle-class families and for upcoming white European immigrants, many Germans, some Italians, some Jews and a couple of us Hispanics.

My father did have that other *comunidad* in his work life. Every morning he left the Estates for a Latino area in Brooklyn, a place my mother called "a bad neighborhood." Summers I went to work at his office, driving with him through block after block of brick apartment buildings bracketed by intricate fire escapes, nowhere a tree visible. But the lively and populous street life seemed far more enticing than the lonely, deserted lawns back in Queens. At El Centro Medico the nurses were all Dominicans or Puerto Ricans with sometimes an Argentine or Chilean lording it over us with her lisp and blonde hair. No matter: Papi was boss, and I was *la hija del doctor*. His patients brought me *pastelitos* and *dulce de leche*. The guys flirted with me, tossing out their *piropos* ("Ay, look at those curves, and my brakes are shot!"). I loved the place, though I admit, too, that I was very aware of my difference: At night, we drove back home to a welcome of sprinklers waving their wands of water over our lookalike lawns. We were of another class, in other words, a difference that was signaled the minute I walked into our house and my mother instructed me to wash my hands. "You don't know what germs you picked up over there."

But any *comunidad* we would have joined would have been temporary anyway. Worried about the poor reception and instruction we were receiving at the local school, my mother got scholarships for us to go away to school. We were cast adrift in the explosion of American culture on campuses in the late '60s and early '70s. Ethnicity was in; my classmates wore long braids like Native Americans and peasant blouses from Mexico and long diaphanous skirts and dangly earrings from India. They smoked weed from Mexico and Colombia and hitchhiked down the Pan American highway and joined the Peace Corps after college to expiate the sins of their country against underdeveloped and overexploited countries like, yes, the Dominican Republic. More than once I was asked to bear witness to this exploitation, and I, the least victimized of Dominicans, obliged. I was claiming my roots, my Dominicanness, with a vengeance.

But what I needed was to put together my Dominican and American selves. An uncle who lived in New York gave me a piece of advice embedded in an observation: "The problem with you girls is that you were raised thinking you could go back to where you came from. Don't you see, you're here to stay?"

He was right; we were here to stay. But the problem was that the American culture as we had experienced it left us out, and so we felt we had to give up being Dominicans to be Americans. Perhaps in an earlier wave of immigration that would have sufficed—a good enough tradeoff, to leave your old country behind for the privilege of being a part of this one. But we were not satisfied with that. The melting pot was spilling over, and even Americans were claiming and proclaiming not just their rights, but the integrity of their identities: Black is Beautiful, women's rights, gay rights.

What finally bridged these two worlds for me was writing. But even in my writing, I had only the models that had been given to me in school, books by the great writers, mostly white male American and British. And so, for many years, I didn't have a vocabulary or context to write about the issues I had faced or was facing. I didn't know it could be done. I had never seen it done. I had, in fact, been told it couldn't be done. One summer at Bread Loaf, a poet stated categorically that one could write poetry only in the language in which one had first said Mother. Thank God, I had the example of William Carlos Williams to ward off some of the radical self-doubt this comment engendered.

How I discovered a way into my bicultural, bilingual experience was paradoxically not through a Hispanic-American writer, but an Asian-American one. Soon after it came out, I remember picking up *The Woman Warrior* by Maxine Hong Kingston. I gobbled up the book and then I went back to the first page and read it through again. She addressed the duality of her experience, the Babel of voices in her head, the confusions and pressures of being a Chinese-American female. Wow! The silence within me broke.

With her as my model, I set out to write about my own experience as a Dominican American. And now that I had a name for what I had been experiencing, I could begin to understand it as not just my personal problem. I combed the bookstores and libraries. I discovered Latino writers I had never heard of: Piri Thomas, Ernesto Galarza, Rudolfo Anaya, Jose Antonio Villareal, Gary Soto. But I could not find any women among these early Latino writers.

The '80s changed all that. In 1983, Alma Gomez, Cherrie Moraga and Mariana Romo-Carmona came out with *Cuentos: Stories by Latinas*. It was an uneven collection, but the introduction, titled "Testimonio," was like a clarion call: "We need *una literatura* that testifies to our lives, provides acknowledgement of who we are: an exiled people, a migrant people, *mujeres en la lucha* . . . What hurts is the discovery of the measure of our silence. How deep it runs. How many of us are indeed caught, unreconciled between two languages, two political poles, and suffer the insecurities of that straddling."

The very next year Sandra Cisneros published her collection of linked stories, *The House on Mango Street*; Ana Castillo published her book of poems, *Women Are Not Roses*; I published *Homecoming*. Up at Bread Loaf, I met Judith Ortiz Cofer and heard her read poems and stories that would soon find their way into her books of poems, stories and essays and her novel *The Line of the Sun*. Cherrie Moraga, Helena Maria Viramontes, Denise Chavez. Suddenly there was a whole group of us, a tradition forming, a dialogue going on. And why not? If Hemingway and his buddies could have their Paris group and beat poets their Black Mountain School, why couldn't we Latinos and Latinas have our own made-in-the-U.S.A. boom?

Still, I get nervous when people ask me to define myself as a writer. I hear the cage of a definition close around me with its "subject matter," "style," "concerns." I find that the best way to define myself is through the stories and poems that do not limit me to a simple label, a choice. Maybe it is part of my immigrant uneasiness at the question, in whatever form, "Do you have something to declare?" Maybe, too, after years of feeling caught between being a "real Dominican" and being American, I shy away from simplistic choices that will leave out an important part of who I am or what my work is about.

Certainly none of us serious writers of Latino origin wants to be a mere flash in the literary pan. We want to write good books that touch and move all our readers, not just those of our own particular ethnic background. And speaking for myself, I very much agree with the advice given to writers by Jean Rhys, "Feed the sea, feed the sea." The little rivers dry up in the long run, but the sea grows. What matters is the great body of all that has been thought and felt and written by writers of different cultures, languages, experiences, classes, races.

At last, I have found a *comunidad* in the word that I had never found in a neighborhood in this country. By writing powerfully about our Latino culture, we are forging a tradition and creating a literature that will widen and enrich the existing canon. So much depends upon our feeling that we have a right and responsibility to do this.

May 14, 1995

John Banville

"I've always tried not to play the Irish card," says John Banville, one of the most imaginative literary novelists writing in the English language today. "The real charm of the Irish is evasiveness. Irish writers are best when they're ambiguous. Maybe I'm a sour old bastard, but I don't understand the current obsession with heart-on-the-sleeve Irish sentimentalists. I don't see myself as an 'Irish writer' with a 'gift of gab.' It's bad for the work. Good writing is good writing. Period."

Banville's writing is emphatically good. Excellence, in fact, may be the only predictable thing about it. His novels are anything but similar, ranging from *Doctor Copernicus*, a richly textured tale about the shy, sexually conflicted 16th-century scientist, to *The Book of Evidence*, his feverish Booker Prize-winner, narrated by a murderous madman. Banville can be dense, steamy, lyrical, cracked, but he is almost always original, having produced an array of works impossible to categorize: among them *Ghosts*, a contemplative story about a tour group run aground on an old man's island; *Mefisto*, which treats a modern-day Faust pinned between mathematics and crime; *Athena*, a piquant story about a woman who appears to have stepped out of her lover's canvases; and *The Untouchable*, about a Cambridge aesthete who turns out to be a spy.

Banville was born in 1945 in Wexford, a small town with big history: It had been a Viking settlement before the Norman invasion. "One's past is always a kind of medieval world," he says. "But the town of Wexford was deeply medieval. I think it's why Doctor Copernicus and Kepler came so naturally to me."

His father was a "white-collar worker" in a garage supply business, his mother a strong force in persuading her three children to move on, aim high. There were no books at home, no music, but the nuns in Banville's school were thorough and inspiring—"English classes were always taught by interesting people, and the libraries were a window to another world. I can still smell the books. I wanted to be part of them. From the start, I wanted to be a writer."

His parents had hopes he'd be an architect some day, and so he tried his hand at painting. "I had no sense of color, no gift. But it turned out to be a useful thing to do: It made me look at the world in a different way." Painting came to play an important part in his writing: Many of his novels are set in the world of art.

He refused to go to university, a decision he has always regretted. "I couldn't contemplate being dependent on my parents any longer," he says in grim defense. He took a job instead as a clerk with Ireland's national airline, Aerlingus, because it offered him a chance to travel and gather material for stories. In 1968, at the height of that unruly decade, he found himself in Berkeley, Calif., where he met his American wife.

His first novel, *Nightspawn*, was published in 1971, and it was followed quickly by a spate of others. By 1980, he had begun work as an editor at the *Irish Press*, a newspaper run by Eamon De Valera's party. When his *The Newton Letter* was made into a movie, he left journalism but quickly found out he couldn't make a living on fiction alone. He was hired as literary editor of the *Irish Times*, a post he manned for a decade before stepping aside last year. Today he is chief literary critic for the *Times*, and continues to live in Dublin.

"I've never been able to live off my novels," he says. "I've always had to fit them in. I've always been a night-worker." There is nothing melancholy in his voice when he says it. For all the travail, for all its limited financial reward, he has had his share of laurels; critics hold him in high regard, and he has been awarded Britain's top literary prize.

"There's a little quotation I've found," he says when he is asked to consider the great recent successes of writers like Frank McCourt (*Angela's Ashes*). "It's from Nietzsche, and goes something like this: 'Before you can get the crowds to cry Hosanna, you must ride into the city on an ass.' Isn't that it, now? Isn't that just the way it is?"

M. A.

Living in Irish, Writing in English

BY JOHN BANVILLE

What is it about the Irish that makes them so gifted as writers in English? What is the magic at work that has produced such extraordinary figures as Shaw, Yeats, Beckett and Heaney?

Somewhere in one of his very many books, Anthony Burgess attempts to illustrate the revolution James Joyce wrought in English prose by translating the first paragraph of Ulysses into standard English. One fine summer morning, on the roof of a tower overlooking Dublin Bay, Malachi "Buck" Mulligan was preparing for his morning shave—that kind of thing. It was an amusing exercise, but it had a sharp point. What it showed was not only how innovatory Joyce's style is but also that the English employed—one might even say invented—by Irish writers is an entirely separate medium from that used by their colleagues on what many English people still refer to as "the mainland," even though most of Ireland has been independent of England for more than 70 years.

Considering its size and situation, an offshore island of an offshore island, with a population of a few millions, Ireland has a remarkably rich literature. Even if we ignore writing in the Irish language—hard to do, for there is still a small but thriving literature in Irish—Latin and Norman-French, and concentrate only on the past couple of hundred years or so, the record is impressive. We have four Nobel laureates—Shaw, Yeats, Beckett and, most recently, Seamus Heaney; Wilde, Synge and O'Casey are giants of world drama. In our own time, fiction writers such as John McGahern and William

Trevor are international figures, while in Derek Mahon, Michael Longley, Thomas Kinsella and Paul Muldoon we have four of the world's finest living poets. Why? How?

It is a question worth pondering, not out of national pride—there are many aspects of life in this little country sufficiently shaming to cure us of any temptation toward chauvinism, literary or otherwise—but because the search for an answer leads out of books and into life, which is the proper direction to take for writers and readers alike.

The assimilation—or imposition—of the English language in Ireland, effectively completed after the Great Famine of the 1840s, was a painful but productive process that wrought deep changes both in the Irish national sensibility and in the language itself. Hiberno-English is a wonderfully versatile yet often treacherous literary tool. The subtlety, richness and volatility of English as written in Ireland is the result of an alchemical fusion, as it were, between two wholly dissimilar methods of linguistic interpretation of the world and our being in it. Standard English as we received it in Ireland was, like Latin, an implement of bureaucracy, a mode of command; the building and maintaining of an empire requires a language capable of reducing itself to essentials without losing any of its coherence and concrete force. "O, rocks!" as Molly Bloom memorably said, "tell us in plain words," unconsciously reminding us of her girlhood spent as the daughter of a military official on Gibraltar's stony outpost of empire.

If English is the language of the colonist—one of the first words Crusoe taught Friday to speak was "Master"—lending itself to directness and clarity and well suited to the imperative mode, Irish is an altogether different tongue, convoluted in its grammar and syntax, onomatopoeic rather than descriptive, and oblique to the point of evasiveness. Certain straightforward statements of fact are impossible in Irish: For instance, one cannot say "I am a man" but must use a formulation that roughly translates as "I am in my manness." It is a language the fluid structures and formulaic elaborations of which seek to apprehend reality not by the narrational method of standard English but in the manner of a fine-meshed yet amorphous net thrown over the stubbornly solid objects that make up the commonplace world.

And that mesh or grid of the old Gaelic tongue is still there, a sort of "deep grammar" underlying the peculiarly airy constructions of Hiberno-English. I believe it is this intermeshing of the two languages, with all its political, psychological and epistemological consequences, that goes a long way toward explaining the continuing extraordinary richness of Irish writing. Fiction, drama and poetry in Ireland, even when it is seemingly at its most engaged, is primarily, I am convinced, a linguistic endeavor.

Take the case of Samuel Beckett. Since *Waiting for Godot* in the 1950s brought him to the attention of a wide if largely bemused audience, he has been regarded as the Great Pessimist, whose Manichaean vision of humankind's benighted condition in the world demanded extreme and fractured styles of linguistic expression. To conceive of Beckett's work in this way, however, is to view it through the wrong end of the telescope. From the start his concern was with language itself, its possibilities as a key to the House of Being, its areas of recalcitrance and exhaustion, its capacity to aestheticize and therefore in some sense redeem quotidian reality or, viewed from a bleaker standpoint, inauthenticate and betray it. Thus at an essential level his increasingly refined raids on the inarticulate are no more than technical exercises. No more, and no less: What is remarkable, what is well-nigh miraculous, is that from these seemingly sterile forays he should bring back a representation of humanity and the world so persuasive and of such thrilling poetic intensity.

By a combination of stratagems—going into exile, writing in French—Beckett made of himself a thoroughly cosmopolitan artist, although his Irishness is always and everywhere apparent in his work. For the writer living and working in Ireland, however, the linguistic peculiarities in which, and under which, he labors bring with them peculiar disadvantages. For instance, although Ireland has a native publishing industry, it is still a youthful growth, and the Irish writer, especially the Irish novelist, who is aiming at an international audience—and what writer would wish to be read only in his own country?—must look to London for a publisher. The consequence is that when an Irish novel is published, its first reception, so important in these days of dwindling shelf-space in the bookshops, depends almost entirely on London book reviewers, most of whom, perhaps understandably, regard fiction written in Hiberno-English as either insufferably "poetic" or quaintly comic.

English novelists for the most part follow Orwell's dictum that the novelist's prose should be a clear pane of glass though which the story can be clearly viewed; for the Irish novelist, on the other hand, language is not a sheet of glass but a lens, and a lens, as we know, not only magnifies but inevitably distorts. It is precisely that distortion, the product of willed linguistic ambiguity, that the Irish novelist aims for and revels in.

Since I am a novelist, or at least, that appellation having become problematic in recent decades, a writer of fictions, I have concentrated here on the novel, though I believe that the things I have said so far apply equally to all forms of what academe calls "creative" writing. However, though we seem to produce poets and dramatists at a steady and unvarying rate, the past 20 years or so have seen the appearance of an extraordinary number of new novelists. To try to list them would be foolhardy—I would be bound to omit someone—but one has only to look at recent long- and short-lists for major literary prizes, not only in Ireland but also in England and Europe, to be struck by the preponderance of Irish names—many of them, incidentally, female; the growing strength of women writers is the most marked Irish literary development of recent years. To pose the question again: How on earth do we keep producing so many writers?

Besides our fascination with language, there is I believe a second factor which, however paradoxical it may seem, contributes to our productivity in the novel form, and that is the lack of a strong Irish tradition of fiction writing. Or, perhaps I should say, we have no tradition of minor fiction writing, as England and America have. The contemporary American or English writer whose talent is less than great has a large number of predecessors against whom, unconsciously or not, he can measure himself. In Ireland, however, though we have our Carletons and our Edgeworths, they are isolated figures, more like sports of nature than parts of a tradition; when we look back, what we see are the giant figures of Swift, Wilde, Joyce, Elizabeth Bowen, Beckett. No petty people they.

To have to measure oneself against such colossi is at once liberating and daunting. They can seem sustaining ancestors, or they can be like Easter Island statues, vast, mysterious, unavoidable, looming over the land and darkening it. But however we, their heirs, may regard them, they are a standing example to us that the Irish voice speaking through English is distinctive, resonant and carries far, and, beyond that insular boast, that language, even one imposed by colonizers, is the supreme mode of interpretation of this baffling world into which we find ourselves so unceremoniously thrown.

September 19, 1999

III

Hunkering Down

Wendy Wasserstein

Patricia Cornwell

Stanley Karnow

David McCullough

Ray Bradbury

Edmund Morris

Michael Korda

David Chanoff

Wendy Wasserstein

"What's a nice Jewish girl like me doing in a Christmas piece like this?" asks Wendy Wasserstein, turning her well-tuned antenna momentarily on herself. Her wit can be fiendish, but one soon realizes that her sharpest ridicule is for herself. She has a ringing talent—a distinctly Jewish gift—for making puckish fun of her life and then sitting back and enjoying the racket of her own laughter.

She was born in the Flatbush area of Brooklyn in 1950, the daughter of a perennial dance student and a ribbon manufacturer. Her mother, Lola, is "a total eccentric, a wonderfully colorful character" who even now (in her seventies) still struts through Manhattan in chin-to-toe leather, headed for tap class and blowing kisses all the way. Wasserstein's father holds the patent for putting wire in decorative ribbons. "Why, this is our time of year!" says Wasserstein with a girly twinkle, and you can almost see how somewhere between wacky and real she has found fertile ground for art.

She went to yeshiva school until the third grade. "But Lola had me lying to the rabbis, telling them I was going off to temple when I was really going off to the June Taylor School of the Dance . . . I knew early on something was very wrong with that." By second grade she was into more intricate fibs: She told her mother she was in a school play. "Lola asked so many questions that I started to make up the play as I went along. On the appointed day, she put my hair in ringlets, dressed me in the obligatory velvet dress, and then showed up in school to see me perform . . . But she didn't miss a beat. 'Oh, there's no play?' she said to the teacher. 'It must be one of my other kids, then.' And the moral of the story was clear: Plays were worth a lot of fuss."

At the Brooklyn Ethical Culture School, Wasserstein learned more about the theater, and her parents took her regularly to Broadway and

Radio City Music Hall, but it was at The Calhoun School for girls that she began to write.

She studied intellectual history at Mount Holyoke from 1967–1969, then spent her junior year at Amherst studying playwriting with nearby Smith College's Len Berkman. Amherst was her first experience away from an all-girl environment. It was also a time of self-discovery: "There was that innate confidence Amherst boys had. The girls I'd known may have had all the intellectual resources, but none of that confidence." Wasserstein emerged from college fascinated with the role of men and women in American society.

She went on to City College of New York to study writing with Israel Horovitz and Joseph Heller. Wasserstein landed at the Yale Drama School after that, along with many other bright theatrical lights of her generation: Meryl Streep, Sigourney Weaver, Robert Brustein, Ted Talley, Albert Innaurato, Glenn Close, Jill Eikenberry and Christopher Durang. But when she graduated in 1976, "It was like coming out of stained-glass school. Nobody was posting job listings saying 'Playwright wanted.' "

It was Lola who got Wasserstein her big break: She handed the receptionist at Playwrights Horizons Wasserstein's *Uncommon Women and Others*. The receptionist, in turn, handed it to the literary manager, Andre Bishop. It was read there, produced at the Phoenix Theater in 1977, and then made into a TV movie. But none of this was steady income.

Wasserstein squeaked out a job "as a gofer" for the Eugene O'Neill Theater Center. "We got 2,000 scripts a year. My job was to schlepp the scripts to readers all over the city. Needless to say, I got well-versed in who was writing what in America, and I began to realize that I wasn't seeing any plays that reflected the women I knew."

By 1981, she had another play to her name, *Isn't It Romantic?* about a fledgling TV writer whose parents want her to marry a nice Jewish doctor. It was staged in 1983, and she was given a grant to go to London, sit in a rooming house, and write another. This time she focused on a group of '60s women who want to have it all—professions, families, good hair.

It was called *The Heidi Chronicles*, and when it was produced on Broadway in 1988, it took practically every prize available: the Pulitzer, the Tony, the N.Y. Drama Critics, the Drama Desk, the Susan Blackburn Award. "The only thing I'd ever won was a babka at the local bakery!" *Heidi* was made into a TV movie with Jamie Lee Curtis.

Her next play was the 1992 box-office phenomenon *The Sisters Rozensweig*, a story about three Brooklyn-born siblings who meet in London to celebrate the 54th birthday of the eldest. It starred Jane Alexander and Madeline Kahn.

An American Daughter (1996) was, according to Wasserstein, "a darker story, a critical look at the left–about a woman whose carefully crafted life suddenly begins to unravel." But she returned to comedy in *Shiksa Goddess* (2001), a collection of mordantly funny pieces, siblings to the one you will read below.

Like her plays, Wasserstein can be both hilarious and dead sober. Summing up her career, she goes from chandelier-rocking jollity to the intensity of Medea: "You see, what I've really wanted all along is to see more women in major roles, more women taking curtain calls. They haven't been doing that in great numbers. I cannot help feeling that if someone isn't actively looking for them, they simply won't be there. Where will we be then?"

And suddenly neither one of us is laughing.

M. A.

Holidays at The Keyboard Inn

BY WENDY WASSERSTEIN

Here's a really great holiday vacation. The day after Christmas I get out my suitcase, stuff it with a sweatshirt for a daytime look, a cashmere cardigan for nighttime glamour—both of these definitely oversized, preferably enormous—add a flannel nightgown, and head for a deserted, unfamiliar college town.

I check in advance that the good local innkeeper can provide me with an IBM Selectric typewriter. Of course I know I should really use my Powerbook and coordinated Word Perfect, Scriptbetter, PlayDoctor, and Plotpositive software. But hey, I'm having myself a merry little Christmas and I get to be as cyber-stupid as possible. If I want to hand-feed a machine with erasable typing paper, it's my process and I'm welcome to it.

Generally, I arrive after lunch. After check-in, I quickly unpack and move the furniture around so the typewriter has an inspirational view of a pseudo-Oxford gargoyle, a library, or at the very least an evergreen. Finally, I place the manuscript-I've-deliberately-isolated-myself-to-complete on the desk and flee. After all, no one can write without Ricola sugar-free cough drops. Just ask Joseph Conrad.

Empty streets are festooned with Dickensian decor. Ye Olde Campus Bookstore carries every Christmas cat calendar published; the Republican Women's Cat Calendar, the Gay/Lesbian Cat Calendar and the Environmental Cat Calendar. I gather my necessities and spend 20 minutes debating the purchase of a 10-dollar, locally made pottery mug. Finally, I decide I don't deserve it until later in the week, when I've completed my mission. Before returning to my room, I stop in at the local all-natural pizza, pasta, and yogurt parlor for the tallest non-fat extra-foam decaf cappuccino east of Seattle.

Once back, I finally face my manuscript and make my first observation. A holiday trip is no place to start work. One's mind drifts too easily to family, friends, Prozac and *It's a Wonderful Life*. But New Year's Day is the best possible deadline for the somewhat stalled and uncompleted. Before leaving town it's a swell idea to call an editor or producer and promise them something tangible January First. It certainly solves the entire "What to do on New Year's Eve" dilemma. (The playwright Terrence McNally—*A Perfect Ganesh, Master Class*—

and I were once on our way to a New Year's Eve party when the anxiety of mutual deadlines overcame us. By midnight we were typing in separate rooms, he in black tie and I in pearls and blue velvet.)

Confronting the semi-existent play, the pulse rises. Will it be possible to ever finish? Is it worthwhile enough to finish? To relieve the uncertainty, an hour call to a friend vacationing on the Neva or in Saint Grappa, an island only known to platinum American Express Card owners, is an absolute necessity. By the end of the call it's at least cocktail hour and time to make the Scarlett O'Hara pledge, "Tomorrow is another day."

A simple rule for holiday writers: Cocktail time is time for physical fitness. Since the purpose of the trip is to work, it's best not to set relaxing precedents. Hollywood screenwriters may at sunset innately desire to bench-press Harley Davidsons with inspirational music playing in the background, but those of us with at least three fewer zeros after our names would always choose a martini instead. Best to fight the inclination. Best to go for a run on an unlit back road chased by barking dogs to a place you don't know. Orion, on an early winter night, is spiritually and artistically inspirational. Orion on an early winter night with wet shoes, frozen hands, no one to talk to, is reason enough to go home, have a drink and start writing

Ken Ludwig, the Washington author of the Broadway play *Moon Over Buffalo,* told me during rehearsals this fall that the problem with being on the road is "having dinner alone." For the holiday writer the joy of being on the road is having dinner alone. Dinner is a time to sit beside tomorrow's intended workload, ignore it, and listen carefully to all the surrounding conversation. It's time to judge harshly the surrounding couples in L. L. Bean turtlenecks and duck boots and fantasize about their sex lives. Do they leave the duck boots on? And, of course, it's time to mislead the very pleasant law student/waiter into thinking you've landed in this place as a cross between Blanche DuBois and Dolores Claiborne.

Since this is a work week, late night entertainment is simply out of the question. After dinner a brief diversion to the message desk is sufficient, and then up to the room. As for television, best to remote control John Sununu's holiday greeting and the private party girls at 1-900-BE-MERRY in favor of revisiting classics. For instance, I suggest dipping into *The Shoemaker's Holiday,* Thomas Dekker's 1600 Elizabethan comedy, and a sure lights-out in under five minutes.

Next morning the serious work begins. No more excuses, no more excursions. The still-unopened manuscript is cracked, the seat at the typewriter is occupied, the power button is turned on. Retyping the last scene to get back in the groove is not as hideous as anticipated. The work is not totally unsalvageable. It's even decent. Of course, it's entirely possible a ghost-writing elf popped into the holiday writer's hotel.

The next week is spent in an obsessive haze of writing, rewriting; a chicken sandwich in the room, another walk stopped midway by barking dogs, another "I rely on the kindness of strangers" dinner, and another scene of *Shoemaker's Holiday* before bed. If I were a man I wouldn't shave both for the Hemingway effect and to avoid the hassle. Since I'm a woman, by the fifth day I hardly dress.

All week I promise myself a movie on Thursday night. But as with Moscow for the three Chekhovian sisters, I know I'll never get there. By Thursday I decide I hate whatever it is I've written, that I've lost my talent, and furthermore I begin inventing my worst-nightmare notices. I get into bed with a case of Diet Coke and watch QVC until four o'clock in the morning. I get to sleep only when I am the happy owner of two $64 ruby rings and a total fitness abdominizer.

By morning I know it's time to force myself outside. I even put on mascara for the occasion. I take myself to the campus library and join in the communal contract for concentration. Leaving the room, I leave behind my fear and am able to focus again. I'm back on track. Life will be bliss when I put these pages in an envelope and they are out of my sole possession.

Now my work and I are one. There is no alienation on my part. I am not for one moment self-flagellating or lonely. On the contrary, I have a company of characters who are leading me to their final destinations. Of course, since I write plays, our journey together will not be over when I finish the script; most likely it will last another two years. We will be together for casting, previews, rewrites, and hopefully we will still like each other by opening night. They are my responsibility and my undoing—they are my alternative family. After all, we're spending the holidays together.

I plan to celebrate the night I finish, but I never do. Instead, I arrive at dinner with my completed work and begin to cut, mangle and torture it until it is legible only to me and a kindergarten class of the very differently gifted. As the waiter brings me a final dessert—on writer's holiday, calories, cholesterol and nicotine are freebies—he asks me if I've had a nice stay.

"Yes," I smile at him and I think now I've merged with Maggie Smith in *The Prime of Miss Jean Brodie*. "I've had a wonderful time. Happy New Year!"

Looking back at my plays, I remember an inn or a hotel room associated with each one. At some crucial point I took myself to the Hanover Inn, Hanover N.H.; the Inn at the Market, Seattle, Wash.; the Old Parsonage Inn, Oxford, England; the Duke Diet and Fitness Program, Durham, N.C., and my all-time favorite, the Savoy Hotel, London. There's nothing like finishing a play overlooking the Thames and the flashing lights of the Royal National Theatre. It's a honeymoon.

In the middle of these holiday excursions, my mind wanders to what an odd life writing is. Wouldn't it be far healthier to spend the week in the company of real, not imagined, family and friends? I make a plan to integrate my life next year. Set scheduled time for work, personal life and harpsichord lessons. Then time passes. Unfinished work accumulates. The phone keeps ringing, and I plan my next writing-woman's holiday.

December 18, 1995

Patricia Cornwell

One July morning in 1993, Patricia Cornwell made the trip to Knoxville to visit a research facility criminologists call "the body farm." It was one of those suffocating days when air hangs over Tennessee as uncertainly as a feather over a furnace. "I was driving along with the windows down, trying to find some air to breathe. As I approached the place, it hit me. The smell. It drifted toward me over the fence." The place stores corpses—44 of them to be exact—in every state of decay: curled around steering wheels, impaled on stakes, left to sizzle in the sun. The point was to study the ever-elusive "time of death," to learn how to sift through the wreckage of a violent crime and determine exactly when and how the dying began. Cornwell descended on this laboratory of horrors with all the intensity of a believer on a pilgrimage to Lourdes. Her 1994 novel, *The Body Farm*, was the result.

"It was gruesome, stunning," she says of the eerie display in Knoxville, "but the place wouldn't exist if there weren't something terribly wrong with us—with our society." For someone with so much mettle, so much resolve, there is the faintest hint of a wobble in her voice when she speaks of death.

Cornwell is the author of a string of phenomenally successful novels featuring the diligent forensic pathologist Dr. Kay Scarpetta. *Post Mortem* (1990), her first, won the Edgar, Creasey, Anthony and Macavity awards, as well as the French *Prix du roman d'aventure*. The rest have followed like annual events: *Body of Evidence* (1991), *All that Remains* (1992) and *Cruel and Unusual* (1993). *The Body Farm* (1994), *Unnatural Exposure* (1997), *Southern Cross* (1998), *Black Notice* (1999), *The Last Precinct* (2000). When she wrote the following essay, she was at work on her 1995 novel, *From Potter's Field*.

Cornwell was born in Miami in 1956, the daughter of a lawyer and a secretary. Her dream as a child was to become an archaeologist—dusting the bones, reconstructing the past. But she graduated from Davidson College with an English major instead; her first job was night-shift copy aide for the *Charlotte Observer*'s TV guide. "I would work from 4 a.m. to noon, then go around to all the desks and beg people to assign me stories. They would toss me things no one else wanted: Boy Scout conventions, stamp collectors' conferences . . ." Within six months she was made a reporter. Within a year she was covering crime.

"Imagine this 23-year-old skinny blonde thing running around the newsroom with a radio banging against her leg. I fell in love with the job. At first the cops hated me because they hated the newspaper. But I got tough and they got soft. I started riding with them. Eventually I found myself wanting to solve crimes more than I wanted to report them."

She left the *Observer* to write *A Time for Remembering* (1983), a biography of Ruth Bell Graham, wife of the evangelist Billy Graham. And then three crime novels followed, but she couldn't get any one of them published. Determined to find a vocabulary and context for her fiction, she took a job first at a morgue and then in a medical examiner's office in Richmond. She was there for four years as a computer analyst when she looked about her and realized what she had done. "I had been an award-winning crime reporter, I had a nonfiction book to my name, and here I was, facing utter despair and a creme de menthe office wall." It was then that she got some very good advice. "Try again," said an editor at Mysterious Press, who had written her the most helpful rejection letters, "but this time write about what you see." Cornwell went back to work and changed her perspective to first-person.

The product of her efforts, *Post Mortem*, was rejected by seven houses. "Too monochromatic," one publisher wrote back. "Who wants to read about a morgue?" But Scribner's decided to take a chance. A year later the book was an international bestseller.

Cornwell has since worked as a volunteer with the Richmond Police Department and learned alongside FBI agents at the Academy in Quantico. Today, she owns a company that sells security services. Her novels are studies in postmodern verismo; each is grounded in a real crime and debuts the use of some emerging forensic technology.

But it is more than curiosity that drives her. "My mother paints in her spare time," she reflects. "I remember standing in front of one of her night scenes once. There was a full moon in it, and everyone around me saw the image differently. To others it was charming and harmless. To me it was gothic, scary. I've never stopped wondering why that is."

What is it that draws this outwardly delicate woman to the arena of violent death? "Fear," she answers quickly. "I have to take it apart, conquer it, perform an autopsy. Fear is behind it all. Fear is my enemy."

M. A.

The Passionate Researcher

BY PATRICIA CORNWELL

I remember working on my first novel while a senior at Davidson College in North Carolina. The apartment I rented that year had no heat. I often typed late at night with my winter coat on and could see my breath. That first book, blessedly, was never published and is not worth remembering. But the words of a sage, older friend I will not forget. "Writing," he said to me, "is a way of having experiences without scars."

I thought this a wonderful insight at the time. I could write about any subject, even murder, and not suffer. I did not have to get close. I could sit at my desk and simply imagine the morgue. Of course I was wrong.

So now I will tell the way it really is when I sit down to write novels about Kay Scarpetta, medical examiner: I am a reporter; I am Dr. Scarpetta's feet, hands and eyes. I gather facts like shards of brilliant, bloody glass and fashion from them a window. On the other side is a dimension of life, powerful in its darkness and exhausting in its extremes. I have come to know that side profoundly well because listening to secondary accounts about the tracks that crime leaves was not and will never be enough. I must see, smell, hear and touch the evidence for myself.

When I first wrote crime fiction in the early '80s, the stories turned to air in my hands. I could not grasp the characters nor understand what they felt. My voice had no authority, and even after laboring to create a world, I could see it was not good. I needed more than library articles and interviews. I began working very hard for the legitimacy that would earn me passage into the places I needed to see—places I still find painful to traverse.

Sometimes I spent 12 hours a day in surgical scrubs, assisting forensic pathologists as they performed autopsies in a Richmond, Va., morgue. I will never forget the first time I placed my gloved hands in a chest cavity and was startled to find that the blood was cold.

Death becomes very real when it has been refrigerated, and no matter how many times someone may have told me that bodies in the morgue are stored this way, the reality did not grab my soul until I felt the cold firsthand. Since those early days of research, I have camped in the shadow of violent death and befriended the troops of stalwart spirits and great minds who war against it. I am forever changed.

Memory for me is like one of those Civil War greenhouses sadly built of daguerrotypes instead of glass panes. If I walk into my thoughts and quietly sit, I suddenly find myself surrounded by haunting faces and harrowing tableaux. I conjure up soldiers who have run into bayonets—bodies of young people who fight believing they will never die. I see mere boys giving their last Rebel Yell, and they are not so different from last week's teenager who decided to stand up suddenly in the back of a pickup truck, not realizing it was about to go under a bridge. I remember he came to the morgue with a dented can of Old Spice deodorant in one pocket, 35 cents in the other.

In the greenhouse of my memories I have worn a police uniform and driven an unmarked car. I have directed traffic during Richmond summers when heat shimmered like snow in a relentless sun, and carbon monoxide fumes made me light on my feet. I remember being ridiculed, almost run down and verbally abused for being "a cop." I remember the turgid bureaucracy of a police department that first sent me out into rush hour without training.

I have said goodbye in the morgue to a homicide detective who was my friend, and stared stunned at the small hole in his chest. In these ways I have come to understand Pete Marino, the homicide detective in my books; I know he would not speak to me had I not lived in his world and done my best to learn its language.

Benton Wesley, the FBI profiler in my novels, makes demands of me that are more tolerable. The FBI Academy at Quantico is the finest law enforcement facility in the world. To go there is to feel one is at Oxford University or in a monastery where doors are never locked because the people are so good. The academy is rarified, scholarly. Yet, ironically, the cases studied by the Investigative Support Unit concern some of the most evil people in the land: Ted Bundy, Jeffrey Dahmer, John Wayne Gacy.

The public has heard of them—these creatures who inevitably find their way onto the cover of People magazine after murdering 33 victims or cannibalizing the lovers they bring home from the bar. But what I find worse is the monster no one reads about or sees on the six o'clock news. We would like to think that the ones we know are all there are.

There are other monsters—other cries that no one hears: the girl jogging; the newspaper boy riding his bicycle; the old woman who lives alone; the child wandering off in the mall while his mother pays the cashier. They become statistics, case numbers, photographs passed around a conference room.

I am told my novels are different from traditional mysteries, and I would agree. It would be misleading for me to claim to be an expert in such a masterful, old genre. But I have become—for reasons even I do not fully understand—a passionate student of crime. No matter how well I may do, I can never forsake the work that got me where I am—the dogged research into time of death, the slide in the lab, the slab in the morgue.

Now I am at work on my sixth Scarpetta novel. The research has not changed. The new novel began on a snowy night in the subway tunnels of New York City as I stepped over syringes and crack vials. I wore a surgical mask and gloves, and rats ran over my boots. The next morning I went to the Office of the Chief Medical Examiner where a corpse was being autopsied, and I realized that the man on the table was the police officer who had been slain the night before. This frigid fact-gathering trip ended with a flight over New York's Potter's Field—the vast common grave for unclaimed bodies and criminals. From the air I watched prisoners burying simple pine boxes on a barren island where the dead are stacked on top of each other and many have no names.

I tried to sleep in that vibrating Bell Jet Ranger, cold air blowing on my neck. I thought about what it was I had seen that day. I felt dirty, exhausted, depressed. For more than 10 years I have put myself through the same thing and wondered if I should stop—or at least, ease up.

I cannot. If I stop seeing, hearing, touching, there will be no story. I will be a writer with nothing to say—a violin with no music to play. The journeys I find myself taking inevitably unfold the story, and the characters who accompany me always reveal more to me with time.

July 31, 1994

Stanley Karnow

"The kind of writing I do," says Stanley Karnow, "is a constant struggle between me and material." Ninety-five percent of what is in his files never gets onto the printed page. Though as a journalist and historian, Karnow deals with the facts of a story, he does not see himself as a thresher of information. He claims to use his intuition as much as any novelist in a creative trance. "When I'm doing my best work," he says, "I'm not in control."

As a young reporter in Paris, Karnow once asked the Cubist Georges Braque how he decided on his images. Braque responded, "If I knew what was going to come out, young man, I wouldn't paint it." "The funny thing," says the packrat documentarian, "is that, in my work, I feel exactly the same way." According to Karnow, good contemporary history is written by instinct. The magic comes when you unexpectedly pull something from the morass.

He was born in Brooklyn in 1925, the son of a machinery salesman and a Hungarian-born mother. "I was a typical Jewish kid in a lace-curtained, cloistered environment. It didn't take long for me to realize I wanted out." He was bitten by wanderlust early, reading newspaper dispatches from faraway places, fantasizing junkets as a starry-eyed boy.

For his bar mitzvah, he was given a portable typewriter. After that, hardly a day passed that he didn't write. By high school he was sports editor of his newspaper. But when he read Vincent Sheean's *Personal History*, the memoir of a globetrotting reporter, he knew he had found his career.

He began training for radio at the University of Iowa, but then transferred to Harvard, where he earned a degree in European history and literature. "I've never believed in journalism school," he says. "What a good reporter needs is a solid and broad education: a base in the liberal arts. The rest comes with the territory."

At Harvard, he was an editorial and feature writer for the Crimson. From there he was drafted into the Second World War. He served as a U.S. Army weather observer, cryptographer and unit historian, and it was in these roles that he fulfilled his boyhood dream of traveling to exotic climes: He was posted in Asia, sent off to live in the mountains between India and China. "The army for me was a chance to read," he says. "I didn't hear one shot fired. I would go down to headquarters, pick up box after box of paperback books, a couple cases of beer, and then head up the hill to consume it all." When he returned to Harvard and graduated in 1947, he knew he'd go back abroad.

He went to Paris for a summer and stayed for 10 years. He studied at the Sorbonne and married the daughter of experimental novelist Nathalie Sarraute. (He described his early days in Paris in a book he co-wrote with his wife, *Paris in the Fifties*.) He was then hired by Time magazine. At Time, he wrote about cuisine, wine, sex, crime and politics. Within a few years he was writing about war. By the end of the '50s, Karnow had covered Algiers, was remarried and "suitcasing" through Africa, and had relocated his family to Hong Kong. When the Vietnam War started in earnest, he was there to see it unfold. When he grew weary of all the rewriting—"sausage-making"—in the *Time* editorial process, he took a job covering the war for *The Washington Post*. In 1970, in his mid-40s, he returned to the United States. After one stint with NBC and another with the *New Republic*, public television gave him his biggest break. He was asked to do a documentary on the Vietnam War.

The book that accompanied that documentary was *Vietnam: A History*, a work that, since publication in 1983, has sold just under 2 million copies and won him the Pulitzer prize. Karnow has also written a book on the Philippines and is at work on a monumental history of Asian Americans. "I'm starting with the first alleged trip across the Bering Strait some 30,000 years ago," he says. Like his Vietnam chronicle, the book is being mined from great mountains of string.

"I could never go back to reporting now," says Karnow. "I'm too used to a historian's pace. Not to mention that I would never approve of it: I'm the toughest boss I've ever had."

M. A.

From Packrat to Historian

BY STANLEY KARNOW

Back in the early 1950s, when I was a novice foreign correspondent, Theodore H. White—a veteran journalist and, later, author of *The Making of a President, 1960*—cautioned me, "Never throw anything away. You may be able to use it again." Heeding his advice, I filled boxes with duplicates of my dispatches, notes, memos, letters, sketches, calendars, photos, even trivia like faded theater posters, vintage wine labels and embossed menus from banquets. I schlepped bulging cartons with me from Paris to North Africa to Hong Kong and ultimately to my home in suburban Washington. They languished unopened until I made the transition from journalist to historian, and found myself sitting on a treasure trove waiting to be mined.

I am not the only packrat journalist around. David Halberstam's *The Best and the Brightest*, Christopher Ogden's *Maggie* and Neil Sheehan's *A Bright Shining Lie* are works that richly display this tendency: mountains of material crafted into bestsellers that reflect their authors' days in the news business. The same can be said, to some degree, about Ward Just's perceptive Washington novels. The practice dates back to Theodore Dreiser, Bret Harte, Frank Norris and Mark Twain.

Good reporters are perennial adolescents—restless, skeptical, petulant, compulsively inquisitive. Whether they serve at home or abroad, they enjoy unique privileges. They stride the corridors of power, witnessing major events. They hobnob with presidents and royalty: the glamorous, the celebrated, the mythical. Many of them are chronic adventurers who cannot resist the urge to risk their skins in war. Such had been my life, and I adored every minute of it until I reached my mid-40s. By that point, I had been rushing around Europe, Africa and Asia on suitcase assignments for years. My legs were giving out. Rather than retire to a university or a golf course, I began to ponder the idea of shifting to a career in books.

Initially, I assumed that in order to make that transition I had merely to delve into the crates cluttering my basement. They contained anecdotes, insights, vignettes of the exotic places I had visited and my impressions of the extraordinary and ordinary people I had encountered as I roamed my beat. Particularly valuable were my recollections of sounds, smells and atmospheres. But, like other correspondents, I had operated under tight deadline pressures and space limitations that prevented me from examining things thoroughly. At first, too, I was only vaguely acquainted with the wide range of traditions, cultures, customs and languages of the regions I covered. Clearly I had barely scratched the surface in my reporting. I was well aware that in order to write a book I would have to probe deeper.

Nor was I sure I had the patience and discipline to organize and classify all the odds and ends in my vast repository and then proceed to sit at my computer for months. Writing books is the loneliest of occupations, akin to long-distance running—not exactly my idea of fun. I was also afraid of the process, persuaded that my prose would be engraved in granite, that I would no longer be able to dash off pieces, as I habitually did for newspapers and magazines. Equally difficult would be the task of constructing a narrative that was both dramatic and credible. But I forged ahead anyway, deciding to try my hand at it.

Soon I discovered that I would need an assistant to organize all my boxes of material. Bright young college graduates are a glut on the market, and I had the pick of the crop. Many were aspiring journalists willing to accept relatively low pay in hopes of picking up tips from a veteran, and I depended heavily on their help. They tended to go from the tedium of scouring my files to much more exciting jobs. One of them even joined the Peace Corps. But I don't think I could have sorted out all that history by myself.

In 1959, after working in *Time*'s Paris bureau for a decade, I had been transferred to Hong Kong, where I switched to the *Saturday Evening Post* and later to *The Washington Post.* My territory included Vietnam, and, with intervals, I covered the escalating war there for nearly 20 years, accumulating rumors, opinions, real and bogus information. I saved records of chats with peasants in remote villages, jotted down anxieties as I accompanied American troops on missions through the countryside. As the conflict dragged on, I attended the conferences at which President Lyndon Johnson, Robert McNamara, General William Westmoreland and their entourage, equipped with charts and statistics, promised imminent victory. I happened to be in Saigon in 1968, when the Tet offensive erupted, shattering the rosy assertions and shocking a pessimistic U.S. public.

But I realized as I prepared my book on Vietnam many years later that my boxes lacked the answers to numerous questions. I rummaged through in an attempt to fathom the decisions made by Presidents Truman, Eisenhower and Kennedy that propelled the United States into Southeast Asia. I needed to learn more, for example, about the ambiguous Tonkin Gulf incident, which Johnson had used in 1964 to maneuver Congress into authorizing him to deploy American forces in Vietnam. It was vital, as well, to assess the influence exerted by the press—especially television—on U.S. opinion. Another subject worth exploring was the impact of the anti-war movement. I also felt that I did not fully understand Richard Nixon's dual policy of intensifying the war while seeking to achieve peace.

To fill these and other gaps, I tracked down State Department, Pentagon and CIA officials who had previously been reluctant to speak freely. The postwar climate had changed and many of them, now relaxed, disclosed what I already suspected: They initially had either been lying or, at the very least, blurring the truth when they issued optimistic predictions. I also combed archives and libraries, and, as formerly secret documents became available, I scanned them for precious details.

During the war, I had observed enemy soldiers rush to their deaths as they struggled against America's overwhelming military superiority to gain what often seemed to be a minor objective. The phenomenon had bewildered me, and afterward, in an effort to appreciate their awesome fearlessness, I returned to Vietnam several times. There I interviewed, among others, General Vo Nguyen Giap, the legendary communist commander. As we sipped tea in his modest Hanoi villa, he discussed the strategies he had employed to vanquish France and later the United States. Finally, I asked him how long he would have gone on fighting. His voice rising to a pitch, he thundered in French, "Ten, 20, 100 years, whatever it took to win, regardless of losses." So it was more than saving string or diving into history; it was going back to check and recheck the sources.

I devoted 8 years to my Vietnam book, and have revised it twice since its publication in 1983. My books on China, America's relations with the Philippines and my salad days in Paris have also been marathon endeavors that required me to dig into all the reporter's notes I had preserved. In retrospect, I owe Teddy White a debt of gratitude for his tip. Otherwise little might remain of my experiences as a foreign correspondent: a few yellowed clippings, some misty memories, and a story to swap over a drink.

April 26, 1998

David McCullough

Hemingway had the hunt. Capote had the parties. Tolstoy had the farm. Sometimes it's the pastime that tells you most about the work. In the case of David McCullough, it's the painting. A passion for it informs his writing: His prose is detailed, textured, visual.

McCullough is one of our most gifted living writers. He has given us history as well as biography: Among his books are *The Great Bridge: The Epic Story of the Brooklyn Bridge*; the panoramic *Path Between the Seas: The Creation of the Panama Canal*; the National Book Award winner *Mornings on Horseback* (about Theodore Roosevelt); the harrowing *Johnstown Flood*; and his current bestseller, *John Adams*. He has an unerring sense of narrative pace, an uncanny ability to reduce the mess of history to a clean arc, a memorable tableau.

He was born in Pittsburgh in 1933, one of four sons of an electrical supply wholesaler. "My father was a salesman, a natural storyteller," he says, "and he was totally against FDR. My mother thought FDR could do no wrong. They were both quite hard of hearing, so you can imagine: The decibel level at our dining room table was high." Small wonder he grew up knowing history could be lively.

He went to the nearby Shady Side Academy, believing he would become a painter someday, but Yale changed his mind. "Yale in the '50s was like attending a trade school for New York publishing. There were so many writers there. I never dared say I wanted to be one, but when I graduated, I automatically drifted in that direction: I became a trainee at Time-Life." A job at *Sports Illustrated* followed. When Kennedy became president, McCullough was "swept by the spirit of the times" and came to Washington, where he landed a job at the U.S. Information Agency, editing a magazine for the Arab world. He immersed himself in histories:

Bruce Catton's *A Stillness at Appomattox*, Shelby Foote's *Fort Sumter to Perryville*, Barbara Tuchman's *The Guns of August*. He began moonlighting for *American Heritage* magazine. And, on his lunch hours, he began research for his first book.

"I write to find out," he says. "There isn't anything in this world that isn't inherently interesting--if only someone will explain it to you in English, if only someone will frame it in a story." Does he prefer to write biography or history? "You have more freedom in history; you don't have to stick to a protagonist; the ground rules are more lenient. In biography, on the other hand, the life gives you that spine."

He is grateful to have begun as a journalist. "It encouraged me to walk the ground, see the place, project myself into another time. Nothing had to happen the way it did, you know. People didn't know how it all would end." His goal is to capture that sense of immediacy—to paint a way into the past. "Of course the art has had an influence on me," he says. "Wasn't it Conrad who said, 'I want to make you see'? I want to do that. I want to give people words that will make them see."

M. A.

Climbing into Another Head

BY DAVID McCULLOUGH

For about 6 years now, in the time it's taken to write my biography of John Adams, I have largely abandoned reading anything written in our own day. For along with research of the kind to be expected with such a book, I have been trying as much as possible to know Adams through what he read as well as what he wrote, and the result has been one of the most enjoyable forays of my writing life.

I say I've been trying as much as possible because to read all that this remarkable man read is beyond almost anyone's capability. It would require, as it did for him, a life span of nearly 91 years and an ability, not to say desire, to devour books as few mortals ever could. Starting at about age 15, Adams "read forever," as he said, and more broadly and more deeply than any other American of that bookish era, even Thomas Jefferson. To keep pace with Adams would also require a command of Greek, Latin and French, all of which he read continuously and most happily right up to the point when he could no longer see to read.

Adams's first book was a schoolboy copy of Cicero's *Orations*. A lifetime later, in their famous exchange of letters, he and Jefferson compared notes on Cicero and others of the Romans, or discussed the proper pronunciation of certain Greek phrases. "Your Father's zeal for books will be one of the last desires which will quit him," Abigail Adams told their son John Quincy, as Adams, in his 81st year, launched eagerly into a 16-volume French history.

Though Abigail read no language but her own, her love of reading was hardly less than that of her "dearest friend." Indeed, the bonds of literature were no small part of their extraordinary love for each other, starting with their courtship. She read at every chance and could quote from Shakespeare and other favorite poets more readily than he, and all to his delight.

Having, like Abigail, no fluency in Greek or Latin and only the rustiest of French, I have been reading Thucydides, Tacitus and Marcus Aurelius, as well as Rousseau and Voltaire, in the translations available in the superb Penguins Classic series. But it has been in the great works of English literature, available also in the Penguin series, that I felt most able to "find" him and his world to a degree not possible in other ways. What is more, it has enabled me to immerse myself, to marinate my head, in the vocabulary of the 18th century, and particularly as the excellent notes in the back of each volume provide definitions of many delightful and unfamiliar words long out of usage. "Spatterdashes" are leggings to protect stockings from mud and dirt, in case you didn't know. A "cabinet" is a small private room; "diabled" means cursed, noisome, ill-smelling, and when John Adams called the Quakers of Philadelphia "dull as beetles," he was only employing a familiar expression.

I have been reading, one after another, books of the kind most of us remember, if at all, from high school or college English courses long past, when the likes of Pope, Swift, Defoe and Samuel Johnson were required, and we were probably too young to realize just how marvelous they are.

The basic John and Abigail Adams Reading List (for summer or life) would include, for fiction, Jonathan Swift's *Tale of the Tub*, a book Adams adored; both *Tristram Shandy* and *A Sentimental Journey*, by Laurence Sterne; and *Clarissa*, Samuel Richardson's highly popular, mammoth novel wherein the story is told entirely with letters. Richardson, Abigail Adams advised a niece, had done more to teach "the talent of letter writing" than any other writer she could name. In Richardson's hands events unfolded in letters written "to the moment," as things happen. "My letters to you," Abigail told her sister Mary, "are first thoughts without correction."

For my own part, the most engaging and in many ways the most valuable of the novels is *The Expedition of Humphrey Clinker*, by Tobias Smollett, another of John Adams's favorite authors. Published in 1771, it, too, is a tale told through the device of letters and a book so full of spirit, so wise and entertaining, that I read it twice, and will, I'm sure, return to it often again. It is the 18th century as a show of constant commotion and change. The descriptions of London are as vivid as any to be found, and many of the observations by its winsome central character, the cantankerous, clear-eyed Matthew Bramble, could be those of Adams himself. Consider Bramble's (Smollett's) views on the evils of political parties, the partisan press and politicians who pander for votes—views that Adams came to agree with, and then some:

> The spirit of party is risen to a kind of phrenzy, unknown to former ages, or rather degenerated to a total extinction of honesty and candor. You know I have observed, for some time, that the public papers are become the infamous vehicles of the most cruel and perfidious defamation. . . . Notwithstanding my contempt for those who flatter a minister, I think there is something still more despicable in flattering a mob.

For nonfiction prose I would include on the list Edward Gibbon's *Memoirs of His Life*; Edward Burke's brilliant *Reflections on the Revolution in France*; Henry St. John, Lord Bolingbroke's famous essay "The Utility of History"; and Adam Smith's *Wealth of Nations*, which was published in the same year as the Declaration of Independence. Whether either of the Adamses ever read Goethe's lovely *Italian Journey*, published 10 years later, I can't say, but it's hard to imagine Adams, one of the record-breaking travelers of his time, passing it by, and certainly what Goethe has to say about life is in tune with much Adams himself felt. Adams, too, might have written as Goethe did: "The observation that all greatness is transitory should not make us despair; on the contrary the realization that the past was great should stimulate us to create something of consequence ourselves."

Of the poets John Dryden must figure prominently, as well as Milton, James Thomson, Defoe and, of course, Shakespeare. "Let me search for the clue which lead great Shakespeare into the labyrinth of human nature," young John Adams set down in his diary in a tiny hand. "Let me examine how men think." Abigail, in 1776, writing to her husband in far-off Philadelphia in advance of the Declaration of Independence, reminded him in the words of Act IV, Scene III of Julius Caesar, that "There is a tide in the affairs of men, Which, taken at the flood, leads on to fortune. . . . We must take the current when it serves, Or lose our ventures." In 1805, at age 70, Adams read all of Shakespeare twice through again.

Of the poets of the 18th century, to Adams's mind it was Alexander Pope who ranked first. In his early efforts as a published writer, Adams had been advised that nothing so helped one gain a command of the English language as frequent readings of Pope—advice he took much to heart. Through his whole life, he was to read and re-read Pope, and especially the *Essay on Man*, which he drew on repeatedly to make a point. Years later after the Revolution, Adams and Jefferson took several days off from their diplomatic rounds in London to tour England's new-style gardens then much in fashion, both men having been enlightened on the subject by what Pope wrote of the splendors of Stowe and his own garden by the Thames at Twickenham.

Once, after giving his son John Quincy several fine volumes of Pope, Adams counseled the boy that it was essential that he read poetry every day—and for pleasure. "In all the disquisitions you have heard concerning the happiness of life, has it ever been recommended to you to read poetry?" Adams asked, adding the memorable line, "You will never be alone with a poet in your pocket."

While I can't say I've been carrying a poet in my pocket all along these past six years, I can affirm that more often than not the book in my pocket—or briefcase or glove compartment—has been something that Adams read. At hand at the moment, for example, as I write this in my Washington hotel, is a well-worn, heavily underlined copy of Laurence Sterne's *A Sentimental Journey*, which includes a wonderful line that applies directly to so much about the outlook of John and Abigail Adams, and that we can all feel a lift from in our own time, more than 200 years later: "What a large volume of adventures may be grasped within this little span of life by him who interests his heart in everything."

July 1, 2001

Ray Bradbury

You might think that a man who wrote 30 books, 20 plays, 2 musicals, 2 space-age cantatas, 12 books of poetry, 3 books of essays, half-a-dozen film scripts and 500 short stories would need a vacation now and then. Not Ray Bradbury. "I've never had a vacation in my life!" he says exuberantly. "Why should I? I've never worked!"

For Bradbury, writing is playing. No suffering, slavish wordsmith he. "I don't think I know what writer's block is," he says. "I never had it. My typewriter goes everywhere I go. I get up at 3 a.m. every day, head for the keyboard, laugh a lot, then go back to bed." It takes him 2 hours to write a poem, half a day to finish a short story, 9 days for a full-scale novel. His secret? "Let your subconscious take over; keep your intellect out of the way. Be passionate about what you're doing. Look at it this way: When you start a love affair, the last thing you want to be is critical, right? And if you're starting a business, the last thing you want to do is second-guess yourself, heh? Write, that's what I say. Don't look back, just write, Ray. Go and write."

And so he has. From the first day he set a story to paper at the age of 12, he hasn't stopped. *The Martian Chronicles, The Illustrated Man, Fahrenheit 451, Dandelion Wine, The Halloween Tree, October Country, Something Wicked This Way Comes*: These are but a few of the classics that bear his name, and they are remembered by many with a reverence approaching love. Now 82 years old, Bradbury remains, as science-fiction critic Damon Knight called him, "the poet of 20th-century neurosis . . . the isolated spark of consciousness . . . the grown-up child who still believes." He is, in short, America's one-man fantasy factory.

He was born in Waukegan, Ill., on Aug. 22, 1920. His older brother had died in the great flu epidemic of 1918. His little sister succumbed a few years later. When the Depression hit and his father lost his job as a pole-climber for the power and light company, the family headed west, first to Arizona, then to California. "We had all of $40 to our name for 4 people," Bradbury recounts, "and couldn't afford a car. My father walked all around Los Angeles looking for work; he couldn't find it. He came home one day and sat in the kitchen, the tears dropping off his nose."

But Leonard Bradbury eventually found a $14-a-week job and was able to provide for his wife and 2 sons. "Thank God for that," says Ray Bradbury today, "because it was staying in California that enabled me to do what I dreamed of doing."

His mother's motion-picture addiction had a profound effect on him. By high school, he was seeing 10 to 12 movies a week, befriending the movie theater managers, sneaking his way past the box office by running errands and doing favors, then hanging out in front of the Uptown to get autographs of the greats—Helen Hayes, Clark Gable, Laurel and Hardy, Norma Shearer. He began collecting comic strips, gathering illustrations, corresponding with cartoonists and writers and heading for cover in the library when the bullies came around to taunt him for being so small and so very strange.

His high school English teacher became his friend for life; it was she who encouraged him to keep on writing, though it was clear enough to him that the stories he valiantly submitted to Esquire and other magazines were second-rate. His glamorous aunt—a costume designer, art-gallery fanatic and avid reader—became his benefactress; she took him to the 1939 World's Fair, and, at the age of 87, was still attending his readings, bringing fudge and crying.

By the time he was 19, Bradbury had introduced himself to the great science-fiction writer Robert Heinlein, "who became my teacher and accepted me into his group, although I was lousy." Rejected by the army for his poor eyesight, he continued to live at home, sell newspapers on the street corner and find himself in lively conversation with John Barrymore, Edna May Oliver and other Hollywood notables. By 20, he had several stories accepted by Script magazine; by 25, he was a regular contributor to Weird Tales.

He left home at 27 to marry Maggie, a young woman working in a local bookstore. The store owner had asked her to keep an eye on Bradbury, whom he suspected of coming around to steal books. "I'm going to the moon some day," Bradbury told her when he lured her out for a cup of coffee. "Wanna come?" Fifty-five years and 4 daughters later, they are still together.

Bradbury's first big break came when radio dramatist Norman Corwin invited him to New York City in 1949 to introduce him to an editor at Doubleday. "Take all those space stories of yours," the editor instructed him when he learned Bradbury had no novel to offer him, "tie them into a tapestry, make it look like a novel, and call it *The Martian Chronicles*." The rest, says Bradbury, was easy.

Despite the wildly fanciful adventures for which Bradbury became known, he has never driven a car: He still has nightmares about the carnage of a highway accident he witnessed as a child. And until he was 62 years old, he never flew in an airplane. But he has been a consultant to the World's Fair, designed a ride for Disney World and helped engineer California from shopping malls to rapid transit.

Now a grandfather of five and firmly grounded in a global network of friends he has cultivated for more than 50 years, Bradbury continues to be a fount of the written word. Even when the word is *about* Bradbury. The year 2002 marked the publication of a biography of the man by Jerry Weist. Its subtitle, "A Journey to Far Metaphor," and its introduction were supplied by none other than the subject himself.

M. A.

Hunter of Metaphors

BY RAY BRADBURY

I first met film director Sam Peckinpah some 20 years ago when he expressed a desire to film my novel *Something Wicked This Way Comes*.

"How will you do it, Sam?" I asked.

"Tear the pages out of your book," said Sam, "and stuff them in the camera!"

And so it was that I discovered, late in life, the obvious fact that most of my stories were written to be filmed. Examining an average page, I found that each paragraph was a long shot, a medium two-shot or a close-up. So it was easy to screenplay my tales, or write them for my TV series. The scenes paragraphed themselves. I was astounded at Peckinpah's insight. How come he knew what I was? How had I become a screenwriter without knowing it? Where did it start, to end like this?

It started the day I became the Hunchback or perhaps the day I descended the stairs in my grandma's house, her black opera cape slung on my shoulders, the Phantom himself.

I was a child of movies. My mother ate them like popcorn. So in 1923 when I was 3, I got trotted off to the flickers (they still flickered then) to see Lon Chaney, *Lost World* dinosaurs and *The Cat and the Canary*. In the first grade my mother picked me up after school 3 days a week and hurried me one block to the Academy theater for late matinees of *Ben Hur*, *King of Kings* or *The Johnstown Flood*. By the time I was 10 I had seen practically every silent film ever made, plus Al Jolson and all those sound films that shattered the Silents.

I was walking backwards up a dark theater aisle when, in 1928, I stood riveted by Disney's *Skeleton Dance*. I froze in place, until my hunger-enraged father lunged in to drag me home to dinner. I joined my local movie houses's Mickey Mouse Club and in a few short years saw 300 five-minute Disney shorts without blinking.

Sundays, aged 14, I loitered in the local museum basement, where a mere dozen *Steamboat Willie* and *Skeleton Dance* cartoon cels were locked under glass. Somehow I felt that if I stared long and hard enough, the cels would float up into my eyeballs and there, locked forever, be mine.

Fixated patience gave me my reward. In 1965, at lunch one day in his office, Walt Disney recalled my defending Disneyland against a few jealous intellectuals and untidy Philistines and said: "Ray, you've done so much for us. What can we do for you?"

"Walt," I said, "open the vaults."

Walt dialed a number and said, "Ray's here. Open the vaults."

A little later I rose from the vaults, arms brimmed with treasure: cartoon cels by the dozen from *Snow White, Sleeping Beauty, Alice in Wonderland* and *Fantasia*. I staggered off the lot capsized with images, not imagining their worth some day, but thinking, I'm 14 years old and those museum cartoon cels, unreachable, under glass, are now mine!

Along the way to Disney's tombs, consuming all the optic-nerve junk food I could find, I was stunned by the covers of *Amazing and Wonder Stories,* published when I was 8, with their military architectures, fabulous towers and incredible city canyons. In 1929 Buck Rogers, in a single daily strip, focused my life forever. From there on, it was the future and only the future. My fifth-grade friends snorted at my madness, so I tore up my Buck Rogers collection, broke into tears, saw that I had destroyed my life, called my friends what they were—idiots—and resumed my fixation on Buck, Wilma, Killer Kane and the Tiger Men of Mars, and thus came back to life.

In those same years Edgar Rice Burroughs's John Carter, Warlord of Mars, flew to the Red Planet and asked me along. With us, I learned later, flew astronomer Carl Sagan, novelist Arthur C. Clarke, Bruce Murray, president of Jet Proposition Lab, and all the astronauts who footprinted the Moon.

So what was I doing, all unaware? Collecting metaphors.

Lord, I didn't even know what a metaphor was. But, hell, I collected 'em anyway. I saw the world as a brightly lit sweet shop where you stared, pointed and cried, Gimme one of these and two of those!

And I remembered King Tut, who came from hiding in 1923 and stunned my imagination with his feat of playing dead for 3,000 years. I ran on stage with Blackstone to help him vanish an elephant. I wandered through Chicago magic shops to touch but not buy tricks that controlled existence.

Metaphors. Symbols, bright objects for jackdaws like me to seize and make nests of.

The Chicago Century of Progress Exposition knocked me down in 1933, and suddenly there were all those impossible architectures, the shapes and colors of future cities, no sooner reared then razed. A vast turntable carried me into the first animated three-dimensional robot-dinosaur show. I walked backwards so I could stay in one place while the turntable whisked everyone else back to reality. After an hour of me walking backward, the show proprietors ran in cursing to eject me. I never forgave them.

At night I refused to go home on the midnight trolley to Waukegan, 33 miles north of the fair, wanting to hide in those incredible towers and future attics and wake up in 1999. My father dragged me out to the train and rocketed me back to 1933. Later, I forgave him.

About this time, a living metaphor arrived: Mr. Electrico, a traveling carnival illusionist, visited Waukegan and sat fused in his electric chair as a billion or so volts of electricity rampaged through his body. Lifting his sword, he tapped my nose. The blue fire sluiced in to spark my ears and comb my hair as he cried, "Live forever!"

That seemed a great idea. But how was someone supposed to do it?

The next day, soon after a favorite uncle's funeral, driving back from the graveyard, I told my father to stop the car. He let me out to plunge downhill toward the carnival, running away from death, I see now, running toward life—electricity—and a carnival magician who had promised me immortality.

And there he sat on his platform by his electric chair. He did not tell me how to live forever, I was too shy to ask, but he did introduce me to all those strangely contorted people behind the scenes in the tent, then walked me down to sit me on the lakefront sands and listen to my large philosophies.

"You know," he said, at last, "we've met before."

"No, sir" I said.

"Yes," he said, "you were my best friend at the battle of the Ardennes Forest in October 1918 and, wounded, died in my arms that day. Now here you are with a new name, new face, but the soul shining out of your face is the soul of my lost friend. Welcome back to the world."

Astounding. The night before he had offered me electrical immortality. Now he put the other bookend in place: I had lived before.

Within 2 months of my last encounter with Mr. Electrico, I wrote my first stories of landings on the moon and arrivals on Mars. God bless Mr. Electrico, who sent me on the journey.

Just ahead I encountered Ray Harryhausen, who animated 16-millimeter film dinosaurs in his garage. We promised, in our loving friendship, to grow old but never grow up. I would write dinosaur screenplays which he would spark to life. Which is exactly what happened.

In 1950 I published a tale about a dinosaur falling in love with a lighthouse, thinking that its foghorn voice was the lonely sound of another beast lost in time and summoning him near. Then I dined with John Huston, gave him all my metaphorical tales, told him I had seen *The Maltese Falcon* 20 times and begged for employment. Huston read my stories in Africa (where he was filming *The African Queen*) and wrote to me, agreeing that someday we would work together. Returning to Hollywood in August 1953, he called me to his hotel, put a drink in my hand, leaned over me and said, "Kid, what're you doing in the next year?"

"Not much, Mr. Huston," I said. "Not much."

"Well," he said, "how would you like to come live in Ireland and write the screenplay of *Moby Dick*?"

"Gee, Mr. Huston," I said, "I've never been able to read the damned thing."

There was a long silence and then Huston said, "Tell you what . . . go home tonight, read as much as you can, come back for lunch tomorrow and tell me if you'll help kill the White Whale."

I went home and said to my wife, "Pray for me."

"Why?" she said.

"Because," I said, "I've got to read a book tonight and do a book report tomorrow."

I did just that, got hired and took my wife and daughters to live in Dublin for most of the next year.

One night, sipping my least favorite drink, whiskey, I turned to Huston and said, "How'd I get this job? Out of all the writers in the world, why me?"

"It was that story of yours about the dinosaur and the lighthouse," said Huston. "I felt the ghost of Melville there."

But how could that have been?

The answer came when I researched Melville's life. His metaphors were my metaphors. His midwives were mine. The Old Testament of my young years was his. Shakespeare had embraced me as a teenager. Shakespeare had fallen late on Melville. Nearsighted, unable to read the small type of his age, Melville found a large-type edition of *Hamlet, King Lear* and *Othello* when he was 30. In a Shakespearean frenzy he threw most of his whaling gear out and, pummeled by Job and Ecclesiastes, birthed the White Whale, flukes, Spirit Spout and nightmare panics in less than a year.

So there you have it, dinosaurs when I was 6, Daniel in the lions' den, chariot Elijah and Mickey Mouse when I was 9, Hamlet's father's ghost at 16. From such metaphors, then—kept, nurtured and delivered forth in my story the "The Fog Horn" (film: *The Beast From 20,000 Fathoms*)—came my first screenplay, *Moby Dick*.

The young collector of Popeye, Flash Gordon, Prince Valiant and Tarzan delivered forth those storyboard intuitions. (Every comic strip is a storyboard scene for a screenplay, large or small, so that as you grow up you learn screenwriting day by day in your local newspaper or from Greek and Roman myths cheek-by-jowl with same.)

The youthful reader of Emily Dickinson, John Donne and Robert Frost delivered forth those images to the unflickering screen of 1953. As I have often said, if I taught cinema my students would write haikus and shoot one-minute films based on those superbly clear poetic snapshots. Shooting haiku in a barrel is how I put it. Compacting reality into 17 syllables or 60 film seconds. Pure metaphor, out of the poet's head and onto the screen.

In the years since, I have learned to watch those metaphors drift in my subconscious in the relaxed hour before dawn, instructing me for my day's occupations. In that early-morning theater, trapped between my ears, the old images of hunchback, phantom, dinosaur, world's fairs, red planets and apeman perambulate as they wish. I do not own them. They control and bid me jump to run and trap them with my typewriter before they sleep.

It is from this interior theater that I learned what to do when, confronted with 800 pages of Melvillian novel, I read and re-read some sections 50 times until a dawn came in London 40 years ago when I sat up in bed, stared at the mirror and said, "I am Herman Melville!" Out of bed, I wrote the last 30 pages of the screenplay in 8 hours. All the metaphors within metaphors within metaphors fell into place.

If you wait long enough, I learned, and stuff your eyeballs with shapes, sizes and colors, the gumball machine in your skull lends you gifts at the drop of a penny.

And so it seems Sam Peckinpah was right. Rip my pages and stuff them in the camera, for they contain all the bright trash and compacted truths of a life that refused to stop its constant hyperventilation.

All the sources I have named, magnificent or vaudeville secondhand, have been my traffic cops. This way, not that, that way, not this, they have cried, at last echoing my long-lost magician's advice: "Live forever!"

Stand back. I'm still trying.

September 11, 1994

Edmund Morris

If Washington, D.C., can be said to have a scribe, he is surely Edmund Morris, biographer to presidents, habitué of the White House, sage of American leadership. He is, in person as in work, a minimalist—lean in physique, terse with words, spare in production. When he wrote this essay, despite a 20-year reputation in his field, he had one published book to his name, *The Rise of Theodore Roosevelt* (1979). By the following year, and after 13 years of careful study, he had a second: *Dutch: A Memoir of Ronald Reagan* (1999). Today, only a handful of years later, he has a third book to show: the second volume of his Roosevelt memoir, *Theodore Rex*.

There is a curious and seemingly serendipitous quality to Morris's rise as biographer. He is not a homegrown historian, bred and steeped in a collective memory of this land. He is a naturalized American born in Kenya, raised in South Africa, a '60s college dropout, a writer of ads, a latecomer to the capital. But with luck and the considerable gift for a story, he has achieved a kind of stardom: His first book won him a Pulitzer Prize; his second, a multimillion-dollar contract. There is good reason for his success: For all the seeming spareness, there is a scholarly heft to Morris, and a canny ability to turn a prism on the familiar.

His father was an airplane pilot, chief of East African Airways, a flier who marked out skyways over Africa: He remembers being taken from Nairobi to Dar es Salaam, hearing wind rush into the cockpit, feeling envy for the very tactile, romantic world his father inhabited. He was, however, too absent-minded a child to aspire to something as technical as flight. He lived in books, dreamt of becoming a famous pianist, and then aspired to something more abstract: a life up north, in a latitude where he felt history was being made.

After a year at Rhodes University in South Africa, he moved to England to try his hand at copywriting. He wrote ads for airlines, motor oil companies, small manufacturers, capping his career with a manual for the "Heatrae," a natural gas boiler that was popular at the time. When he married an English schoolteacher, Sylvia Jukes (a future biographer herself), and came to New York, however, everything changed.

He began writing for a number of major advertising agencies—Foote, Cone & Belding; Ogilvy & Mather, among them—but had no taste for corporate life. One employer after another ended up firing him. "God was trying to tell me something," he says. "And then, when I started to write as a freelancer, my ads kept mutating into articles." He and his wife took what work they could find, collaborating, for instance, to produce travel tapes for TWA. Then, as the bicentennial year of 1976 approached, Morris decided to act on his newfound infatuation with America: He wrote a screenplay about "an all-American subject": Theodore Roosevelt. The script never sold, but he took his prodigious research and worked to turn it into a biography. By decade's end, it was done: a prizewinner, bestseller, staple of the history lover's bookshelf.

When he wrote the essay that follows, he was contemplating the imminent publication of his authorized biography of Reagan. He told me he thought he knew why he was able to slide so easily from writing ads to writing about presidents. "I learned the essence of literary communication in writing about men's clothing for the Zulu market in Durban. I had to move a product in short and simple words. If 75 sports coats a week didn't move, my ad had failed. Literature is the same: Words move products. It doesn't really matter if those products are cultural or emotional or satirical. If your words aren't plain enough to move your readers, your books will fail. It's as clear as that."

When *Dutch* was published, Morris returned to his task of completing the second volume of the Roosevelt biography. *Theodore Rex* was published in 2001, and immediately climbed onto the bestseller lists. Currently, he is writing the third installment.

In all his work on political titans, it is not the careers he finds compelling, it is the men themselves. Morris claims to be resolutely apolitical, finding the task of revealing character infinitely more interesting than that of recording a career. What does he contemplate writing about in the future? Something entirely different, he indicates, with his customary and courtly archness. Something he's always had it in mind to do. A book on astronomy, perhaps. With a bit of poetry in the title. *Rushing Starlight*?

M. A.

Following the Script

BY EDMUND MORRIS

The English novelist Howard Spring is forgotten now even in England, although he was popular a generation ago. I devoured several of his long novels then, but recall little of them except the haunting quality of their titles: *Time and the Hour, There Is No Armour, These Lovers Fled Away*. Yet—such are the vagaries of memory—I can recite to this day a paragraph of self-description that Spring contributed to the back cover flap of *The Houses in Between*, under a mildly owlish photograph of himself:

> I can think of nothing more pleasurable than to sit down of a winter's night, before a bright fire, with a ream of clean paper before me, and ink, and my old wooden pen. It cost me a penny when I was a boy, this pen, and with a relay of steel nibs, it has lasted me the whole of my writing life."

I at once embraced Spring's ideal of "pleasurable" employment as my ideal too, and vowed that I would one day live and work like him. Winter nights were in short supply in equatorial Africa, where I grew up, but paper and ink and wooden pens were not, so I perpetrated many novels (mainly about airplanes) and poems (mainly about girls), in handwriting so dreadful that my mother decided to teach me the Spencerian script she had herself been taught as a child.

"Nobody will ever read your stories," she sensibly remarked, "if your writing looks like a *siafu* fell into the inkwell and had to walk across the page to dry himself off."

She was alluding to the large red "safari" ant, disturber of many a Kenyan picnic, and the aptness of her simile, not to mention its originality, persuaded me to practice looping *f*s and *l*s and upslashing *q*s—separately at first, then conjunctively—in a lined exercise book whose coarse paper made the smallest blot balloon to Rorschachian proportions. Mother would write words like hopscotch on the right-hand page with her Parker 51 (black and sleek, chrome-capped, discharging graceful curlicues of Royal Blue Quink), while I scratched painful imitations on the left, my own dribbly black ink dampening my finger ends and invariably running out just as I was trying to negotiate the difficult transition from *p* to *s*. After several months, mastery suddenly came, and I developed a flowing orthodox script, about as impersonal as the copperplate of a clerk.

In this hand, at high school, I experimented with blank verse, and under the influence of Dylan Thomas came up with a line that I believed might qualify me for the Poet's Corner in Westminster Abbey. It ran as follows:

Her eyes were portals full of rushing starlight.

I declaimed it to the chaps in Form 2A, and they reacted with loud raspberries. "Here comes old Rushing Starlight!" they would yell, whenever they saw me after that. Pitying them for their ignorance of the finer points of poetic style, I consoled myself with dreams of having a study like Howard Spring's one day—paneled, book-lined, secluded—where I could be alone with my starlit thoughts. And paper, and ink.

It took a while, but in 1976, through the generosity of the Theodore Roosevelt Association, I was given use of its defunct library adjoining TR's Birthplace Museum, in what is now called the Flatiron District of Manhattan. I had gotten a contract to write a "short, popular" biography of the 26th president, and needed an office in town that would meet the above specifications. To my delight, this one did. It was oak-lined from floor to ceiling, hung with heavy drapes, stacked with nice peppery-smelling old volumes, and furnished with a massive desk and couch. There was even a fireplace, but I was forbidden to bring in logs, for fear of burning down a National Historic Site.

As for paper, I discovered while dusting some shelves a stash of thick, marble-smooth certificate bond, 11 and a half inches by 17, untouched since 1938, proof positive that God had brought me to this place for a good reason. I discarded the top scarred sheet and the bottom scuffed one, vacuumed the edges of the others, and when I had finished sneezing, sat down and wrote the word "Prologue."

After that, inspiration deserted me. I spent the rest of the day listening to the chimes of the Metropolitan Life clock tower on 23rd Street, the only outside sounds that penetrated the library. Its silence, and the blank space shimmering on my desktop, made me understand for the first time the full horror of the phrase writer's block.

Indeed I remained blocked for the next several days, to the point that my stomach muscles began to mime the Laocoön—the nearest, alas, that my body has ever gotten to Greek sculpture. One morning I tried to relax on the couch, closed my eyes, and of course in walked P. James Roosevelt, president of the TRA, on one of his rare visits to town. "Getting a lot done?" he inquired pleasantly.

That afternoon, perhaps because of the shock, words began to uncurl from the nib of my fountain pen. (What a splendid term: fountain pen, the source from which prose flows, except in a dry season). I enjoyed the soft wet scratching sound of fresh letters as they linked up—no longer in copperplate, but in adult handwriting that was at least clear and evenly suspended above the whiteness below: sentences skeining west to east, a book in flight. I grew to love the silence, even the mini-silences that swelled between one word and the next, and to this day, when words won't come, I listen for them rather than look for them. Sooner or later one that sounds right will whisper itself onto the page.

After about 6 months, the National Park Service sent in a young maintenance man. "Scuse me sir, I gotta take down them drapes for dry cleanin'."

"Go ahead," I told him, and continued to work. He mounted a step ladder and detached the curtains, ring by ring. I sensed that he could not wait to unhook them all. His movements became more and more agitated. Eventually he said, in a voice high with panic, "Man, it's so quiet in here! Ain't you got a radio?"

"Every word that you write," St. Bernard of Clairvaux once observed, "is a blow that smites the devil." Four years and 250,000 blows later, *The Rise of Theodore Roosevelt* was done, and the devil smitten into temporary retreat. Since then I have been able to afford my own paper, and splurge on the occasional bottle of Waterman's Jet Black. My study is not paneled, but Howard Spring occasionally visits en esprit, and he seems to find it congenial.

Looking at myself in the mirror recently (on a bad gray hair day) I noticed that I have begun to look like him. Maybe in time I'll be able to match his splendid fecundity. If not, I can always blame this pen. Now, if I could only find out where he bought his steel nibs. . . .

September 27, 1998

Michael Korda

What book made you a lover of words, spurred you to frame a lifetime around them? It is not an unreasonable question: a little literary hoop presented to every participant in this Writing Life series, from James Michener to Umberto Eco, with telling results. But Simon & Schuster editor-in-chief Michael Korda sniffs when the interrogative is put to him. No book, he says, "I was not interested in books as a child." No story, no film, no bedtime tale.

It is clear that it's personalities—not artifacts—that lure Michael Korda into his office every day. It's the people who write books, build them, live off them, buy them. For Korda, the making of a book is a drama like no other—churning with patter, sets, recognition scenes and, most important, players.

"I never thought about books or stories until I found myself sitting at a desk at S&S," says Korda. "And then I instinctively understood what I was supposed to do."

It is a disingenous remark. The truth of it is that Korda was well tutored in the art of the book and the contours of the craft well before he arrived at that desk as a 24-year-old. He was the son of Hollywood set designer Vincent Korda and stage actress Gertrude Musgrove, nephew of the famous film producer Alexander Korda and his movie star wife Merle Oberon. He spent a European childhood listening to the table conversation of Lillian Hellman, Orson Welles, Graham Greene.

It was Greene, in fact, working on *The Third Man* with Korda's uncle, who handed the 15-year-old Korda his first pre-luncheon martini, took him on a boyish binge to a "de luxe" brothel in Nice, initiated him into the seductions of the cigarette, and then insisted the boy chauffeur him around Antibes. Watching Greene rise at dawn, unscrew the cap of his fountain pen, write a deft 500 words and then stop cold—mid-paragraph, if need be—to go out and watch the world go by, Korda decided that perhaps a life contemplating the narrative arc might not be so bad. It was all about being someone like Greene, cutting a figure: a prosifier before breakfast, a flaneur in the afternoon, a clever dinner guest at night. And it was all about people. Famous people.

Little wonder that it is famous people Korda has published ever since. The roster is formidable: Charles de Gaulle, Leonid Brezhnev, Ronald Reagan, Henry Kissinger, Richard Nixon, David McCullough, Cher, Jacqueline Susann, Mary Higgins Clark, Jackie Collins, Larry McMurtry, Tennessee Williams, Carlos Castaneda and countless others. More than the books, it is the authors he wants to talk about in any given interview, and Korda does it ebulliently, imitating Reagan's throaty whisper, describing dour Kissinger as a genuinely funny man, gushing about Cher. He is a fierce partisan about his stable, somewhere between priest and parade captain—unwilling to tell the press exactly what he does for any given manuscript ("I would never! I clam up!"), and yet shameless in his pursuit of publicity once a book is ready to go.

Having been Korda's colleague at Simon & Schuster years ago, I know full well what he is capable of doing with a red pencil. He has been known to tell an author: "You know the part between page 18 and 92? Well, let's make it into one very good sentence." He is known for his ability to transform a 600-page lemon into something publishable over a weekend; known for story ideas, which he hands novelists over the lunch table at the Four Seasons as easily as he passes the salt; known for his rousing presentations to world-weary, achy-footed sales reps, who have had it with books, have had it with their mousey literary defenders, have had it with starry-eyed hype. (Korda is the only editor I've ever known to get real applause at a dreaded sales conference.)

Korda is best at commercial fiction and politics—a range that allows him to publish powerful men and glitzy women—Hollywood archetypes, after all. He is, by his own admission, less able with literary novels.

Except for Graham Greene, who came to be published by Korda in the last 15 years of his writing career, Korda has not done particularly well in that genre. He has published Tennessee Williams and Phillip Roth, but the books they produced for Korda were among those writers' worst. Perhaps the editor a literary novelist needs is precisely not one who is most engaged in people, but one obsessed by art—one who would take on this interview's first query with relish—one who could point to the beginning of his career by citing a passionate encounter with a book.

Korda stands, nevertheless, with the great editors of the day. But he has, along the way, broken an unspoken vow among them: Never, never write your own book. He has published a string of fiction and nonfiction, some failures and some blockbuster bestsellers. Among his most successful: *Queenie*, a novel based on the life of Merle Oberon; *Power! And How To Get It*; *Charmed Lives*, his memoir of growing up in a notoriously difficult and glamorous family. Then there was *Man to Man*, a brave account of battling prostate cancer. Since this essay, he has published three more: *Another Life* (1999), a memoir of his 41 years at S&S, *Country Matters* (2000), about life in his country farmhouse, and *Making the List* (2001), a history of the bestseller list.

Born in England, schooled in Switzerland, molded by Beverly Hills, trained by the Royal Air Force, graduated from Oxford in French and Russian, Korda is not the typical bookworm, laboring ignominiously in a dusty office.

"You want to hear the best quote in all of publishing?" he asks giddily at the end of the interview, by which time he is laughing uproariously at his own anecdotes, mimicking authors with uncanny precision, twisting in his chair with excitement. "It's from Dick Snyder, when he was still at S&S: Some editor tells him, 'I don't know about this book, Dick. I'm having second thoughts.' 'Shut up!' says Dick. 'If we own it, we love it!' 'If we own it, we love it,' the editor repeats it again and again. Isn't that grand?"

M. A.

Headbirths: Bookish Midwifery

BY MICHAEL KORDA

It has always been hard to define exactly what a book editor does, even for many editors themselves. There is a story, possibly apocryphal, that when Rupert Murdoch acquired Wm. Collins, Ltd., the distinguished British publishing house, he walked through the editorial department and saw office after office of people sitting at their desks reading. "Tell them to get to work," he is alleged to have snapped. "They can read on their own bloody time."

Well, that's part of the problem, of course. A lot of an editor's job does in fact consist of reading, maybe the most important part, though book publishing is full of executives who still haven't figured that out.

Even back in the supposedly "good old days," when Bennett Cerf and Donald Klopfer, the co-founders of Random House, were still running the company from adjoining desks, encouraging editors to rush into their office whenever they had a good idea, editors were still regarded by management with a certain degree of suspicion. From the vantage point of the executive floor, the view has always been that book publishing would be a great business if only it weren't for the authors, and some of this attitude extends, inevitably, to the editors as well, partly because they work directly with writers (toward whom they are constantly being accused by management of being too sympathetic or easygoing), and partly because, like their writers, they are seen as a bunch of unruly children, the grown-ups being, of course, the people who wear suits and deal in numbers, not words.

This is understandable. In an era when most book publishing

houses have been bought up by companies that are part of the mainstream business world, it's hard to explain to the new owners or the stockholders that in this business the difference between a good and a bad year may come from an unknown housewife somewhere, typing away on her first novel at the kitchen table while her children are at school, or from a young assistant editor just out of college who's reading a magazine on free time and thinks the writer in it may have some potential.

This kind of thing—the young housewife I am thinking of was Susan Howatch, at work on *Penmarric*, a family saga set in the north of England; the assistant editor is Laurie Chittenden, of Simon & Schuster, who discovered Richard Paul Evans's *The Christmas Box* on her lunch break—is difficult to sell to hard-headed businessmen and investors as a serious, grown-up way of doing business, or a sensible part of the Great God Business Plan. Editors know it is better to be lucky than smart.

"The Golden Age of Book Publishing," when the editor dominated or seemed to dominate the process of book publishing, was in fact fairly brief. It began with Maxwell Perkins of Scribner—the first editor whose name anybody can remember, who edited Hemingway, Fitzgerald and Wolfe—and ended in the 1970s, when book publishing changed from a cottage industry to a big business.

It is hard to imagine that any publishing company today would give an editor the kind of authority that Perkins had to deal with his authors in the '30s and early '40s, or would patiently wait for years while Robert Gottlieb, when he was a young editor at Simon & Schuster in the 1960s, edited, re-edited and polished Joseph Heller's *Catch-22*. Today Perkins would have had a dozen people second-guessing him, not to speak of innumerable committees and focus groups trying to tell him what to tell his authors to do, and Gottlieb would have been told to stop playing around and get Heller's novel published on the next list, ready or not.

When I started work at Simon & Schuster in 1958, my father, while relieved that I had found a job, was puzzled by what I was actually going to be doing. "Editing?" he asked. "But my poor Miki, at your school they always complained to me that you couldn't spell or punctuate." This was true enough— though perhaps not a fair criticism coming from my father, who himself couldn't spell or punctuate in the five languages he spoke.

Fortunately for me, I started out as a very junior editorial assistant at exactly the moment when Gottlieb was editing *Catch-22* in the office next door. Since I had been assigned the painful task of rewriting the revision of a vast volume on religion by a Unitarian minister, with orders to pay special attention to grammar and punctuation, about which I knew nothing, and a warning to work—on pain of death—in pencil so my boss could erase what he didn't agree with, it was fascinating to see Gottlieb, the editorial equivalent of a beau sabreur, fiercely at work with a pair of scissors cutting pages to ribbons, Scotch-taping the pieces together in a different order, throwing out whole sentences, paragraphs, even pages, and rewriting boldly in ink.

Here was editing as a form of drama—for as Gottlieb completed his revision of each page, he read it aloud to a small audience of his admiring acolytes. Sometimes, if they disagreed, a frown would cross his Napoleonic brow and he would tear the page apart and begin again; otherwise, it was handed to his glamorous assistant, the first woman in book publishing to have a telephone and typewriter in a matching designer color, who retyped it. This, I felt, was real editing, and I longed to follow in his footsteps. Spelling and punctuation didn't seem to interest him much at all, to my relief.

I soon had the opportunity to put "the Gottlieb method" to work. There were scads of authors, I discovered, whose work not only demanded but urgently required bold surgery, ranging from a complete rethinking of the plot and vigorous cutting to a complete line-byline rewrite, sometimes both. Some writers rebelled at this treatment, others simply expected it as a matter of course (What else are editors for?), but all of them blithely assumed that the finished product was theirs alone. Perhaps the first, and most important, thing I learned about editing is that the editor invariably neither takes nor gets any credit—his or her work is invisible, anonymous and unsung, and never more unsung than by those who need it most.

Other authors, of course, like Graham Greene, whom I would eventually publish for nearly 20 years, neither needed nor accepted editorial changes. Greene's manuscripts arrived on my desk with a forbidding, neatly typed note on the title page that read, "Please do not change any of Mr. Greene's punctuation or spelling!" When his previous publisher, Tom Guinzburg of Britain's Viking Press, had expressed some doubt about the title of one of Greene's books, he had received a terse cable in reply that read: "EASIER TO CHANGE PUBLISHER THAN TITLE. GREENE."

There was a world of difference between being Graham Greene's editor, therefore, and working with Jacqueline Susann, say, who liked to have me sit across from her in her pink bedroom at the Navarro, on Central Park South, so I could read each page as it came from her pink typewriter (on pink paper) and edit it on the spot.

Jackie was not only open to plot suggestions—even of the most drastic nature—but positively demanded them. One of my early notes about *The Love Machine* reads simply, "Lesbian scene earlier?"; another reads "Rape flashback?" I had a lot of trouble making sense of Amanda's compulsive, obsessive love for icy-cold TV-executive hunk Robin Stone, and also with the scene in which Christie, the comedian, argues with his girlfriend while seated on the toilet. "Can I write, 'He's taking a dump'?" I remember Jackie asking me at one point.

On the subject of Amanda's motivation, Jackie finally lost her temper and said, "She knows he's a [expletive], but she gets hot . . . every time she sees him, all right?"

Vigorous editing she accepted, but she liked to argue points of character motivation and plot, sometimes acting out the parts herself. In such arguments she was profane, passionate and often angry, and expected to receive as good as she gave. Namby-pamby discussions didn't satisfy her at all. She figured she hadn't gotten the best out of you unless there was a screaming fight.

On anything to do with her female characters, however, she was usually unmovable, on the grounds that she knew more about what made women tick than I did, which made sense to me. Jackie was, after all, the poet laureate of attractive young women hopelessly in love with men who were world-class [expletives], and the special combination of tough independence in everyday life and total masochism in their personal relationships was exactly what made her popular with millions of women readers who saw in her characters some element of their own lives (or dream lives), but rendered in a more glamorous form. Jackie not only knew for whom she was writing, she knew what they wanted to read—and understood from the first that her women readers would be a lot less shocked by her frankness about sex, drugs, abortion and obsessive love than male publishers (and reviewers) were likely to be. When warned that one of the book clubs might not take her novel because the management was afraid that it was too shocking (the book club's initial readers, all women, loved it), Jackie said "F - - - 'em! I don't write for middle-aged men in suits. I write for women on the subway." (The club took it anyway, a victory for Jackie and those initial readers.)

As for her method of research, Jackie had a habit of scrawling notes to herself, snatches of dialogue or character sketches on cocktail napkins and nightclub menus with what looked like an eyebrow pencil. These she inserted in the manuscript at the appropriate points, as reminders.

(I had thought that this was unique, but years later Joan Collins, whose autobiography and first novel I edited, turned out to have the same habit—a showbiz thing, I guess.)

The thing is, there are no rules about editing. You do what you have to do to produce a book, and very often with an impossible deadline because there's a commitment to a book club, or the big retail chains, or Oprah, or because the publication date is critical and involves a major, expensive promotion that can't be delayed or moved—Mother's Day, or Christmas, or Thanksgiving. Thus, in a state of white-hot panic, I have worked with Cher in her bedroom in a New York hotel, on Joan Collins's novel on the floor of the boudoir of her home, on her sister Jackie's novels while sitting by her Beverly Hills pool, on a Mary Higgins Clark novel while in bed recovering from major surgery, and on ex-Godfather Joseph Bonanno's memoirs of his life in the Mafia in his fortress-like house in Tucson. "Don't come back without the book!" is the name of the game, the only thing that counts.

The notion of the editor as a judicious figure hunched over his or her desk, chewing on a sharp pencil and worrying about commas and the state of literature, has very little to do with the reality of the job. The successful editor is at once an impresario, with some of the tasks of a Hollywood producer in the old days of the studios, an arbiter of taste, a counselor, a 24-hour-a-day cheerleader, and the kind of old-fashioned "plot-doctor" whom theatrical producers used to bring in at the last minute when a play bombed in Boston and New Haven and clearly needed a complete rewrite before it opened in New York.

Showmanship is definitely required, since the editor has to be able to enthuse sales reps and marketing staffs, normally pessimistic about the chances of any book, and needs to be able to explain at the drop of a hat the plot and special appeal of a book in less than 30 seconds and in words of one or two syllables.

Patience, the ability to take risks and to keep calm in the midst of crisis, a real love of reading and a respect for writers, and above all the gift of being able to see what's wrong with a book (and what it might take to fix it), together with a full reservoir of enthusiasm and the kind of personality that can persuade a reluctant writer who thinks his or her book is finished to undertake one more rewrite—these are the qualities an editor needs. A range of interests and a certain adaptability help. I have edited simultaneously the work of Henry Kissinger and Cher, and gone straight from editing a Pulitzer Prize-winning historian to working on Esther Williams's Hollywood recollections.

I still haven't learned how to punctuate or spell, but that doesn't seem to have held me back a bit.

January 31, 1999

David Chanoff

What kind of expert would you hire if you wanted to delve into a Famous Psyche, unearth the meaning of his life and set it down for all posterity?

One might not be enough. You'd do well to hire 10: a rabbi to gain the eminence's confidence, a lawyer to get his signature, a psychologist to plumb his head, a sleuth to follow his heart, a researcher to dig out documents, a scholar to sift out facts, a talker to free his tongue, a mimic to capture its timbre, an editor to organize the story, a wordsmith to make it flow. And, when everything was said and done: a crack-shot negotiator to defend every hard truth you managed to squeeze onto the page.

Then again, you could skip the 10 experts and hire David Chanoff.

Chanoff is a master among ghosts, a writer who slips from voice to voice, skin to skin, and strides away with sheaves of history.

He didn't plan it that way. Chanoff had always thought of himself as an academic—someone whose notion of adventure was plunging into his desk chair.

He was born in Philadelphia in 1943, the son of a labor relations economist and a dental hygienist. His father was a second-generation Slavic American whose first language was Yiddish and whose roots were in the rough-and-tumble ghetto of South Philadelphia. "My father, despite his poverty and the lure of the street gangs, put himself through college. He memorized more poetry and more prose than anybody I have ever known. He had a tremendous love for literature, and long recitations would just spring from him naturally in the course of conversation: Heine, Wordsworth, Shakespeare, Keats, all the British and American poets. I was fascinated by his ear and his linguistic sensitivity, especially since I knew all about his background. I think it was that element in him that made me realize how complex most people are. And how important language can be in their lives."

Chanoff attended public school in Philadelphia and studied English at Johns Hopkins in the '60s. In 1973 he completed a doctorate at Brandeis, writing his dissertation on John Dunne. "It gave me a sense of what it means to look at a life," he says.

About the same time, Chanoff became interested in education. He had no children of his own, but began participating in discussions with fellow graduate students: What is real learning? If you prod a child's natural curiosity, will it spur the kind of intensity that leads to the most valuable kind of learning?

They decided to find out, and so founded the Sudbury Valley School in Framingham, Mass. It was a highly experimental school then: no curriculum, no authoritarian structure, no requirements that the students—ages 4 to 18—did not impose themselves. Today it is a thriving institution with 150 students.

Chanoff taught at Sudbury for many years, supplementing his meager income by teaching part-time at colleges around Boston. He had a Finnish wife by then, Liisa, and, with three children, they soon had all the demands of an active household. He became an instructor of English as a Second Language, first at Tufts and then at Harvard. "That was probably one of the most important experiences for me as a writer. It forced me to think a great deal about modes of expression."

At Harvard he met Doan Van Toai. "He was one of the most interesting voices in postwar Vietnam," Chanoff says. "A student radical who had been through it all and had ended up in prison in the most terrible of circumstances. He came to me in 1982 and said he was writing an article, could I help with the English?" Their first piece was published in the *New York Times*; their second in the *Wall Street Journal*; another made it into the *New York Review of Books*.

Before long the Chanoff-Toai collaboration blossomed into *A Vietcong Memoir* (1984), written with former Vietcong minister of justice Truong Nhu Tang. After that came *The Vietnamese Gulag* (1985), Chanoff's account of Doan Van Toai's years in prison. Their next book, *Portrait of the Enemy* (1986), was a composite of many North Vietnamese voices.

And then Chanoff began to be sought out by others. Bui Diem, chief of staff of South Vietnam's last civilian president, got him to write his recollections of the war, *Into the Jaws of History* (1987). Gen. Ariel Sharon called on Chanoff to help him write *Warrior* (1989), even as Sharon was carrying out his duties in Israel's cabinet.

Then followed *Slow Burn* (1990), with Orrin DeForest, chief of CIA operations in the Vietnam War's crucial Military Region Three; *Into the Heart* (1991), with Kenneth Good, about an anthropologist's 12 years with a tribe of rainforest nomads; *The Line of Fire* (1993), with Adm. William Crowe Jr., former chairman of the Joint Chiefs of Staff; *Never the Last Journey* (1995), with Holocaust survivor Felix Zandman; and *Joycelyn Elders, M.D.* (1996).

"I lead a quiet life," Chanoff tells me. "I sit in my study and look out my window and write about people trekking through the Amazon, fighting battles in the desert, rising from sharecropper to surgeon general. These are people of action. Not people of introspection, like me. What I can do is put their life in order, give significance to what they do, maybe even open them up. And sometimes in the process, things that were unresolved in their lives get resolved. The writing makes them whole. It is an amazing thing to be party to."

M. A.

Guided by Voices: The Work of a Ghostwriter

BY DAVID CHANOFF

Ghostwriters are people without a proper name, a little like significant others. Everyone knows ghosts are out there, but no one is exactly sure what they do or what to call them. "Collaborator" sounds a little too fancy; it's also vaguely sinister. "Ghost" denotes the ectoplasmic, something not quite real. Children growing up don't think of becoming ghosts. Neither do most writers.

Most ghosts fall into the trade by accident. A good opportunity comes along just when your novel-in-progress has developed terminal rigor mortis or the day after your movie deal got dumped into turnaround. Journalists are especially prone. Most would kill to write their own book, and suddenly here's a book to write, even if it's not exactly theirs. A new ghost may not be very forward about admitting what he does. He's still likely to claim he's a novelist, even after he's slipped into the nether world of the writing profession.

For years ghosts were truly ghosts, unseen and rarely noted. For the most part, that's changed now, though on occasion there's still an egregious omission: the talented Robert Lindsey, for example, who strove mightily to inject life into Ronald Reagan's autobiography but didn't get a cover mention, or the famously uncredited Barbara Feinman, who helped Hillary Clinton with *It Takes A Village*. More often, though, today's publishers put the ghost right up there on the jacket directly under the celebrity author's name just to the right of "with" or the dearly coveted "and."

Today a few ghosts even achieve a fame of their own, most notably William Novak, whose credits include bestsellers with Lee Iacocca, Tip O'Neill, Nancy Reagan and Ollie North. On occasion a principal author might even give all the credit to his writer, as O. J. Simpson did last month during the civil trial when he vigorously denied having had anything to do with his autobiography at all. He was a football player, he said, not a writer.

Ambiguity, of course, is the curse of ghostwritten books. Readers are always a little doubtful as to who actually might have said what. Good collaborators, though, aspire to transparency. What the ghost wants most is to be a clear channel of expression for his principal's experiences and reflections.

That can be an unexpectedly complex task. Adm. William Crowe

Jr., former chairman of the Joint Chiefs of Staff, used to joke that when people start thinking back on their careers they tend to have increasingly vivid memories of events that never happened at all. They may also have almost no memory of events everyone else wants to hear about. When collaborator Joe Persico asked Gen. Colin Powell to talk about Vietnam, Powell's first impulse was to give only his name, rank and serial number. Powell's Vietnam story ended up as arguably the most powerful part of the book, but it took some doing. I once asked a Viet Cong guerrilla leader who had spent 6 agonizing months blazing the Ho Chi Minh Trail to tell me what it was like. It was hard, he said. "Well," I prodded, "what did you eat, for instance?" "Rice," he said.

Like a biographer, a collaborator needs to do the background research that will stimulate, sharpen and check memories. But the main business of collaboration consists of extended discussion. In a recent book with former surgeon general Joycelyn Elders, we recorded 60 tapes, about 100 hours of face-to-face conversation. That's a lot, but my sense is it's fairly typical.

Given all the talk, the collaborator's basic obligation is to be an intelligent interlocutor. This means getting up to speed fast in whatever field your principal has made his or her life's work. You may not have spent half a lifetime inside the Beltway, but if your principal is a Washington pol you better be able to think like someone who has.

If the first challenge is learning what you need in order to talk, the second is knowing how to sit back and listen. That voice coming at you contains a world. It's not merely telling you things, it's telling them in a way that reveals the habits of mind and quality of feeling that give your subject his uniqueness. That's all in there, wrapped in an idiolect of vocabulary and syntax and inflection. Getting the key to it gives you access to a mind. Even better, once you've broken the code, you can present this person to the world in all his recognizable distinctiveness. Capture the personal voice and you've gone a long way toward capturing the person.

This isn't a matter of merely quoting verbatim. The spoken and the written word are not the same. The trick is to use the building blocks of the spoken language to convey not the thing itself but the authentic tone of the thing. If there's an art to collaboration, this is the center of it. Genesis translator quotes Boris Pasternak in saying that the average translator gets the literal meaning right but misses the tone. And tone is everything. Tone is the life-rhythm of the mind.

I don't know a ghost who doesn't pray for a subject with a powerfully individual voice. Who wouldn't love to work with the raucous blare of Richard Marcinko, the Rogue Warrior, or the hammer-and-tongs growl of campaignmeister Ed Rollins? Joycelyn Elders has that kind of unique voice, a swelling, rhythmic, in-your-face voice, a voice you hear once and never forget. Whatever else a book by Joycelyn Elders had to do, it had to speak with that voice.

Getting the voice takes close listening; I think of it as the linguistic side of the empathic personality, which is the collaborator's characteristic trait. In a *Book World* article last fall, Scott Turow (author of *Presumed Innocent* and *The Burden of Proof*) wrote about the "fundamental act of imaginative translation, of taking to heart what it's like to stand in someone else's shoes." (See page 106 in this collection.) Collaboration doesn't presume the creative flame that impels an artist, but it does demand a very similar act of imaginative translation.

Turow was talking specifically about the problem of white novelists creating black characters and, by extension, male writers creating female characters, old writers creating young characters and so on. Are we at heart insular and self-absorbed creatures or boundary-crossers capable of compassion? If a collaborator doesn't assume the latter, he's in trouble from the start. The same is true for his partner, though most principal authors probably don't give much advance thought to this question of intimacy. One of several fortunate exceptions in my experience was Ariel Sharon, the stormy petrel of Israeli warfare and politics. When we first sat down to talk, I wanted to begin chronologically. Instead he started telling me the story of his first son's death at age 11 in a gun accident, the deepest pain of his life. It took me a while to understand that he was putting both of us to the test. Would he be able to say to me what needed to be said? Was I a person who could listen to such things from him? Usually the interviewer tries to draw emotions out of his subject. He reversed the roles.

I was lucky in that my first collaborations were with foreigners. Sometimes I felt I needed a personal anthropologist to guide me through the social and psychological thickets, but afterward I knew that boundaries were made to be crossed. Read David Hackworth's scorched-earth description of war in Korea, then look at the sweet jacket photo of his collaborator, Julie Sherman, and you'll see what I mean. Principals often want to work with someone who shares a background: Women might look for a woman collaborator, blacks might feel more comfortable with blacks, Jews with Jews. There's no getting around the immediacy of such connections. But true mutuality is based on something deeper.

I've thought about this question a lot recently. My previous book was with Felix Zandman, a Fortune 500 CEO and Holocaust survivor who spent a year and a half hiding from the Nazis in a shallow grave beneath the floorboards of a Polish peasant's cottage. My instinct was not to do this book; Holocaust stories are notoriously hard to sell. But when it came out that Felix had grown up in the Jewish city of Grodno, I had no choice. My grandparents were from Grodno, and many of my relatives died there. Although Felix Zandman and I had never met before, we were *mishpuchah*, family.

This wasn't the case with Joycelyn Elders. Some people were surprised at a collaboration like this, none more than one elderly, vision-impaired relative of hers in southwestern Arkansas who squinted hard at me and asked, "Are you Bill?" He couldn't imagine what white man other than Clinton Joycelyn might have been schlepping around Arkansas' Blacklands. What I didn't know at the start was that Elders's life among the ill and dispossessed had freed her from the chains of race and gender to a degree I've never experienced in anyone else. Up close, that was a quality you couldn't miss; it gave her an unself-conscious grace and unlocked communication.

Writing is a living process. It invariably affects those who do it seriously. There's a commonplace that autobiographies are always self-serving. But confessional writing can turn into many things besides apologia—therapy, for example, even sacrament. Accompanying another person on that kind of journey is rare in life. It's a ghost's peculiar privilege.

January 12, 1997

IV

Old Bottle, New Wine

E. L. Doctorow

Umberto Eco

Stanley Elkin

Ned Rorem

Richard Selzer

Reynolds Price

Cynthia Ozick

Gloria Naylor

Donald E. Westlake

Barbara Mertz

E. L. Doctorow

When Edgar Lawrence Doctorow was writing *Ragtime* (1975), his most celebrated novel, he puzzled over one tiny point of American history. He wanted to move his character from Depression-weary New York City to Lowell, Mass., via trolley, "from one town to the next, tossing a buffalo nickel in at the end of every stop on the interurban trolley line." The trouble was that he didn't know whether such a trip would have been possible.

He was roaming the inner recesses of the library one evening, pondering the difficulties of that question, when suddenly he caught sight of a brazenly orange book leaning toward him from the business shelf. "It was the color that drew me," he says, still marveling at the mystical nature of the moment. "When I picked it up, I saw that it was a corporate history of the trolleycar business. Exactly the stuff I needed."

That vignette says much about Doctorow. Although his books are steeped in history—cameos of New York in a very specific, very interesting time—they are more the products of his own life and imagination than of any elaborate research. Doctorow summons history as he needs it, wrestling it to fit his own vision, his own mythology, of America. "I don't think of myself as a historian in any sense—my books are not thorough, not exhaustive. But you know, when you're working well, the things you need—like history—come to hand. It's as if you were a magnetic field. Things fly out of the air at you."

He makes it sound easy, but, in fact, Doctorow is a deliberate, hardworking man. His 40-year marriage, his gentle humor, his impeccable manners, his grant-endowed career all attest to a cautiously crafted life.

He was born in 1931 and grew up in "a richly informed household" in the Bronx, the second son of second-generation Americans of Russian descent. His father, the proprietor of a Manhattan music store, was so renowned for his knowledge of the obscure that Rubenstein, Horowitz,

Heifetz, Stokowski and Toscanini would wander in to seek his advice. And home was full of books.

At the Bronx High School of Science, Doctorow distinguished himself in poetry, painting and music composition. He read indiscriminately—from pulp fiction to sports biographies to Cervantes. But perhaps the most motivating event in his creative young life was when his older brother came home from the front lines of World War II to sit at the family kitchen table and write a book. "He never published it, but he made writing—which for me had always been a dream—a reality."

Doctorow then went to Kenyon College to study with poet John Crowe Ransom. When he graduated in 1952, he applied for Columbia University's graduate program and got in with the help of Robert Penn Warren.

Within 1 year Doctorow was drafted to serve as a high-speed radio operator in the U.S. Army Signal Corps in Frankfurt, Germany. When he returned to New York he got a job as a staff reader for Columbia Pictures, whose cowboy movies inspired him to write a novel about the West, *Welcome to Hard Times* (1960). "Being a motion picture reader was a wonderful apprenticeship for a writer. For three years I got my hands on everything that was being published. Seeing how much bad stuff was coming out gave me great confidence."

He got work as an editor at New American Library, where he edited everything from Shakespeare to the Mentor Science Library to Ian Fleming's James Bond novels. In 1964 he became editor in chief of Dial Press, "a feisty little house, in which I got to edit James Baldwin, Norman Mailer, Tom Berger and Bill Kennedy," among others. While at Dial he wrote and published his next novel, a science fiction story entitled *Big as Life* (1966).

Married, with two small children and an editorial career on the rise, Doctorow was quite unexpectedly offered a position as writer in residence at the University of California at Irvine. "I consulted the I Ching, and it said, 'You will cross a great water.' My wife promptly responded, 'That's the Mississippi. Let's go.' "

Doctorow's next work, *The Book of Daniel* (1971), which was inspired by the Rosenberg spy trial of the '50s, established him as a major American writer. Since then, his novels have garnered the nation's highest literary honors and been hailed for their gritty vision of old New York: *Ragtime* (1975), *Loon Lake* (1980), *World's Fair* (1986), *Billy Bathgate* (1989) and *City of God* (2000)

He has never left his editorial persona completely behind, and still speaks of his books in terms of rewriting and polishing: "I can't think of one of my pages that has gotten by with less than 6 or 8 drafts," he says. Days after he delivered *Loon Lake* to his publisher, he took back the manuscript for 6 weeks and rewrote it from an entirely different point of view.

Speaking of his novel *The Waterworks* (1996), he admits readily that he struggled with the voice through several drafts until he finally hit upon the perfect narrator: a New York newspaper editor just after the Civil War. "Once you get the diction and the voice right," he says, "the rest of the book"—the plot, the history, the context—"follows. Each book may have a different career in you, but language precedes, and ultimately controls, the book you set out to write."

M. A.

From Will-of-the-Wisp to Full-Blown Novel

BY E. L. DOCTOROW

A book has its origins in the private excitements of the writer's mind. The excitements are private because they're incommunicable unless they're rendered, given extension and resolved as a book. They are powerfully felt, even epiphanic responses to what may be the faintest or most fleeting stimuli . . . an image, the sound of a voice, a kind of light, a word or phrase, a bar of music, even an unwritten-upon page.

And they come unbidden. Years ago, driving in the Adirondack mountains, I passed a road sign that said "Loon Lake." I've always been moved by that part of the country but my strong feelings for its woods and streams suddenly intensified and seemed to cohere on those two words, which I said aloud as if they were the words of a poem. I wrote a novel that was in a sense an exegesis of the—for me—poetically charged words "loon lake." They became my title, and were endlessly suggestive, yielding a period of time, the Great Depression, a setting, the remote mountain retreat of a very wealthy man, and a number of characters of different moral sizes—that man, his aviatrix wife, a drunken poet, a party of hoodlums and two hobo children—as in a mural.

Of course not all, in fact very few, of the writer's private excitements are resolved as books. Most are forgotten as soon as they occur. But I imagine them as a kind of groundsong, as constant and available as the sensation of life itself.

An earlier novel, *The Book of Daniel,* was conceived during a period of enormous national torment, the late '60s, with the war in Vietnam raging and the divisions among our generations deeper than at any time since the Civil War. Another private excitement of the writer is his sudden awareness of the historically systematic unfairness of things. This particular resolution into pain of an intellectual commonplace can hardly be suggested by the word excitement. The writer writes from an almost biblical anger, which is not much different from despair. It is a dire, driven state of mind that professes and, at the same time, refuses to accept the truth that, as individuals, humans are pitiful, and as groups, inhuman. *The Book of Daniel*, a novel reflecting on an espionage conspiracy trial in the '50s, and its aftermath in the '60s, was composed out of that unassuageable feeling. But what made it possible was an image in my mind of 2 children in their winter coats and hats, being held aloft over the heads of a crowd at a political street rally and passed forward to the speaker's platform.

It was not a blank page but a blank mind that led to *Ragtime*—the emotional exhaustion that came inevitably after the completion of *The Book of Daniel*. The blank mind, when it has no wish to think or improve upon existence, grants you a simple unreflective being that is very pleasant and peaceable. Fortunately it doesn't last. One day I was sitting in my study, on the top floor of my house in New Rochelle, and I found myself staring at the wall. Perhaps I felt it was representative of my mind. I decided to write about the wall. And then about all the walls together. "My house was built in 1906," I wrote. "It is a great, ugly three-story manse, with dormers, bay windows, and a screened porch. When it was new the shingles were brown and striped awnings shaded the windows. . . ." I then imagined what New Rochelle looked like when the house was new. In those days trolley cars ran along the avenue at the bottom of the hill. People wore white in the summer. Women carried parasols. I thought of Teddy Roosevelt, who was president at the time. And the blank page of my mind began to fill with the words of a book.

But wherever books begin, in whatever private excitement of the mind, whether from the music of words, or an impelling anger, or the promise of an unwritten-upon page, the work itself is hard and slow, and the writer's illumination becomes a taskmaster, a ruling discipline, jealously guarding the mind from all other, and necessarily errant, private excitements until the book is done. You live enslaved in the book's language, its diction, its universe of imagery, and there is no way out except through the last sentence.

As a writer I have developed the habit of signing myself over to fictional narrators, perhaps from the belief that they can explicate my private excitements better than I can. Another way to say this is that no matter what elevated state of inspiration you might find for yourself, you can't write the book until you find the voice for it. As it happens, there is just one voice and one voice only for a given book and you must ventriloquize until you find it.

The impetus for *Billy Bathgate,* I think now, may have been a measure or two of the tune *Bye Bye Blackbird.* In my mind as I hummed it was an image of several men in formal evening clothes standing on the deck of a tugboat. I didn't know what they were doing there, but the person I designated to leap aboard just as the tug was leaving its pier on the East River, and tell me who they were and what they were up to, was a teenaged boy, a rhapsodist of criminal life named Billy Bathgate who, as it turned out, had attached himself to the infamous gangster Dutch Schultz.

I have recently finished a novel entitled *The Waterworks* and I'm not sure I have sufficient distance to speak of it its origins coherently. Its narrator is a newspaper editor named McIlvaine. He is a chronicler of bizarre and ominous events. The year is 1871. New York in the post-Civil War teems with maimed veterans, beggars, newsboys, flower sellers and millenarians. The Tweed Ring is running things. A class of new wealth and weak intellect goes nightly to its balls. The booming city is building itself northward with a kind of dark genius of technology. It transports water to its reservoirs, gas to the streetlights, and its high-speed printing presses turn out tens of thousands of papers for a penny or two each.

What excited me into the composition of this book? I can't be sure. I did write a story some years ago with the same title: A model boat sinks in the water of a reservoir and moments later the boat's owner, a child, is found drowned in the sluice gate of the adjoining waterworks. In fact, where the New York Public Library now stands at Fifth Avenue and 42nd Street, there stood for the better part of the century behind thick stone walls 40 feet high, an enormous holding reservoir. Perhaps this put me in mind of my city as it was in the 19th century.

Or perhaps it was a night a few years ago when a thick fog dropped over lower Manhattan, erasing the World Trade Center, the Woolworth building and, in fact, the entire 20th century skyline, until only the grandeur of 19th century New York was visible, and I walked through the ironfront district in Soho with a great private excitement, because I knew I was seeing the city that Herman Melville saw, and my namesake Edgar Allan Poe, when he was sober.

April 17, 1994

Umberto Eco

So, *okay*—as Umberto Eco loves to say, punctuating his exchanges with verbal astringents and evincing a brisk understanding of how American conversations work—why does a man, a professor of philosophy at the University of Bologna to boot, decide to write a novel at the age of 50? Well, he confesses, it was a midlife thing. "Some men at that age take up with chorus girls. I wrote a novel instead."

Now 61 and the author of two unlikely blockbusters—*The Name of the Rose* (1982, 9 million copies in 36 languages) and *Foucault's Pendulum* (1989, 7 million copies in 27 languages)—Eco is a feisty blend of philosopher and entertainer, scholar and shtickmeister. He has the sort of agile mind that can decipher 14th-century texts in the morning and be translating Woody Allen by afternoon.

He was born in the Italian village of Alessandria in 1932, the only son of an accountant at an iron bathtub manufacturer. One of his grandfathers was a typographer, the other a tailor. His sister grew up to become an actress; he was the first in his family to attend a university.

Eco was 7 years old when World War II began, 13 when it was over, and he witnessed war with a combination of terror and wonder. He would summon those memories four decades later for the pages of his second novel. Once the bombing ended, Eco decided to dedicate himself to Italy's national organization for Catholic youth. He traveled the country, mobilizing other young people to join. By 21 he was president of that organization and writing a dissertation on St. Thomas Aquinas to prove his ardor, but it was also about then that he experienced a radical change of heart about faith. "My group—a conglomeration of students, workers and peasants—suddenly shifted from one commandment to another; from facts to socio-political concerns. I never went back."

He worked for Italian state TV in "routine jobs," then joined the army, where he was given a wide berth to study medieval philosophy and aesthetics. "Like a government grant!" he exclaims delightedly. After that he spent 17 years as an editor for Bompiani, one of Italy's most distinguished publishers. Eventually, he left to become a full professor at the University of Bologna, where he teaches to this day. By now, the savvy reader of Eco will have recognized how avidly Eco has scavenged his own experiences for his novels: his dazzling recreations of medieval life, his shrewd insights into the peculiar labyrinths of publishing, his cameraman's sense for the inherent drama of a good whodunit.

But for all the literary éclat of *The Name of the Rose*, the movie version was disastrous. "I don't want to play the role of betrayed author," Eco says, "but frankly, that movie is someone else's work, not mine." As a result, he has staunchly refused to sell *Foucault's Pendulum* to Hollywood.

Eco's books have seen their share of adversity. Two months after the Italian publication of *Pendulum*, the pope himself dismissed Eco as "the mystifier deluxe," a dangerous individual who saw human life "as moving inevitably toward death and nothingness" (a quote almost identical to a line in *Pendulum*). And although that novel was generally greeted by positive reviews, Salman Rushdie—in hiding for the threats leveled at him by the Ayatollah—publicly declared it "mind-numbingly full of gobbledygook of all sorts," and then went on to proclaim, "Reader: I hated it." Eco says, "Basically, Rushdie called it bullshit."

Did he ever confront Rushdie on the matter? "Pah," Eco responds affirmatively, and you don't have to see him to know his arms are swinging. "So, it's like this: We meet in Paris at an Academie function. Mitterrand brings us face to face. There is a moment of dead silence, embarrassment and then I put out my hand and say, "So, *okay*, I'm Eco. You know . . . the bullshitter?"

M. A.

Reincarnation, Translation and Adventure*

BY UMBERTO ECO

There are writers who do not bother about their translations, sometimes because they lack the linguistic competence, sometimes because they have no faith in the literary value of their work and are anxious only to sell their product in as many countries as possible.

Often the indifference conceals two prejudices, equally despicable: Either the author considers himself an inimitable genius and so suffers translation as a painful political process to be borne until the whole world has learned his language, or else the author harbors an "ethnic" bias and considers it a waste of time to care about how readers from other cultures might feel about his work.

People think an author can check his translations only if he knows the language into which he is to be translated. Obviously, if he does know that language, the work proceeds more easily. But it all depends on the translator's intelligence. For example, I do not know Swedish, Russian or Hungarian, and yet I have worked well with my translators into those languages. They were able to explain to me the kind of difficulties they faced, and make me understand why what I had written created problems in their language. In many cases I was able to offer suggestions.

The problem frequently arises from the fact that translations are either "source-oriented" or "target-oriented," as today's books on Translation Theory put it. A source-oriented translation must do everything possible to make the B-language reader understand what

*Translated from the Italian by William Weaver, who also translated Umberto Eco's novels, *The Name of the Rose* and *Foucault's Pendulum*.

the writer has thought or said in language A. Classical Greek affords a typical example: In order to comprehend it at all, the modern reader must understand what the poets of that age were like and how they might express themselves. If Homer seems to repeat "rosy-fingered dawn" too frequently, the translator must not try to vary the epithet just because today's manuals of style insist we should be careful about repeating the same adjective. The reader has to understand that in those days dawn had rosy fingers whenever it was mentioned, just as these days Washington always has D.C.

In other cases translation can and should be target-oriented. I will cite an example from the translation of my novel *Foucault's Pendulum,* whose chief characters constantly speak in literary quotations. The purpose is to show that it is impossible for these characters to see the world except through literary references. Now, in chapter 57, describing an automobile trip in the hills, the translation reads "the horizon became more vast, at every curve the peaks grew, some crowned by little villages; we glimpsed endless vistas." But, after "endless vistas" the Italian text went on: *"al di la della siepe, come os servava Diotallevi."* If these words had been translated, literally "beyond the hedge, as Diotallevi remarked," the English-language reader would have lost something, for *"al di la della siepe"* is a reference to the most beautiful poem of Giacomo Leopardi, "L'infinito," which every Italian reader knows by heart. The quotation appears at that point not because I wanted to tell the reader there was a hedge anywhere nearby, but because I wanted to show how Diotallevi could experience the landscape only by linking it to his experience of the poem. I told my translators that the hedge was not important, nor the reference to Leopardi, but it was important to have a literary reference at any cost. In fact, William Weaver's translation reads: "We glimpsed endless vistas. 'Like Darien,' Diotallevi remarked . . . ." This brief allusion to the Keats sonnet is a good example of target-oriented translation.

A source-oriented translator in a language I do not know may ask me why I have used a certain expression, or (if he understood it from the start) he may explain to me why, in his language, such a thing cannot be said. Even then I try to take part (if only from outside) in a translation that is at once source- and target-oriented.

These are not easy problems. Consider Tolstoy's *War and Peace*. As many know, this novel—written in Russian, of course—begins with a long dialogue in French. I have no idea how many Russian readers in Tolstoy's day understood French; the aristocrats surely did, because this French dialogue is meant, in fact, to depict the customs of aristocratic Russian society. Perhaps Tolstoy took it for granted that, in his day, those who did not know French were not even able to read Russian. Or else he wanted the non-French-speaking reader to understand that the aristocrats of the Napoleonic period were, in fact, so remote from Russian national life that they spoke in an incomprehensible fashion. Today if you reread those pages, you will realize that it is not important to understand what those characters are saying, because they speak of trivial things: What is important is to understand that they are saying those things in French.

A problem that has always fascinated me is this: How would you translate the first chapter of *War and Peace* into French? The reader reads a book in French and in it some of the characters are speaking French; nothing strange about that. If the translator adds a note to the dialogue saying "*en francais dans le texte*," it is of scant help: The effect is still lost. Perhaps, to achieve that effect, the aristocrats (in the French translation) should speak English. I am glad I did not write *War and Peace* and am not obliged to argue with my French translator.

As an author, I have learned a great deal from sharing the work of my translators. I am talking about my "academic" works as well as my novels. In the case of philosophical and linguistic works, when the translator cannot understand (and clearly translate) a certain page, it means that my thinking was murky. Many times, after having faced the job of translation, I have revised the second Italian edition of my book: not only from the point of view of its style but also from the point of view of ideas. Sometimes you write something in your own language A, and the translator says: "If I translate that into my language B, it will not make sense." He could be mistaken. But if, after long discussion, you realize that the passage would not make sense in language B, it will follow that it never made sense in language A to begin with.

This doesn't mean that, above a text written in language A, there hovers a mysterious entity that is its Sense, which would be the same in any language, something like an ideal text written in what Walter Benjamin called *Reine Sprache*, The Pure Language. Too good to be true. In that case it would only be a matter of isolating this Pure Language and the work of translation (even of a page of Shakespeare) could be done by computer.

The job of translation is a trial-and-error process, very similar to what happens in an Oriental bazaar when you're buying a carpet. The merchant asks 100, you offer 10, and after an hour of bargaining you agree on 50.

Naturally, in order to believe that the negotiation has been a success you must have fairly precise ideas about this basically imprecise phenomenon called translation. In theory, different languages are impossible to hold to one standard; it cannot be said that the English house is truly and completely the synonym of the French maison. But in theory no form of perfect communication exists. And yet, for better or worse, ever since the advent of Homo Sapiens, we have managed to communicate. Ninety percent (I believe) of *War and Peace*'s readers have read the book in translation, and yet if you set a Chinese, an Englishman and an Italian to discussing *War and Peace*, not only will all agree that Prince Andrej dies, but, despite many interesting and differing nuances of meaning, all will be prepared to agree on the recognition of certain moral principles expressed by

Tolstoy. I am sure the various interpretations would not exactly coincide, but neither would the interpretations that three English-speaking readers might provide of the same Wordsworth poem.

In the course of working with translators, you reread your original text, you discover its possible interpretations and it sometimes happens—as I have said—that you want to rewrite it. I have not rewritten my two novels, but there is one place which, after its translation, I would have gladly rewritten. It is the dialogue in *Foucault's Pendulum* in which Diotallevi says: "God created the world by speaking. He didn't send a telegram." And Belbo replies: "*Fiat lux*. Stop."

But in the original Belbo said: "*Fiat lux*. Stop. *Segue lettera*" ("*Fiat lux*. Stop. Letter follows." "Letter follows" is a standard expression used in telegrams (or at least it used to be standard, before the fax machine came into existence). At that point, in the Italian text, Casaubon said: "*Ai Tessalonicesi, immagino*." (To the Thessalonians, I suppose.) It was a sequence of witty remarks, somewhat sophomoric, and the joke lay in the fact that Casaubon was suggesting that, after having created the world by telegram, God would send one of Saint Paul's epistles. But the play on words works only in Italian, in which both the posted letter and the saint's epistle are called "*lettera*." In English the text had to be changed. Belbo says only "*Fiat lux*. Stop," and Casaubon comments "Epistle follows." Perhaps the joke becomes a bit more ultraviolet and the reader has to work a little harder to understand what's going on in the minds of the characters, but the short circuit between Old and New Testament is more effective. Here, if I were rewriting the original novel, I would alter that dialogue.

Sometimes the author can only trust in Divine Providence. I will never be able to collaborate fully on a Japanese translation of my work (though I have tried). It is hard for me to understand the thought processes of my "target." For that matter I always wonder what I am really reading when I look at the translation of a Japanese poem, and I presume Japanese readers have the same experience when reading me. And yet I know that, when I read the translation of a Japanese poem, I grasp something of that thought process that is different from mine. If I read a haiku after having read some Zen Buddhist koans, I can perhaps understand why the simple mention of the moon high over the lake should give me emotions analogous to and yet different from those that an English romantic poet conveys to me. Even in these cases a minimum of collaboration between translator and author can work. I no longer remember into which Slavic language someone was translating *The Name of the Rose*, but we were wondering what the reader would get from the many passages in Latin. Even an American reader who has not studied Latin still knows it was the language of the medieval ecclesiastical world and so catches a whiff of the Middle Ages. And further, if he reads *De pentagono Salomonis* he can recognize pentagon and Solomon. But for a Slavic reader these Latin phrases and names, transliterated into the Cyrillic alphabet, suggest nothing. If, at the beginning of *War and Peace*, the American reader finds "*Eh bien, mon prince* . . . ," he can guess that the person being addressed is a prince. But if the same dialogue appears at the beginning of a Chinese translation (in an incomprehensible Latin alphabet or—worse—expressed in Chinese ideograms) what will the reader in Beijing understand? The Slavic translator and I decided to use, instead of Latin, the ancient ecclesiastical Slavonic of the medieval Orthodox church. In that way the reader would feel the same sense of distance, the same religious atmosphere, though understanding only vaguely what was being said.

Thank God I am not a poet, because the problem becomes more dramatic in translating poetry, an art where thought is determined by words, and if you change the language, you change the thought. Yet there are excellent examples of translated poetry produced by a collaboration between author and translator. Often the result is a new creation. One text very close to poetry because of its linguistic complexity is Joyce's *Finnegans Wake*. Now, the Anna Livia Plurabelle chapter—when it was still in the form of an early draft—was translated into Italian with Joyce himself collaborating. The translation is markedly different from the original English. It is not a translation. It is as if Joyce had rewritten his text in Italian. And yet one French critic has said that to understand that chapter properly (in English) it would be advisable to first read that Italian draft.

Perhaps the Pure Language does not exist, but pitting one language against another is a splendid adventure, and it is not necessarily true, as the Italian saying goes, that the "translator" is always a "traitor." Provided that the author takes part in this admirable treason.

December 19, 1993

Stanley Elkin

Stanley Elkin was the author of 17 books: 10 novels and 7 collections of shorter pieces. Even his most serious works are funny, irreverent, abristle with linguistic acrobatics. His heroes are the powerless but shrewd, seeking revenge against their mortality with little more than a mouthful of fast-talk.

Elkin's work earned him a National Book Critics Circle Award for his novel *George Mills* (1982), a place in the American Academy and Institute of Arts and Letters, and 3 nominations for the National Book Award, the most recent of these for his novel *The MacGuffin* (1991). Before his death in 1995, he was a professor at Washington University in St. Louis, where he taught writing for 33 years. Just months after he died, he won the National Book Critics Circle Award, posthumously, for *Mrs. Ted Bliss*.

When Elkin wrote the following essay, at 62, he was wheelchair-bound, a hostage to his "handicap and footicap," as he has one of his characters say in his book of novellas, *Van Gogh's Room at Arles*. He was shameless when it came to drawing on his life to shape his art, throwing his multiple sclerosis and all its encumbrances into the alloy of Elkinalia, letting it fizz out into his writing where it would.

He was born in the Bronx and grew up in Chicago, the eldest child of a costume jewelry salesman. That fact may best explain Elkin's craft, for a spieler's tongue lived in the man. "Less is more," a brash young editor once told him when faced with endless fugues of Elkin-prose. "Less is not more," Elkin barked back. "I believe more is more. Less is less. And enough is enough."

Just after his death, I wrote an appreciation for Elkin, which was published in the Style section of *The Washington Post*. I reproduce it here, in its entirety:

JUNE 5, 1995: The last time I saw Stanley Elkin, we were speeding through a late Manhattan night in a van. I was in the front next to the driver, looking out at the street ruts winter had left behind. Stanley was in an open space in the back, strapped into his wheelchair, which was, in turn, yoked to the floor. It was 1992, and we were returning from the National Book Award ceremony in a funk. It was the third time he had been nominated for the award, and the third time he had lost.

Bumping along in the dark, trussed up in his tux with a runner-up medal festooning his neck, Stanley was inconsolable. As the road got worse, I could hear his hands thwack against the armrests and his head flop from side to side. Soon he was bobbing like a balloon in the wind. "Goddamn New York potholes!" he finally roared, half in a rage, and half with diabolical glee. It was vintage Elkin—a moment that could have been pulled from the life of Bobbo Druff, city commissioner of streets and luckless hero of *The MacGuffin*, his novel that hadn't taken the prize that year.

Stanley Elkin died last week in St. Louis of complications arising from his 23-year struggle with multiple sclerosis. He was 65. Merle King Professor of Modern Letters at Washington University and easily one of the greatest virtuosos of the American language, he produced 10 novels, 2 volumes of novellas, 1 volume of short stories, 1 collection of essays, and 3 published scripts.

I was Elkin's editor for a time—an oxymoron if ever there was one, for Elkin's books needed no editing. They sprang full-blown from the man's head, magical riffs of irreverent wisdom. Their heroes, like him, are the powerless but shrewd, setting out into an unjust world like Brooklyn-bred Don Quixotes: off to tilt at windmills with little more than a mouthful of fast talk.

For all his yearning to be known by the greater American public, however, Elkin remained a writer's writer: an artist who was envied and exalted by the literary world, but whose works went undiscovered by the common man they strived to depict. Cynthia Ozick said of him, "Stanley Elkin is no ordinary genius of language, laughter, and the irresistible American idiom; he is an ingenious genius—an inimitable sword-swallower, fire-eater, and three-ring circus of fecund wit."

Elkin was born in the Bronx and grew up in Chicago. He was the eldest son of a costume jewelry salesman, a hereditary fact that predisposed him (he always said) to looking at words as if they were glittering gewgaws ready for the stringing.

After graduating from South Shore High School in Chicago, he attended the University of Illinois at Urbana-Champaign, where he completed a B.A. (1952), a master's (1953) and a doctorate (1961) in English. He served in the U.S. Army from 1955 to 1957. He was a visiting professor at many colleges, including Yale, Smith and the University of Iowa, but for most of his career he was an English professor at Washington University in St. Louis, where he taught writing until his death last Wednesday.

Although he could be seriously funny, much of Elkin's work is about the angst at the heart of American mass culture. *Boswell*, his first novel (1964), tells the tale of a modern-day biographer whose gnawing sense of his own mortality and mediocrity leads him to surround himself with bizarre people he perceives to be famous. His second book, *Criers and Kibitzers, Kibitzers and Criers* (1966), is a much-loved collection of 9 short stories—sketches of an array of oddballs—that Harvard's Helen Vendler has likened to a dazzling show of "naked bravado and ostentation."

George Mills (1982), the novel that won Elkin the National Book Critics Circle Award, is about 40 generations of workers who are all named George Mills and who are all trapped in their blue-collar jobs. In *The Magic Kingdom* (1985), a group of terminally ill children is taken to explore the surreal landscape of Disney World. In *The MacGuffin* (1991), the aforementioned Bobbo Druff combs city streets in an existential daze and wonders when the traffic and his life got so far out of control. Among Elkin's most recent works are *Pieces of Soap* (essays, 1992), *Van Gogh's Room at Arles* (novellas, 1993) and the novel *Mrs. Ted Bliss* (1995).

When Elkin was nominated for the PEN/Faulkner award in 1994 and didn't win, his daughter Molly (one of three children Elkin had with his wife, Joan), went to the ceremony in his place. "My father couldn't be here," she told the audience, "because of his debilitating disease. . . . Oh, I don't mean that one," she added when a knowing hush descended on the room. "I mean his writer's ego." He couldn't bear the torment of watching someone else get the glory again.

And yet, it was that not-getting-the-glory-thing that sharpened his wit and fed his imagination. Here Stanley Elkin ultimately found a victory: He became America's past master at taking defeat and weaving it, word by word, onto filaments of gold. "As long as you've got your health," he wrote, "you've got your naivete. I lost the one, I lost the other, and maybe that's what led me toward revenge—a writer's revenge anyway, the revenge, I mean, of style."

M. A.

Master of My Universe

BY STANLEY ELKIN

In the middish '60s, after I received tenure, was promoted to associate professor and, in the words of a friend, had risen to the middle of my profession, I took all my untenured colleagues to lunch in the old Santoros tavern, only across the street from the university, but so far removed from it in ambiance and spirit it might have been any back room in the world, smoke-filled and with a smell of testosterone hanging in the air like the balls of beer.

I'd gone there for a reason, which I announced as soon as the pitchers came and my friends had settled into their hamburgers. I'm no good sport, I told them. There's no such thing as a free lunch, I told them, and I was buying theirs on condition that they vote for me when the ballots came next week that would determine which four faculty members would be elected to the English Department Executive Committee.

I made them promise. Sure, they said, no problem, I was a shoo-in. They gave their word of honor. They crossed their hearts.

When the votes were tallied I received only one vote—my own, of course. It forever changed my view of politics and taught me a good lesson—that you can't put any trust in a campaign promise.

I had wanted to be on the executive committee because I thought that that's where the beans got spilled, where all the secrets and private opinions were laid out on the table after the last players folded and you got to see who held what.

I deserved to be defeated. I did. Not because I'd sought to win through corrupt means, or even that I'd not gone far enough and sprung for mixed drinks and a better lunch in a classier restaurant. I deserved to lose because I had no idea about the purpose of politics, which ain't about anything so crass as meaning of course, but about power, the ability, I mean, to get things done, to shove the population around in a kind of human chess.

And anyway it's so abstruse, too abstruse for the likes of me, who hasn't the lore of Robert's rules, cloture, quorum, nor any of the Tables of Governance—ochlocracy, plutocracy, pantisocracy. Or can distinguish the pitch between socialism, bolshevism and syndicalism, republicanism and federalism, Wellesley and Radcliffe.

You think no?

I go to English Department meetings. Someone or other is up for tenure. In the 33 years I've been at Washington University, in the 27 or 28 I've been eligible to vote to grant or deny it, I've never, not once, either recused myself or cast a negative vote against anyone's tenure.

I could say, I suppose, that I believe in some which-of-us-would-'scape-whipping principle of live-and-let-live, but it isn't that so much as my simply zoning-out when it comes not to the pluses-and-minuses, all those on-the-one-hand-but-on-the-other-hand arguments of the logician's balanced scales, some claustrophobic maze of procedure in which I get lost every time out. Also, I'm a sucker for the other guy's ardor and argument, every opinion canceling its neighbor to a stalled standstill like the push/pull mechanics of my isometric will.

Yet the writer's soul is, at bottom, political as a president's. He deals out of a benign autocracy, home rule, some best-sense fascism of the heart. All I mean, of course, is his imagination, his license to legislate worlds, reality, nature, truth; if not obliged always to hold up a mirror to these things, then at least to make them interesting when he doesn't.

The First Amendment, freedom of speech, is not just the prerogative of writers, it is their absolute mandate and fiat, the most profound law by which they live, sworn to its service and leaving as little wiggle room as a Commandment.

Very high-minded such talk, very noble such writerly ideals, trippingly to the tongue, a riff of lip service, yet something to it, I think, the great ambition of literature—to wield the power, to get things done, "to make," as the Sondheim lyric has it in *Sunday in the Park with George*, "a hat where there never was a hat!" This last seems so true and moving to me it could almost serve as a definition of all art.

Because that's precisely the writer's job, his only politics, not to ordain taste or teach the aesthetic forks, enjoin the ladderly etiquettes of beauty, fluency or any of the eye's upper elegances and spiffy stations of grace, not even to redress grievance, but to legislate the infinite details of the world, to inventory the vast holdings of the human heart and work its combinations like a safecracker, giving everyone, everyone, the best lines, putting the best face on the worst actions, pleading the case of the guilty as well as the innocent, as if literature were a sort of litigation, due process, *le filibuster juste* if it comes to that, and all the rest of the high higgle-haggle of philosophy.

April 18, 1993

Ned Rorem

"It is a truth universally acknowledged," says the American composer Ned Rorem, "that the entire solar system is torn between two aesthetics: French and German. Virtually everything is one or the other. Blue is French, red is German. No is French, yes is German. Formal gardens are French, oceans are German. The moon is French, the sun German. Gay men are French, lesbians are German. Crows' feet are French, pigs' knuckles are German. Schubert on his good days is French, Berlioz is forever German. Jokes are French, the explanation of jokes is German. If French is to be profoundly superficial, like Impressionism, which depicts a fleeting vision of eternity, then German is to be superficially profound, as when Bruckner's music digs ever deeper into one narrow hole. If you agree with all this, you're French. If you disagree, you're German."

It is a point Rorem makes in his bracing autobiography *Knowing When to Stop* (1994), and it is a point that is wholly Roremian: delightful for its cleverness and spontaneity (very French), but fierce, even leonine, in its claim on truth (100 percent German). The fact is that for all Rorem's Americanness, he is both sides of his own equation: a man whose music can be as ethereal as Ravel's and as cerebral as Schoenberg's; a prose writer whose words may strut and flirt across a page, but whose elegiac themes are never far beneath. There is heart, there is brain. Charm and gravity. *Savoir vivre* and *Drang*.

Rorem was born in Richmond, Ind., and raised in Chicago—the only son of liberal, even left-wing Quaker parents. His father was a professor of economics at the University of Chicago and the conceptualizer and founder of Blue Cross. His mother felt keenly about supporting women's suffrage, gay rights and birth control, but confined her opinions to her family and directed her drive and intellect to the raising of her two children. Theirs was not a stodgy home. Socially conscious, educationally upper class, they were "bohemian in the safe style of university denizens." Too WASP to kiss or hug, they nevertheless "paraded nude" among themselves; and they did it in such a "businesslike" manner that it was a shock to learn that other families did not behave in the same way.

From nursery to high school, Rorem attended Friends' meetings with his parents and older sister and studied at an experimental school run by the faculty of the University of Chicago. It was a remarkably mixed institution—largely Jews and blacks—and he was blind to the differences among his playmates until he left its halls. "Only when I went out into the world did I learn how sexy and interesting those differences really were."

He was given all the music lessons he asked for. By 10 he proclaimed himself a composer. By 13 he was reading André Gide, and when his parents took him to France later that year, he fell in love with the country. But his real love affair with France would not flower for another 15 years.

At 16 he graduated from high school and began his studies at Northwestern University's music school, "but I soon felt that I was straining against the faculty. I urgently wanted to learn the music of my time and place—not the classics." It is a position he has held fast for almost 60 years, and one he speaks on today with almost missionary fervor: "Serious contemporary concert fare has all but vanished during the past 20 years," he says; and it has done so "in the ken of even the most educated laymen. Intellectuals who appreciate the arts of past and present know their Dante as they know their Dinesen, and adore Praxiteles as they adore Pollock; but when it comes to music they may thrive on Vivaldi or even Mahler but not on these men's living equivalents—we contemporary composers are not even a despised minority, for to be despised you must exist."

Within 2 years, he left Northwestern for Philadelphia's Curtis Institute of Music (his father had sent them a sheaf of his compositions). But even in the creative atmosphere of Curtis he felt too constrained by his teachers. Before a year was up, he left Philadelphia, and, against his father's wishes, went to New York to work as Virgil Thomson's manuscript copyist. "I still tend to take music schools with a big grain of salt," he says. "They're good at smelling a rat and pointing out solutions, but they can't make a composer out of someone who isn't."

But Manhattan in the '40s offered a young composer a different kind of schooling: Rorem befriended Aaron Copland, Paul Bowles, John Cage, Eugene Istomin, Billie Holiday. He had his first homosexual affair, learned how to drink, enrolled in Juilliard, took odd jobs as a rehearsal pianist, and was hired and fired by Martha Graham.

By 1949 he was in Paris, fulfilling a long-lived fantasy of submerging himself in that culture. ("I was already French," he wrote.) There he met Truman Capote, Francis Poulenc, Jean Cocteau, James Baldwin, Samuel Barber. He would write about the musical and sexual encounters of that heady time in *The Paris Diary* (1965), an unprecedentedly honest memoir that would reach cult status in pre-Stonewall days.

Established as a solid, productive writer of music, Rorem went on to publish many books, among them *The New York Diary* (1967), *Critical Affairs* (1970), *Setting the Tone* (1983), *The Nantucket Diary* (1987), *Settling the Score* (1988), *Other Entertainment* (1996), *Lies* (1999) and *The Later Diaries* (2000). Not incidentally, he won the Pulitzer Prize for his *Air Music* in 1976 and is widely acknowledged today as one of America's greatest living composers. Author of hundreds of compositions, from songs to chamber music to full symphonic works, Rorem now lives and works in New York City and Nantucket.

In 1994, he published *Knowing When to Stop*. Despite its juicy revelations ("I have been in bed with four *Time* covers: Lenny Bernstein, Tennessee Williams, Noel Coward, and John Cheever"), the book was most notable for its wry and probing reflections on an American life in music.

What Rorem's writing does best is express an angst about the shrinking world of the musical mind. "There was a time," he says, "when the performer and the composer were one and the same: Beethoven, Chopin and Debussy all played their own works. Not so now. My good neighbor (violinist) Itzhak Perlman makes in one night what a composer makes in one and a half years of work." Today the performer is a star; the composer hardly exists. Writing a symphony in the America of the '90s, it seems, does far less for one's pocket or ego than writing a book or painting a canvas.

And then there is the question of American musical confidence: "Americans know they're better than the rest of the world in bombs and budgets, but retain a vague inferiority vis-à-vis the musical arts, still feeling that European repertories, not to mention European conductors, are better than ours."

Well, this is all fearfully serious. Gloomy even. Downright German. Which prompts me to inquire, "So which side of you, Ned Rorem—the composer or the writer—is French?"

It stumps him only momentarily. And then he starts in: "Well, if prose is German and music is French—although subdivisions of prose, like essays, are French, while subdivisions of music, like symphonies, are German; and Schubert, say, though anatomically Austrian, was, in his economy, Frenchish, while Franck, though biologically Belgian was, in his profligacy, Germanic—then, maybe, according to my own definition . . ." Here, he stops.

"Wait, let me put on my thinking cap. But which one? I do wear two, but never both at the same time."

M. A.

Sounds and Sensibilities

BY NED ROREM

I am a composer who also writes, not a writer who also composes. The distinction lies not in how I spend my time but in how I subsist. Born in 1923, I was early entranced with all the arts, as much a doer as a consumer. It was less a question of declaring "I want to be an artist when I grow up" than "I am an artist, so how do I grow up?" (Arguably, no artist grows up: If he sheds the perceptions of childhood, he ceases being an artist.)

I showed little gift as a painter, but I did scribble tragic poems and garish novellas, practiced the piano (mostly what was then termed "modern music"—Debussy, Poulenc, John Alden Carpenter) until I was good enough to improvise my own notions, then inscribe them. My parents, albeit liberal WASPs in a capitalist culture, had mixed feelings about an artist in the house—How would he earn a living!—but remained unstintingly supportive. It was a matter of tossing a coin between whether I'd pursue formal studies in words or in music.

Music won. By age 20 I was a professional composer—that is, commissioned for what I loved doing—without compromise. By 30 I had published dozens of songs (today an unsalable commodity), plus longer works including one opera, and was supporting myself, if meagerly, through performance fees and handouts from here and there. At 40 I was independent, with a small but solid reputation worldwide. Today I still live from the just rewards of my labor. If I can't be certain about future income from commissions, I do have enough to see me through for a bit, and also I teach and lecture a little, as do most composers to break even. But so precarious is the lot that if I didn't have some weekly guarantees (a new piece in print, name in the paper, fan letters) that I'm needed, I'd throw in the sponge.

Meanwhile, ever since tossing that coin, I've hesitated to remove the other hat. I've kept a journal all those years, and occasionally write an essay for some specialized magazine. But not until 1965, with the publication of *The Paris Diary* when I was 41, did I become a professional author. Within 3 months I received more mail about this one book than I had received about all my music in the preceding 20 years. Priorities began to shift. If total strangers were going to read me, then perhaps I'd better make the prose less rhapsodically self-indulgent and more firmly objective. As for the music, which had hitherto been (so I imagine) elegant, pristine, well-chiseled, I consciously tried for more . . . well, for more ugliness, more space and more madness. And so, the Good Ned of Notes entered a destabilizing mirror while the Naughty Ned of Verbs exited. The two changed places permanently and, with benign schizophrenia, have run on parallel tracks ever since. They seldom meet.

Except for Paul Bowles, am I the only composer splitting his time between words and music? Other composers do write prose (Schumann, Berlioz, Debussy, Thomson), but the prose has always been about music—their own or other people's. (Mendelssohn: "It's not that music is too vague for words, it's too precise for words.") Bowles's prose is plotted stylized fiction serving quite another purpose. And yes, other composers do write fiction (Wagner, Mussorgsky, Menotti, Blitzstein), but their fiction is for singing, for librettos, in service to their primary craft. (Interestingly, when poets compose, as Hopkins, Pound, Paul Goodman have done, the result invariably falls flat. Lionel Barrymore too wrote music, so did Hitler. That's another story.) My prose, like Bowles's, is not consciously related to music, except when I'm reviewing; it follows some other urge, impossible to define. As a wearer of two hats I do know this: The arts are not interchangeable; if they were, we'd need only one.

Who is my audience? Certainly it's divided. Those who read my books (let's say, to be kind, 10,000 during the season in which the book comes out) don't overlap with those who hear my music. Of the 15,000 souls present at recent performances of my English Horn Concerto with the New York Philharmonic, and of the 80,000 more who will hear it during that orchestra's upcoming tour, maybe 1 percent knows I write books, and one-tenth of that percent has read one of the books. As for that mob that hears the music, how many actually listen? How many will forget my name the next day? How many—100? 50?—will buy the recording, assuming a recording ever appears?

"Do you set yourself to music?" people sometimes wonder. Whatever my songs are worth, the words of the 200-odd authors I have musicalized have never been less than first rate. I set words I feel can take a change, seeking not to improve so much as to reemphasize them. Music can't broaden their meaning, only heighten their meaning. Occasionally the words benefit from the change; but although they might not inherently need the change, I must feel that they need it.

Now, to write words with the intention of setting them to music would be to write words I intend, by definition, to change. Only a dreary text could emerge from so inhibiting a task. Nor could I musicalize words I had written at another time and for their own sake, since those words would not exist if I had been able (at that other time) to express their sense in notes.

There is already an arrogance in any composer who presumes to set a poet to music. To direct this arrogance toward his own texts is beyond even me.

The IRS, learning that I write both words and music, is at a loss. So they say: We'll place you in the category of "Other Entertainment." Which, by the way, is the title of my forthcoming collection of essays.*

January 14, 1996

*Editor's note: And indeed, *Other Entertainment: Collected Pieces* was published in 1999.

Richard Selzer

Imagine, if you will, the hands of these writers: Keats, Chekhov, Rabelais, William Carlos Williams, Maimonides, Somerset Maugham, Arthur Conan Doyle. What could they possibly have had in common? They were wielders of the pen, yes. But they were doctors' hands, too, as adept in lancing a boil or delivering a newborn as in looming thread after thread of gossamer prose. That is not to say that any one of them consciously set out to infuse literature with medicine or science with art.

But that is precisely what Dr. Richard Selzer means to do. He began writing in the fifth decade of his life, even as he was at the peak of a long career as a surgeon—in a practice that took him from prostatectomies to plastic surgery, from trimming bowels to pinning hips.

"I try to render the facts of medicine in compelling settings," he says, "but I admit I always have an eye on making art. I realize that the word may sound high-falutin', suspect even, but as I strive to make my work real, I try to take the high road, to remember that I am the living descendant of an accomplished line of doctor writers. I feel I am part of that continuum."

It is not a pompous claim. Selzer is as awed by his two professions as he is intense about the possibilities of their fusion.

He was born in Troy, N.Y., in 1928, the son of a physician and a saloon diva. Both his parents had emigrated from Russia as children. His father had grown up in New York City and gone to the medical school at McGill University in Montreal. His mother, "a woman of immense beauty and flamboyance," had been raised in the Montreal ghetto, and had sung her way out via Montreal's bars. When his father heard his mother warble *Pale Hands I Loved Beside the Shalimar* in a nightclub one evening, he was smitten for life. They were married, bought the sort of car two penniless newlyweds can afford, and struck out for Manhattan. At Troy, they ran out of gas. The doctor hung out his shingle, thinking they'd stay long enough to fill a tank, but they remained for 20 years. "By that slender thread, I hang," says their son, for, according to him, it was working-town America that shaped him.

Selzer's father had always wanted him to be a surgeon—said he had the hands for it. But Selzer was more attracted to the notion of following in his mother's footsteps; he loved her outrageous wit, her sense of style, her world of art song and high culture. His father's death when he was 12 changed it all: Selzer chose medicine. "It was my way of keeping him alive."

"I became a bookworm," he recalls. He thrived in school, excelled in the pre-med program at Union College, and went on to Albany medical school, minding his mother through a series of husbands—"picking up the pieces of her progressively unstable life."

In his third year of medical school, he walked into the classroom of a thoracic surgeon who represented "everything an ugly little shrimp like me yearned to be: bombastic, macho, fearless, witty, a little cruel, a lot handsome." The man promised to help Selzer get into Yale if Selzer would pledge to study surgery. "The only thing I'd ever done with my hands was turn the pages of a book," says Selzer, but he seized the opportunity. He completed an internship at Yale, served in the Korean War, learned to perform colon operations as well as mastectomies, and began a wide-ranging medical career.

In 1968, he wrote his first book, *Rituals of Surgery*. Then a string of books followed, among them *Mortal Lessons*, *Confessions of a Knife*, *Taking the World in for Repairs*, *Down From Troy*, *Raising the Dead* and *Imagine a Woman*. He has taught writing and medicine at Yale. He has written about autism, AIDS and cancer and always, he has done so with a deep reverence for the process: the terrible responsibilities of a doctor, the heart-lifting faith of the stricken.

"The word 'patient' comes from the Latin *patiens*, which means to suffer," he points out. It is a word distinct from "client" or "customer" or "spectator" or "reader." "We doctors have patients, and they suffer." A doctor's knowledge of pain and loss, in other words, is at the heart of what Richard Selzer writes. It is a condition Chekhov or William Carlos Williams certainly would have understood.

M. A.

Writer with Scalpel

BY RICHARD SELZER

Writing came to me late. I was 40 when I began to teach myself the arachnoid knack of spinning words. My equipment consisted of my discipline—surgery—a relish for language, and a pen. Hardly reason to take off my hospital mask, don tights and dare the high trapeze of prose. But from that first day, I loved the warmth of the process, the awkwardness, the wobbly first steps of authorship. What emerged on the page was an account of what Jonah must have experienced as he was swallowed by the whale. Since I knew what the gastric mucosa looked like better than the original Bible storytellers, the belly of my whale had a good deal more authenticity. That fact alone was thrilling.

I wrote in longhand then and still do. The pen is the writing instrument most congenial to my hand. It has the same length and heft as a scalpel, though one is round and the other flat. Ply either one, and something is shed. From the scalpel, blood; from the pen, ink. I like to watch words issue from my fingers, like a secretion from my body. The word processor does not exist that offers so personal a sense of discharge. Then, too, there are the quick, tiny hisses as the flat of the hand moves across a page from left to right, to say nothing of the long, delicious hiss from right to left when you start a new line. Each time I write a story or an essay in longhand, I feel a triumph over the technological preeminence of the computer keyboard.

In the 1960s, it was rare for a surgeon to become a writer, but I decided to write about what I knew: my work as a doctor. The two careers cross-fertilized each other. My medical situations and portraits were as factual as I could make them, but I learned to betray facts with the "gentle treason of poetry." Highly suspect behavior for a member of a male priesthood, such as surgery was 30 years ago.

"Come! Come!" my colleagues scolded. "Stick to your last. Isn't surgery enough for you?" But it was too late. I had succumbed to the irresistible urge to record stories that were being enacted every day at the hospital. Like Ulysses, who had melted wax poured in his ears so as not to hear the song of the sirens, I warded off their warnings. I persisted. There was only one person who did not dismiss me outright: myself. From this I learned that a writer must have some measure of will, that he or she must exhibit the requisite courage to put work forward despite any fear of rejection. Something of a trickster's appetite for triumph is necessary in this.

I make rather more use of the English language than less. I'm about as far from a minimalist as you can get. A full-throated ease is what I strive for, not often achieved. Is this outdated? Perhaps. But I doubt that there's any such thing as progress in art. Are the cave paintings at Lascaux more outdated than the paintings of Picasso? I find the former even more compelling for the patina of their 20,000 years.

A good deal of what I do is in the form of a diary. My present project is to prepare my diaries for publication. On the face of it, this doesn't make much sense. First you tell a notebook all your secrets, and then you publish it? In fact, I have come to diaries both by nature and by training. Every doctor is a diarist: You keep a daily record of your patients' illnesses, setting down the vital signs, the physical findings, the patient's "complaints." You order tests, prescribe medications, express disappointment at worsening and joy upon recovery. Such "keeping" seems to me a higher genre than mere storytelling; there is a life at stake at the center of each tale. Walt Whitman, upon first witnessing the wounds and suffering of the Civil War soldiers, cried out: "This bursts the petty bonds of Art!" I would agree. The best writing I have ever done in my life may have been done in medical charts where the patient is the hero, a character whose very existence is a work of art. It is the only writing I've done that is devoid of vanity and pomp. Still, those were case histories and, as I am now retired from my work as a doctor, I don't write them any more. I write stories that reach for privileged moments of revelation, as when a cleft lip, say, or an ingrown toenail, or a torn rag of flesh takes on a certain radiance. In such moments, flesh becomes the spirit. Unlike a CAT scan or an MRI, these stories don't look for concrete answers. Their aim is more difficult to define; they are apt to be ambiguous. As a writer, I have learned that some life mysteries aren't meant to be solved; they're meant to make us wonder at them.

Writing, for me, is what purring is for a cat. It represents pure pleasure, and there is no purer pleasure than chasing after the nature of a bodily thing and nailing it to a page. To do so, I have often made use of the rich language of medicine. In the 1930s, my father was a general practitioner in Troy, N.Y. He practiced downstairs. Our family lived upstairs. At night, after office hours, my brother Billy, who was 8, and I, 7, would sneak down to his consultation room and to the glass-front cabinet where he kept his medical texts. Our favorite was the *Textbook of Obstetrics and Gynecology*. It was there that I first became aware of the richness of medical language. There were words such as "cerebellum," "carcinoma" and "sphincter" (which Billy told me was a lady who never got married). Father wanted me to become a surgeon; Mother, who was a singer, hoped I'd become a poet.

When I was 12, he died, long before my eyes had had their fill of him. That was when I decided to take up his trade.

Medicine has enlarged the language, offering words such as "cough," "asthma," "hiccup"—all derived from the sounds of the sick. There is an onomatopoeic high when old King Lear appears onstage carrying the corpse of Cordelia, and cries like an animal in pain, "Howl! Howl! Howl!" The symptom of suffering lies outside the precinct of language. It cannot be rendered. In such moments, only howled vowels will do.

Twelve years ago, after 3 decades of hurly-burly surgery, I retired. I felt rather like a camel who suspects his master is overloading his poor hump. He turns and looks sadly upon the piled load, sighs at the injustice. All at once, the amperage of my life dropped to 20 watts. I found that dim twilight ideal for entering a writing life. Now there is time to indulge my eccentricities. I carry an amulet in my pocket; I put on my lucky hat, the one that keeps my thoughts from flying off the top of my head. I'm quite sure that I write better by candlelight or if it's raining. That sort of thing.

Unlike surgery, there's a good deal of waiting around in writing. A whole day will go by at my desk, where I sit, instrument in hand, without so much as one keepable word issuing in a tidy, cursive coil.

"Here, Ariel!" I cry, but the Muse comes not to me. After such a day, I fall into bed like an apple from a tree, with the same thud, only to awaken to an angel holding a perfect sentence out to me on a silver tray. A writer's mind is like flypaper—it traps whatever happens by, an object, an expression, a bit of dialogue. Not long ago, a woman came to visit and was taken to the garden to see my wife's pride and joy: the daylilies.

"Daylilies!" cried the woman, "How they garnish a salad!"

"Old cow!" said Janet later. "Thinks only of grazing." Now show me the writer who wouldn't die to have written that. Or this, in a 19th-century textbook of parasitology: "Tapeworms may be harbored for years, and except for the inconvenience of the gravid segments crawling out of the anus, the host continues in robust health, enjoying both food and drink." I think I'd rather have written that than the whole of the Encyclopaedia Brittanica.

There seem to be two phases that occur before and after writing. First, there is the mysterious quicksilver of inspiration, an altered state of consciousness that may be biochemical in origin. The second is the tinkering with the text. Both give a good deal of pleasure, although there is such a thing as too much tinkering. A sheepdog that turns obsessive can worry the sheep until they won't graze, only stand huddled and trembling.

Once, I lived for the sense of urgency in surgery. Don't imagine that writing is a more lighthearted pursuit. Nor is it easier to perform, but rather harder to make come out right. The technique in either is intricate, painstaking. In surgery, the body of the patient is opened up and put together again. In writing, the whole world is taken in for repairs and then put back in running order, piece by piece.

July 19, 1998

Reynolds Price

Fatherhood and sexuality figure large in Reynolds Price's life. Both are certainly at the epicenter of his novel *The Promise of Rest*. One could argue with equal vehemence that the story is about the death of a young gay man or that it is about the unfolding of a father's love. It concerns, anyway, two subjects Price knows better than most: the cost of unremitting pain and the resilience of the human heart. The plot is devastatingly simple: Wade Mayfield, a 24-year-old New York architect, learns he has AIDS; his father, a poet-professor, brings him home to die.

Price was born in Macon, N.C., in 1933. His father, Will, was a recovered alcoholic, a traveling salesman who peddled electric appliances and counted himself a Baptist. His mother, Elizabeth, was a protofeminist, a strong character who called herself Jimmy, bridled at the narrow world of Southern women and raised her two sons Methodist. Theirs was a modest home, where "religion was the only source of shouting matches." His parents were not avid readers, but when his stories, essays and poems began to get his high school teacher's attention, they gave him unequivocal support.

In 1951, Duke University offered him a scholarship, and he went off to study with William Blackburn, the professor who had nurtured William Styron and Peter Maas, among others. Three years later, when he learned that his father had lung cancer, Price went home to care for him. Will Price died in his son's arms.

Reynolds Price returned to Duke, and Jimmy Price took a job in a boy's clothing store in order to support her sons. She worked there well after her eldest became a prize-winning author.

During his senior year at Duke, Price wrote a short story about two boys that so moved Blackburn that he showed it to Eudora Welty. Welty was immediately taken by Price's craft and put him in touch with her agent, Dirmud Russell of Russell and Volkening. It was the start of a lifelong friendship between Welty and Price, and herald of a long partnership between Russell, Price and Atheneum Publishers.

In 1955, after graduating summa cum laude, Price traveled to England to study at Oxford, where he received encouragement from W. H. Auden and Stephen Spender. He returned to Duke three years later to embark on a teaching schedule that has lasted 37 years and a publishing career that has produced more than two dozen books.

Price's first novel, *A Long and Happy Life* (1962), received the William Faulkner Award and has never gone out of print. Subsequent works include *A Generous Man* (1966), *Love and Work* (1968), *Kate Vaiden* (which won the National Book Critics Circle Award in 1986) and *Blue Calhoun* (1992). *The Promise of Rest* is the first of his novels to be published after the demise of Atheneum and concludes his "Great Circle Trilogy," which interweaves *The Surface of Earth* (1975) and *The Source of Light* (1981). In 2002, he published *Noble Norfleet*, a coming-of-age story that addresses the Vietnam War years. He has written two memoirs: *Clear Pictures*, about his early life, and *A Whole New Life*, about his 10-year battle with spinal cancer. In the course of his writing career, he has produced essays, short stories, poems, plays and screenplays; he has even written lyrics for singer James Taylor.

Now a paraplegic confined to a wheelchair, Price continues to teach courses on writing and Milton at Duke. He is an intensely religious, deeply private individual, who is inclined to believe that homosexuality is largely a personal matter. "Cancer forced me to reinvent myself," he says. "This is a different Reynolds Price you see here. A post–1984 version. A waist-up model. A Reynolds Price junior."

He has had to be father to a whole new man.

M. A.

A Chronicle of the Plague Years

BY REYNOLDS PRICE

When I was overrun by spinal cancer in 1984, I withdrew to my home for more than a year. In stunned depression and the need to focus all my strength on rooting out an inoperable monster, I chose not to see most of my old friends, acquaintances and colleagues. Seclusion seemed my best hope for that white-hot aim. The drastic simplification may have worked. For whatever reasons, in any case, I've survived the onslaught for more than a decade; but it was some 2 years after the discovery of my cancer before I learned of an assumption made by many of my unseen friends and colleagues—they thought I was dying of AIDS.

A number of my old friends were indeed dead, or fading, in the brutal plague; and my unthreatened friends might well have been right—I might easily have been infected in those oblivious years of the '70s and early '80s when the virus arrived and extended its secret presence among us. In fact, it spared me. By the time I learned of my luck in the matter, however, more of my friends were ill; and hardly a month goes by, even now, that I don't learn of another who's joined the enormous, still burgeoning family whom AIDS has consumed.

As those friends have begun the slow leaving that AIDS demands, I've found myself attempting to write of their fate and their ongoing life. First, I managed a few slender poems about their bravery and their deaths; then I wrote 2 short stories (one of which, called "An Evening Meal," I'd attempt to save in any disaster that threatened my life's work).

But my balked affections and the bitter helplessness each of us feels—or will feel soon now—needed more room to state the sorrow of so much dying, so much stubborn courage, and the often heroic kindness of loved ones. It was only some 3 years ago, in the early '90s, that I found my mind beginning to urge me to deal, in the serious space of a novel, with the merciless waster and its long-range meaning for every American, every human on Earth.

One aspect of the threat has barely been considered. In the past 30 years—within the generous confines of the English language and the tolerance of American law—fiction, poetry and drama have been called on to respond to 2 concurrent challenges. The first came early in the 1960s. With the collapse of the last barriers to a writer's freedom in describing sexual acts, our literature faced a prospect so broad as to seem overwhelming. And in fact a great many writers have been overwhelmed.

We don't need to venture as far as the repellent depths of *American Psycho* to recall instances from the past 3 decades in which gifted writers have seized the barbed hook of sexual freedom and promptly choked or regurgitated in awful plain view. Any seasoned reader can provide his or her examples of otherwise admirable novelists, poets and playwrights who have flung themselves on the heady challenge—a challenge longed for through centuries of severe repression—and wound up achieving little more than embarrassing displays of personal craving or idiosyncratic itch.

A handful of serious writers have achieved real gains, in fiction at least—oddly, verse and drama have proved less lucky (drama continues, obviously, to be bound by the limits on the legality and decorum of public performance, and mainline American poetry has skirted the risk). To name a few winners from a very small field, I'd begin with John Updike in the first volume of his Angstrom series—*Rabbit, Run* (later volumes, as the Angstroms grow increasingly unattractive with age, have achieved less enlightenment from the couple's sexuality). James Salter in his brief novel *A Sport and a Pastime* and Scott Spencer in *Endless Love* each coaxed narrative compulsion and usable light from the beautiful, eminently watchable bodies of their young protagonists. Toni Morrison, while less direct in her portrayals than those 3 men, has derived much of the power of her *Song of Solomon*, *Tar Baby*, and even her baleful *Beloved* from a close attention to the bounty won through physical love by her straitened characters.

Despite the rarity of individual success, it's unquestionable that—in the past 30 years—the novel has made strides toward the goal of a rewarding aesthetics of the body in its acts of pleasure and procreation. The fact that a torrent of bores and occasional felonies has likewise poured from the attempt is lamentable but was only to be expected after such an oppressive wait, and I've yet to be convinced that badly deployed and unrevealing sexual candor in fiction is likely to harm substantial numbers of readers. Meanwhile, in theory, the vast subject lies available for use and mastery.

But a second, and equally large, challenge to writers is upon us and—despite a few dispatches from pioneers—has barely been acknowledged, much less confronted, in serious American writing. The challenge was stealthily rolled toward us by the surfacing of the HIV virus in the early 1980s; and more than a decade later, we continue to work blindly inside an AIDS pandemic that not only has devastated central Africa, southeast Asia and the male homosexual population of America and Europe but also is now the major cause of death among all Americans under the age of 40—men, women and children of whatever income or persuasion.

The defiant reality is simple to state: The sexual acts by which all human beings propagate, delight and console themselves most profoundly are potentially lethal. Any American older than 50 may ask "What's new about that?" I, for instance, was born in 1933 and had reached the near edge of sexual maturity myself before penicillin became available in the mid 1940s to stem the curse of syphilis, which had not only decimated humanity for centuries but had killed a great many artists of all sorts.

Diagnosis is scarce for writers, painters and composers of any century before the 20th (some say there is evidence in Shakespeare's work to indicate that he suffered from syphilis); but a glance at the death roll of 19th-century artists alone makes a point that was largely forgotten in the light of penicillin's brief triumph. That roll includes—among many others—the certain names of Schubert, Schumann, Baudelaire, Flaubert, DeMaupassant, Gauguin, Verlaine, the 20th-century Isak Dinesen; and quite possibly Beethoven, Wilde and Rimbaud. One could argue that a tormented sexuality festers at the root of a great deal of their work—as it does in the work of their near-successors, who began to publish only a few decades before the penicillin rescue: Eliot, Hemingway, Fitzgerald, Faulkner, a more recent writer like Norman Mailer (who matured in the safety zone but whose mind was formed before 1945) and even my own contemporaries Updike and Roth, who like me were near adolescence when the rescue arrived.

It was a brief rescue, as we now know so bleakly. Given current estimates for the efflorescence of the HIV virus in America in the late 1970s, it's suddenly clear that we—plus a good deal of the rest of the Earth—had 30 quick years of safety from the only venereal disease that had killed significant numbers in modern history. And in retrospect, we can see that the heady sexual freedoms of the 1960s and '70s flowed almost entirely from the fragile umbrella spread over us by a small battery of antibiotics, all desperately impotent against HIV.

Given the weight of human history, neither the civil law that governs private relations nor the personal literature of physical conjunction had sufficient time in 3 decades to elaborate sufficiently upon what sane citizens were learning from the wide spectrum of sexual choice. We were only in the near outskirts of the understanding we'd desired for so long when the bludgeon of AIDS reared up and stalled our best hopes—hopes that have labored under pain through much of the life of our species.

Even now, well over a decade into the plague, the most notable aspect in the response of American literature to the reality is a scarcity of attempts to confront it. If we look to what might be called mainline, wide-audience American writers—male and female—it's quickly clear that only in the theater, though not at all in film, has a sizable body of distinguished work accumulated, most notably in Tony Kushner's *Angels in America* and in Terence McNally's several eloquent approaches. Elsewhere, numbers of poets have written elegies for dead friends, and Thom Gunn has produced a handful of fiercely elegant lyrics from the San Francisco eye-of-the-storm. There have been riveting memoirs from men and women with HIV infection, notably Paul Monette's two furious books *Borrowed Time* and *The Politics of Silence*. But with a few exceptions from the work of new young writers, the novel by veteran American writers—a form that is so often the bellwether of seismic change in our national psyche—has been virtually silent. To the best of my knowledge, my own recent novel *The Promise of Rest* is the first by a senior American writer to set an AIDS life and death at its center. We may argue that even 10 years is a short time for a subject to result in mature and thoughtful work from anyone, of any age. But the large fact is that HIV infection itself is not the most gravely neglected subject.

What's gone almost entirely unexamined in our recent literature is the giant threat of AIDS to devastate once again, in a country that's always poised on the edge of hateful Puritan reaction, our sense of the sexual body as a source of high pleasure and profound understanding—a spur for not only our art and compassion but for what John Milton called "those thousand decencies that daily flow" from the intimacy of 2 willing bodies. Think of the mysterious darkening of the clean-lit sexual exuberance of Shakespeare's early comedies and histories into the diseased horror of plays like *Troilus and Cressida*, *Othello*, *Hamlet* and *Lear*. Think of the long pall of erotic disease in the poems of Baudelaire, the physical revulsions of his master Poe and even the fascinated helpless gaze of so recent a writer as Graham Greene at a magnet that was nonetheless lethal.

If AIDS continues to advance among us—and it gives no sign of turning aside—it is inevitable that it will pollute the mental territory we claimed for sane carnality in our years of antibiotic respite. Worse still, our dawning sense of the body as a benign instrument will be gravely enveloped when more and more people come to see one another as sources of danger, even death. And while fidelity to the demands of a certain time and place has never been enforceable in literature—serious writers write not to order, but from old compulsions—surely it's among the waiting duties of our best writers to provide whatever understanding, sympathy and mitigation their work can retrieve from the pall of so much darkness.

June 18, 1995

Cynthia Ozick

Word-spinner, image weaver, philosopher of uncompromising moral force: If there is such a thing as a literary pantheon in America, then Cynthia Ozick is surely its Athena. One of the finest essayists in the English language, Ozick casts sentences that fairly pulse with the electricity of a highly charged mind.

And yet Ozick's work is only marginally known. Her obsessive care for the heft and texture of her words—her meticulous approach to craft—has served to produce only a slender thread of literature in a nonstop writing life of 66 years. To date she has but three novels (*Trust*, 1966; *The Messiah of Stockholm*, 1987; *The Shawl*, 1989), five short story collections (*The Pagan Rabbi*, 1971; *Bloodshed*, 1976; *Levitation*, 1981; *The Cannibal Galaxy*, 1983, *The Puttermesser Papers*, 1997), 4 books of essays (*Art and Ardor*, 1983; *Metaphor and Memory*, 1989, *Fame and Folly*, 1997, *Quarrel and Quandary*, 2001) and 1 play (*Blue Light*, 1994) to show for half a century of hard work.

She admits to laboring over her sentences, polishing their turns to a lapidary finish. "The sentence is my primary element, my tool, goal, bliss," she says girlishly. "Each new sentence is a heart-in-the mouth experiment." But there is a lingering sense in this rumination that her kind of fastidiousness at the micro level of writing has its liabilities. "Emily Brontë's one novel, *Wuthering Heights*, was a miracle," she says. "If Balzac had written a single novel he would have been a minor writer. There is a definite relationship between being major and having a profusion of work to show. You could write one exquisite thing, but you would never be considered more than a minor writer for having done it. Your career would lack the necessary lavishness. And lavishness has never been my portion in life."

But what Ozick may lack in lavishness she makes up for in appetite.

She was born in Depression-era Manhattan, the daughter of 2 pharmacists—cousins who had emigrated from the same little Russian town in Belarus. The 2 had come to America separately and were thrown together when he fell ill with the 1918 influenza epidemic and she was enlisted to help care for him. They married shortly thereafter.

Like other Jewish families from Russia, the Ozicks had many pharmacists in their ranks. A tsar's decree prevented Jews from studying medicine above certain levels. Those with an inclination to science, like the Ozicks, had to make do with a mortar and pestle.

They had a son in 1922 and Cynthia in 1928, and 2 years later, the family moved to New York City's Pelham Bay area, then "a wilderness with meadows, wildflowers and open spaces." The Ozicks worked long hours in their corner drugstore, rarely returning home until the wee hours of the morning, leaving the children in the trust of their grandmother, who, as fate would have it, was a keen student of the Bible and a woman with a gift for telling stories.

One of the stories Grandmother Ozick told was of how the family came to have its name. It was during the time that Jewish men were forcibly drafted into the Russian army at the age of 4 and made to serve in it until they turned 35. But the tsar's ukase had an ameliorative element: Families with only one son would not have to give up their children. Knowing this, the original Rozicks, a couple with 2 male infants, decided to separate and so make two families with single, undraftable sons. One "family" removed the R from the front of their name; such was the genesis of the Ozick line.

Cynthia Ozick's was a classic Depression childhood. Though comfortable enough, the family lived a frugal, austere life. Ozick's greatest pleasure was the library truck that passed through her neighborhood from time to time. The librarian would pull up, cast boxes of children's books out on the ground, and Ozick would scramble through the mud to pick out the volumes she would inhabit that week.

She grew up thinking that she was slow and "profoundly inferior." She remembers being punished for her quiet refusal to sing religious Christmas carols in the school choir. P.S. 71 was not a welcoming place for a skinny, frightened, Jewish girl.

She applied and got into Hunter College High School by the skin of her teeth—getting coached in math in order to make the grade. Once there, however, she flourished. She wrote incessantly, becoming "the editor of everything in sight." It was during her senior year there (1945–1946) that she learned of events that would color her thinking forever: the news about the Nazi death camps.

But it wasn't war or politics that lured her. She was "too deep in the id" for that. Literature was what she craved, and plumbing the human calamities that make it.

At New York University she entered an English honors program that had only one other student, whom she never saw. She consumed huge lists of reading in utter isolation—everything from Beowulf to Wordsworth. Her thesis was on Blake, Shelley and Coleridge.

By 1949 she was a teaching assistant at Ohio State University, doing detailed research work on Henry James's correspondence and writing *Mercy, Pity, Peace and Love*, a sprawling "attempt at a Jamesian novel" that devoured 7 years of her life. She eventually returned to Pelham Bay, married a law student and set up house under her parents' roof.

By 1958, when she and her lawyer husband were on their own, Ozick decided to set the gargantuan novel aside and start a novella. Eight years later that "momentary diversion" became her first published novel, *Trust*.

Since then she has slipped from genre to genre, blithely unwilling to believe that a true belle lettrist need limit herself to any one.

Her play, *Blue Light*, was produced off-Broadway in 1994. In it, slick talkers try to convince a death camp survivor—whose baby was torn from her arms, dashed against a fence and electrocuted—that the Holocaust never happened. They tell her that she must learn to be skeptical about "history"; that the world would be a better place if we forgot the whole thing. The play may be a different medium for Ozick, but it is a theme she has explored before, especially in *The Shawl*, and she finds the challenge of the play format exhilarating.

"I am a literary obsessive," she says firmly. "I believe a writer can weave in and out of genres—do it all. It is a gluttonous point of view, to be sure. Then again, when it comes to writing, that is what I truly am and nothing less: a glutton."

M. A.

On Being a Novice Playwright

BY CYNTHIA OZICK

I remember precisely the moment I knew I wanted to write a play: It was in an out-of-the-way theater, the Promenade, on Broadway in the '70s, somewhere in the middle of the second act of *The Common Pursuit*, a melancholic comedy by the British playwright Simon Gray. The play was a send-up of the passionate Cambridge cenacle attached to *Scrutiny*, that fabled literary periodical presided over by F. R. Leavis, an eminent critic of 40 years ago; it followed the rise and fall and erotic history of its madly literary protagonists from cocky youth to sour middle age. Madly literary myself, I sat electrified in the seductive dark of the Promenade, flooded by an overpowering wish: Some day!

And I remember precisely the moment I discovered the first sinister fumes brewed up by those liars and obfuscators who dare to term themselves "revisionists," but are more accurately named Holocaust deniers. It was the late summer of 1961. My husband and I had just rented an apartment in a building so new that the fresh plaster, not yet fully dried, was found to be congenial to a repulsive army of moisture-seeking insects rather prettily called silverfish. How to rid ourselves of this plague? Off we went to the town library, to look for a book on household infestation. The helpful volume we hit on happened to be translated, and very nicely so, from the German. It recommended a certain gas with a record of remarkable success in the extermination of vermin. An asterisk led to a slyly impassive footnote at the bottom of the page, utterly deadpan and meanly corrupt: "Zyklon B, used during the Second World War."

How the delectable theatrical dark came to be entangled with the dark of Zyklon B, the death-camp gas, I can hardly fathom; but when, after years of feeling unready, I did finally undertake to write a play, it turned out to be tempestuously and bitterly political—nothing in the least like that dream of literary laughter the Promenade had inspired long before. Its salient theme was Holocaust denial: a trap contrived out of cunning, deceit and wicked surprise. Yet a not inconsequential literary issue has from the start stuck to the outer flanks of my play, and continues to dog it: the ill-humored question of the playwright's credentials.

I brought it on myself, as people say: After all, it is one thing to go about, as I have, satirizing oneself as an Elderly Novice, and another thing to be taken at one's word. The adjective stands incorrigibly—all these white hairs. But the noun? Without making much of a reputational dent in my own generation—nobody's household name—I have nevertheless been publishing stories, novels, poems and essays for nearly 4 full decades. So I seized on "novice" with a zealot's teasing glee: Here was an untried genre, a fresh form, a dive into difference. And more: that mysterious hiatus in the dark, that secret promissory drawing of breath just before the stage lights brighten.

Of course there is nothing new in a writer's crossing from one form into another; no one is startled, or aggrieved, by a novelist turned essayist, or by a poet who ventures into fiction. The radical divide is not in the writer, but in the mode, and mood, of reception.

Reading is the expression of a profound social isolation. As in getting born or dying, you are obliged to do it alone; there is no other way. Theater—like religion, its earliest incarnation—is a communal rite. Study a row of faces transfixed in unison by a scene on a stage, and you will fall into a meditation on anatomical variety irradiated by a kind of dramaturgical monotheism: the infusion of a single godly force into so many pairs of luminously staring eyes.

Theater is different from fiction, yes; but neither is a novice the same as an amateur. An amateur worships—is glamorized by—the trappings of an industry, including the excitements of being "inside." Theater industry (or call it, as anthropologists nowadays like to do, theater culture), with all its expertise, protocol, hierarchy, jargon, tradition, its existential hard knocks and heartbreak, its endemic optimism and calloused cynicism, its experience with audiences, its penchant for spectacle, still cannot teach a writer the writer's art—which is not on the stage, but in the ear and in the brain. Though a novice playwright will certainly be attentive to "technique," to "know-how," real apprenticeship is ultimately always to the self; a writer's lessons are ineluctably internal. As a beginning novelist long ago, I learned to write dialogue not in a fiction workshop ruled by a sophisticated "mentor," but by reading Graham Greene's *The Heart of the Matter* over and over again. There were uncanny reverberations in those short, plain sentences, and a peculiarly suspenseful arrest of a character's intent. The perfected work was the mentor.

Let me not arrogantly misrepresent. There is plenty for an uninitiated playwright to learn from the living air of a reading, a rehearsal, a developing performance in the theater itself; and from an actor's cadence or lift of the eyelid; and from an impassioned talk with a seasoned playwright (and no one is more openly generous than lifelong playwrights, who are a band of mutually sympathizing cousins); and above all from a trusted and trusting director who recognizes the writer as writer. Besides, a novelist's perspective is hardly akin to a playwright's. Novels are free to diverge, to digress, to reflect, to accrete. Proust is a gargantuan soliloquizer. Tolstoy encompasses whole histories. George Eliot pauses for psychological essays. A novel is like the physicist's premise of an expanding universe—horizon after horizon, firmament sailing past firmament. But a play is just the reverse: the fullness of the universe drawn down into a single succinct atom—the all-consuming compactness and density of the theorist's black hole. Everything converges in the dot that is the stage. A novelist seeking to become a playwright will uncover new beauty—structure and concision; the lovely line of the spine and the artfully integrated turn of each vertebra.

Yet always a gauntlet is thrown down before the newcomer playwright (especially one who has arrived from the famously sequestered craft of fiction), and that is the many-fingered image of "collaboration." I want to say quickly—against all the power and authority of theatrical magnates and magi, against the practice and conviction of all those who know more and better than an uninformed interloper like myself—that the term "collaboration," as I have heard it used again and again, is a fake, a fib and a sham. The truth stands clarified: No matter what the genre, a writer is necessarily an autonomous, possessed and solitary figure generating furies. Imagination is a self-contained burning, a fire that cannot be fed from without. The idea of a "collaborative art" is an idea out of Oz—that is, it supplies you with a phony wizard haranguing into a megaphone. No one can claim ascendancy over a writer's language or imagination, and anyone who tries—and succeeds—is an invader, an editor or just a run-of-the-mill boss. Writers cloutless and consequently docile will likely acquiesce but what will come out of it is what editors and bosses always get: something edited, something obliging. An artificial voice. A dry wadi where the heart of a river might have roiled. In the name of a putative collaborative art, a novice playwright (even if an old hand as a writer) will be manipulated by the clever, patronized by the callow, humiliated by the talentless. Generations of clichés will pour down. To become master over a writer is not, as it happens, to become a master of writing.

But if the notion of a collaborative art is simply an authoritarian fiction, the experience of skills in collaboration is the rapt and gorgeous joy of theater—the confluence of individual artists, each conceptually and temperamentally singular. The brainy director's orchestral sensibility; the actors' transformative magickings (a gesture over nothingness will build you the most solid phantom table conceivable); dramatic sculptures hewn of purest light; inklings sewn into a scene by the stitch of a tiny sound; a dress that is less a costume than a wise corroboration; a set that lands you unerringly in the very place you need to be; and the sine qua non of the producers' endlessly patient acts of faith—all these carry their visionary plenitude. The novice playwright (and the veteran, too, I believe), will fall on her knees in gratitude.

To return to the matter of credentials. A bird can fly over any continent you choose; it's the having wings that counts. A writer can be at home in novel, story, essay or play; it's the breathing inside a blaze of words that counts. However new to theater culture, a writer remains exactly that—the only genuine authority over the words and the worlds they embody.

January 15, 1995

Gloria Naylor

"I am a black female writer and I have no qualms whatsoever with people saying that I'm a black female writer. What I take umbrage with is the fact that some might try to use that identity—that which is me—as a way to ghettoize my material and my output. I am female and black and American. No buts are in that identity. Now you go off and do the work to somehow broaden yourself so you understand what America is really about. Because it's about me."

So said Gloria Naylor in the PBS series on African-American culture *I'll Make Me a World*, and it fairly sums up her dismay at the marginalization of black literature by America's mainstream. Yet few have done more than this writer to make the culture of black America live on a page. With 5 published novels to her name, Naylor has taken firm ground in African-American letters, and, as her essay suggests, she is eager to stake out new ways to give life to her craft.

She was born in New York City in 1950, but she claims her writer's heart "was conceived" in Robinsonville, Miss., where her parents once worked as sharecroppers. Her mother had little education but loved to read. In a brief speech that *Book World* printed in 2000, Naylor characterized her mother's love of books as so intense that she worked extra hours in the fields to earn enough to join a mail-order book club. (Libraries in the South would not admit blacks at the time.) When her mother encouraged her to read, Naylor listened. And when her mother handed her a journal and urged her to write down her 12-year-old's thoughts, she took the advice.

The family moved to Queens in 1963, and shortly thereafter Naylor's mother became a Jehovah's Witness. Five years later, Naylor followed. The missionary work nudged her out of a natural shyness and forced her to travel and meet people, but it also sealed her into a hermetic world, where she remained unaware of the boom of black literature that was exploding around her. When, in time, she left the Witnesses disillusioned and anxious about the world she felt was passing her by, she began full-time work as a switchboard operator. In off hours, she studied writing at Medgar Evers and Brooklyn Colleges. She will say that it was in 1977, when she read Toni Morrison's *The Bluest Eye*, the first book she'd ever read by an African-American woman, that she was suddenly suffused with hope. She began to see the possibility of spinning tales about what she knew, to conceive of herself as a real writer. When she submitted a short story to *Essence* magazine, the editor convinced her she had a career.

Naylor finished her first novel, *The Women of Brewster Place*, a heart-wrenching story of seven women in a seedy urban neighborhood, just as she began graduate work at Yale. When it was published in 1983, it won rapid fame. Five years later it was made into a movie starring Oprah Winfrey. Naylor has followed that success with more novels about love and survival in America: *Linden Hills* (1985), *Mama Day* (1988), *Bailey's Cafe* (1992) and, most recently, *The Men of Brewster Place* (1998). Apocalypse, morality, transcendence, redemption—echoes, perhaps, of her days as a Witness—are what take center stage in her novels. But it is racism and politics that lurk in the wings.

She has reason for this. To be black in America, according to her, is a political construct. Just as it took time to feel she had a voice, she says, "we have yet to feel within this country that we are home."

M. A.

Acting Out, Letting Go

By Gloria Naylor

When I first conceived of my fourth novel, *Bailey's Cafe*, it was a different experience from the others. I was haunted by a vision of a lone man on stage playing the saxophone. When this image refused to vanish, I took it to mean that this material was to serve me for both a novel and a play. I was a bit daunted by the fact that I had never written a play, but I also knew you don't tamper with the call of the muse.

My first order of business was the novel, a path I had walked down before in the bliss—and agony—of solitude. In about a year *Bailey's Cafe*, the novel, was completed. It was a mystical place, set on the margin between the end of the world and infinite possibility. Each character had a chapter and a reason for stumbling into this cafe, which was their last chance to gain redemption or a byway for them to go hurtling off the end of the world. They all came singing the blues, which gave me the structure of the novel and—I thought gleefully—the structure for the play. (I was still gleeful at this point.)

I sat down and wrote the first draft of the play, which was given a reading at Lincoln Center. The assistant art director for the Hartford Stage Company was at that reading, and we agreed to have the world premiere at his theater. The play would need revisions, of course, which I acknowledged eagerly; I knew all about revisions, didn't I? I did them all the time, after all. A novelist's life is mostly revisions. But what I hadn't counted on was "other people" having a part—a lot of other people. Bringing the page to the stage was a process that I simply couldn't do alone—a lesson I was to learn slowly, and sometimes painfully for all involved.

A novelist's life is a solitary one. You work in a universe that, for lack of a better metaphor, makes you God; and there are no sidekicks, no archangels or seraphim to send out on duties to help with the creation. If a novel was analogous to a play, I was the director, the actors, the set designers and even the wardrobe mistress. I provided the music and lights, if need be. You learn that in creating a new world from raw space it's all on your shoulders, and in the beginning you play to an audience of one. This can be both exhilarating and frightening, but the bottom line is control. And I wasn't aware of how much of a controller I was until I embarked on the road to becoming a playwright.

Auditions were fun and just like the movies, I thought. You sit behind a long table with the director and watch a bevy of talented people parade before you as you try to match the characters in your head with the actor that's standing before you. It was like playing with dolls, live dolls, who only wanted to please you. With the cast finally assembled, we began rehearsing. I can't remember if the rehearsal period was 4 weeks or 6 weeks; it all melds in my head as one long night when I returned to my studio apartment in Hartford, chained to my laptop until the early hours of the morning, "fixing" things. If the actor stumbled over a line, I fixed it; if the director wanted more drama in a scene, I fixed it; if the dramaturge found an interchange too long, there I was, at night, fixing it.

It never occurred to me to allow some of these issues to just rest and have the other players in this game smooth out those rough edges. If there was a problem, the whole world depended on me to make it right. And so there I was the next morning with laptop in tow and disk in hand, with new revisions. A few things encouraged me in all this excess. One, the playwright is the final word in repertory theater, and holds a great deal of weight even in commercial theater. When I came to rehearsals with new scenes, the actors discarded everything they'd done previously and read those scenes. Which leads me to Number 2, the instant gratification: whatever I wrote at night was realized within hours right before me. No waiting months or even years for feedback as when you're writing a novel. No, here was a captive audience—and captive they were, as I drove everybody crazy, even during preview week. I wrote a whole new beginning and ending with only 2 days left before opening night.

I realize that what I was trying to ward off was the inevitable. I could not control the outcome of this process with just words. And all the other players could not control it either. The actors could act, the director could direct, the set designer and the wardrobe designer and lighting specialist could all do what they had to do, but no one person could make "it" happen: The play's the thing, a much more experienced playwright than myself once wrote, and indeed it was. And what was even more frightening was the fact that the play, once it was shined and polished, still needed an audience to be complete. Four hundred more participants in this drama that I could not control.

But why was this any different from writing a novel? I'm experienced enough to understand that you reach a point in writing a novel when you're no longer in the driver's seat. The book takes on a life of its own, and characters can stubbornly refuse to do what you want them to. It's part of the magic of creation. But I think that, way deep down, I know that it all still hangs on me. I'm the last one left holding the bag. With the theater I'm only the first one with the goods, and they have to be given into many other hands to be realized. And while I can "fix" a paragraph or a page, or even a whole chapter, there is nothing I can fix once that theater begins to fill with people. It was like being in free fall; you're in the front seat of the roller coaster, it's the apex of the 90-foot drop, and down you go. Your stomach gives way, your head gives way, and wonder of wonders, you're flying. (I have always hated even the idea of roller coasters.) So I spent the rehearsal period cognizant only of the drop, the helplessness of being 90 feet in the air with only a laptop between me and all sorts of imagined disasters. It took opening night to bring me back to the wonder of it all.

There is little like the excitement of opening night. Expectation is thick in the air; the empty stage pulses with the promise of unimagined possibilities as you await the arrival of the last—and most important—players in your drama: the audience. True, on opening night the audience contains a disproportionate number of your family and friends; you can only hope enough of them owe you money so that they will be kind. But they all become part of the faceless mass as the lights in the theater dim and the humming of hundreds of voices becomes a hush. And so it begins, the play. And as the action progresses, there is nothing so sweet as hearing an audience laugh in the places they're supposed to, be quiet and moved in others. Their energy spurs on the actors, who rise to the occasion to return that energy to the audience. What's no longer just my words but rather its own entity—its own creation—unfolds before my eyes and ears. At that moment I finally come to understand what it would be like to enter the heads of hundreds of readers as they move through my novel; it's there and up-front. And on that night I fall in love with a new way to use my power with words. Not the end-all, but the engine that carries hundreds of people on the road to a new type of magic.

October 29, 2000

Donald E. Westlake

In the late '60s, the literary agent Henry Morrison held a weekly poker game for a revolving table of authors. He called it "Hack," Henry's Active Clients. To get in, you were asked to make a list of all the works you'd ever published. If you could list them, you'd be shown the nearest exit. Suffice it to say, Donald E. Westlake not only made it into Hack, he claims to be its charter member. No one, least of all Westlake himself, could possibly remember everything he's written—under any one of his names.

How many books has he published? "I'd guess 70 or so," he says. The truth is, he hasn't counted. At the age of 69, the grandmaster of mystery boasts more novels than years of life on this planet.

He was the son of a traveling salesman and a clerk-typist in post-Depression Albany. The boy grew up a reader, loving stories far more than the grim realities of the day. "But I kept thinking the books I read followed the wrong story line," he says. He found himself wanting to follow the minor characters. The frustration was impetus enough to make him grow up and write.

"I wanted to be Dashiell Hammett. *The Thin Man* was like nothing I'd ever read. Nothing happens on the surface. Everything happens underneath. The main character was once a private investigator; he isn't any more. He's lost it—would rather not think about it. I loved that underwater feel. Hammett makes you feel you're looking down into something. Nabokov does it, too. Anyone can make a guy go into a room and pull a gun. But to make a reader feel as if he's seeing something he's not supposed to—now that's something."

Westlake never completed college. He credits his high school English teacher, Sister Mary Carmel, with giving him the best advice a writer could have. "'Use active verbs,' she said. "Nobody just walks in. They slink in, stride in, scurry."

He joined the Air Force at 19, served in Germany in the early '50s, worked in New York as a "slush-pile reader" for the Scott Meredith agency. When he placed his first science fiction story in a magazine, Westlake celebrated by taking 204 rejection slips down from his wall. When he convinced Random House to take his first novel, he began a career as one of the most popular writers in America.

"I write from 10 at night to 4 in the morning," he says, "about 7,000 words at a time. It's like being in the basket of a blimp, working at that hour. It's wonderful. There's just one little room with me in it, and I'm sailing through the night wherever the story will go. Just me, alone."

Oh, and Richard Stark, too. And Curt Clark, and Tucker Coe, and Timothy J. Culver. All the writers, in other words, that Westlake has ever been.

M. A.

Pen Names Galore

BY DONALD E. WESTLAKE

There are several reasons for publishing under a pen name, and I, a frequent fighter under colors not my own, have at one time or another done so for most of those reasons.

The first and most obvious is concealment, either because you're writing something of which you're not proud, or because contractual obligations keep you from publishing here or there, or because the divorce isn't final. (But not to hide from the IRS; they have nom de plume sniffer dogs, I believe.)

I have had, in my writing life, motives of concealment that have led me to pseudonymity and that I do not intend to discuss. You do understand.

Fictitious names on one's fiction can also be caused by fecundity.

In my earliest writing years I madly loved writing (I still do but more calmly now), and as is usual with new lovers I wanted to do it all the time. I was writing lots of short stories then, but magazines frown on the idea of running more than one piece under the same name in the same issue. So I flung all kinds of monikers on the excess, in order to have 2 or even 3 stories published in a clump. The editors knew all these people were me but didn't care, just as long as the bylines were different. I remember one of them was published as being by James Blue, my cat at the time.

Another reason for anonyms is what I think of as the General Motors strategy. You can tell the difference between a Chevrolet and a Cadillac, or at least you used to be able to, even though you know they're both really by General Motors. The company's most successful recent use of this nom de commerce approach has been the Saturn.

Writers do the same thing, use a second name to let the potential reader know what sort of book is on offer here. My friend Evan Hunter, for instance, is Ed McBain when he wants you to know he's writing a police procedural.

The first of my alter egos to have any staying power was created for this reason. It was 1961, I was publishing 1 hardcover mystery novel a year with Random House, and I was throwing off short stories like sparks from a pinwheel, but it wasn't enough.

I decided I'd like to write some paperback originals as well, preferably for Gold Medal, at the time the cream of that crop. I intended to use a very lean, emotion-free prose to produce a book that would be both tough and laconic. To remind myself what I was up to, I decided that the pseudonym's last name should be Stark, like the writing. For the first name, I kept thinking of Tommy Udo, the cold killer played by Richard Widmark in his astonishing debut in *Kiss of Death*. "It is clear," James Agee wrote, "that murder is one of the kindest things he's capable of." Tommy Stark sounded wrong; too English or something. Udo Stark sounded Martian. What the hell; I became Richard Stark.

Richard Stark wrote a hardboiled novel about revenge, robbery, murder, betrayal and stuff like that. I think some of the characters even wore fur. The lead was also the villain, so nasty and cold-blooded I didn't even bother to give him a first name. Parker, I called him, and *The Hunter* I called the book, and at its end the police gathered Parker up and took him away forever.

The first thing that happened in Richard Stark's nascent career was that Gold Medal rejected the book he'd written for it. This was disconcerting. However, Pocket Books, no fly-by-nighter either, took *The Hunter* on, and a grand editor there named Bucklin Moon called me to ask, "Is it possible for Parker to escape at the end, and you could give me 3 books a year about him?"

Three books a year! I could stop writing short stories! (Which I almost did.) That pace did soon slacken, naturally (q.v. "new lovers," above), but still, over the next 12 years, Richard Stark did write 20 novels, 16 of them about Parker, who never did get a first name, and 4 about an associate of Parker's (he doesn't have friends) named Grofield, first name Alan.

From the outset, Richard Stark did very well. He wrote more than I did, got more fan mail, and by the end of the '60s he was earning more, principally because the movies got interested. In 1967, that first Stark novel became one of the seminal movies of our time, *Point Blank*. Not bad for a 25-cent paperback whose anti-hero was supposed to have been carted off to prison at the end of what was to have been his only appearance in print.

But here at last we come to the downside of pen names. (There's always a downside to everything, have you noticed?) *Point Blank* was a big hit and became the critics' darling, but any time I wanted to bask in the reflected glory I first had to go through this explanation: You see, well, Richard Stark, in fact, that's me. No, honest.

More movies were made, some like *Point Blank* to make me rue the pseudonym, others to make me grateful for it, and then, in 1973, Richard Stark the author, if not the motion-picture source, dried up.

Why that happens, why a writer can suddenly no longer do what was easy or at least possible yesterday, no one knows, but when it occurs it isn't pleasant. I tried to return to Parker several times, but every attempt was poor pastiche, the work of some fourth-rate imitator, so finally I gave it up.

At which point, the General Motors strategy showed its versatility. My own name was getting better known by now, as Mr. Stark faded into history, so when Avon decided to reissue the Parker novels in the mid-'80s they asked if they might use my name as well as Stark's on the books, and I agreed. After all, Stark was never going to write again.

And then, a couple years ago, he came back. I hate to sound like an idiot savant here, with no control over or understanding of my own oeuvre, but in fact the ability to think and write like Richard Stark went away and then came back, 23 years later.

Actually, Richard Stark did do some writing in those years; it's just that he didn't write about Parker, so he didn't get to use his name. When I wrote the screenplay for *The Grifters* from Jim Thompson's gritty novel, the director Stephen Frears insisted that Stark had done the job and wanted Richard Stark to be the writing credit. I had to point out that Richard Stark wasn't a member of the Writer's Guild. Since I was, I couldn't very well permit Stark to scab.

But now, with the return of Stark, the General Motors strategy is complete. The pen name is on the book, but it conceals nothing. It merely says, "This is Westlake when he's writing about Parker." Which is also nice because the movies' interest has returned as well. That first Parker novel, filmed as *Point Blank* in 1967, has just been made as a movie again, this time as *Payback* with Mel Gibson. And this time I can bask without explanations.

Fifteen years ago, I found yet another reason to John Doe it. I think it's fairly common for people in the creative world who've had some success to wonder if they could do it all over again. The world changes; if I were starting now, what would happen?

I decided to try a new style and a new name with a new publisher, just to see what would happen. The publisher agreed to keep silent about this writer's identity, but, when the time came, he reneged. There was a brief period when the new writer was out there on his own, during which he got some nice reviews and a movie option, but then the publisher's double-dealing put an end to the experiment. And the pseudonym.

I've had other General Motors names, but once I hid myself because the book was just too silly. It was a paperback from New American Library, meant to be a parody of Arthur Hailey-type extravaganzas (*Airport*, *Hotel*), and it was called *Comfort Station*. Set in the men's room in Bryant Park next to the main library on 42nd Street in New York, it was written by "the vibrant J. Morgan Cunningham," and in conjunction with it I got to do something almost no writer has ever achieved. On the cover it said, "I wish I had written this book.—Donald Westlake."

May 2, 1999

Barbara Mertz

Chances are you've never heard of Washington writer Barbara Mertz—a surprising lapse, since her Amelia Peabody mysteries and gothic romances have been popular summer reading for 3 decades running. Amazon.com credits more than 350 entries to her name.

Ah, perhaps not to her name exactly. Mertz is the engine behind two popular pseudonyms: Elizabeth Peters and Barbara Michaels. Under cover, she publishes 2 novels a year.

As Elizabeth Peters, she writes archaeological mysteries set in Edwardian-age Egypt, featuring the spunky, meddlesome Amelia Peabody: among them, *The Last Camel Died At Noon*; *The Snake, The Crocodile and the Dog*; *He Shall Thunder in the Sky*; *The Lord of the Silent* and, most recently, *The Golden One*.

As Barbara Michaels, her more lucrative persona, she is known for a singular brand of romance that interlaces suspense with the supernatural: *Into the Darkness*; *Ammie, Come Home* (Barbara Stanwyck starred in the film version, *The House That Wouldn't Die*); *Shattered Silk*.

Under the name Mertz, she has published only serious nonfiction: *Temples, Tombs and Hieroglyphs* and *Red Land, Black Land: Daily Life in Ancient Egypt*.

She is an Egyptologist with a Ph.D. from the University of Chicago. Her mother was a schoolteacher; her father, a printer. Born in 1927 in the tiny town of Astoria, Ill., she credits 4 big reasons for choosing to write the way she does: a lifelong obsession with mummies; a childhood compulsion to shoulder large bags from the library; simple boredom; and, fourth, a divorce—an overnight catapult into single motherhood. When, at almost 40, she looked around for work she might do, stories were her only stock in trade.

"There are lots of connections," she says, "between Egyptologist and mystery writer—it takes a certain kind of mind. You have to love puzzles, love a treasure hunt." As for the romance writing, she has been known to say that if she's going to fantasize, she might as well go all the way: with pretty heroines and knee-knocking adventure. "Honestly, honey," she tells me, "I couldn't write a straight novel if I tried. I wouldn't have the audacity to write about angst."

M. A.

Summer Lite

By Barbara Mertz

I've never understood why summer reading should be different from winter, spring and fall reading. For those of us who have been hooked on books since childhood, there are few pleasures to compare with reading. It's an obsession, a compulsion, an addiction. We do it all the time—winter and summer, day and night.

Summer is the time when our bodies relax and go on holiday; the implication seems to be that our brains should do the same. Even admitting that this is the case, is it permissible only after the summer solstice? It seems to me that we need relaxation and entertainment even more in winter, when the winds howl and we suffer from colds, flu, light-deprivation and the bitter knowledge that we won't see a daffodil for months.

Still, I know what people mean by summer reading. Light reading. Popular fiction. Books that don't tax the mental processes. Fluff. Fun reading. The kind of books some people hide behind copies of Proust so they won't be accused of being lowbrows.

The kind of books I write.

As a writer of popular fiction, I don't resent the implication that my books are read for pleasure rather than for edification. What I resent is the implication that the two goals are incompatible, and that "summer reading" is enjoyed only by those who keep their brains in first gear. What is the definition of pleasure anyhow? I don't derive pleasure from descriptions of autopsies, the handiwork of depraved serial killers or the interminable angst of adolescents. On the other hand, I rather like mummies. Chacun à son gout.

However, I read about mummies for edification as well as for pleasure. I have written about mummies a lot, in two nonfiction books about ancient Egypt and in my series about a turn-of-the (last) century family of Egyptologists. The Amelia Peabody mysteries are funny (so I've been told), romantic, replete with wild adventures—and, of course, mummies. Popular fiction they certainly are, but any man who calls them fluff does so at his peril. I work too hard on those books to accept that put-down. Since they are historical mysteries, the events of the period must be accurately described. In the course of the series, I have researched the history of Egyptology, the nationalist movement in Egypt, the women's movement in England and Egypt, World War I (campaigns, weapons, uniforms) and a dozen other subjects that mercifully escape me for the moment. I even read *Seven Pillars of Wisdom*. Well . . . not all of it. Has anyone in this generation actually read all 650 pages' worth of Lawrence's somewhat overblown prose? (That's T. E. Lawrence, of Arabia, not D. H.)

Luckily for me, I enjoy doing research like this. Even if I didn't, my readers would insist I get my facts right. Their brains operate at full speed, winter and summer, and they are alarmingly well informed. No matter how esoteric the subject, one of them is bound to know more about it than I do, and if I make a mistake, I hear about it. I once placed my archaeologist family at one of the most obscure sites in Egypt. I make a point of visiting all the places I describe, even though many of them have changed beyond recognition in the past century;

but this time I cheated. I had not been to Mazghuna. I didn't particularly want to go to Mazghuna. So far as I knew, no archaeologist had been at the cursed place for years.

Two weeks after the book was published, I received a polite letter from a polite colleague politely informing me that my description of the terrain was not entirely accurate. He'd been there.

The point is that some, at least, of the books labeled light reading or popular fiction can be as solid and informative as works of nonfiction. (Yes, I slipped up on Mazghuna. To err is human.) I read biographies, memoirs and histories of the period about which I write, but I also read the contemporary novels—the popular fiction of the time. In some ways they give a more accurate impression of how people lived and felt and thought than do scholarly tomes—and they are usually much more entertaining. Some of these novels, former bestsellers, have held up amazingly well. Dated they may be, but then so am I. Buchan and Haggard, Anthony Hope and Sax Rohmer have provided me with many hours of informative entertainment—and, to be honest, a few ideas. (I have no scruples about borrowing a good idea. It's not plagiarism. Honestly. The books in question are out of copyright.)

I've been asked by interviewers whether I have ever considered writing a "serious" book. I never hit any of these amiable souls with my machete, because they mean it as a compliment (I think). But the answer is that all my books are serious. It's hard enough to fill 600-plus pages with words that are correctly spelled and make sense. (Don't tell me about Spellcheck; mine irritably rejects words like "canopic" and allows me to substitute "their" for "there.") Inventing believable characters, creating a convincing background, and tying all the plot strands into a nice, neat knot in the last chapter are serious business.

Sometimes the hardest part is deciding not what to put in but what to leave out. One is sorely tempted, especially in historical fiction, to beat the reader over the head with one's erudition. "I really know a lot about this subject; see how clever I am?" The writer has to ask herself how much information the reader needs, and take care not to show off. As for plot, it is nothing more nor less than a story—a narrative, held together by logical sequence and believable motivation. But if you think it sounds easy, take a closer look at those two adjectives—"logical" and "believable"—and give me a logical reason for a heroine to go off by herself in the middle of the night to a lonely spot in the desert when she knows there is a murderer on the loose.

I can't think of one either. But I've had a lot of fun trying.

We writers of pop fiction have one advantage over our more respectable colleagues, though. "Serious literature" carries its own cachet; some people buy and read such books to impress their friends, or because they've been told they will improve their minds. On the other hand, those who read our books do so because they want to, not because they ought.

I no longer read to improve my mind. I figure it's probably about as good as it's ever going to get. Some of the books I read are purely for research. I mean, who could really relax with a box of chocolates and a volume entitled *British Military Intelligence in the Palestine Campaign, 1914–1918* or *Mastabas of Cemetery G6000*? But when I settle down on a cold winter's night or a hot summer afternoon (probably with that box of chocolates), I choose a book that won't do a damned thing for me except provide entertainment. It could be anything from *Harry Potter* to Terry Pratchett to Jane Austen (for the umpteenth time) to Durrell's Alexandria Quartet or Mary Renault's *The Last of the Wine* or Isak Dinesen's *Out of Africa*. Or something about mummies.

Storyteller is an ancient and honorable title. Far be it from me to suggest that only we writers of lowbrow fiction deserve it, but deserve it we do, and the proof is found in the letters we get from readers telling us that our tales have given them enough pleasure to let them forget, if only for a few hours, that something in their lives has gone badly wrong—a painful illness, a nasty divorce, the death of a loved one, despair, depression. I can conceive of no higher compliment. Temporary escape from a reality too painful to bear isn't cowardice; it is needed respite. And even if your reality isn't so bad, what's wrong with a little fun? Enjoy your summer reading without repining or apologizing. I would be happy to recommend a good book about mummies.

June 17, 2001

V

Facing the Facts

David Halberstam

Dominick Dunne

Tracy Kidder

Carl Sagan

George P. Shultz

Jimmy Carter

Stacy Schiff

Kay Redfield Jamison

Jonathan Raban

E. O. Wilson

Bill McKibben

David Halberstam

There is a pioneer's intensity in David Halberstam—a tireless will to push on, stretch out; a hunter's sense for the hidden fragility in things that claim power; an eye for seeing large cities where others only see stones. He is the author of 16 books, among them his Pulitzer Prize-winning *The Best and the Brightest* (1972) about the Vietnam War; *The Powers That Be* (1979), about the American media establishment; *The Reckoning* (1986), a dual history of the Ford and Nissan companies; and *Summer of '49* (1990), a paean to American baseball. These are big books in every way: fat bestsellers fashioned from mountains of accumulated detail, hearty slices of big-picture America. Halberstam's book, *The Fifties*, published just before he submitted this essay, is no less in scope. A massive cultural history of the decade, it seeks to trace the roots of our current national psyche and explain how we have become what we are today. Since then, he has written *October 1964* (1994) , *War in a Time of Peace* (2001) and *Firehouse* (2002).

Born in New York City in 1934, Halberstam was the grandson of a Hassidic rabbi and the son of an itinerant army doctor. He graduated from high school in 1951 and went on to Harvard, where he became the editor of the *Crimson*. Upon graduation in 1955, he headed South, attracted by the issues of social conscience abrew there. As a *Nashville Tennesseean* reporter for 4 years, he covered civil-rights stories, among them the case of Emmett Till, the 14-year-old black boy who was murdered because he whistled at a white woman. Halberstam concedes now that, although he reported it, he did not comprehend the historical force of that story until many years later. Not until he sat down to address it in *The Fifties*.

In 1960 he was recruited by the *New York Times* and shipped out to the Congo. Within a year he was reporting from Vietnam, writing front-page pieces that claimed the war was "on its way to becoming a first-class failure." Halberstam's pessimism led President Kennedy to approach the *New York Times* to ask for his recall. Halberstam stayed in Vietnam but eventually returned to the United States in 1964 to report on civil-rights developments in Mississippi. In 1966 he became the *Times* correspondent in Poland, but he was expelled shortly thereafter for writing that the communist government was a farce—an invisible occupation without roots in Polish soil. Known by now for his inclination to write longer stories, he left the *Times* in l967 for *Harper's* magazine, where he stayed until the publication of *The Best and the Brightest*.

The Fifties, Halberstam says, is as close to autobiography as he will ever come. In it, he has tried to take history one step further, making players out of things and events: the mechanical cotton picker, the birth control pill, the computer, Levittown. "These were all factors of my life and times—I could well have put them into my own story—but I've chosen an exterior rather than an interior stance." As usual, his book is comprehensively reported: It is journalism writ large.

But already, when he wrote the following piece, he was thinking ahead, pushing on. There was a quick book he had in mind about the Yankees and the Cardinals. And then a big one after that: "Did you ever stop to think what became of the young blacks who took part in the sit-ins in the early '60s? The kids who stood up to all the beatings? I was there. I was just a kid reporter myself. I covered them. Well, what became of those people? That's what I want to find out."

M. A.

History Is Their Beat: The New Journalist Historians

BY DAVID HALBERSTAM

In early 1966 when I was stationed for a brief time in Paris for the *New York Times*, I went to dinner with two friends, Sanche de Gramont (later Ted Morgan), who had been my opposite number in both the Congo and Vietnam when he was with the *Herald Tribune*, and Bernard Fall, already surfacing as the leading journalist-historian of the Vietnam War. Like most people who had covered that war, the three of us carried the memory of it with us at all times. That night we went to a Vietnamese restaurant favored by Bernie. Not surprisingly, we spent most of the evening talking about Vietnam, excavating territory we already knew extremely well, searching for even the tiniest truth that we might have missed.

Near the end of the evening, Sanche changed the subject. When 2 years earlier the *Herald Tribune* had begun to move into its terminal stage, he had left to go to work for the *Saturday Evening Post* as a contract writer. Already frustrated with the form of daily journalism, he had decided not to try either the *New York Times* or *The Washington Post*, both of which, I suspect, would have welcomed him; he was self-evidently gifted as a journalist, intellectually superior, absolutely fearless, and had already won the Pulitzer Prize. Eventually he was going to move from magazine writing to full-time book writing, he said that night. Not just books done in his spare time, an extension of his existing journalism, which many of our generation, including me, had already done, but books that were a record of contemporary events—books that would make him in a real sense a historian. Theodore H. White, he noted, was already creating this kind of career.

It was, he said, the most natural of career progressions. Most of us were already restless with the form of journalism and the very definition of what did and what did not constitute news. In addition, those of us who had had good assignments early in our careers would not, he predicted, warm to the idea of returning from tours in Vietnam to cover luncheon meetings in New York. There was a point now where contemporary history and serious journalism intersected, and, increasingly, journalists were beginning to move in the direction of history.

Bernie Fall readily agreed. Indeed, he noted, he was just about to publish a book that as far as he was concerned completely validated what Sanche had said. It was a considerable jump over what he had done in the past—and for the first time he felt more like a historian than a journalist. It was a detailed account of the battle of Dien Bien Phu. He had gone out and interviewed everyone he could who had been a player in that tragic event. The result was a book called *Hell in a Very Small Place*. He was quite excited by the jump he had taken in his own career, and with good reason, for it was by far his best book, and it became a classic with an enduring life of its own. It was the work of a man consumed by an event, a summation of all the years he had invested in Indochina. Tragically he was killed a year later in Vietnam, and other books he mentioned that night, perhaps one about France during World War II, never came to fruition.

What was stunning to me about that night was that Sanche was saying things I was already thinking. By then I had been a daily reporter for some 11 years, 6 of them with the *Times*, and I was almost painfully restless with daily journalism. In addition, back in the United States, contemporaries like Gay Talese and Tom Wolfe were becoming architects of a vibrant and significantly richer nonfiction magazine journalism that broke most of the existing rules of what magazine reporting was supposed to be. In the end they were producing, in quite separate ways, reportage that seemed to have the texture and originality of fiction.

Talese, with a style that I think of as journalism *verité*—staying with his subjects until he caught them in moments of candor, and not as they and their public relations people wanted them defined—was probably the most influential figure of that early breakthrough in nonfiction letters. (Wolfe's work was too idiosyncratic; only fools or geniuses dared think of emulating him.) A generation of young reporters read Talese's work, understood instantly why and how he had broken out of the traditional form, and immediately wanted to emulate him. It was an important moment; in the past, young reporters, restless with what they were doing and wanting to make their names and expand their horizons, had sat around in America's city rooms dreaming of writing the great American novel. Now they sat around and dreamed about the nonfiction books they would one day write. The latter dream was, I suspect, in many cases a great deal closer to possibility than the earlier one.

Within a year I was a contract writer for *Harper's* magazine. On my last day at the *Times*, I remember explaining to Abe Rosenthal, then the paper's chief news executive, why I was leaving—the lament of the reporter restless with the form. The things that interested me, I told him, interested me a lot more than a typical 600-word *Times* story would allow, and the things that did not interest me, did not interest me at all. At *Harper's* I gloried in the greater amount of time and space I had to work on a piece but I remained restless. Three years after the dinner in Paris I cut back my responsibilities at *Harper's* to begin legwork on the book that became *The Best and the Brightest*.

So as Sanche spoke that night, there was a sense of hearing in his words the echo of my own frustrations and ambitions, except that he seemed far more confident about the process and was describing the future in clear intellectual terms. Now, 2-and-a-half decades later, his words seem particularly prophetic. He is Ted Morgan today, having Americanized his name with an anagram, and he has written biographies of Churchill and Roosevelt and Maugham among others (my favorite of his is a book he did on the Beats disguised as a biography of John Burroughs). His most recent work, *Wilderness at Dawn*, is an extremely well-reviewed book on the settlement of the North American continent. As he suggested more than 25 years ago, there has been a dramatic increase in the number and the quality of books of contemporary history or biography by daily and magazine journalists who in many cases left secure jobs in institutional journalism to pursue book ideas that had obsessed them for several years.

There are, I suspect, a number of reasons for the flowering of nonfiction books by writers trained in journalism. The most obvious is the fact that starting in the early- and mid-'50s the young people going into journalism were far better educated than their predecessors. In the postwar years, as America rose to great power and as more and more papers hired more Washington correspondents and foreign correspondents, journalism attracted better-educated reporters to report to better-educated readers. This was to be, though few of us knew it when we entered what was still a poorly paid profession, a media age in which the status and influence of journalists increased exponentially. More, the society was becoming infinitely more affluent in general, and that affluence was being felt in the book business. More people were reading better books, and that meant there was more money for writers than ever before. When I first graduated from college, a freelance writer was usually someone who had to write 5 or 6 pieces he or she did not care about in order to get the money and the time to do the 1 piece that truly mattered. By now that had dramatically changed.

In addition, I think we caught a giant wave which we in no way understood at the time. That wave was the impact, not so much on us, but on our potential audience, of the network news shows. Some of television's impact was obvious: First, that print was no longer the most immediate carrier of news, and that therefore print reporters had to extend their horizons and do things television could not do; and second, that in its hunger for material, television, with its countless early morning and late night news-and-variety shows, was beginning to introduce writers to a large audience, and embellish their careers by making them into (very) minor celebrities on the occasion of the publication of their books. (Soon book publishers, learning that this phenomenon was taking place, took it one step further: In addition to television's taking the nation's writers and turning them into minor pseudo-celebrities, publishers started taking the nation's celebrities, with their greater access to these talk shows, and turning them into minor pseudowriters.)

But what I and most of my colleagues did not entirely understand at the time was the larger effect of television on the society. That was its role in greatly expanding our audience by greatly expanding the interest in public affairs. There, every night in the homes of ordinary people, the most dramatic events of an era were being acted out—first and most obviously, in the civil-rights struggle and soon in Vietnam. People who had not been that interested in public affairs in the past were now hypnotized by what was taking place in their homes. And the viewers were becoming a much better potential audience for book writers.

To understand in the simplest way the effect that television and its capacity to amplify public events had on the book business, it is necessary only to compare the astonishingly rich and diverse shelf of nonfiction books on the Vietnam War with the comparatively thin shelf of books on the Korean War. The Korean War, coming as it did before the revolution in the communication industry, stirred neither publishers to print a great deal about it nor readers to feel they had to know a great deal more about it. It is certainly arguable that this national audience by the late '70s became glazed or at least somewhat blasé, and less interested in serious public affairs as story after story flashed across the screen. But in that first decade and a half of public affairs coverage, the audience remained almost innocent—curious and eager for ever more information.

The writers who came to maturity and benefited from this new interest in public affairs were a diverse group, and generalizations about them can be dangerous. Most of us came from city rooms, and most of us had put at least a decade in our apprenticeships, honing our skills before we left institutional journalism behind. The main skill that the traditional historian brought to contemporary history was an ability to work in the archives. The main skill that the journalist-historian brought to the same field was the ability (and the luxury of time, for we were not burdened by classroom responsibilities) to do an endless number of saturation interviews on our subjects. We had the ability to draw information out of people who were not always eager to talk and the ability to line up interviews sequentially in such a way that each interview helped unlock a succeeding interview. Intuitively we knew where to look. Somehow along the way, we had picked up considerable skills in doing legwork. In my own case I know exactly what happened; I worked on the *Nashville Tennessean* when I was young, and I was well aware that doing legwork was the weakest link in my professional abilities. So I set out quite consciously over a period of 4 years to study those reporters who were our paper's best legmen—to see how and why they were good.

In addition, the city rooms of America were excellent places in which to learn how to improve your writing. Most of us during those long apprenticeships had learned our craft; we knew how to make our work more readable by weaving anecdotes into the narrative and by writing biographical sketches of our principals. We learned the simplest of rules—the better the legwork, the richer it was in detail and anecdote, the better the writing always seemed to be.

America's new affluence made our lives considerably easier. If we had started out with small advances on our books, say, $10,000 in the beginning, then the rewards were there if we persevered. By the time we reached our third or fourth book, we were getting advances—hard- and soft cover—large enough to let us take on one project and stay with it for 4 years or more if need be. It did not mean that we became rich, but it did mean that we had the greatest luxury of the self-employed writer, the time to do the book to our own specifications.

The other thing I think most of us had was an obsession with our subjects. More often than not, our signature books were a carry-over from some subject that had intrigued us back in our days as young reporters. "What is it that makes a bestseller, anyway?" a colleague of mine had once quite brazenly asked Teddy White. White's first book about China's collapse, *Thunder Out of China*, had been a bestseller and contained all of his passionate reporting that Henry Luce had censored and kept out of *Time* and *Life*. White had surprised us both with his answer: "A book that burns in your belly—something that has to be written before you can go on to anything else." What many of us in the early days lacked in professional skills, we made up for with passion. Certainly that was true of me when I started out to write *The Best and the Brightest*. I had already dealt with Vietnam over a period of some 7 years, and the question of how it could have happened, how men who were ostensibly the ablest people to serve in a government in this country could have been the architects of so terrible a disaster, quickly became an obsession.

I had no idea that *The Best and the Brightest* would turn into a considerable commercial success. That seemed unlikely in my opinion and that of my publisher. But I was somehow confident that it would be enough of a success, critical or otherwise, to allow me to get enough money so that I could keep on writing books. That was the real definition of success: the ability to keep on going. Even as I was doing it I had no idea, as Sanche had suggested just a few years earlier, that what was happening with me was typical of what was happening with many others like me—and that we were making the transition from journalism to contemporary history at what was almost the perfect moment.

REPORTERS AS HISTORIANS

Here are some examples I've chosen of former newspaper reporters who have written books that sit comfortably on the history or biography shelf:

- Taylor Branch—*Parting the Waters: America in the King Years* (1988)
- Robert Caro—*The Power Broker: Robert Moses and the Fall of New York* (1974)
- Richard Kluger—*Simple Justice: The History of Brown v. Board of Education and Black America's Struggle for Equality* (1975)
- J. Anthony Lukas—*Common Ground: A Turbulent Decade in the Lives of Three American Families* (1985)
- William Manchester—*American Caesar: Douglas MacArthur* (1978)
- David McCullough—*Truman: A Life* (1992)
- Richard Rhodes—*The Making of the Atomic Bomb* (1987)
- Neil Sheehan—*A Bright, Shining Lie: John Paul Vann and America in Vietnam* (1988)
- Randy Shilts—*And the Band Played On: Politics, People, and the AIDS Epidemic* (1987)
- Bob Woodward and Carl Bernstein—*The Final Days* (1976)

July 4, 1993

Dominick Dunne

"People tell me things," says the protagonist of Dominick Dunne's *A Season in Purgatory*. "They always have." And so it is with Dunne himself, confidant of the upper class, chronicler of their scandals—an American Trollope for our times. "I've been like that all my life," Dunne says. "When I was a child, I would get brought down to meet the dinner guests. The next morning I would say to my mother, 'Did you know that Mrs. So-and-so's husband has been missing for weeks?' 'How do you know that?' she'd say, her mouth wide open. 'Well,' I'd say, 'her best friend told me so last night.' "

A dinner party is still archive and trench for this writer; soirees are to Dunne, according to Truman Capote's biographer Gerald Clarke, "what the plains of Africa were to Hemingway or the bottom country of Mississippi was to Faulkner."

"I'm simply a very good listener," says Dunne. "And listening is an underrated skill. If you really listen—if you're really interested—someone is bound to talk." He has often compared the process to a Catholic confession: "Someone once told me that I looked like a defrocked priest," he says, laughing, "and, well, you know, a priest never says, 'You've got to be kidding,' when a person tells him something awful. Somewhere along the way I learned that."

It is not an image plucked from nowhere. Catholicism has played a large part in Dunne's life. Born into a well-off Irish Catholic family (his brother is John Gregory Dunne, author of *True Confessions* and *Harp*), he grew up in West Hartford, Conn., where to be Catholic was to be marginal indeed. Dunne's grandfather, Dominick Burns, emigrated during the potato famine and took up work as a butcher. By the end of his life, he had made a fortune as the president of a bank and been knighted by the pope. Dunne's father, in turn, was a successful heart surgeon. But the Dunnes continued to live on the periphery of Hartford society—outsiders to its tight circle of moneyed WASPs. Marginalization was grist for Trollope, though, and so it would be for this latter-day novelist of manners and misbehavior.

Dunne never dreamed of being a writer. As a child he put on plays, much to the chagrin of his father, who called him "a sissy" and beat him until his ears turned purple. During his senior year in high school in 1944, 18-year-old Dunne was drafted into the army and fought in the Battle of the Bulge. He won a Bronze Star for bravery.

He returned to attend Williams College and blaze a career in television. He was stage manager first for the *Howdy Doody Show* and then for the *Robert Montgomery Show*. In 1954, Dunne married the daughter of an Arizona rancher. They had two sons, Griffin and Alex, before moving off to Hollywood. There, in the '60s, Dunne produced such films as *The Boys in the Band*, *The Panic in Needle Park* and his sister-in-law Joan Didion's *Play It as It Lays*. There too the Dunnes had a third child, Dominique, who would grow up to play the teenage girl in the movie *Poltergeist*.

By the early 1970s, Dunne says, he was a hopeless alcoholic. His marriage disintegrated. Ostracized for telling too public a joke about a Hollywood power-broker, he left Los Angeles in 1979, heading north until his car broke down in a ramshackle town in Oregon. Six months later he emerged sober with a manuscript under his arm. *The Winners*, his novel about a young actress who is bullied out of town by her agent, was published in 1982. "It was a terrible book," says Dunne. "It deserved to flop." But by then he had a better idea: He embarked on *The Two Mrs. Grenvilles* (1985), a story based on the real-life 1955 murder of millionaire William Woodward Jr. by his chorus-girl wife. During the 4 years it took to write the novel, however, tragedy struck twice: First, his youngest brother committed suicide. Shortly thereafter—and he alludes to this staggering loss in his essay—his daughter Dominique was strangled by her former lover, John Sweeney.

Devastated, Dunne was sharing his sorrow in a friend's kitchen 3 nights before Sweeney's trial, when a young Englishwoman, a guest, turned to him and said that he should write about it. More to the point, he should write about it for her. The woman, Tina Brown, went on to become the editor of *Vanity Fair*, and Dunne's piece about the trial and sentence, "Justice," ran in her debut issue of that magazine. It became a book by the same title in 2001. Eventually Dunne covered other trials for *Vanity Fair*: Alfred Bloomingdale's mistress's (on whom *An Inconvenient Woman* (1990) is based), Claus von Bulow's, the Menendez brothers', and William Kennedy Smith's, to name a few. Several became books.

In 1986 his daughter's murderer was released after serving 2-and-a-half years. For a time, Dunne and his sons were obsessed with the man—tracking his whereabouts, gathering information on his habits. They have since let it go. "I may have doubts about our judicial system, but I have come to believe in ultimate justice," he says. He directs his energies in other ways. As a director of the National Victim Center, he counsels bereaved families. But Dunne's moral outrage continues to bubble up in his novels. Under the gloss of each of his "entertainments" lurks a stinging morality tale.

As he writes here, Dunne's *Season in Purgatory* had a curious effect on its model, the stalled murder case of 15-year-old Martha Moxley, who was last seen alive with Thomas Skakel (a nephew of Ethel Kennedy) at a 1975 Halloween party in Greenwich, Conn. The police never questioned Skakel extensively after the night the girl's body was found; they never searched his house. When Dunne's novel began prompting "people to tell him things," he reported the information to the authorities. That in turn triggered new reporting in the *Boston Globe*, the *New York Observer*, the *New York Daily News* and the *Greenwich Times*. As a result the Connecticut police reopened the case. On June 7, 2002, Thomas Skakel was convicted of Martha Moxley's murder.

This is a fascinating example of how the written word can have an impact on the machinery of the real world. Of course, Dunne had no way of knowing the outcome of the case when he wrote the piece that follows, but there is little doubt that his writing set people to asking the relevant questions.

M. A.

A Novel Approach to Reality: Basing a Story in Facts

By Dominick Dunne

I am a late-life writer. I had a long and varied career in show business that began with *The Howdy Doody Show*, which I stage managed, and more or less ended with *Ash Wednesday*, an Elizabeth Taylor movie that I produced. There were telltale signs that the Industry, as people out in Hollywood call it, had had enough of me. But the fact is, I had also had enough of it. Inner voices were urging me to move on.

In 1977, in the waning years of my movie career, an event occurred in Hollywood that had nothing whatever to do with me, but had a profound effect on my future career as a writer, although I did not realize it at the time. A studio head, for reasons known only to himself, forged a check in the amount of $10,000 in the name of an Academy Award-winning movie star. The movie star became aware of the forgery when he received a W-4 form requesting that he pay tax on that amount. Like a good citizen, he investigated, refused to be sweet-talked out of his quest to get to the bottom of the mystery, and persevered in his probe, but to no avail. Rumors were rampant on the Hollywood circuit of financial malfeasance, but nothing appeared in the Los Angeles papers.

Concurrently, in an extraordinary coincidence of timing, the wife of the same studio head brought out a book she had written, a shopping guide for rich women, called *New York on a Thousand Dollars a Day, Before Lunch*. Hollywood is not a place where writers have ever been held in the highest esteem, so it was something of a surprise to me to see that every studio head and important figure in the industry turned out, with wives, at the launch party to celebrate the publication of that book. Could it be that *New York on a Thousand Dollars a Day, Before Lunch*, on its own, would have that kind of draw? Even the dimmest observer could understand that the ranks were closing round one of their own to protect him. Even the dimmest observer could see that the newspaper of the town was ignoring the story about the forged check. I knew all the participants in the affair—the studio head and his wife and the movie star and his wife. Needless to say, I was riveted.

Coincidence is a daily occurrence in my life. A few days later, I was paged during lunch in the Polo Lounge of the Beverly Hills Hotel, where I was talking with my agent about the desperate situation of my non-existent producing career. The bellboy told me that a man wished to speak to me in the lobby. The man, John Berry by name, was a reporter from *The Washington Post*. It developed that he had been a roommate of my youngest brother at Georgetown University and recognized the family resemblance when he saw me in the hotel. He and his partner, Jack Egan, were out there, he said, to write a story on the studio head and the forgery case. It seemed that the movie star's wife, a socialite actress with powerful Washington connections, had appealed to Katharine Graham for her newspaper to investigate the case, as the Los Angeles papers were not. He told me that he and his partner were having no luck at all in their investigation. All doors were closed to him. Telephone calls were not returned. He asked me if I knew anyone who knew any one who, et cetera. One thing about my life is that I've always known someone who knew someone who, et cetera.

I spent the next 10 days with the reporters watching them go about getting their story. It awakened in me an excitement I had long since ceased feeling for the picture business, and I kept thinking to myself, "I could do what these guys are doing." They broke the story, which eventually became a national one. A bestselling book, *Indecent Exposure*, by David McClintock was written about the case. Ultimately, the studio head, David Begelman, had to resign from Columbia Pictures, but he shortly thereafter became the head of MGM. On the other hand, the victim, Cliff Robertson, became the bad guy for blowing the whistle. Despite having won an Academy Award, his Hollywood film career was effectively over. (Not to mention his marriage to Dina Merrill.) There was a lesson here.

Two years later, I left Hollywood for good and embarked on a new career as a writer. What I had witnessed running around with the reporters from *The Post* became the foundation stone of nearly everything I have written since, in nonfiction for *Vanity Fair* or in fiction in my novels. I had learned that there are a different set of rules for the rich and powerful in a criminal situation. The ranks close. Things can be kept out of newspapers. Police can be told to look the other way.

Reality has always had a strong influence on my plots. A personal tragedy in my own life brought me into contact with the American justice system. It has drawn me ever since. Each book I have written has been based on an actual crime that occurred in the world of America's rich and powerful. Justice, or the lack of it, has been my particular obsession—people who get away with things, or people who go unpunished or underpunished from the prosecution that would be the fate of a less privileged member of society. After covering so many high-profile trials, I have become cynical enough to know that acquittals often have little to do with innocence. They have to do with megabucks defense attorneys who outclass by far the bright young 3-years-out-of-law-school prosecutors the state so often puts forward. Sometimes I feel the overworked prosecutors do not have the same passion to convict that defense attorneys have to acquit. I am interested in cover-ups.

I am interested in affluent families who do not want a murder in their midst to be solved for fear of exposing embarrassing circumstances. I am interested in pressure being brought to bear. I am interested in the machinery of the rich and powerful when they come together to protect one of their own.

The tragic event at the center of my novel *A Season in Purgatory* is based on an unsolved murder in a fashionable New England town in the 1970s. The brutal and savage death of a 15-year-old girl from an affluent family shocked the community as it had rarely been shocked. She was bludgeoned with a golf club. When the club broke from the force of the blows, the shorter end was used as a dagger and she was stabbed through her neck. Yet, to this day, nearly 18 years later, no arrest has ever been made. There have been whispers. There have been rumors. "So and so did it," people from that town will tell you. But the mystery remains. My version of what came after the actual murder is a fictional one. The trial and resolution that I have written never happened.

In my investigation, I came to know the mother of the victim, who subsequently moved to another state. The unsolved murder of her daughter was like an open wound she carried with her every day, living as she then did in close proximity to kids, some of them suspects, going on with their lives as if nothing had ever happened. Certainly, in the back of my mind, there was always the hope that the book would serve as a spotlight on the old case and that her daughter's murderer would be brought to justice, even after 18 years.

And indeed fiction has a way of jarring the truth loose.

During a 22-city book tour to promote the book, I grew used to people coming up to me, identifying themselves as having come from the city where the murder took place, and giving me bits and pieces of information about the night it happened. Some of it was pertinent, some not. "Two boys did it, not one," said one person. Another told me it was three boys. "They were drunk. They were drugged," she said. Everything I heard I shared with the police. A new theory being circulated was that an employee in the household did it. The truth of the matter is that I don't know who did it. It could be any of them, or all of them, or none of them. What I do know is that people who had information did not share it with the police, "not wanting to get involved," as each said to me.

I have found, writing about the rich and powerful, that as much as some in their ranks will reach for the convenient cover-up, others will instinctively move toward truth. And yet, wanting to help, they are afraid of the consequences—they almost never want to be identified as sources of information.

Reporters from several newspapers have now taken up the case, however, hounding the police and the family lawyer of one of the suspects for answers. These days I am feeling hopeful that some resolution will be forthcoming. And that is a satisfying thing for a spinner of tales to be able to say.

August 1, 1993

Tracy Kidder

There is a halting quality to Tracy Kidder's voice—a reserve that underscores his love of precision. He is a man who reveals far more of himself in what he says of other lives and other work than in what he seems willing to say about his own.

These are the facts of his life: He was born in New York City in 1945. The middle son of a lawyer and a schoolteacher, he grew up in Oyster Bay, Long Island, and, at the age of 14, went off to board at the elite Phillips Andover school, although he admits this last with something resembling an apology. "Perhaps because it says so much about what I really am," he offers when I ask him why.

At Harvard he learned to love writing. He managed to get himself into a class taught by poet and translator Robert Fitzgerald, who became his mentor and beacon for the next decade. When an excited 19-year-old Kidder submitted a short story to him for the first time and asked Fitzgerald what he thought of it, the professor said, "Not much," and pointed to the wastebasket. Kidder persisted, nevertheless, writing "a great deal of fiction about sensitive young men." To this day, he says—long after Fitzgerald has left this life and Kidder has left the short story form behind—he is still trying to write something that would please his old teacher.

Kidder graduated in 1967, just as the Vietnam War rocked into high gear. He landed in Vietnam as a U.S. Army lieutenant in the intelligence corps. When he got out in 1969, he headed home to Long Island to write about it. "The result was a really bad novel about experiences I never had in Vietnam. About combat. I remember an awful, sickening feeling when I looked at my year's work—all 362 pages of it—and realized I had it all wrong."

He put the manuscript on a shelf, got married and went to the University of Iowa Writers Workshop. There he made lasting friendships with serious writers. "I came to the conclusion that perhaps I had had too happy a childhood to write good fiction. An older writer-friend said to me at about that time that if he could start all over again, he would try nonfiction—there was so much interesting stuff going on in the world. It got me thinking."

In 1974, he published his first book, *The Road to Yuba City*, about a murder case in California. "It was flawed," he says sharply. He was trying to get too much of himself on the page.

And then came *The Soul of a New Machine* in 1982. "With that book I realized how tremendously liberating nonfiction was. Suddenly I had all kinds of lives to immerse myself in other than my own." Kidder looked at the computer industry as no one else had, weaving together its minutiae to make a penetrating portrait of a way of life. The book won him a Pulitzer Prize.

From there he went on to write *House* (1985), in which he mapped out the building of a family's home, and *Among Schoolchildren* (1989), in which he described a year in the life of a fifth-grade teacher. A writer of bestsellers now, he became known as the quintessential observer of ordinary people at work. The book he had published most recently when I interviewed him in 1993 was *Old Friends*, which tells of his year among the residents of Linda Manor, an old age home in Massachusetts. It is about work of a different kind, he says. "Old people have nothing to do but try to make meaning out of their lives. They have a job in the deepest sense of the word." He rewrote the manuscript 10 times before he submitted it to his publisher. "I don't mean just tinkering," he says, "I mean starting over again, rethinking it all more carefully." Since then, he has written *Home Town* (1999), about that quintessential New England community, Northampton, Mass.

The writing life, says Kidder, is not orderly. Nor is it fair. "I don't recommend it to young people. The ones who ignore me and go ahead and do it anyway are the real writers." Orderly or not, his career is all about discipline. And, unlike his manner of speaking, the voice he has found to reveal the intricacies of other people's lives is anything but halting.

M. A.

Making the Truth Believable

BY TRACY KIDDER

When I started writing nonfiction a couple of decades ago there was an idea in the air, which for me had the force of a revelation: that all journalism was inevitably subjective. I was in my 20s then, and although my behavior was somewhat worse than it has been recently, I was quite a moralist. I decided that writers of nonfiction had a moral obligation to write in the first person—really write in the first person, making themselves characters on the page. In this way, I would disclose my biases. I would not hide the truth from the reader. I would proclaim that what I wrote was just my own impression of events. In retrospect it seems clear that this prescription for honesty often served as a license for self-absorption on the page. I was too young and self-absorbed to realize what should have been obvious: that I was less likely to write honestly about myself than about anyone else on earth.

I wrote a book about a murder case in a swashbuckling first person. After it was published and disappeared without a trace, I went back to writing nonfiction articles for the *Atlantic Monthly*, under the tutelage of Richard Todd, then a young editor there. For about 5 years, during which I didn't dare attempt another book, I worked on creating what many writer friends of mine call "voice." I didn't do this consciously. If I had, I probably wouldn't have gotten anywhere.

But gradually, I think, I found a writing voice, the voice of a person who was informed, fair-minded, and always temperate—the voice, not of the person I was, but of the person I wanted to be. Then I went back to writing books, and discovered other points of view besides the first person.

Choosing a point of view is a matter of finding the best place to stand, from which to tell a story. The process shouldn't be determined by theory, but driven by immersion in the material itself. The choice of point of view, I've come to think, has nothing to do with morality. It's a choice among tools. On the other hand, the wrong choice can lead to dishonesty. Point of view is primary; it affects everything else, including voice. I've made my choices by instinct sometimes and sometimes by experiment. Most of my memories of time spent writing have merged together in a blur, but I remember vividly my first attempts to find a way to write *Among Schoolchildren*, a book about an inner-city teacher. I had spent a year inside her classroom. I intended, vaguely, to fold into my account of events I'd witnessed there a great deal about the lives of particular children and about the problems of education in America. I tried every point of view that I'd used in previous books, and every page I wrote felt lifeless and remote. Finally, I hit on a restricted third-person narration.

That approach seemed to work. The world of that classroom seemed to come alive when the view of it was restricted mainly to observations of the teacher and to accounts of what the teacher saw and heard and smelled and felt. This choice narrowed my options. I ended up writing something less comprehensive than I'd planned. The book became essentially an account of a year in the emotional life of a schoolteacher.

My choice of the restricted third person also obliged me to write parts of the book as if from within the teacher's mind. I wrote many sentences that contained the phrase "she thought." I felt I could do so because the teacher had told me how she felt and what she thought about almost everything that happened in her classroom. And her descriptions of her thoughts and feeling never seemed self-serving. Believing in them myself, I thought that I could make them believable on the page.

For me, part of the pleasure of reading comes from the awareness that an author stands behind the scenes adroitly pulling the strings. But the pleasure quickly palls at painful reminders of that presence—the times when, for instance, I sense that the author strains to produce yet another clever metaphor. Then I stop believing in what I read, and usually stop reading. Belief is what a reader offers an author, what Coleridge famously called "That willing suspension of disbelief for the moment, which constitutes poetic faith." All writers have to find ways to do their work without disappointing readers into withdrawing belief.

In fiction, believability may have nothing to do with reality or even plausibility. In nonfiction, it has everything to do with those things.

I think that the nonfiction writer's fundamental job is to make what is true believable. But for some writers lately the job has clearly become more varied: to make believable what the writer thinks is true (if the writer wants to be scrupulous); to make believable what the writer wishes were true (if the writer isn't interested in scrupulosity); or to make believable what the writer thinks might be true (if the writer couldn't get the story and had to make it up).

I figure that if I call a piece of my own writing nonfiction it ought to be about real people, with their real names attached whenever possible, who say and do in print nothing that they didn't actually say and do. On the cover page of my new book I put a note that reads, "This is a work of nonfiction," and I listed the several names that I was obliged to change in the text. I feared that a longer note would stand between the reader and the spell that I wanted to create, inviting the reader into the world of a nursing home. But the definition of "nonfiction" has become so slippery that I wonder if I shouldn't have written more. So now I'll take this opportunity to explain that I spent a year doing research, that the name of the place I wrote about is its real name, that I didn't change the names of any major characters, and that I didn't invent dialogue or put any thoughts in characters' minds that the characters themselves didn't confess to.

I no longer care what rules other writers set for themselves. If I don't like what someone has written, I can stop reading, which is, after all, the worst punishment a writer can suffer. But the expanded definitions of "nonfiction" have created problems for those writers who define the term narrowly. Many readers now view with suspicion every narrative that claims to be nonfiction. But not all writers make up their stories or the details in them. In fact, scores of very good writers do not—writers such as John McPhee (*Coming into the Country*), Jane Kramer (*The Last Cowboy*), J. Anthony Lukas (*Common Ground*). There are also special cases, which confound categories and all attempts to lay down rules for narrative. I have in mind especially Norman Mailer's *Executioner's Song*, a hybrid of fact and fiction, labeled as such, which I loved reading.

Most writers lack Mailer's powers of invention. Some nonfiction writers do not lack his willingness to invent, but the candor to admit it. Some writers proceed by trying to discover the truth about a situation, and then invent the facts as necessary. Even in these suspicious times, a writer can get away with this. Often no one will know, and the subjects of the story may not care. They may approve. They may not notice. But the writer always knows. I believe in immersion in the events of a story. I take it on faith that the truth lies in the events somewhere, and that immersion in those real events will yield glimpses of that truth. I try to hew to a narrow definition of nonfiction partly in that faith and partly out of fear. I'm afraid that if I started making things up in a story that purported to be about real events and people, I'd stop believing it myself. And I imagine that such a loss of conviction would infect every sentence and make each one unbelievable.

I don't mean to imply that all a person has to do to write good nonfiction is to take accurate notes and reproduce them. The kind of nonfiction I like to read is at bottom storytelling, as gracefully accomplished as good fiction. I don't think any technique should be ruled out to achieve it well. For myself, I rule out only invention. But I don't think that honesty and artifice are contradictory. They work together in good writing of every sort. Artfulness and an author's justified belief in a story can produce the most believable nonfiction.

September 5, 1993

Carl Sagan

It was hard to believe, when I interviewed him for this series, that 1994 marked Carl Sagan's 60th year on earth. Hard because despite his litany of accomplishments—from his work for NASA to the TV success of *Cosmos*—he was still going at science with all the bubble and energy of an obsessed boy.

He was born in Brooklyn in 1934, the son of a fabric cutter in a garment factory. His father had emigrated from the Ukraine and worked his way through poverty, ushering at a movie theater when money was particularly scarce. His mother was Austro-Hungarian, a storyteller who entertained her 2 children with flights of the imagination. Some day, the Sagans hoped, their son would hold a full-time job.

Books opened the door to Sagan's future. At the age of 7 he took a streetcar to the New Utrecht branch of the New York Public Library and checked out his first science book. It was about stars. "I felt a sense of vertigo leafing through it. How could these huge bodies—these suns—hang in that immensity of black vacuum?" He began to frequent libraries to satisfy his curiosity.

"School was little more than a detention camp," Sagan says. "There was schoolyard violence, a rigidly enforced system of intimidation—reading became my way out." By 12 he was onto H. G. Wells and Jules Verne, but longed for the concrete vocabulary of hard science.

By the age of 17, he knew astronomy was his field, although he had never attended a class on the subject. He won a scholarship to the University of Chicago. By 1954 he had his B.A. and by 1960 a Ph.D. in astrophysics from Chicago.

It was a propitious time to be doing science: Sputnik had prompted the U.S. government to pour money into scientific research. NASA was hiring, and it took Sagan on as a consultant. In the early '60s Sagan went from research fellow at the University of California at Berkeley to assistant professor of genetics at Stanford to pursuing astronomy at Harvard. By the end of the decade he was a professor of space science at Cornell.

Sagan always had a missionary's zeal about pushing science into the public arena. He argued to send cameras on NASA's early missions, a position some colleagues criticized as skylarking or grandstanding. "There were those who thought of science as a priesthood, and I battled this," he told me.

When Hollywood and bestselling novelists finally discovered scientific subjects, however, he decried the inaccuracies promulgated by sloppy writers. "It's too easy for bad science to drive out the good . . . and for scientists then to feel they should turn around and make a conscious effort to mystify it all over again—to guard the treasures." At NASA he played a leading role in the Mariner, Viking, Voyager and Galileo expeditions, blending scholarship with what James Michener called his writerly "iridescence."

At the time of his death in 1996—two years after he wrote the essay that follows—Sagan had authored more than 700 articles and 20 books, including *Broca's Brain* (1979), *Contact* (1985) and *The Dragons of Eden* (1977), for which he won the Pulitzer Prize. In 1980 he created *Cosmos*, an award-winning TV series that was seen by more than 500 million people in 60 countries. The book was a bestseller for 70 weeks.

He has 5 children whose ages range 32 years—the youngest 2 are the product of his 17-year marriage to TV producer and author Ann Druyan. Sagan and Druyan co-wrote *Comet* (1985) and *Shadows of Forgotten Ancestors* (1992). When asked if having a daughter made him ponder why there are fewer women than men in science, he responded, "We've persuaded them that they're not hormonally suited for it. It's a national stupidity of ours and we've lost access to half the population in the process."

When I interviewed him, Sagan was the director of the Laboratory for Planetary Studies at Cornell and had just won the 1994 National Academy of Sciences' Public Welfare Medal—the NAS's highest honor. He had just begun a new novel, a love story he was co-writing with Druyan. The year he died, he published *The Demon-Haunted World: Science as a Candle in the Dark*, with which he clearly was wrestling when he fashioned this piece for The Writing Life.

And what was the secret to Sagan's protean creativity? "Multiplexing. Have several projects going at all times. When you get stuck in one, move on. But always leave yourself room." Room? For what? "For something that makes no sense at all. Every night no matter what, for instance, Annie and I always leave room for five good games of pinochle."

M. A.

Describing the World As It Is, Not As It Would Be

BY CARL SAGAN

I was lucky enough to be a child in a time of hope. I wanted to be a scientist from my earliest school days. The crystallizing moment came when I first caught on that stars are mighty suns, and how staggeringly far away they must be to appear to us as mere points of light. I'm not sure I even knew the word science then, but I was gripped by the prospect of understanding how things work, of helping to uncover deep mysteries, of exploring new worlds—maybe even literally. It has been my good fortune to have had that dream in part fulfilled. Doing science is still among my chief pleasures.

For me, popularizing science—writing so as to make its methods and findings accessible to non-scientists—then follows naturally and immediately. Not explaining science seems to me perverse. When you're in love, you want to tell the world.

But there's another reason: I have a foreboding of an America in my children's or grandchildren's time—when we're a service and information economy; when nearly all the key manufacturing industries have slipped away to other countries; when awesome technological powers are in the hands of a very few, and no one representing the public interest can even grasp the issues; when people have lost the ability to set their own agendas or knowledgeably question those in authority; when, clutching our crystals and consulting our horoscopes, our critical faculties in decline, unable to distinguish between what feels good and what's true, we slide, almost without noticing, back into superstition.

We've arranged a civilization in which most crucial elements—transportation, communications, and all other industries; agriculture, medicine, education, entertainment and protecting the environment; and even the key democratic institution of voting—profoundly depend on science and technology. We have also arranged things so that almost no one understands science and technology. We might get away with it for a while, but eventually this combustible mixture of ignorance and power is going to blow up in our faces.

I know of no area of human endeavor in which science has not had at least one important thing to say. Of course, there is much about which even experts are ignorant; this will probably always be the case. Science is far from a perfect instrument of knowledge. It's just the best one we have. In this respect, as in many others, it's like democracy.

The predictive powers of science are astonishing—in foretelling eclipses, say, or the sex of an unborn child. There isn't a religion on the planet that doesn't long for a comparable ability—precise, and repeatedly demonstrated before committed skeptics—to prophesize future events. No other human institution comes close.

One of the reasons for its success is that science has built-in, self-correcting machinery at its very heart. It takes account of human fallibility. One of its commandments is, "Mistrust arguments from authority." Too many such arguments have proved too painfully wrong. Authorities must prove their contentions like everybody else. This independence of science, its unwillingness to pay automatic obeisance to conventional wisdom, makes it dangerous to doctrines less self-critical.

Because science carries us toward an understanding of how the world is, rather than how we would wish it to be, its findings may not in all cases be immediately comprehensible or satisfying. It may take a little work to restructure our mindsets. But when we penetrate the barrier, when the findings and methods of science get through to us, when we understand and put this knowledge to use, many feel, if not wild exhilaration, at least deep satisfaction. This is true for everyone, but especially for children—born with a zest for knowledge, aware that they must live in a future molded by science, but so often convinced by their culture that science is not for them. I know personally, both from having science explained to me and from my attempts to explain it to others, how gratifying it is when we get it, when obscure terms suddenly take on meaning, when we grasp what all the fuss has been about, when wonders are revealed. We are reassured: We're not so stupid after all. We can influence the decisions touching on science that will determine our future. And we're moved—because in its encounter with Nature, science invariably conveys reverence and awe.

Being human, scientists are not perfect. Scientists have, both inadvertently and intentionally, developed formidable, downright mythical powers of destruction. The technological perils that science serves up, its implicit challenge to received wisdom and its perceived difficulty, are all reasons for some to mistrust and avoid it. You can see the disquiet easily enough in the image of the mad scientist on Saturday morning television, or in the plethora of Faustian bargains in popular culture, from Frankenstein to Dr. Strangelove to Jurassic Park.

Here are some of the reasons that a concerted national effort is needed to write clearly about science—in radio, TV, newspapers, and classrooms, but especially in widely available books—to bring science to every citizen:

- It makes the national economy and the global civilization run. Other nations well understand this. This is why so many graduate students in science and engineering at American universities—still the best in the world—are citizens of other countries. Science is the golden road out of poverty and backwardness for emerging nations. The corollary, one that the United States sometimes fails to grasp, is that abandoning science is the road back into poverty and backwardness.

- It alerts us to subtle dangers introduced by our world-altering technologies, especially to the environment.

- It teaches us about the deepest issues of origins, natures and fates—of our species, of life, of our planet, of the universe. In the long run, the greatest gift of science may be in teaching us, in ways no other human endeavor has been able, something about our cosmic context, and about who we are.

- The values of science and the values of democracy are concordant, in many cases indistinguishable. Science confers power on anyone who takes the trouble to learn it. Science thrives on the free exchange of ideas; its values are antithetical to secrecy. Science holds to no special vantage points or privileged positions. Both science and democracy encourage unconventional opinions and vigorous debate. Both demand adequate reason, coherent argument, rigorous standards of honesty and evidence. Science is a baloney detector, a way to call the bluff of those who only pretend to knowledge. The more widespread its language, rules and methods, the better chance we have of preserving what Jefferson and his colleagues had in mind. But democracy can also be subverted more thoroughly with the tools of science than any pre-industrial demagogue ever dreamed.

In all of these uses of science, it is insufficient to produce only a small, highly competent, well-rewarded priesthood of professionals; some fundamental understanding of the findings and methods of science must be available on the broadest scale.

As nearly as I can see, the only secret in popularizing science (or anything else) is remembering what thinking went on in your head when you first really understood whatever it is you're now explaining, especially (1) what misunderstandings needed to be cleared away, (2) what metaphors and analogies proved helpful and (3) what reassurance had to be offered. The effort involved is slight, the benefits great. Among the potential pitfalls are oversimplification, the need to be sparing with qualifications (and quantifications), inadequate credit given to the many scientists involved and insufficient distinctions between helpful analogy and reality. Doubtless, compromises must be made.

Like some editors and TV producers, some scientists believe the public is too ignorant to understand science, that the enterprise of popularization is fundamentally a lost cause. Among the many criticisms that could be made of this judgment is that it is self-confirming.

Most scientists, I think, are comfortable with the idea of popularizing science. (Since nearly all support for science comes from the public coffers, it would be self-defeating, an odd flirtation with suicide, for scientists to oppose competent popularization.) What the public understands and appreciates, it is more likely to support.

Newspaper articles or TV programs can strike sparks as they give us a glimpse of science, but—apart from apprenticeship or well-structured seminars—the best way to popularize science is through books. With books, you can mull things over, go at your own pace, revisit the hard parts, compare texts, dig deep. As a youngster, I was inspired by the popular books of George Gamow, James Jeans, Arthur Eddington, J. B. S. Haldane, Rachel Carson and Arthur C. Clarke. The popularity of well-written, well-explained books on science that touch our hearts as well as our minds seems greater in the last 20 years than ever before, and the number and disciplinary diversity of scientists writing these books is likewise unprecedented. Among the best contemporary scientist-popularizers, I think of Stephen Jay Gould, E. O. Wilson and Richard Dawkins in biology; Steven Weinberg, Alan Lightman and Kip Thorne in physics; Roald Hoffman in chemistry; and the early works of Fred Hoyle in astronomy. Isaac Asimov wrote capably on everything. (And while requiring some calculus, the most consistently exciting science popularization of the last few decades seems to me to be Vol. I of Richard Feynman's *Introductory Lectures on Physics*.) Nevertheless, current efforts at science popularization are clearly nowhere near commensurate with the public good and the national need.

An extraterrestrial being, newly arrived on Earth—scrutinizing what we mainly present to our children in TV, radio, newspapers, magazines, the comics and many books—might easily conclude that we are intent on teaching them murder, rape, cruelty, superstition and consumerism. We keep at it, and through constant repetition many of them finally get it. What kind of society would it be if, instead, we drummed into them science and a sense of hope?

January 9, 1994

George P. Shultz

If it is true, as Napoleon said, that diplomats are little more than policemen in grand costumes, he did not anticipate George Pratt Shultz in the role. Although our former secretary of state is said to have turned up once at the State Department in a pair of bumble-bee-patterned trousers, there is no pyrotechny and strut in the man. Surely the flamboyant emperor would have been taken aback to find world politics in the hands of such a steady-eyed equilibrist.

Nor was Shultz ever groomed for a career in diplomacy. An economist and businessman, he had no diplomatic experience before President Ronald Reagan handed him the task of negotiating our foreign policy during one of the most decisive decades in recent history.

Shultz was born in New York City in 1920, the only child of Birl and Margaret Shultz. When George was 3, the little family moved to a modest home in the affluent suburb of Englewood, N.J. His father had just founded the New York Stock Exchange Institute, a training school for employees of the exchange. A quiet and studious man, Birl Shultz was also a caring father who took his boy to the office on Saturday mornings, taught him to respect the workaday world and infected him with a passion for football.

Shultz's mother was the daughter of a Presbyterian minister. Her parents died when she was young, and she was sent from Idaho to New York to be raised by her uncle, an Episcopal reverend. "I was greatly affected by those people," Shultz says of her family. "The church was a big part of my life. My mother was a careful person who liked making everything just right."

When Shultz was 12 and the Depression sank to its worst, he launched a newspaper to earn some extra cash. Its price: 5 cents a copy. As he made his sales pitch at one front door, the resident pulled a *Saturday Evening Post* out from under his arm and said, "See this, boy? It costs 5 cents. What's your paper got that this one doesn't?" It was Shultz's first lesson in the marketplace.

The Depression eased and his parents shipped him off to the Loomis School in Windsor, Conn. From there he went to Princeton, where he studied economics and public policy. "I was an okay student," he says, and his college cohorts agree he was no academic star, but he was diligent and capable and fared well enough.

He played football for Princeton, hoping to make the lineup in his senior year, but he clipped his knee in a scrimmage and ruined his chances. "It was one of the great learning experiences of my life," he says. "I became a backfield coach, and ended up teaching the freshmen how to be better players. It made me understand that managerial jobs can be key."

During his junior year, he traveled to Tennessee to see at first hand the progress generated by the New Deal's Tennessee Valley Authority. "The hillbilly family I lived with had no education, but they were smart as whips. They knew what the government wanted to hear and told them just that. Living with them I learned to be skeptical of statistics."

By the time he graduated in June 1942, World War II was in full swing. Shultz joined the U.S. Marines and led a platoon through numerous skirmishes in the Pacific, culminating in their participation in the bloody battle for the Palau Islands.

During an R&R stop in Hawaii, he and his buddies headed for the nearest military hospital, figuring on finding some pretty nurses there. He met and fell in love with Helena Maria O'Brien that day—and he and "O'bie" have been together ever since.

When the war was over he returned to Boston and enrolled at the Massachusetts Institute of Technology, continuing to live in the Navy Yards and report to the Marines even as he did his doctorate in labor economics. When he married O'bie in 1946, he counted on her nursing career to help support them both, but she quit her hospital job at the end of her first day and began taking courses on her G.I. bill at the Fanny Farmer cooking school. "She'd come home having produced and consumed these five-course meals, from hors d'oeuvres to dessert. I ended up starved all the time."

He received his Ph.D. from M.I.T. in 1949 and stayed on to teach industrial relations. In 1955, he took a year's leave to be on the staff of Arthur Burns, then chairman of the President's Council of Economic Advisers. From there, Shultz's career was a steady rise: dean of the University of Chicago's Graduate School of Business, labor policy adviser to both the Eisenhower and Kennedy administrations, secretary of labor under Nixon, director of the Office of Management and Budget, and secretary of the treasury. After Watergate, Shultz joined the Bechtel Corporation, an international engineering firm. Seven years later Reagan made him secretary of state.

It is said that Shultz surprised everyone in Foggy Bottom by appearing one day in the aforementioned bumble-bee pants. It is also said that he is little affected by the pretensions of the world around him. Throughout the Reagan years, the Shultzes lived in a unassuming house in Bethesda, and if they had guests at their old second-hand wooden dining room table, it was—more likely than not—their neighbors.

What did Shultz think of Clinton's foreign policy track record when I interviewed him in 1994? "There are points of light," he said in an interview from his office at Stanford's Hoover Institution. "The Middle East is one. There are struggles, but there is forward motion. South Africa is being transformed. Latin America is looking positive: NAFTA and GATT are important steps. But we [America under Clinton] did not step up to the Bosnia problem. We have misread how to handle Russia and North Korea." He believed that we had dealt too narrowly with one individual—Yeltsin—and hadn't treated Russia as the great power that it was. "We have focused too much on aid, and we haven't delivered on our promises," he said.

Turmoil and Triumph is Shultz's memoir of his days as foreign policy helmsman. A massive book of almost 1,200 pages, it says much about Shultz's personality: Like him, it is deliberate, thorough, solidly responsible, and, perhaps except for its girth as Daniel Webster, another secretary of state, might have put it—the very essence of "wholesome restraint."

M. A.

The Political Memoir: Taking Note of History

BY GEORGE P. SHULTZ

When I left Washington in January 1989 after serving for over 6 and a half years as secretary of state, I had no plans to write a memoir. I felt that memoirs could easily become self-serving. What's more, I was exhausted and wanted to do something else—to get away from the pressures of the job. I would turn my documents over to the historians and let them write the record of foreign policy during the Reagan years.

But soon my energy returned. And as my historian friends pointed out to me, there would be no substitute for providing my own perspective. When I became secretary of state, the world was in turmoil, and when I left office the Cold War was all over but the shouting. As Dean Acheson's *Present At the Creation* had chronicled the birth of the Cold War, I could chronicle its demise and burial.

My adrenalin started to rise as I looked back over what had happened on my watch and delved into my vast records, including over 22,000 pages of notes taken in tiny, yet highly readable handwriting by my executive assistant, of everything that was said in my office—

actual dialogue—and my accounts, usually dictated right after the event, of what had transpired in meetings held elsewhere.

These notes captured, too, my own thoughts there and then, about the events and the players. They constitute a remorselessly precise record and vivid picture of a slice of history in the making: As such, they provided me invaluable and unique raw material from which I could draw. In addition, I had all the official papers that flowed into and out of my office, including memoranda of conversations (almost verbatim) of my meetings with other key leaders. With these in hand, I set to work.

An experience earlier in my life wound up giving me a pattern of behavior that helped me not only while I was in office but also while writing about those events. I was invited in 1968 to be a fellow at the Center for Advanced Studies in the Behavioral Sciences, a quiet, isolated haven on the Stanford campus where some 50 scholars a year from around the world are invited to come and do whatever they want. No duties. Some people called it the Center for the Leisure of the Theory Class. When I arrived, the director took me to my study. The room was small, about 15 feet to a side, with one glass-paneled door that overlooked the San Francisco Bay. A simple desk and chair, a side chair and a little settee were the furnishings. That was it. I looked around and I said, "Where's the telephone?"

"There is no telephone," he said with a smile. "If you get a call, a buzzer will sound, and you go down the hallway to a little booth to take the call." I looked at the telephone booth. It was the only unpleasant, clammy place in the whole complex. "If you want to make an outgoing call," he told me, "you can use a pay phone, and you'll need to have the right amount of change."

"If you don't have the money to pay for a telephone, I'd be glad to pay for the installation," I told him.

"No, we don't believe in telephones. Try it. You'll like it." He laughed.

After a couple of weeks, it dawned on me that for the first time since I was a graduate student, I was working completely from the inside out. What I did was what I decided to do, not what somebody rang me up on the telephone and asked me to do. I carried this lesson over into my later work. In any day, or certainly in any week, I would block out periods of time when nothing was scheduled and I wasn't going to deal with the things in my "In" box. I was going to sit with a piece of paper and think ahead about key problems, ways of getting at them, what I wanted to work on, and what I wanted to cause others to work on. In other words, work from the inside out.

In moving from doer to writer, I could stretch those blocks of unscheduled time into days and weeks. I spread out voluminous material on the large conference-room table where I worked. As I read through what I had at hand for a particular chapter, I took time to think about it. After I inhaled the material and searched out still more, sometimes from the public record, sometimes from my assistant's notes and my other archival sources, I made an outline and then started writing. I could see how the writing forced me to be more rigorous, to rethink, to look up new information, to check facts meticulously, to recognize where a piece was missing, here and there, and where the logic was flawed.

As I tried to portray the scene as I had found it, to create for the reader a living history of my days in office, I inevitably needed to set forth not only the ideas and issues but also the interplay among the key players, the clashes of personalities, the interagency warfare, the reality of the scene as I tried to forge a strategy in what was a highly contentious administration.

Perception and reality were sometimes strikingly different. The more I studied the summit meeting in Reykjavik between President Reagan and General Secretary Gorbachev, the more I realized the importance of this point. That historic event is generally remembered as a failure, to some a disappointment, to others an alarming exercise in real negotiations by leaders themselves. But the reality, as I develop in a chapter entitled, "What Really Happened at Reykjavik," is that this summit was one of the most important and amazing events in the diplomacy of the Cold War. The achievements at the Reykjavik summit were greater than those in any other previous U.S.-Soviet meeting. The basic structure of the two key arms-control treaties involving intermediate range (INF) and strategic (START) nuclear missiles were worked out there, and the Soviets agreed for the first time to make human rights a recognized and regular part of our agenda—an astonishing breakthrough. Agreement was not consummated at Reykjavik but, once on the table, the Soviet concessions bargained out there could not be taken back. We had seen their bottom line.

Why then the perception of the Reykjavik summit as near disaster or near farce? There are many reasons, but as I pondered and even got a videotape of the end of that meeting and of my own press conference right afterwards, I could see one important reason more clearly. We had worked hard for an agreement and, for a time, thought we might have one. In the end, we did not get there. I was later asked why I had looked tired and disappointed at my press conference. "Because I was tired and disappointed," I answered. That immediate popular perception of disappointment and the downcast appearance of Reagan and Gorbachev as they parted left the impression of failure and that impression hardened over time into accepted truth.

Years later, when Gorbachev visited me at Stanford University, I asked him what he considered the turning point in U.S.-Soviet relations during his tenure in office, he answered without hesitation, "Reykjavik." I agreed: I thought that at the Reykjavik summit we had in fact arrived at an enormous turning point. I recognized full well that the nuclear age could not be abolished or undone: It was a permanent reality. But we could at least glimpse a world with far diminished danger from possible nuclear devastation. And in this memoir, I could at least try to set the record of Reykjavik straight.

The process of writing is a process of learning. I puzzled long and hard over President Reagan's visit to the German military cemetery in Bitburg and its implications. My memory of the immense stress and controversy surrounding the visit in May 1985 before the Bonn summit was vivid. But as I looked carefully into my notes and the surrounding cables and records, I realized more fully than I had even at the time the tremendous pressure that Chancellor Helmut Kohl had exerted on President Reagan to go through with this highly controversial visit. Kohl, an ally who had stood firmly against intense Soviet pressure and domestic discontent and deployed intermediate-range missiles on German soil at the end of 1983, sent President Reagan a long and tortured cable. Cancellation of the president's scheduled visit to the Bitburg cemetery, he argued, would be fateful. The Kohl government would fall, he bluntly told our ambassador, Arthur Burns. As I read the notes of my conversation with Arthur and reread the long cable Kohl sent to President Reagan at a most critical moment, I could see in retrospect far more than at the time, the impact of the cable's emotional content on the president.

Notes and records more than memory deepened my appreciation of the president's dilemma. I wound up devoting a full chapter to the Bitburg visit, the story of how a decision, made before all the facts about this German cemetery were known, unfolded and unraveled almost uncontrollably, showing the power of history in present events.

My one frustration in the writing was my inability to reprint the full text of the Kohl cable to Reagan, so that readers could feel its impact upon the president for themselves. In the required process of clearance of my manuscript before publication, this was the only real change forced on me. The State Department decided to seek the German government's permission for me to publish the cable, and the German government declined, despite the fact that the existence of the cable and selected portions of it had been made public contemporaneously by the West German government itself. In any case, notes and records made possible the writing of what was for me a gripping and instructive account of a compelling event that was, at the time, inexplicable to many.

I mentioned earlier the tools of remembrance that I was fortunate to have at hand. I should say especially fortunate since I quickly became aware of how easily my memory could play tricks on me. But this was a memoir that, far less than most, had to rely on mere memory. These records are relentless, and they held me to a high standard of accuracy and candor. Their precision is rare and perhaps, in this context, virtually unique. That fact came to life as I worked on my congressional testimony about the Iran-Contra affair. That record provided me the capacity to be more specific and coherent than other witnesses, who had to rely more heavily on memory, even though my own involvement in the Iran-Contra affair (I had consistently and vigorously opposed any effort to trade arms for hostages) was peripheral, and even though my knowledge was, in many ways, fragmentary. Nevertheless, my records became important in the unfolding of events, the analysis of them, the hearings about them and the prosecutions connected with them.

Suddenly I found that these notes, full of very blunt and sensitive observations, sometimes made in frustration by me, were called for in their entirety by the Independent Counsel's office. The notes were not only taken, but many of my most candid observations, which I thought were made in the privacy of my office, became public. A lot of people thought I had been crazy to have someone in my office scribbling away constantly, taking down exactly what people said and when. These notes enabled me to create with accuracy a history with the richness of actual dialogue. But the fact that any such notes can be made public certainly puts a damper on the taking of such a complete record in the future. In fact, I question whether such detailed notes will ever again be taken.

I noticed this problem in other contexts when I was in office. If a cable came in from an ambassador with a highly critical or sensitive set of observations about the country where the ambassador was stationed, the existence of this cable would often become the subject of rumor. Adamant demands from Congress for that cable would almost inevitably follow, along with threats of retaliation, such as refusing to confirm anybody for any ambassadorial post anywhere, until it was produced. I would rebuff these pressures because the release of such a cable would mean, of course, that the ambassador's role would be diminished, sometimes even ended. Nonetheless, the pull-and-haul had its impact, and candor in the cables inevitably suffered.

The result was increasing reliance on telephone diplomacy, with all its imprecision and vulnerability to misunderstanding. The result is that there is now a widespread, conscious reluctance to create records—and a disposition to destroy them if taken—in our society, whether in business or politics. What I worry about is our ability to portray history accurately if such records are not at hand and the statesman tries to rely heavily on his or her own memory, which is often flawed in significant ways. A living history requires tools of remembrance. Moreover, so much of what we do today depends upon our understanding of the past. If we lose that past, we are also going to lose one of the important handles on the future.

March 13, 1994

Jimmy Carter

"I come from a family of habitual readers," said Jimmy Carter, speaking to me from his office in Atlanta, out of which he conducts possibly the most active and versatile post-officio life of any modern American president. "My mother started that habit at the dinner table. Everybody read their own book while they ate. We do it in our house even now."

The reading habit served him well in school. He was, according to an "old-maid teacher" he remembers most fondly, the star reader of his little rural school in Plains, Ga. When he was 8 or 9 his godmother gave him a leather-bound set of the classics, complete with a bonus book of short stories by Guy de Maupassant. By 12, he had gone through them all, savoring especially *War and Peace*, *Don Quixote* and *Jane Eyre*. Regularly winning accolades for reading the most books in a given school year, he would take home prizes in the form of prints of famous paintings and hang them proudly on his wall.

Writing followed naturally. He entered "ready writing" competitions—"aggressively competitive contests" in which teachers would scrawl three topics on the blackboard and students would race to fashion 1,500-word essays around them. He would win those too.

But he had other ambitions. By 6 he was out on the roadside selling boiled peanuts out of a little red wagon. By 9 he'd saved enough money from those sales to buy bales of cotton and hoard them in his father's warehouse until the prices quadrupled. Even then he claims he could tell the good people from the bad: The good were the ones who bought his peanuts. The bad were the ones who did not. That rule stuck with him through a naval career, a governorship, the 39th presidency, and his current work as house builder, college teacher and international crisis negotiator for the nonprofit Carter Center: He fights ardently for the principles he believes in and those who are with him are on the side of the angels.

That firm notion of right and wrong Carter attributes squarely to his religious family, which had more than a slight missionary bent—his sister Ruth Carter Stapleton was a staunch evangelist, his mother a Peace Corps worker in old age, and he himself did missionary work for the Southern Baptist Convention. He taught Sunday School to the officers' daughters when he was a student in the U.S. Naval Academy. He teaches it now at the Maranatha Church in Plains. And little wonder he's so good at it: The rhythm and rhetoric of a lay preacher are the bedrock of his language.

To this day, he and Rosalynn Carter read a chapter of the Bible aloud every night. Sometimes they read it to each other in Spanish, checking the words they don't know against the English on facing pages.

Books are his consuming passion, said Carter when I interviewed him for the series. He had just finished Doris Kearns Goodwin's biography of the Roosevelts, *No Ordinary Time* ("I enjoyed it"), and said he makes a point of reading most everything that is published about the presidency. But his tastes are far-ranging. "I've immersed myself in voluminous reading on Bosnia, and on Ireland. I've been fascinated by books about the Sudan—about Muslims and the Middle East in general. For enjoyment I read John le Carré, John McPhee, Stephen Jay Gould. I like their sense of style."

And poetry? "Dylan Thomas. I've read 26 books about him." Those 26 still sit on his shelves, within arm's reach of other favorites—books about the conquest of human disease, or woodworking, or flyfishing . . . "There are so many of them," he says wistfully. "I'm still bringing them all to the dinner table."

These days he might bring some of his own. Since writing this essay for The Writing Life, Carter produced two enormously popular memoirs, *An Hour Before Daylight: Memories of a Rural Boyhood* and *Christmas in Plains*.

M. A.

President in Search of a Publisher

BY JIMMY CARTER

As a high school student I read voraciously and competed in writing contests. In college, while studying to be an engineer, I was taught to write as crisply and clearly as possible. Since then, in a late-blooming writing career, I have progressed from dutifully producing books that have promoted my political aspirations or met my financial obligations, to writing just for the enjoyment of it. From the pragmatic to the poetic, it has been a continuous learning experience.

My first book was a campaign autobiography, *Why Not the Best?* It was written on yellow scratch pads on airplanes and in hotel rooms. It was early 1975, and I was traveling around the country looking for voters, but with little attention from the public or news media. I had plenty of time to write.

Having studied typing and shorthand in high school, I did my own stenographic work on a portable typewriter during weekends at home. When it was finished, I called some small publishers in Georgia, none of whom would print the book. Finally, Broadman Press in Nashville looked at a few chapters and agreed to publish it. They print all the Southern Baptist literature, and I had some influence with them as a member of the Baptists' Brotherhood Commission. There was no thought of an author's advance, but I received a percentage of the volumes printed. I gave these to potential political supporters and sold a few at my early political rallies.

After I won the primaries in both Iowa and New Hampshire,

Broadman could not print my book fast enough, and so they arranged with Bantam Books to do a mass printing in paperback. Almost a million copies of that edition were sold, as people scrambled to learn something about a relatively unknown Georgian who might become president. Bending over backwards to be ethical, I put all the author royalties into a benevolent foundation. Also, I had a thriving agricultural business, Carter's Warehouse, and didn't particularly need the money.

As president, I placed my business in a blind trust, and heard no more about it during my term in office. After my defeat in November 1980, the trustee told me that my farm operation had had some bad years and was almost a million dollars in debt. We were lucky enough to sell the entire business, and Rosalynn and I signed book contracts for our memoirs that would provide the much-needed cash to save our home and land.

Writing the memoirs as a defeated incumbent was a somewhat bitter and difficult task for me, and I was soon in a quandary about how to address some of the more politically sensitive or personal issues. The historian Arthur S. Link offered to assemble at Princeton University about a dozen authorities on presidential biographies and memoirs, and Rosalynn and I spent a very fruitful day with them. Their advice was not to be defensive, not to distort the facts or try to write a complete history of my administration, but to tell about the personal and interesting things that had not previously been published.

I spent 8 to 10 hours a day writing on a word processor, selecting excerpts from 6,000 pages of my typewritten diary notes. I had not read these entries since I had made them; they described events in the Oval Office and on presidential trips as they occurred during my 4 years in office.

I wrote the first draft of *Keeping Faith: Memoirs of a President* within a year and completed the manuscript 6 months later. I broke the monotony of research and writing by making furniture in my nearby woodworking shop. In fact, I designed and built more than 30 pieces—enough tables, chairs, beds, benches, cabinets, chests and accessories to furnish an entire house.

As an engineer who had long been interested in literature, I considered myself able to write in a clear and logical manner, and resisted Bantam's suggestion that I work closely with one of their editors. However, when Nessa Rapoport was assigned to this task, she quietly transformed my understanding of writing a book. She was meticulous and persistent, and her comments and questions were incisive, probing and aggravating, but always stimulating. Nessa helped me to clarify obscure passages, fill gaps in the narrative, eliminate superfluous words and sentences, and arrange the text in an orderly manner. She forced me to search for exactly the right words to explain why I had done certain things and how I felt about having done them. I learned that good writing requires a lot of effort, but can be rewarding.

The book tour was really my first exposure to the public after I left the White House, and it was gratifying to welcome the crowds that came for a copy and an autograph. For 11 weeks, *Keeping Faith* was on the bestseller list, although it never managed to climb above Jane Fonda's first workout book.

Why Not the Best? and *Keeping Faith* were written as a matter of duty, to further my political career or for income, but most of my other books have been for my own pleasure. I learned a great deal about myself in *Outdoor Journal* as I struggled to describe what motivates me to climb a mountain, spend hours in the total isolation of woods and swamps, attempt to master the technique of flyfishing, or to balance the interests of a conservationist with those of a hunter.

In truth, my writing has given me an education that I never received at the Naval Academy or in graduate studies in nuclear physics. I learned to appreciate personal research when I conducted personal interviews for *Turning Point*, a history of my first campaign for the Georgia senate. Thirty years after that dramatic political confrontation, it was surprising to discover how different the facts and documents were from some of my "vivid" memories.

Among many things, the presidency gave me unlimited access to top leaders in the Middle East. I had never fully understood the complexities of the conflicts there until I traveled extensively in the region and listened to presidents, prime ministers, faction leaders and private citizens in Israel, the West Bank and Gaza. Egypt, Jordan, Syria and Lebanon give their own totally differing perspectives on the same basic issues. In *Blood of Abraham*, I tried to present these views as accurately as possible, without distorting them with my own editorializing.

My worst experience as an author was writing a book with Rosalynn. Our *Everything to Gain* almost broke up a 40-year marriage. It was amazing to find how differently we remembered the important events of our lives together, and how differently we reacted to them. As the writing progressed, we couldn't speak to each other about the book, and could communicate only by writing vituperative notes back and forth on our word processors. Rosalynn treated my portions of the text only as rough drafts, but hers as having been carved in stone, just come down from Mount Sinai! Finally, our editor suggested that the more controversial paragraphs be allotted to just one of us, and identified in the final text with either a "J" or an "R." We'll never be co-authors again!

I wrote *Talking Peace* for young people of high school and college age; my purpose was to describe the causes of conflicts and how they might be prevented or resolved. It gave me a chance to report some of my personal experiences in the field, and to tell something about the work that the Carter Center does in peacekeeping, promoting human rights and monitoring elections worldwide. Having taught at Emory University as a distinguished professor for almost a dozen years, I have enjoyed seeing this book (as well as *Keeping Faith* and *Blood of Abraham*) used extensively in high school and college classrooms.

The most profound development in my writing, however, came when I decided to take up poetry in a serious way. I had written a number of poems during my life and was infatuated with the work of a few poets, but I wanted to learn more about the technique of poetry writing. I was fortunate to have two University of Arkansas professors who took me under their wing. I was an eager student, and they inundated me with textbooks and literary criticism and, perhaps most important, passed judgment on my verses.

This was a new experience for me. I became fascinated with the words themselves, and was able to draw new meaning from the poetry of Dylan Thomas, Theodore Roethke, Langston Hughes and many others I had long enjoyed. As I searched for the exact word or juxtaposition of words to express a concept or feeling, I was forced to examine ideas and thoughts relating to my own life that I had never been willing to confront or explore. Rosalynn was surprised at some of the things I wrote and would often say, "I never knew you felt this way." On occasion, I replied, "Neither did I."

When I finally completed a few poems—after months of struggle and 15 or 20 revisions—I was very reluctant to expose them to the public. But one of my mentors, the poet Miller Williams, called me one day to say that he was submitting several to a poetry journal. One was accepted, and subsequently about a dozen were published in respected magazines.

This increased my confidence, but when I offered the collected poems to my longtime publisher, he rejected the idea, saying that poetry books didn't sell and implying that if I published them I might expose myself to ridicule. When he finally changed his mind and *Always a Reckoning* was published, it became a bestseller. The brief promotional tour was an emotional experience; the crowds were so large they were almost unmanageable. Many people asked me to autograph a particular poem instead of the title page. My daily mail almost doubled with readers who wanted to comment on particular verses. There was an intensity of personal reaction I had never known among my readers.

Early in the mornings and during the brief interludes between my duties at the Carter Center and at Emory University, I continue to write poetry, and I have two other books under way. One is based on tape recordings of my weekly Sunday School lessons, including more than a dozen I taught at First Baptist Church in Washington while president. The other is an account of my life on a Georgia farm during the Great Depression, with a focus on what I saw as a strangely intimate interrelationship between black and white families, both children and adults. This was in the days when sharecropping was the highest ambition of day laborers and when no one questioned the total official segregation that existed. It is an intriguing subject, and I'm taking my time with it.

Every book has its own challenges and particular pleasures, and each has taught me something important about myself and the magic of words. I have come a long way, but I still have much to learn. That's what makes the journey worthwhile.

July 2, 1995

Stacy Schiff

There are those who shout from the sidelines—according to an old adage—and those who run the race. There are those who recognize brilliance and those who dare to attempt it. There are either commentators or doers. Critics or artists. And—as the rule says—coaches cannot run, critics cannot do, and editors cannot write.

But every now and then someone upends that rule: Joan Didion. Janet Malcolm. Umberto Eco. Toni Morrison. E. L. Doctorow.

And Stacy Schiff. Thirteen years before she wrote this essay, she was an "entry-level" editorial assistant at Basic Books—answering phones, typing rejection letters, reading the slush pile—all for $9,000 a year. By 1995, she was the author of a much praised biography of Antoine de Saint-Exupéry. The proposal for the book that followed—a biography of Vera Nabokov (Vladimir Nabokov's wife, helpmeet and inspiration)—had just been sold on both sides of the Atlantic for a hefty six-figure advance. When *Vera* was published, four years after this piece appeared in *Book World*, the *New York Times* hailed it as "a triumph." *Book World* reviewer Michael Dirda had a more critical view.

Schiff was born in 1960 in Adams, Mass., a little town nestled in the Berkshires. Her mother was a French teacher, her father a businessman. By 15, she was at Andover; by 1982 she had graduated from Williams College with a major in philosophy and art history.

After 1 year at Basic in New York, she was hired by Viking. There she acquired and edited what all young editors buy and edit: first novels that never go anywhere. But soon she was given larger responsibilities: a collection of stories by Marianne Wiggins; Barbara Leaming's biography of Orson Welles (which she pared down from an original almost twice its size).

In 1986, she moved to Poseidon Books, a Simon & Schuster Imprint that no longer exists. Her mandate was to publish 12 authors a year, and within her short tenure there she brought in Phillip Lopate and Marian Thurm. The only writing she did was to be found on book jackets, marketing notes and in other people's books. Her strengths, she now recognized, were her abilities to hone sentences into models of clarity and wrest lean books from overwritten reams of paper.

Poseidon could not keep her. By 1988 she was a senior editor at Pocket Books, running its Washington Square Press.

One day she stumbled onto the fact that there was no biography of Antoine de Saint-Exupéry in print. "I started to research it, sneaking over to the public library at lunch time." She thought of mentioning it to a literary agent to see if together they might find a willing author. Like any good editor, she was conditioned to offer up her best ideas for adoption.

"But something kept me from giving Saint-Exupéry away. I became obsessed. I had begun to think it might be nice to be attached to one big thing."

Having read proposals for 8 years, Schiff knew just how to write one. And having dealt with many an agent, she knew just how to find one. In 1990, she left her editor's job, married a Frenchman and settled down to a life of writing books and raising children.

What was the most difficult part of that transformation? "Finding that I couldn't do for myself what I had so ably done for my authors," she says. Namely, judge her own work.

Which is all to say that she discovered the iron corollary to the rule she had just disproven: Even editors—if by some miracle they do become writers—can find themselves in need of editors.

M. A.

Biographer, Get a Life

BY STACY SCHIFF

No one reads the obits like the out-of-work biographer. For a few months last year I devoured them, not with the expectation that they would deliver up my next subject, but to be reminded of how we measure a life, how we assign it shape and texture, to marvel over the neat, black-and-white portraits to which the muddle of existence can be reduced in the end. For devotees of capsule histories the society page has its attractions as well, though it seems to me more properly the province of the fiction writer: Its columns bubble with as yet unlived—if delicious to imagine—drama. Having read of a particularly improbable match, how are we to repress the urge to listen in on the strained conversation at the head table? The biographer is too much wed to his facts to indulge in such luxuries. He labors—or is meant to labor—not in the fragrant ether of raw possibility, but in the hard, cold caverns of fact.

The relationship that binds the biographer to his subject has often been compared to a love affair and frequently been observed to mimic its development. Has anyone yet commented on what happens when it is over? After all, the analogy ultimately falls apart. All lives of historical subjects end the same way: With a light or a heavy heart, biographer kills off subject. And then what to do? Leon Edel has described the quiet events of the morning of Jan. 12, 1971, when he wrote the last lines of his magisterial 5-volume account of the life of Henry James. After several hours at his desk he typed James's prophetic line, "I reach beyond the laboratory brain." (It is the penultimate line of the biography.) He stood up. He stretched. Emptiness quickly gave way to euphoria: "Suddenly I was a man of leisure. I shaved; I picked a bright holiday necktie. Dressed as if for festivities. I took a long walk . . . went to my club and drank an aperitif." His friends' concern for his newfound state of bachelorhood leaves him dumbfounded; he cannot understand why they speak as if he has lost his freedom when he feels so certain he has gained it. But how did he—so eloquent in his description of his empathy with James, even if, as he makes clear, the empathy was with James's story rather than with James himself—suddenly live without his companion of 20 years, this other life?

Biographical subjects are partners you carry around with you for 5, 10, 15 years. You do things for them you would not do for your devoted spouse or lover. You drink their drinks. You visit their favorite museums, walk their favorite walks, read their favorite books. You develop a social competence in their sports. You adopt their obsessions as your own. (Pity the Lewis Carroll biographer.) For a little over 4 years I lived with the French author and aviator Antoine de Saint-Exupéry, of whom I completed a biography last spring. Happily I submerged myself in flying manuals. I suffered through much of Gide. I learned a great deal I wish I could unlearn about expert card tricks. For months I casually dated my checks "1944." On one occasion I consulted a therapist on Saint-Exupéry's behalf. And I spent a long winter afternoon with a cardboard sent to his Central Park South apartment from an Eighth Avenue drycleaner: On it had been folded a shirt he had worn. Magic dust fell off the relic and into my hands, the kind that whirled in the air in the apartments of the women with whom Saint-Exupéry had slept. In the early days that magic would dust the air if—in an unlikely file in an underheated archive—the name "Saint-Exupéry" so much as appeared on a page.

You carry—tote, lug, shepherd, escort, follow—a biographical subject around for years, and yet in the end you don't give birth to him, only to an account of his life. You suffer postpartum for the manuscript—not everyone recovers as quickly as Edel, but sooner or later everyone recovers—but what you feel for the subject is something else altogether. On some levels the disengagement qualifies as divorce: The book may be finished before the relationship. And in any event the separation is far from final. The finished book bears, will always bear, both of your names. It came as a shock to me to see "Schiff" and "Saint-Exupéry" on a mock-up of the spine of mine, but there we are, linked for life. What I felt was some combination of bereavement and withdrawal, what the analyst might feel for the patient at the end of a long-term therapeutic relationship. The proper analogy hardly mattered; the absence weighed on me. I didn't find myself mourning or grappling with disengagement as much as I found myself missing the unpredictable roommate who could be relied upon to leave the toothpaste uncapped.

Living with Saint-Exupéry had not been a perfect joy. He smoked too much. He whined. He disappointed, he deceived, he ducked. I lost him at times; I tried to at others. Often enough I wanted to shake him by the wide shoulders, set him on the straight and narrow. (The image in itself speaks to the limits of biography: What would the hulking French Catholic aristocrat have made of the admonitions of the American Jewish woman a foot shorter than he, from a world he neither knew nor could have imagined, who seemed so interested in his every move?) At times, unprofessionally, I wanted to mother him, not his story. But if I lost sight of Saint-Exupéry, I never lost interest in him. Throughout the years I walked into the room with the absent-minded aviator on my arm or on my mind, I remained mercifully immune to biographical subject-envy. Then I became jealous of anyone who so much as has a subject. I came up for air, which was for many months all I wanted to do, but Saint-Exupéry was for so long the prism ("prison," I very nearly typed, and could have) through which I saw the world that things began to look very gray indeed. The air felt thin.

I have at times thought that if anything were to happen to my husband—who had his own relationship with the man who came to live with us for 4 years, which he is quick to admit was at least 1 year too many—I would have to move in with his best friend. Together we could sift through the relics. Now I notice an unwillingness on my part to stop corresponding with those close to Saint-Exupéry, those related to him. A woman with whom he had had an intimate relationship in 1943—and whose heart he broke—was widowed this summer. She had met her husband the evening after Saint-Exupéry made his precipitous departure from her life; in tears over the Frenchman, she had looked especially ravishing. My grief at her recent loss is greater than I would have expected, tinted with an understanding of the blow Saint-Exupéry dealt her 50 years ago, which she never forgot, and which of course colored many of her recollections. I think we have always felt a solidarity in our devotions to the man, different though they may have been. Now that the biography is finished it has grown. We have each lost him as well.

And so the anxiety of waiting for the book to be published paled in comparison to the anxiety, the ordinariness, of being unattached again, the literary equivalent of walking into the junior high school cafeteria alone, the indignity of calling out, "Single?" in the Christmas chairlift line. New subjects appear and are rejected daily, lovers quickly embraced on the rebound. My plight has turned into a kind of literary parlor game: Find Schiff a subject. Friends have proffered ideas so enticing that Lawrence Bergreen, Justin Kaplan and Ted Morgan have already made of them first-rate biographies. A novelist between books who recently came to visit found that she was far happier to indulge in this high-stakes contest than to think about her own next book. Our quandaries are in fact different: Chroniclers, parasites, "artists under oath," we biographers are less able to help ourselves. The facts dictate our stories; we can illuminate them, we can downplay or emphasize them, we can cunningly juxtapose them, we can set them in context, but we cannot hatch them. Our imaginations are tied. We work with pre-fab beginnings, middles and ends. We can turn a lesser life into a great book, or a great life into a lesser book, but we are inevitably beholden to the life. The value the biographer adds to his account has nothing to do with the raw material, everything to do with knowing how to locate it, how to discard much of it (by far the most difficult task), how to order what we have not discarded, where to take a stand, how to write.

Moreover, contemplating a book this time around is like contemplating a second marriage. An eager, blushing (and lucky) bride, I rushed into the first union with my eyes closed. Wiser to the difficulties of the enterprise, more familiar with its rewards, I am fussier now about the person I bring home. "I have learned so many things that will be useless elsewhere," wrote Saint-Exupéry, poised to leave Europe after the fall of France, and the same holds true for the second-time-out biographer. The graveyard of half-written biographies is less crowded than that of half-written novels, but one hesitates all the same to bury a child there. My friends speak as if to a divorcée, counsel me not to "rush into" a new book. But how can I resist when I found the neat little ménage-à-trois my husband and I shared with Saint-Exupéry so consistently rewarding? I have long forgotten the months during which it seemed as if the lifeblood had been drawn from me, infused directly into the veins of a man I have never met, who died before I was born.

And I know now precisely what I want: I have been to the sixth-grade slumber party at which everyone describes the attributes she finds indispensable in the man of her dreams. Subject Number 2 must write as fine a letter as did Saint-Exupéry, must have a sense of humor to rival his, must have lived most of his or her life in a Romance language. That subject appeared on the horizon recently—reappeared, in fact, from behind a crowd of firmly suggested dead and not-yet-dead luminaries, all of whom kept up engaging correspondences in languages I read. Several months ago, nervously, I mailed off a letter to the intended's estate. Immediately—in the post office parking lot, to be exact—my skin began to tingle. Only later did I recognize this for what it was, the frisson of "I am going on an adventure," the flip side of "A charming stranger comes to town." I had sent off a marriage proposal; I had made a modest, first advance to a mail-order spouse. For 2 weeks I tried not to let myself imagine which drawers would have to be emptied, which shrines visited, which languages mastered. I could feel the questions bubbling to the surface; I could taste the challenge. Still, I flirted—brazenly—with other subjects. I did not want to be widowed before my time.

Then one morning a fax arrived, from the keeper of the subject-to-be's archives. "I find your idea appealing and touching," it began, and went on—by way of a few caveats—to end on an inviting note. Shyly I showed the fax to my husband, whom I must have been hoping to catch unaware. Why else would I have waited until he and his briefcase were halfway out the door? "Prepare the guest-room," he called as he raced off, sounding genuinely enthusiastic. Unemployment is unemployment, and after a few off-kilter months probably he too had come to realize that the only way to clear the lingering smell of Saint-Exupéry's cigarettes would be to move a new tenant into his quarters. I watched my husband walk to his car, saw the next 5 or 10 years of my life go down the drain. Then I closed my eyes with relief. And smiled, the crazy smile of the possessed.

August 13, 1995

Kay Redfield Jamison

Physician, heal thyself, goes the familiar adage, and it appears Kay Redfield Jamison has. She is a wounded healer—a psychologist who has felt the ravages of mental illness first-hand. What is so compelling about her case is that the act of writing has figured in her cure. Two of her books, *Touched with Fire: Manic-Depressive Illness and the Artistic Temperament* (1993) and *An Unquiet Mind* (1995), display her heroic efforts to deal with a disease that has plagued her for 30 years. In 1999, she published *Night Falls Fast: Understanding Suicide*.

She was born in Palm Beach, Fla., in 1946, the daughter of an Air Force meteorologist and pilot; her mother was an elementary school teacher. The youngest of 3 children, she recalls her early life as a series of family moves: Puerto Rico, California, Washington, D.C., Tokyo, Washington again, then back to California again, where her father took a job as a scientist for the Rand Corporation. By the time she entered junior high school in Pacific Palisades, young Kay was a bubbly girl with lots of friends and an array of swimming and horseback riding trophies.

"I loved reading poetry and biography as a child," she said, "but I wanted to be a veterinarian. I would traipse around after animals waiting for them to get sick." Her father and his colleagues took that interest seriously and encouraged her dreams of a medical career. By the 10th grade she was on her school's science and math team. By her senior year in high school she was president of the pre-med club.

But that was the year her world turned inside out. At 18—what we now know to be the classic age for the onset of the disease—she experienced her first episode of bipolar manic-depressive illness. It was also about that time that her father was fired from Rand for his brooding and erratic behavior.

She shelved all ambition of going away to college, enrolled at nearby UCLA and took a 30-hour-a-week research lab job to help pay for her tuition. Working manically—wavering between A's and F's—she soared and crashed her way to a degree in psychology. "There were times I was profoundly, suicidally depressed. I have no idea how I got through," she remembers.

Perhaps it was her writing that got her through. Whenever there was a question about grades, she would produce a paper or publish an article. In those works, she would offer ample proof of her depth of knowledge and understanding. By the time she graduated from UCLA, she had placed 15 articles in medical journals.

Jamison's interest in psychology began with questions about measurement—How do animals learn? How do invertebrates perceive? How do octopuses see?—"issues that have no immediate relevance, but are intrinsically fascinating."

She went on to do an M. A. in psychology at UCLA. At Maudsley Hospital in London, she studied the effects of opiates, LSD and marijuana. All this as she struggled with her own recurrent psychoses, careening between her treatment and numerous attempted suicides. By then her interest in psychology took a dramatic turn and the questions came closer to the bone: What is normal, societally acceptable behavior? What is psychopathic? She got her doctorate, became a professor at the UCLA School of Medicine, visiting scientist at the University of Oxford in London, and then founder and director of the UCLA Affective Disorders Clinic.

Today, Jamison is a leading scholar on manic-depressive illness and suicide. The recipient of numerous awards, she teaches at Johns Hopkins University School of Medicine and is an active participant in the Human Genome Project, a research effort funded by the National Institutes of Health to track the genetic structures and functions of the human body. She is married to Richard Wyatt, chief of neuropsychiatry at the National Institute of Mental Health.

Jamison's drive to study and record her condition is helping others to contend with her disease. She is, by force of her own will, both scribe and conqueror of a crippling illness. Seneca wrote in *Hippolytus* almost 2,000 years ago, "The wish for healing has ever been the half of health." He might as well have been writing about Kay Redfield Jamison.

M. A.

From the Clinic

BY KAY REDFIELD JAMISON

When I was a young girl, I almost always had 2 kinds of notebooks going at any one time. The first was filled with detailed observations, and very bad drawings, of animals and plants I saw in our neighborhood and the woods nearby, as well as notes made from various dissections and experiments that I carried out in our basement. Given my age and temperament, these science notebooks were actually quite well organized, almost obsessively so, and the findings and thoughts that I fastidiously jotted down were not only quite logical but almost coolly cerebral in their presentation.

My other notebooks, or journals, really, could not have been more different. They were kept in wildly disparate handwritings, a profusion of ink and pencil colors, and they were filled to the edges with blots, erasures and exclamation points, as well as phrases that had been underlined many times, no doubt because I felt they were of some cosmic importance. Or might be. The outpouring of raw emotions was palpable, a torrent of volatile feelings, triumphs, setbacks and disappointments. School plays I had written were squeezed in higgledy-piggledy next to fragments of anguished poems, scribblings about first loves, and hedged comments about one's friends, realizing that these same friends might, in impulsive moments of diary-sharing, someday read what had been written about them.

The quirky science notebooks of childhood were replaced by uniform, quadrille-ruled, carbon-papered, numbered laboratory notebooks, which recorded years of physics, chemistry and biology experiments. Cloth-covered diaries of elementary school progressed to more elegant, leather-bound notebooks, signaling, or so I imagined, a more serious commitment to the act of writing. I kept these personal journals throughout my school and college days, and long into the long days of graduate school. But my senior year in high school—4 months of intermittent psychosis, bookended by the equal portions of heaven and hell that constitute most of normal adolescence—brought a disquieting and true darkness into the pages of my journal.

Yet, strangely, as my emotional life veered more and more out of control due to severe manic-depressive illness, my personal writing style somehow became more disciplined. Earlier jottings about childish, albeit passionate enthusiasms—vividly recorded alongside the usual hurts and fears of adolescence—gave way to an increasingly disturbed, but far more tightly written, accounting of turmoil, despair and confusion. And then, for many years, my personal journals stopped entirely.

I don't know why I stopped writing, but certainly it was grim enough having to go through the unrelenting cycles of high-voltage intensities, followed by despair and hopelessness, without having to read about them as well. Too, by that time I was trying to survive as a young assistant professor in the shark-infested waters of academic medicine. Such writing energy as I had increasingly went into publishing scientific and clinical articles.

The lulling grace of precision, and the predictable structure of journal articles, made scientific writing a relief and a pleasure. The knitting together of methods, data and interpretation provided not only my livelihood, but an intrinsically fascinating and, at least for a while, safe intellectual harbor. The uniformity of writing style became a kind of a protective armor that allowed me to pass as normal in my professional life. The repeated demonstration of the ability to think clearly and reason logically was what allowed one to earn one's academic spurs. Each time a paper was accepted for publication there was also a subtle reaffirmation of at least some part of the mind's normality.

But, somewhere along the way, writing had ceased to be writing. It had become communicating, the presentation of findings and ideas. The slippage in the pleasure of writing, the lack of a development of a style, had become almost entire. Passionless and straightforward prose, made all the more necessary because my academic specialization had become the illness from which I myself suffered, became the external manifestation of the deep split between my mercurial personal life and my scientific and clinical career.

Finally, after years of struggling with psychotic manias and depressions, lithium restored some vague semblance of a stable emotional life. I obtained tenure with both relief and a new sense of freedom. I gradually became aware that I was incorporating more and more personal material into my professional writing. I was director of the UCLA Affective Disorders Clinic at the time and finding it difficult to convey to the psychiatric residents and interns the subjective experiences of mania and depression. Diagnostic criteria and treatment protocols were reasonably straightforward; the description of pathological mood and thought was almost impossible. In frustration, I decided to write a series of brief essays about my own experiences, eventually incorporating them, anonymously, into my clinical teaching, as well as into a massive medical textbook about manic-depressive illness that I was coauthoring with a colleague. I found that my desire to describe the moods of an earlier tumultuous existence was additionally fueled by the increasing sense of hypocrisy I felt because I had not been open about having the illness I was studying, lecturing about and treating.

I decided, after extensive discussions with family and friends, as well as colleagues at Johns Hopkins, to write an account of my own illness. I was deeply apprehensive that years of clinical writing would make it impossible to find the words to describe such elusive and strange things as mania, suicidal depressions and ecstatic hallucinations. I could not imagine putting in writing those experiences I had spent so many years trying to forget, hide or maneuver around.

Once the decision was made, however, writing proved surprisingly easy. The discipline of the years of more structured writing, much of which was done during far more difficult or intensely emotional times, proved invaluable. I found myself, for the first time in almost 20 years, loving to write again. Years of relative mental stability made the recollection of painful memories easier than I had feared. Indeed, writing put considerable order into a seemingly hopelessly chaotic life. Friendship and love, without my being aware of it, had been continuous strands running throughout my life; so, too, they ended up weaving their way throughout the book.

In order to write about my past, I was again brought face-to-face with the most awful moments of my life; but I also re-experienced those surpassingly beautiful moments of love and mood that had both bewitched and sustained me. Writing about such long ago put-aside feelings and experiences not only gave me back my memories. It also gave me back my love of writing.

August 18, 1996

Jonathan Raban

Sometimes it takes an outsider to see the least visible and most essential things about us: our hopes and fears, the landscape of our souls.

In his National Book Critics Circle Award-winner *Bad Land*—published just before he wrote this essay—British-born, Seattle resident Jonathan Raban steps onto a parched stretch of the American Northwest with all the anticipation of an astronaut lighting on another planet. The sights are strange, the feel is new, and there is no little danger in the air. It is an austere, unwelcoming land and its people are as rugged and forlorn as the earth beneath their boots. And yet it is on the prairie that Raban finds the essence of what it is to be an American: our sense of possibility, our absolute certainty that a new start is as near as the next morning. This is writing with lens and zoom. This is a clear-eyed witness.

Raban was born in a small hamlet outside Norfolk, England, in 1942. His father was off fighting the Germans at the time. Upon his return, the Rabans began "a peripatetic, near gypsy life, criss-crossing the country" from place to place until the father was ordained a priest and given a curacy in Winchester.

The eldest of three children, Raban was sent away to King's School in Worcester, a diehard institution whose first order of business was rugby, and whose educational "goal was to prepare assistant district commissioners for tours in remote outposts of the empire." He was miserable in the extreme. An asthmatic, ungainly child, he was not good at games. But he defended himself well enough with a pen and had a certain flair for the dramatic.

At 16, he threatened to leave boarding school for a post as copy boy at the local newspaper. Scandalized, his father pulled him out and sent him to a coed state school, where he happily turned his sights to a career in the arts.

He attended Hull University in Yorkshire, focusing his studies on literature and drama. After graduation, he joined the Salisbury Repertory Company, but soon realized that although he had a resonant voice, he had no talent for moving about on stage. "I was a gangling, shambling heap—too tall for the lead, near perfect for the second policeman." He found himself spending most of his time trawling the town, begging stage props from old widows. "I went back to university with my tail between my legs."

At Hull again, he did graduate work in Jewish-American literature, feeling the lure of the immigrant experience in novels by Philip Roth, Saul Bellow and Bernard Malamud. "It was the move from old world to new that interested me," he says, and more often than not these tales seemed to have the narrative arc of a love story: first the vision, then the voyage, and "then the disillusion that follows hard on infatuation."

After that, he settled into a college teaching job in a little railway town in Wales. It began well enough: His schedule left him plenty of time to "read novels, write television scripts, and carouse in the local town pub." But when he took a university position in East Anglia, everything changed. There were committee meetings to attend, administrative duties to dispatch and precious little time for books and ale.

By 1969, he quit and moved to London, where he published a book on Mark Twain and started a writing life in earnest, turning out television plays that paid well but were never produced and book reviews that made their way into the London magazines. "My office was a little pub called The Pillars of Hercules," the watering hole for a whole generation of up-and-coming British lights—Julian Barnes, Martin Amis, Ian McEwan.

In 1973, he published *Soft City*, "a book about being bewitched by London and the big city." It was probably then that the wanderlust began, for soon after he was writing travel pieces for *Radio Times*, alongside Angela Carter, Margaret Drabble and Paul Theroux. The magazine sent him to Syria, Monte Carlo, Los Angeles and New York, paying big commissions for slender, penetrating glimpses into these cultures. One particular trip to the Euphrates led to *Arabia* (1979), a cultural portrait written "with much perception and sensitivity," according to *Book World*.

In 1985, he published his only novel, *Foreign Land*. The rest was a string of nonfiction: *Old Glory* (1981); *Coasting* (1986); *For Love and Money* (1987); *God, Man and Mrs. Thatcher* (1989); *Hunting Mister Heartbreak* (1992); and *The Oxford Book of the Sea* (1993). By 1990, he was in Seattle and married. Although the marriage produced a daughter, Julia, Raban and his wife are separated—a result of his itinerant ways, as he tells it in *Bad Land* (1996).

When I interviewed him for the series, Raban was at work on a book about the tumultuous affair between Northwesterners and the sea. "I want to try to capture all the Narcissuses—white and Native American—who have squatted by the pool to peer at their reflections. . . . I want to turn the sea into a place again," he told me. The result was *Passage to Juneau: A Sea and Its Meanings* (1999).

He bristles at the term "travel writing." "There's such condescension in it," he says. And, in truth, there is much more to his work than scenics. He is, by turns, historian, memoirist, social analyst and lyrical storyteller. A modern-day homesteader himself, his books open new windows on this country. He gives us the gift of ourselves.

M. A.

Notes from the Road

BY JONATHAN RABAN

When I travel I keep a notebook—actually a Grumbacher sketchbook, ring-bound, 8 1/2 by 11 inches, with a hundred sheets of heavyweight drawing paper. Blotched and swollen, its pages parting company with their binding-wire, the notebook is my main solace when I dine alone at some cheerless eatery where the only remedy for the microwaved chicken is in the ketchup bottle. Writing in it gives me occupation and identity when I might otherwise recognize myself as an aging, unkempt drifter without visible means of support. So it's scribble, scribble, scribble all through dinner. Into the notebook go long descriptions of landscape and character; some fuzzy intellection; scraps of conversation; diagrammatic drawings; paras from the local paper; weather notes; shopping lists; inventories of interiors (the sad cafe gets grimly itemized); skeletal anecdotes; names of birds, trees and plants, culled from the wonderfully useful Peterson guides; phone numbers of people whom I'll never call; the daily target-practice of a dozen or so experimental similes.

"Looks like you're a rider," says the career-waitress with fried hair, whom I gratefully overtip for not saying "Looks like you're a bum."

From my last piece of serious traveling, a solo round-trip by boat from Seattle to Juneau, Alaska, I came back with 3 notebooks stuffed with such writing—the raw material (supposedly) for the book I am now trying to begin. Home, at this desk, seated at this typewriter, I find myself wading through the notebooks with familiar irritation. If the man who wrote them had been hired by me as my researcher, I'd sack him for gross neglect of duty.

My dim-bulb alter ego. The notebooks expose him as short-sighted and long winded by turns. Bogged down in the quotidian details of his adventure, he can't see the wood for the trees. He travels, but can't remember why he's traveling. He's short of wit, and rarely passes up an opportunity to whine. He asks all the wrong questions (when he remembers to ask any questions at all). He's at his worst when trying hardest to "write": I have to skip page after page of phony lyricism, in search of one memorable fact. The chipped flint of the waves? Give me a break. The mauve ring on the page, left by a glass of British Columbian plonk (than which no plonk in the world is plonkier), is more articulate than my man's laborious notebook-writing. It reminds me that—as he sat at that bar in Prince Rupert, the nib of his Papermate racing across the page—a scene was going on beside his shoulder . . . two angry women; one pregnant, one in fishnet tights . . . They'll find a place in the book; his blessed seascape won't. Why didn't he write about them? Why didn't he listen to the row more closely? Because, in our ill-matched duo, he's the traveler and I'm the writer, and the two are chalk and cheese. He can be a character in my story—a useful stooge—but he can never be its author, for all his tiresome literary pretensions.

Traveling (and one might as well say living) turns us into creatures of hap and contingency. We are forever navigating in fog, where the sensations of the moment are intense, and both our point of departure and our intended destination are lost to view in our concentration on the overwhelming here-and-now. Things are constantly happening, but we're in no position to judge their meaning and significance. The rumble of a ship's engine in the murk may turn out to be the sightless bulk carrier that will run us down and send us to a watery grave. Or it may not. As the case may be. The fogbound navigator, all ears for sounds of distant danger, fails to keep his eyes on the depth-sounder, and runs himself aground on the silent reef. So it is with the poor mutt who keeps my notebooks for me, because the narrative of the journey is kept hidden from him until the journey's over. Blundering through the world in zero visibility, he leaves a record only of his misapprehensions—the scary ship that faded into nothing, the impending storm that never blew, the promising channel that led nowhere. Only by the merest accident (for contingency cuts both ways) does he happen to light, occasionally, on something that will still seem to him important when the voyage is done.

Writing—real writing, in the iron discipline of a book—is the mirror-opposite of traveling. A book is a strictly subordinated world. Its logic, of symbol and metaphor, is at once tantalizingly suggestive and ruthlessly exclusive. From the moment that a narrative begins to develop its own momentum, it insists on what it needs and what it has no time for. It's at his peril that the writer loses sight of where the book began and where it's destined to find an ending. (Endings almost invariably change as the book develops, but the sense of an ending is crucial, even if it turns out to be nothing like the ending.) Writing is—in the terms of Philosophy 101—all cause, cause, cause, where traveling is a long cascade of one damn contingency after another. Good writing demands the long view, under a sky of unbroken blue; good traveling requires one to submit to the fogginess of things, the short-term, minute-by-minute experiencing of the world. It's no wonder that my alter ego and I are on such chronic bad terms.

So—tossing the notebooks into the dunce's corner of my workroom, and feeding a clean sheet of paper into the IBM Quietwriter—I'm at last about to find out what really happened to my mobile, purblind self on his travels; what it all meant, and how his voyage fits into the larger story that the book must eventually unfold. Now—touch wood—comes the interesting bit, where the act of writing itself unlocks the memory-bank, and discovers things that are neither in the notebooks nor to be found in the writer's conscious memory.

You try a phrase out: It rings false. That's not it—it wasn't like that. . . . You have to mail a stack of rejection slips to yourself before you hit on the phrase that rings true, or nearly true. Successive errors narrow the field to an increasingly fine band, then—Snap! When you do find a match between the provisional words in your head and that shadowy, half-buried recollection of events, there's no mistaking it; it's as plain as a pair of jacks on the table. Sentence by slow sentence, you begin to discover the world as it truly was—which is nearly always at variance, and sometimes wildly so, with how it was seen at the time by the dumb cluck with the Papermate.

He has his uses. He can be relied on (generally) for names, dates, the odd line of dialogue, the exact wording of a public notice—the basic facts and figures in the story. But on anything of larger importance, he's a tainted witness, too caught up in the proceedings to give a reliable account of them. For the truth of the matter, go not to him but to the language—testing words against the cloudy stuff of past experience, until you get the decisive fit that signals yes, that's how it was; that's what really happened.

Novelists will understand this process well enough—it's more or less how things come to happen in a work of realist fiction. But journalists—wedded to the notepad, the tape recorder, the "verified quote," the querulous gnome in the fact-checking department—may curl their lips in scorn at my habit of trusting the contents of my head more than I trust the documentary evidence of the notebooks. To them I'd offer this remark, made by the Barbizon school painter Jean Francois Millet: "One man may paint a picture from a careful drawing made on the spot, and another may paint the same scene from memory, from a brief but strong impression; and the last may succeed better in giving the character, the physiognomy of the place, though all the details may be inexact."

Just so. For the next 12 months or so, I mean to leave the notebooks in the corner of the room, to the spiders and the rising damp, and go fishing, instead, in the deep and haunted lake of memory.

Tight lines!

May 18, 1997

E. O. Wilson

If the name E. O. Wilson rings with familiarity—two little vowels, eeh! oh!, heralding a six-legged surname—it is because he is a special breed of scientist. He is an expert in the diminutive but a theoretician of the large: a world-renowned entomologist, prize-winning writer, synthesizer of disciplines, philosopher on the essential nature of man. His range is best captured in the two books that won him Pulitzer Prizes: *The Ants*, a breathtakingly detailed study of insect life (co-written with Bert Holldobler in 1990); and *On Human Nature* (1978), a groundbreaking fusion of behavior and biology—a work that drew a firestorm of anger from those who claimed it suggested that humans were little more than slaves to biology, ultimately governed by glands.

Edward Osborne Wilson was born in Alabama in 1929 but grew up in many places, often moving every year. "I was an only child of a peripatetic father," he says. "I don't know why it was he traveled so much. I never asked." His father was a 7th-grade dropout, a runaway who lied about his age, volunteered for the army, and spent the rest of his days as a U.S. government clerk.

Wilson describes his childhood on the move in *Naturalist*. "I thought my experience unique, but after I published my memoir, I received a large number of letters and calls from others who had had a parallel experience—a solitary boyhood, a fascination with the outdoors—there were even those who knew exactly the same marshes and woods that I did, in equal detail." According to him, the South and Gulf Coast have produced naturalists by the legion.

Perhaps because he moved so often, he found a welcome constant in nature. "Everywhere I went, I found it. I fell in love with it because it was the one thing that was familiar." He adds that his father and stepmother didn't care whether he spent all day outside. "As long as I showed up for supper, they didn't mind. I don't think they understood the extent to which I was venturing out, wading in ponds and pulling out snakes." He excelled as a Boy Scout, read magazines and nature books avidly, pored over *National Geographics*, sketched bugs, but had no special training in the elegant prose for which he is so noted.

Eventually, he was drawn to Harvard, not because of its name ("What did I know? I was pulling hay out of my hair.") but because it had the largest ant collection in the world. "My education was lopsided. I was self-trained, but I had a powerful advantage. Unlike my fellow students, I had an intimate knowledge of what the wild world was about." He received his doctorate from Harvard in 1955 and has remained there since. Today he is Harvard's honorary curator in entomology at the Museum of Comparative Zoology.

Among his many books are *Biodiversity* (1989), *Biophilia* (1984), *Sociobiology* (2000), *The Diversity of Life* (1992) and *Consilience* (1998), in which he posits that the real world is naturally consilient, organized by a small number of fundamental natural laws that govern all questions within it. The book has been attacked by those who claim it dismisses questions of religion. Wilson responds, "I may be wrong. I say that clearly in my book. Twice. The spirit of science is to say you may be wrong. I've never heard the religious say they may be wrong."

When he wrote the following piece, he was at work on *The Future of Life* (2002), in which he argues that the natural world can be saved only through technology and science. "If nature lovers do not embrace the best that science has to offer, everything they believe in is likely to disappear." His is a large ambition: to merge the spiritual with the scientific—the big, that is, with the small. "If you want to understand how the universe is put together, you cannot keep the two separate. You must have both."

M. A.

Natural Selections

By E. O. Wilson

In 1954, as a newly minted 25-year-old Ph.D. in biology, my dream was to hunt for ants in remote, unexplored rain forests. The dream—scientific thema might be the better phrase—was an extension of my experience as a teenage entomologist in the forests and swamps of my native Alabama. To trek across wide, unmapped terrain searching for new species was for me the greatest imaginable adventure. The tropical forests were the wildlands of Alabama writ large. That image was fixed in my mind; it still is. I have followed many goals in my professional life, many of them sublimations of the dream, but if I were given free reign in an afterworld, that is what I would choose to do forever.

It all began in my childhood bug period. My first excursion was in 1939 in Washington, D.C., where my father, a federal employee, had been called for a brief tour of duty. With an excitement I can still summon, I went forth one day from our apartment on Fairmont Street, bottle in hand, to explore the wilderness of nearby Rock Creek Park and bring back specimens of ants, beetles, spiders, anything that moved, for my first collection. Soon I discovered the National Zoo, also within walking distance, and the National Museum of Natural History, a 5-cent streetcar ride away, and began to haunt both. Then I narrowed my focus to butterflies, and with a homemade net began a pursuit of the red admiral, the great spangled fritillary, the tiger swallowtail and the elusive and prized mourning cloak. At this time, thanks to a *National Geographic* article on the subject, I also acquired a fascination for ants.

Returning to Alabama, I escalated my bug period by shifting to snakes. Now I hunted the black racer, the ribbon snake, the coachwhip, and the pygmy rattlesnake. In time I caught, studied and released nearly all of the 40 species native to southern Alabama, though a few I kept for a while in cages I constructed in the backyard. In my senior year in high school, I switched to ants, to my parents' undoubted relief. I had always wanted to be an entomologist. College is coming, I thought. Now is the time to get serious.

At the University of Alabama and later, in graduate studies at Harvard University, I continued to spend as much time as possible outdoors. Then came the golden opportunity that turned dream into reality. I was elected to Harvard's Society of Fellows for a three-year term, with full (well, reasonable) financial support to go anywhere, pursue any subject. So off I went and was rarely seen thereafter at Harvard. At last I could reach the tropical forests—my Louvre, my Library of Congress! After trips to Cuba and Mexico, I departed for a lengthy tour of the South Pacific: Fiji, New Caledonia, Vanuatu, Australia and finally the splendid naturalist paradise of New Guinea.

In the mid-1950s very few young biologists had the means to undertake such a distant expedition. I liked being alone. I savored pristine wilderness, climbed the unexplored center of a mountain range (on the Huon Peninsula of New Guinea), discovered scores of new species and filled my journal with notes on the behavior and ecology of ants. Returning to Harvard, I converted the information into a stream of technical articles. Most were strictly factual or theoretical, their data squeezed into the mandatory straitjacket of scientific writing.

Descriptive field research is sometimes dismissed by laboratory scientists as "stamp collecting." There is truth in the label. Natural history is primitive and simple, motivated, I believe, by an innate human urge to find, name and classify, going back to Aristotle and beyond. The naturalist is a civilized hunter. But there is much more to the science than muddy boots, mosquito bites and new species.

While I was in the South Pacific, my mind was turning over the rich theories of ecology and evolution I had learned in reading and formal study. I was especially fascinated by the idea of faunal dominance. That sweeping concept was developed during the first half of the 20th century, first by the paleontologists William Diller Matthew and George G. Simpson and then, most thoroughly, by Harvard's curator of entomology Philip J. Darlington—whose position I was eventually to inherit.

The theory of faunal dominance holds that while evolution occurs everywhere, certain land masses generate disproportionately more terrestrial and aquatic groups, such as the familiar murid rodents and ranid frogs, which are able to colonize and dominate other land masses. To Matthew and Simpson, who worked on mammals, this staging area was the circumpolar north temperate regions. To Darlington, who worked on the cold-blooded reptiles, amphibians and fishes, it was the tropics of the Old World.

Here, I thought, is a truly Homeric scenario, the stuff of great scientific adventure. The questions it posed were obvious: Why are some kinds of animals dominant, and why do they arise with probability in certain parts of the world? Those are mysteries that seem to be soluble from the fossil record and contemporary natural history. Matthew, Simpson and Darlington had worked with entire groups and a broad brush. I chose to take the study down to the species level, using ants to focus on the region from Asia to Australia and the Pacific archipelagoes. I also brought to bear the ecological data I had accumulated during my field research, something else that had not been done to that time. In a nutshell, I was able to show that tropical Asia is the center of faunal dominance.

Species spread out from there to Australia and the Pacific, with little reverse flow. The pioneer species are generally those adapted to marginal habitats, such as shorelines and riverbanks, from which overseas dispersal is easiest. But once they reach outer archipelagoes, they tend to adapt to the inland forests, where they split into daughter species. Eventually these decline, giving way to new colonists.

In the 1960s this "taxon cycle," as I called it, became part of the inspiration for the theory of island biography developed by Robert H. MacArthur of Princeton and myself. Our conception, which helps to explain the equilibrium and turnover of plant and animal species generally, played a useful later role in general ecology and conservation planning.

None of my reports and theory hinted of motivation, and very little emotion was expressed beyond the occasional "I was interested in the problem of . . ." or "It turned out, to my surprise, that . . . ." I played by the aforementioned rules: Humanistic excursions are not relevant; confession is a sign of weakness and self-indulgence. The audience of a scientific communication is other scientists, and not just any other scientists but fellow specialists working in and around a narrowly defined topic. I doubt that more than a dozen fellow entomologists read my article announcing the discovery of cerapachyine ants on New Caledonia, although the data are still used. The taxon cycle and island biogeography became familiar to a wider circle of biologists but still are unknown to the lay public, and for that matter a majority of scientists, who are preoccupied with their own sectors of the frontier.

Only later did it occur to me to write about these early efforts as a personal history, in a narrative that includes motive and emotion. When I decided to try it, in *Biophilia* (1984) and *Naturalist* (1994), I discovered how difficult it is to compose this form of literature. Not only difficult but risky, opening the author to the indignity of being all too clearly understood. The vast majority of scientists would rather stay inside the guild, so that attempts to cross over from their own research directly to the arts (as opposed to merely playing the cello or admiring modern art) are correspondingly rare.

But the rewards to the broader culture, if the effort has quality, are potentially great. I hope others will try. Thanks to the continuing exponential growth of scientific knowledge as well as the innovative thrust of the creative arts, the bridging of the two cultures is now in sight as a frontier of its own. Among its greatest challenges, still largely unmet, is the conversion of the scientific creative process and world view into literature.

To wring literature from science is to join two radically different modes of thought. The technical reports of pure science are not meant to be and cannot be reader-friendly. They are humanity's tested factual knowledge, open to verification, framed by theory, couched in specialized language for exactitude, trimmed for brevity and delivered raw. Metaphor is unwelcome except in cautious, homeopathic doses. Hyperbole, no matter how brilliant, is anathema. In pure science, discovery counts for everything, and personal style next to nothing.

In literature metaphor and personal style are, in polar contrast, everything. The most successful innovator is an honest illusionist: His product, as Picasso said of visual art, is the lie that helps us see the truth. Imagery, phrasing and analogy in literature are not crafted to establish empirical facts, and even less are they meant to be put into a general theory. Rather, they are the vehicles by which the writer conveys his feelings directly to his audience.

The central role of literature is the transmission of the details of human experience by artifice that intensifies aesthetic and emotional response. Originality and power of metaphor are coin of the realm. Their source is an intuitive understanding of human nature, not an accurate knowledge of the material world; in this respect literature is the exact opposite of pure science. The linkage of science and literature is a premier challenge of the 21st century, for the following reason: The scientific method has expanded our understanding of life and the universe in spectacular fashion across the entire scale of space and time, in every sensory modality, and beyond the farthest dreams of the pre-scientific mind. It is as though humanity, after wandering for millennia in a great dark cavern with only the light of a candle (to use a metaphor!), can now find its way with a searchlight.

No matter how much we see, or how beautifully theory falls out to however many decimal places, all of experience is still processed by the sensory and nervous systems peculiar to our species, and all of knowledge is still evaluated by our idiosyncratically evolved emotions. Both the research scientist and the creative writer are members of Homo sapiens, in the family Hominidae of the order Primates, and a biological species exquisitely adapted to planet Earth. Art is in our bones: We all live by narrative and metaphor.

The successful scientist is a poet who works like a bookkeeper. When his bookkeeper's work is done and duly registered in peer-reviewed technical journals, he can if he wishes return to the poetic mode and pour human life into the freeze-dried database. But chastely so, taking care never to misstate facts, never to misrepresent theory, never to betray Nature.

June 25, 2000

Bill McKibben

Henry David Thoreau once said "It takes two to speak the truth—one to speak and another to hear." As Bill McKibben points out below, something very similar could be said about activist writing. It takes one to foment; but it takes another—sometimes many others—to bring about a result. A writer can craft an argument about a life-and-death issue in the finest, most crystalline prose, but if that argument doesn't inspire readers to action, it will not have done its work.

For McKibben, words weren't always the means to an end. He began his career as a reporter, a quintessential observer. He began life, for that matter, as a reporter's son. His father was a journalist for *Business Week*. When McKibben went away to college, it wasn't far: from Lexington, Mass., to Harvard, where he became the editor of the *Crimson*. From there, it was a short leap to the *New Yorker*, where, at 21, he was producing cameos for "Talk of the Town"—not about celebrities, which is what the column seems to favor these days, but about ordinary life in all its eccentric glory, printed without a byline in sight. These were simple observations, meant to delight and entertain.

McKibben ascribes his transformation from observer to activist to a single article, written for the *New Yorker* when he was not yet 25. The piece focused on his New York apartment, on every article in it and where it came from, so that his tiny world suddenly dilated: to the jungles of South America, to the uranium mines in the Grand Canyon, to the forests of Quebec, to the garbage barges along the Hudson. "It had the effect of making me realize just how related life is. How dependent we are on the physical world." And how finite and consumable that physical world can be.

The epiphany had its effects. When William Shawn, editor of the *New*

Yorker, was let go, McKibben quit his job, moved to a secluded house in the Adirondacks, and began to devote himself entirely to writing about the greenhouse effect, the depletion of the ozone layer and global warming. In less than a year he produced *The End of Nature* (1989), "written in a fever" before his 28th birthday. It was a publishing success and may even have changed the emotional valence of our thinking about the environment, but it didn't have the effect McKibben hoped for. "It became a silent issue," he says. "We've wasted a decade. And, in the interim, chemistry has done its work. People just don't realize. Global warming is a threshold issue. Once we pass it, we can't go back."

McKibben has written several books since *The End of Nature*, among them *The Age of Missing Information* (1992), *Hope, Human and Wild* (1996) and *Long Distance: A Year of Living Strenuously* (2000), but he is still held fast by the topic of his first. There is a fundamental transformation when you begin to worry about the environment, he says, whether you are a reporter or a scientist. You cease to be objective. "It's no longer: Here is the data. It becomes: Here is the data and here's how you should think about it." For this writer, we've forfeited the luxury of time.

M. A.

Speaking Up for the Environment

BY BILL McKIBBEN

I'm writing these words on a plane home from Washington. From a Washington press conference, to be precise, where I was answering questions, making arguments: Drilling in the Arctic National Wildlife Refuge must be prevented, we desperately need a new energy policy, and so on. It didn't knock hoof-and-mouth disease off the evening news, but I was giving it my best shot. And all the while I was wondering, have I turned from a writer into a hack?

In an earlier life, I was on the other side of the microphone. As a newspaperman, as a "Talk of the Town" reporter for the old *New Yorker*, I went to hundreds of press conferences and held my tape recorder up in the air, shouted my share of questions. In a slightly later life, I wrote books and long essays—alone in my study, alone in my thoughts, slogging my way through the long, silent process of putting words to paper. That's still my "job," I guess, and I relish it. I savor the chance to read and ponder and most of all to set words down and make my own stabs at beauty and meaning. The trouble is, my books are about controversial topics, in particular the largest environmental problems like global warming. My reporting and reflecting have left me with a definite point of view. And more and more that point of view seems to lead me out of my study and into another world that operates by different rules.

I knew how it was supposed to work: People would read my words and demand change from their leaders, and that would be that. (I was, perhaps it's worth mentioning, 27 when I wrote my first book). The model, I suppose, was Rachel Carson and *Silent Spring*. And in fact, people did read my books. *The End of Nature* was translated into 20 languages, excerpted in dozens of magazines and newspapers. But things didn't go according to plan. The world didn't change. In fact, for the last decade, even as the science of climate change has grown endlessly more robust, our country in particular has done next to nothing about it. We burn more fossil fuel than we did a decade ago, we block international treaties, we are nothing short of a rogue nation when it comes to global warming. Yet nobody seems too exercised about it all. We go on going on—in the years since I published *The End of Nature* we've transformed our everyday fleet from cars to semi-military vehicles. So what is a writer supposed to do? What are any of us who write about the natural world supposed to do, at a moment when it is under constant and sapping siege from every direction? How loud are you supposed to shout?

It's a hard question for a writer, and not just because of the time and energy that any crusading takes, time and energy most of us would rather devote to, well, writing. More, there's the worry about what will happen if you start to take a public role. Will it cost you the crankiness and whimsy real writing demands? Will you start writing press releases or editorials when you think you're writing short stories or essays? Will you sacrifice the particular, the small, the funny, the idiosyncratic? Will you gloss over your misgivings, subscribe to some party line, listen only to the people whose side you're on? Add to that the worry that you'll lose your credibility with your readers (or your editors).

I came to Washington last year, too, came with the express but apprehensive purpose of getting arrested. It was late spring, and the Alliance for Democracy was sponsoring a small protest in the Rotunda. A couple of dozen of us—including the wonderful Granny D, a 90-year-old woman who had walked across the nation for campaign finance reform—were supposed to hold up signs demanding action on environmental issues. We had a training session the night before in a church basement, and everyone gathered into small groups to talk about what was making them most nervous. There might be violence, said one person. I might not be able to handle jail, said another. When it was my turn, I said: What if people decide I'm a hopeless partisan and stop taking seriously my writing about these subjects? What if they decide I'm a propagandist, not a real writer?

At root, we think of writers as observers. Activists can write, of course, but they're activists using writing as one tool in their kit. Real, serious Writer Writers look on—whether it's from novels or from newspaper columns. They can hold strong opinions, write powerful op-eds, but they tell us what is happening, what should happen. They themselves aren't supposed to "happen." The subspecies "journalist," from which I am descended, is in some fashion not supposed to become engaged in the world around him.

For a long time, though, I've found my literary fellowship among the nature writers. This genre may be America's strongest suit in contemporary letters, our most distinctive gift to world literature. (And it grows stronger all the time: The more our forests and fields and even our genes come under assault, the more the fresh voices emerge to tell a story.) It is a distinctive literary community, in part because it is tight-knit (and even loosely organized, through groups like the Orion Society); in part because it exists mostly outside the academy and hence is less divided by dialectic than other literary tribes. But it stands apart most profoundly because it and its members don't just write about the natural world; they vote with their words—they defend it.

There's Rick Bass, the novelist, essayist and champion of Montana wilderness, working to save the Yaak Valley. Wendell Berry, the Kentucky farmer and chronicler of the fictional town of Port William, who has been working to save family farming for decades. Terry Tempest Williams, the Utah writer and wilderness activist. W. S. Merwin, the Hawaiian poet and rainforest protector. Richard Nelson, the Alaska writer who has worked for years to save the Tongass National Forest from clearcutting. And so on and on and on.

First and foremost they are writers—people who sense the world and describe it, as powerfully as they can. Or maybe first and foremost they are guardians of the places and communities they love. Or maybe—very likely—the roles flip back and forth, enriching each other. For in the act of trying to save something—a forest, a mountain, the climate—you need to communicate with others, and to do that you need to look as hard and as carefully as you possibly can. The greatest of this writing is neither sentimental nor obvious—instead, it is very nearly shamanistic, allowing the natural world to translate itself into English in all sorts of ways. Emotional ways, taxonomic ways, descriptive ways, intimate ways, Olympian ways. It is a community of writers, with all the particulars of their upbringings, tastes, genders, mental states, seeking faithfully to serve as some sort of connection between people and the rest of the world. That faithfulness demands the most scrupulous accuracy—you have to know the tree's resilience, the coyote's circling route, the carbon molecule's structure. But it also demands that you care, which is the highest form of objectivity.

There is no way, in this kind of relationship, to escape a deep political involvement. If you make a visceral connection, one that takes you beyond the solipsism that is a writer's normal friend and enemy, then the defense of those places, those communities, is no longer optional. Not only would you lose the right to write about them, you'd lose the ability. That connection cannot be maintained at an emotional distance. You can defend a place without understanding it—that is sentimental hackwork, and there's plenty of it around. But you cannot understand a place without defending it. And if you understand one place . . . well, suffice it to say that everyone in a community of nature writers comes to each other's aid.

The press conference that brought me to D.C. marked the launch of a book of essays about the Arctic National Wildlife Refuge, assembled in six weeks' time by Alaskans Hank Lentfer and Carolyn Servid. The collection *Arctic Refuge: A Circle of Testimony* includes pieces from Barry Lopez and Scott Russell Sanders, John Haines and Mardy Murie, a long, long list. Some of us had seen the wide coastal plain of the refuge, and some of us hadn't, but all of us were ready to write in its defense, and to talk, and perhaps do more if more was called for. Without that kind of commitment, my writing life wouldn't make much sense.

April 22, 2001

VI

Looking Back

Frances FitzGerald

Carol Shields

Julian Barnes

Jane Smiley

Michael Chabon

Ward Just

Frances FitzGerald

Frances FitzGerald writes about things she doesn't understand. She is not alone in this. Many nonfiction writers are drawn to subjects whose contours and logic they feel elude them. Unfamiliarity is par for the course in a journalist's life. Bit by bit, through research and discipline—by tightening a focus, clarifying the picture for someone else—a writer can arrive at comprehension of the deepest kind. It's work akin to spelunking: You tunnel down with little more than curiosity, penetrate caves, track flumes, and then emerge to illuminate a subterranean world teeming with detail. Initially, FitzGerald decided to write *Way Out There in the Blue* (published in 2000, just after this essay appeared in *Book World*), because she was puzzled by Ronald Reagan. "I felt that by listening to him I would learn something about this country. He didn't appeal to Northeast city people like me. But he had an extraordinary connection to the deep mythology of America. I wanted to know what that was. What bell was ringing with other Americans that I couldn't hear?"

She looks at Reagan via his Star Wars initiative—a quintessentially Reaganesque plan to install a defense shield over the United States. "No other president could have convinced the public of something that didn't exist." Her book is more about him and his administration, she admits, than about American ballistic defenses. The question "Why was this man believed?" pulls FitzGerald into complicated landscapes of history and the American mind.

She has seen those trenches before. In 1972, she published *Fire in the Lake*, a portrait of the Vietnamese and the increasing American involvement in their country. It swept all the prizes the following year: the Pulitzer, the Bancroft, the National Book Award, George Polk and Sidney Hillman awards. Seven years later, she produced *America Revised*, an exploration of the subtle ways school textbooks manipulate history. In 1986, she brought out *Cities on a Hill*, an account of four contemporary American communities that exemplify our penchant for self-reinvention.

FitzGerald was born in New York in 1940. Her parents were intensely interested in foreign policy: Her father worked as a CIA administrator; her mother held a post at the United Nations; her stepfather was a British parliamentarian. She spent her childhood shuttling between New York and Oxford, graduated from Radcliffe in 1962 and began her career by producing pieces about Paris for *New York* magazine and the *Herald Tribune*. In 1966, she decided to go to Vietnam and report about the war; her stories were published in the *Village Voice, London Daily Telegraph, Atlantic Monthly* and *Vogue*. Eventually, she wrote pieces about the Vietnamese for the *New Yorker*. "When the war ended, I felt I'd lost a job," she says.

Today she is a passionate defender of journalism. When asked whether or not the post-civil rights, post-Vietnam spate of journalists has written durable history, she bristles. "How can you possibly denigrate journalism?" she says. "Journalists work on deadline. They uncover things nobody else understands, hidden beneath layers and layers of official deception." They may not get it exactly right, they may chase this way and that, but according to Frances FitzGerald they are the front line of an army. If the truth is an underground labyrinth, journalism is a sharp spade; and if FitzGerald fixes her attention on something she doesn't understand, a great deal of digging is bound to follow. Perhaps even books that endure.

M. A.

The Trouble with Finishing

BY FRANCES FITZGERALD

My fourth book, due out in April, took 9 years to write. My relatives long ago learned not to ask the dreaded question, "When are you going to finish your book?", but 9 years is a very long time, and certainly a record for me. My brother and sisters, some of whose children went through primary and middle school in that period, must have found their kindly restraint somewhat taxing, for when I told them I had finished, all of them exhaled, as if they had been holding their breath, and exclaimed, "How wonderful! You must be relieved! Aren't you thrilled?"

Yes, I said, sure, but it wasn't really the truth. The fact is that I don't like finishing books. For weeks after handing a manuscript over to a publisher, my feeling, and I suspect that of many other writers, is simply that of loss. To a writer a book in progress is, after all, a job, and finishing it is something like getting fired. You're out on the streets and faced with the dispiriting task of looking for another job, when it seems impossible that you will find one—much less one you like as much as the one you have. In the meantime you have to do everything you no longer have an excuse to put off, such as getting the stove fixed and dealing with the insurance company. Then, to a writer a book is much more than a job. It's a companion—albeit a temperamental one you would sometimes like to strangle. It's a virtual world you can call up any time—a world with its own landscapes, its own cast of characters, its problems and its epiphanies. Finishing it means that this world must disappear, this companion must go, and it will be a long time before you can find a replacement.

Some writers always have book projects lined up ahead of them.

They know what their next book will be before they finish the last. This has never happened to me. While I am writing a book, I can't see anything beyond it, and my peripheral vision dims to the point that I can't imagine what other matter might be of any real interest. It's like being at the bottom of the Grand Canyon. Only when I come up do I realize that much has happened while I was down there. On finishing this book, I feel somewhat like Rip van Winkle. Among other things, I am 4 or more Microsoft Word programs behind the times.

Yet even if I knew exactly what I would do next, I think I would like finishing no better. For one thing, it would mean having to think about starting all over when I know perfectly well how long a book takes. After a year or so I happily forget this. Then, too, starting a book is almost as bad as finishing one. There are just too many blank spaces, too many possibilities. A book becomes fun only when it fills out a bit and begins to make its own demands: Listen harder to what this person is saying, what is the butler doing in the bedroom with a revolver?, and please don't put on the Hallelujah Chorus right after *Melancholy Baby*. The best part of a book is the middle, when one is convinced of its earth-shaking importance, intrigued by its smallest puzzles, amused by its slightest jokes. At that point it seems just possible that the book might be a metaphor for everything. Toward the end it becomes clear that this isn't the case, and that it is just a book about something. On the other hand, it has become a manageable and fairly comfortable place with problems on the order of where the sofa ought to go. Then, just as it begins to feel like home, it has to go off to the publisher.

Of course, finishing is better than not being able to finish, but it means breaking the satisfying routine of work. Spending much of the day alone in a room in front of a computer does not seem a wonderful life to most people. "What discipline you have," people say. But writers would do almost anything else if they did not like to be alone in the daytime. By late afternoon, of course, enough is enough, and we can be found prowling the streets or looking for a chandelier to swing from. All the same, the time to write is a luxury—and finishing a book means doing all those things one has so successfully avoided.

When a book is finished, a vacation would be nice, but that can't happen because, although the book has gone, the text of it won't. It keeps coming back in different forms—the copy-edited manuscript, galleys, and page proofs—all of which must be read for errors, even while one is quarreling with the insurance company and desperately calling friends to make a lunch date.

Some writers like reading their galleys and page proofs. I don't. True, the dirty, marked-up manuscript comes back all nice and clean and looking much smarter than it did before. But inevitably there are mistakes, and, as I read it over and over again merely to detect more, the text loses all sense—to the point where it seems like nothing more than a compendium of possible errors and a heap of arbitrarily placed words. While in this process, I realize that my book is becoming a stranger to me, and for the first time I can conceive that there might be other things in the world. This is surely healthy—except that it leads me to wonder why I spent so much time on this book when there are so many other things in the world.

By the time the text has finally gone, months have passed, and still there are 3 or 4 months before publication. At this point postpartum depression can set in in earnest. A vacation is not the solution. The only cure is to plunge into another piece of work or to get as far away as possible: the North Pole, Borneo, someplace where people have no relation to books and won't ask what you're working on now.

If the cure succeeds, you come back refreshed and full of enthusiasm for a new project. However, success means that by the time the book is finally published, it has become a complete stranger, whose lineaments you can hardly recall. Describing it to friends or interviewers is like taking the final exam of a course you took a year before. The ardor that sustained you through the years of writing has long since dimmed; the importance of the book escapes you; the solutions to its puzzles seem obvious and its jokes—well, surely by now everyone has heard them. Then, however well the book is received, no one will ever see it as you once did—or understand why it took you so long.

Still, there is at least one satisfaction in finishing a book, and it is this: A book between covers is a solid object, and having it to pick up and put down tells you that you have made something as substantial as a shoe or plate.

March 19, 2000

Carol Shields

There is a quiet strength in Carol Shields. For all the insecurities she cites in her essay, she has the confidence of an artist who knows her medium and loves her craft. "I always think of writing as making," she has said, and indeed her fictions are as formed as family quilts, small-town miniatures, beaded strings. She hones sentences, hangs one after another, and so constructs familiar worlds. "Early on in my career," she says, speaking from her home in British Columbia, "the critics called me 'a miniaturist,' said that I wrote 'women's books,' 'domestic novels,' as if that were a lesser thing. But I knew then as I know now that the lives of women are serious and interesting." Her stories are largely about families, gardens, love and work, and they range from the historical novel *Swann* (1987) to a book about amorous neighbors—*The Republic of Love* (1992)—to *Larry's Party* (1997) to an epistolary novel *A Celibate Season* (1991) to *Stone Diaries* (1998), which won the Pulitzer and the National Book Critics Circle awards and was short listed for the Booker Prize.

Born in Illinois in 1935, she calls her hometown of Oak Park (birthplace of Hemingway) a "WASP suburb, completely white and somewhat unreal. But it afforded me an enviable childhood. I never had anything but encouragement from my parents or teachers or friends. No one told me to go out and play instead of write. No one ever told me how bad my writing really was. No one mocked me for my bookish interests." Her mother was an elementary schoolteacher. Her father managed a candy factory. She read the *Bobbsey Twins* and *Five Little Peppers and How They Grew* and trotted through public school writing poetry wherever she went, stuffing unfinished bits into her purse.

She studied at Hanover College until she was offered the opportunity to spend her junior year abroad at the University of Exeter. It was there that she met her Canadian husband—a future dean of engineering at the University of Manitoba. Transported to Vancouver, she acquired a new citizenship, a new identity, and began the hard business of combining a writing career with the raising of children. There were five babies in all—one coming quickly after the next.

She wrote when she could—at bedtime, in the kitchen, in transit. She found herself composing lines in her head, committing them to memory, then noting them down at the end of the day. She imposed a rigorous self-discipline: a minimum of 2 pages of writing per night. She managed to place her work in literary magazines here and there. She even tried her hand at a thriller (*The Vortex*), the memory of which she finds embarrassing. Finally, at age 40, she produced *The Box Garden*, and, continuing to deliver on her 2-pages-a-day rule, she has not stopped publishing since. When she wrote this essay, her most recent work was *Dressing Up for the Carnival*, a collection of stories judged by *Book World* to be "an endlessly levitating entertainment." Most recently, she has produced *Unless*, a novel about a mother and daughter who have drifted apart.

A number of years ago, Shields published a short biography of Jane Austen. A fierce defender of the sensory pleasures of reading, Shields resembles no one so much as Austen when she says: "Twenty-five years from now I predict a rediscovery of the book as we know it. Suddenly people will be saying of books: how portable, how compact, how direct, how cost-effective, how intimate, how blessedly silent, how vivid, how individual, how interactive, how revolutionary!" There's nothing miniature about that.

M. A.

The Hardest Critics

BY CAROL SHIELDS

All writers, I suspect, even the cocky and arrogant, dread the period immediately following publication. This is the "fragile time," when we writers are at our most vulnerable. A book has been written, edited, published and sent to the first line of critical appraisal. There is no way, it seems, to circumvent this painful process.

Now might be a good time for that long-talked-about trip to the Galapagos. Or a canoe adventure in northern Ontario. I'm often asked whether I read my reviews. Of course, I read them; I pounce on them, in fact, but I've learned not to stew them up and have them for supper. My rule is to read through them twice, then put them away. If they're good, they warm your shivering limbs but make you big-headed and a pain to those you live with. If they're bad, they make you grumpy, then bring on a paralyzing fit of public embarrassment, which shades, a few minutes later, into courage. Who does this person think he/she is? Why have I risked exposing myself to the critical gaze of ----, who doesn't have the least understanding of the contemporary novel, or to ----, who not only refuses to engage with the novel but shows a glint of the fang, or to ----, who has "just one small quibble" and actually tacks that quibble onto the final paragraph? Doesn't he/she know quibbles should be kept in the desk drawer, along with the paper clips and fresh staples?

If official reviews are awkward, personal reviews are a torment. These seldom come from family members, for it is a well-known fact that a writer's extended family maintains a fairly steady and oddly mysterious silence about any new publication except perhaps for the observation—complimentary or accusing, I'm not sure—that there are a lot of big words in the new book. Family members are more than pleased to display your book on their coffee tables, and they do expect a free copy, even though you explained to them that you are given only a limited number. They demand a warm inscription, but beyond that they have elected, for the most part, a no-comment stance.

This used to worry me: Had I embarrassed my family in some way, just by being published? Are they fearful and protective for my sake? Or do they worry that they may lack a critical vocabulary with which to deconstruct a work of fiction, that they have been made to feel, by me and my big words, humbled and inept? I've decided, finally, that family members refuse to comment on a book simply because they haven't read it, and they haven't read it because they know me, the author, in a particular and highly specified way and prefer not to know me in any other, perhaps more dangerous way. I am the aunt, the cousin, the sister, not someone who moves in a glossy literary world with my photo on a book jacket, a photo that frankly doesn't look very much like me: the puffed-up hair, yikes; the startled, yet pensive look in my eyes; that background of bare branches that probably signify—well, what exactly? Safer to say nothing at all.

Friends and colleagues, on the other hand, feel free to offer a range of comments that center not on an analysis of your new book but on their immediate response to the fact that you have published one. They read a review of it—somewhere, ummm—but what was the title again? Someone is sure to ask you when the paperback is coming out. Someone else tells you earnestly that she has especially requested it at the public library, and this is always expressed as a form of high tribute.

"Interesting approach," you will hear, and that word interesting, so neutral and meaningless, a pellet so carefully considered and tactfully delivered, alerts you to the fact that your book has been found worthless.

"I've bought your book," a friend says, "but haven't got around to reading it yet." You what? You mean you have it in your possession and you haven't been compelled to rip open its covers at once? What is the matter with you? Or with the book? Or with me, the author? Are you trying to tell me something?

"I love it, but love your other book(s) better." This comment comes in a number of versions. "It didn't hold my attention quite the way your last book did." "I had a little trouble relating to the main character this time, but otherwise . . . " "Once I got past the first 200 pages I was really hooked, whereas your other book(s) grabbed me right from the first page."

Full-blown paranoia has arrived. When a friend tells me she has read my book between dinner and bedtime, I can scarcely keep the whine of injury out of my voice: This happens to be a book I spent 2 years writing, I want to say, and you're telling me you scarfed it down in one evening!

"I've bought your book for my mother-in-law/for my sister in Florida/for my daughter." These comments come from men, the same men who tell me their wives/mothers/daughters read all my books.

I've never been able to formulate a polite retort to such remarks, which are delivered with such sincerity and good will and such appalling insensitivity that I can do nothing but gaze at the ceiling, mumbling, muttering, pretending to be somewhere else. Almost all the women writers I know have been stunned by the same line of misjudged gallantry. Is there a response? What is it? Is there some way to express gratitude and indignation in one short, sharp, telling, smiling, knee-capped phrase?

"I would have bought your book," a colleague tells me, "but it came out far too late for my wife's birthday." (I'm still sifting through the many levels of this extraordinary remark.)

"I would have read your book, but I don't have time for fiction."

"I read so much during the day"—this is a favorite of lawyers and business people—"that I can't concentrate on anything but junk TV in the evening."

"I like a good, fast-paced plot." Meaning that your book doesn't measure up in that department.

"Maybe I'm old-fashioned, but I, uh, like a beginning, middle and end." Uh-huh.

"Robert really wanted to come to your launch tonight, but he felt he should stay home to—I know this sounds silly—to paint the fence. While the weather holds, I mean. You know what September is like. He knew you'd understand and he sends his best wishes and love. And admiration."

The post-pub period, luckily, lasts only a short while. The authorly skin thickens, as it must. The book itself recedes, and probably you are already thinking of the next project, and also thinking, logically, calmly, that you don't like half the books you pick up, not even a third of them, so why should you expect every single reader to engage with your work? The reviews, both formal and informal, merge and grow misty.

And, after all, there was that one friend (brilliant, perspicacious) who wrote to tell you that every word in your new book felt weighted with rare gold. Hang on to that; never mind whether it is a genuine response or a slice of royal baloney. You know the rules of self-preservation by now. Take baloney any time it's offered. It's better than the other thing.

There's one more critical assault to come, the academic wave. This could arrive next year, in 5 years' time or in 20 years. Your work has been reassessed. Whole new subtexts have been brought to the surface. That story about the Winnipeg widow has become a textbook example of sexual abuse. It's perfectly obvious that the father figure is dangerous. Really? And the names you've chosen for your characters—Kay, Pat, Al, Ray, Fay, Tom—each of these has meaning, drifted like snow beneath metaphorical sunlight. "I've only wanted to choose some short names," you say—or resist saying. "It's so tiresome to write out a long name a million times."

No one will believe you. "They," out there, want double or triple resonance. You may be tempted to claim their insights or else cry out in support of ignorance. But it is better to keep quiet; let them have their way with your work. One can never dismiss the subconscious, after all. Shake hands with what is offered.

Who knows, in the end, what is true? Not you. Especially not you.

August 13, 2000

Julian Barnes

Clever man, Julian Barnes—a writer who can focus on the small even as he makes you think about the large. He strings words carefully, picking his way to perfection as only finicky linguists can. And yet before you know it, you have followed him into the mess of things—love, death, fidelity, survival—seeing it all with a cool, Olympian eye.

There is, of course, a reason for this. Barnes is both philologist and philosopher, a wordman in search of the great perhaps. Writing as Dan Kavanagh and himself—from *Fiddle City* to *Flaubert's Parrot*—he is also (along with Martin Amis, Ian McEwan and Graham Swift) one of Britain's most consistently interesting novelists. He was born in Leicester in 1946. The son of two teachers of French, he was part of a household that savored words and looked abroad for a perspective on itself. By 12 he had won a scholarship to City of London School, by 15 he was well lodged in its modern language department, "doing" French and Russian because "it seemed the sexy thing to do."

At Oxford University he continued with languages, then switched to psychology and philosophy, thinking that in them he might find "the answers to life." But he found himself peering at earthworms instead, and going from philosopher A to philosopher B's refutation of A, in what seemed to him "a series of unpleasant denunciations." Before long he was back in the comfortable cadences of Montaigne, Montesquieu, Baudelaire, Rimbaud and Mallarmé, "lethargically assuming that he would carry on in academic life." He was quickly relieved of that notion, however, when just before graduation a Pascal expert asked him what he planned to do. "I thought I'd become one of you," he responded brightly. Long pause. "Have you thought about journalism?" It was the height of an Oxford put-down. It was also, however, a perfectly good idea.

Barnes did become a journalist, but not immediately. He was turned down for one job after another, and then just as abruptly offered 2: one as tax collector and another as lexicographer. He took the second. For 3 years he worked on the new supplement to the Oxford English Dictionary (letters A through G), burrowing into Oxford's underground stacks to find every possible usage of a given word. It wasn't long before he was chafing at the small and yearning for the large. That was when he decided to read for the bar.

In the mid '70s, as he was struggling with the ins and outs of contract law, some sympathetic soul assigned him a book to review—*The History of Architectural Restoration*, to be exact. And then there were more assignments: from the *Times Literary Supplement*, the *New Statesman*, the *New Review*, the *Observer*. By 30, he had left lawyering to become a full-time book and television critic, a combination as eminently sensible in England as it is preposterous here. By the time *Metroland*, his first novel, was published in 1980, he had a firm foot in the door of literary London.

Barnes has scarcely looked back since. As Dan Kavanagh, he published a series of sassy crime novels—*Duffy* (1980), *Fiddle City* (1983), *Putting the Boot In* (1985) and *Going To the Dogs* (1988). As Julian Barnes, he went on to write *Before She Met Me* (1982), the much-celebrated *Flaubert's Parrot* (1984), *Staring at the Sun* (1986), *A History of the World in 10 1/2 Chapters* (1989), *Talking It Over* (1991), *The Porcupine* (1992), *Cross Channel* (1996), *England, England* (1999) and *Love, etc.* (2001). His work continues to be elusively autobiographical, deliciously satirical, focused tightly on detail and engrossed in the business of life itself.

A thoroughly literary man, Barnes is married to agent Pat Kavanagh, who, in the ingrown London way of things, has represented a number of Barnes's writerly competitors: Jeanette Winterson, Martin Amis, Ruth Rendell. Kavanagh is almost a decade Barnes's senior. There has always been a fair amount of gossip swirling about Kavanagh and Barnes; then again, it's not as if there has ever been a dearth of gossip in London publishing circles. Asked about this, Barnes bridles. "New York is every bit as tight and incestuous as we are," he says. "You want intrigue? Try being a writer in Paris."

Fifty-six now, and firmly established, Barnes is quite immune to gossip anyway. In the very halls that sniffed at his academic aspirations 30 years ago, professors assign his books. "It makes me feel a bit dead, that," he says wistfully. "I had hoped to remain a moving target for a while."

M. A.

Literary Executions

BY JULIAN BARNES

Most writers spend most of their time being themselves—that's to say, living through the oscillating self-doubt and mild paranoia, the rival temptations of vanity and self-pity (sometimes voluptuously combined), endemic to the profession. This burden of authorial self is normally quite enough for us. Recently, however, I've found myself obliged to be another writer as well: Someone, what's more, who is 50 years older than myself, female and dead. It has not turned out quite as I expected. For the last 25 years of her life I was a good friend of Dodie Smith, the author of a string of pre-war West End hits (*Dear Octopus* is still performed on a regular basis), of the teenage classic *I Capture the Castle* and of *The Hundred and One Dalmatians*, from which Disney made its lucrative film. In 1987, when she was over 90, Dodie asked me to be her literary executor. I immediately agreed, though not from any eager desire to fulfill this function. It was partly out of mild embarrassment (not wanting to think about Dodie being dead), but mainly as a logical consequence of our friendship. When I'd been starting out as a writer, she'd encouraged me; now that she was finishing, it was my turn to help her. Dodie, who was always forthright and unsentimental, insisted on worrying on my behalf: Whether the job would distract me from my own work, what my take should be, and so on. In a follow-up letter, Dodie's husband and business manager, Alec, confirmed the appointment, adding that "Neither Dodie nor I have grandiose ideas of vast sums accruing, or much work entailed."

Alec died the following year, Dodie in November 1990. Neither his letter, nor her will, contained specific directions to the literary executor. So the first thing I did was consult Dodie's friend and literary agent of 60 years, Laurence Fitch. Could he think of any general principles of approach, or indeed of any personal whims or wishes, relevant to the Smith estate? Laurence thought for a while. Eventually he said, "Dodie didn't like the idea of her work being done in Japan." "Why was that?" I asked. "Because she understood that they ate dogs there." This firm prejudice seemed to be my sole guideline.

My first indication that being a literary executor wasn't going to be just a matter of rubber-stamping publishers' contracts came with the disposal of Dodie's papers. She was an inveterate hoarder and had kept everything from batches of first-night telegrams to lengthy correspondences with Christopher Isherwood, John van Druten and others. She also kept carbons of her own letters, so the archive was complete—and vast. All I knew was that for some years she had intended leaving it to Boston University; but there had been a falling-out, and she had changed her mind. She had been approached by English universities (Manchester, I think, and Essex) but had made no decision. The will was silent on the matter.

I asked a London book dealer to handle the potential sale, telling him that as far as I understood the matter the only place Dodie had a prejudice against was Boston. It proved an awkward archive to sell, because of the state of the market, Dodie's standing as a writer (significant but minor) and the exorbitant amount of paper involved. Its state was less than perfect too: Some of the correspondence had been chewed away by mice, and the whole archive was infested with silverfish (Dodie was so resolutely pro-animal that she was also pro-vermin). Eventually the dealer reported. A few institutions might be interested in acquiring the archive as a gift; but the only one willing to offer money was Boston.

First I tried to check my imprecise memory. Her file of correspondence with Boston ended abruptly, yet without clue. Her voluminous diary was no help. I vaguely remembered Alec saying something like "The fellow was a bit pushy," but would swear no oath to that quote. Laurence Fitch couldn't recall any details. What, I wondered, would Dodie have done? Would she have swallowed her pride and taken the money to keep her going for another year or two? Did I have the right to deprive her beneficiaries of the cash? Eventually, I decided that Boston should have the archive, on the grounds that an institution that has paid money is more likely to treasure its acquisitions than one that hasn't. But I was aware that even in my first dutiful act as literary executor there was a possible implicit disobedience.

"Being Dodie" meant making decisions as I imagined she would have done. It meant forgetting, or at least playing down, the interests of the living (beneficiaries, literary agent, potential publishers) in favor of the dead. It also meant forgetting being me. For instance, I am skeptical of literary biography as currently practiced, finding much of it reductive in approach and diminishing to the work. But that opinion was largely irrelevant when asking myself if Dodie wanted a biography written of her. Again there were no instructions. She had herself published four volumes of autobiography, which might indicate that the ground had been pretty well covered but also that no literary-moral objections existed. Still Dodie had been born during Queen Victoria's reign. She was modern in her day, but then most people are modern in their day until the next generation defines the next day. Current biography is unVictorian in its obsessions. Everyone has secrets, and even the most sympathetic biographer might discover something that Dodie would have preferred to keep hidden. There would, I guessed, be nothing especially wicked, but it is still an odd tradeoff to reckon: You authorize a biography to help keep your friend's name alive, but it will, for instance, inevitably discuss her long affair with one of London's top shopkeepers, Sir Ambrose Heal. Dodie, who had a writer's normal vanity, would, I think, have approved of being biographed, though equally, and from the same emotions, have quarrelled with some of her biographer's conclusions.

So my literary impersonation of Dodie continues: an East European sale to approve, some Thai pirating to counter, the notoriously rebarbative business of negotiating with the Disney corporation. The work is considerably more than Alec anticipated, but then he also failed to anticipate Dodie's posthumous earning power. During the last years of her life, her work was bringing in a steady $15,000 or so a year; suddenly (in the wake of the remake of *101 Dalmatians*), her income has surged to 5, and then 10, times this amount. She would have been properly proud, also properly surprised.

And then, the other week, came a call from her literary agent. A Japanese publisher had applied for the rights to publish *The Hundred and One Dalmatians*. The agent, aware of my primary principle of executory conduct, had alerted them to Dodie's stance as a one-woman canine protection league. In reply, a fax had arrived from the Japanese publisher. Our late and distinguished friend was entirely mistaken, he assured us. The Japanese did not eat dogs. Not a bit of it. The Oriental canophages worthy of excoriation were the Chinese.

Well, what would you have done? I thought it over for a few days. It was a serious matter and one given an ironical spin by the book in question. I imagined myself putting the problem to Dodie. "As I see it, Dodie, the Japanese may have eaten dogs at the time you wrote the book. Or some of them may have done. And a few still may do so.

On the other hand, you could take the view that publishing this book over there is likely to advance the cause of dog-loving. It might even diminish the attraction of dog-eating among those few recidivists." Was this casuistry or proper moral thought? In my own mind, Dodie reflected on the matter. Eventually, she made her decision. "Well, all right. On your head be it. But no Chinese rights, do you hear? Not for the moment, anyway." I nodded, and obeyed myself.

May 19, 1996

Jane Smiley

It may have been when Jane Smiley's husband announced he was running off with her dental hygienist in 1996 that Smiley found herself asking the big questions about life, love and work. She can't say for sure. What she does remember are her thoughts as she packed her things—her bestsellers, teaching materials, prizes—and prepared to leave Ames, Iowa, the place that had inspired a near lifetime of writing. What is love, after all? Why are we here? And how did she see her novel *A Thousand Acres* from an eyeshot of 5 years?

The answers to the first 2 questions are pending. The answer to the third she gives below. If she had it to do again, she says, she would take that novel back. It will be hard news for a public that loved the story; for a newspaper that called it "a breathtaking . . . near-epic investigation into the thousand dark acres of the human heart"; for a movie company that made it into a feature film; hard news for the Pulitzer jury and the National Book Critics Circle, who awarded it two of the most coveted American prizes for literature in 1991. But where is it written that bestselling novelists can't grow and move on? Tschaikovsky came to hate his ballet music. Picasso rejected his early traditionalism and changed his name to boot. Things happen. Art is long. Artists change. A failed marriage does tend to turn your brain. Smiley had already learned that much from her parents. Her mother was a WAC in Paris during the Second World War; her father a military officer. They met in Germany, returned to the United States, were married, and a year later, Jane, their only child, was born. A year after that, Smiley's father—a handsome, flamboyant man with post-traumatic stress disorder—deserted them, and her mother marched out to begin a career.

Smiley grew up in a house with her mother and grandmother in a suburb of St. Louis. Her mother became the women's page editor of the

Globe-Democrat. The girl was an addictive reader, favoring works that seemed to go on endlessly, *The Bobbsey Twins*, *Giants in the Earth*, *David Copperfield* and virtually anything that featured a horse. "I was dizzy, out to lunch," she says. "Anyone who says they could have predicted a writing life for me is plain dishonest. I was a goofy, happy kid, coasting along without a goal in sight."

Her easy, Midwestern modesty belies a gritty determination. She graduated from Vassar in 1971, fueled by her mother's dream to write fiction. The newspaperwoman had always admired journalists who wrote books: Martha Gellhorn, John Hersey. She had even tried her own hand, unsuccessfully, at 2 novels. The most respectable thing you can do, the mother counseled her daughter, is write and publish books.

Smiley married in Iowa, had 3 children, helped her husband run a farm, but while she was at it, she also got her MFA and her Ph.D. from the University of Iowa and began a long teaching career at Iowa State. Her first novel was *Barn Blind* (1980), a pastoral story set in a single summer. Then came a string of novels that earned her the epithet "Balzac of the American Midwest": a mystery called *Duplicate Keys* (1984); *The Age of Grief* (1987), a collection of short stories mostly about marriage; *The Greenlanders* (1988), a medieval epic set in Scandinavia; her tragic novel, *A Thousand Acres* (1991); her comic novel, *Moo* (1995); and a romance published the year she wrote this essay, *The All-True Travels and Adventures of Lidie Newton*. Somewhere in all that writing, she married twice again.

While at work on *Horse Heaven* (2000), a novel about horse-racing, Smiley found herself thinking a great deal about gambling and commitment. It's only natural. If your third husband had run away with your dental hygienist, you might be thinking along the same lines. "Life is all about fully committing yourself to things you can only partially know. I was committed to that man, but I learned I didn't know him as well as I thought I did." Circumstances change. Things happen. Spouses run off.

It's enough to make someone forswear an enduring book.

M. A.

Taking It All Back

BY JANE SMILEY

The second scariest thing I learned in graduate school was that William Butler Yeats continually rewrote his poems all the way until his death. I always thought this sounded like a doubling and tripling of labor—how would you produce anything new if you had to keep updating the old, and how would you ever know when to stop? It was a Borgesian nightmare. But the scariest thing I learned in graduate school was that Geoffrey Chaucer disavowed almost all of his works on his deathbed, even, and maybe principally, *The Canterbury Tales*, because they were too secular. However awful it would be to have your life's work turn into a never-ending cycle of revision, it would be far worse to regret it entirely, an act of retrospective despair and a rejection of the faithful reader. I didn't want Chaucer to have disavowed his works. It shook my faith in them. I expect writers whom I love to agree with me about the lovable qualities of their writings. They may evince a becoming modesty, but deep in their hearts, I want them to find the same truths and beauties I find there. I may love this character a little less whom they love a little more. I may see greater depths of style in this book while they see it in another, but what can literature be but a form of communication so extended and elaborate that after the author and I have contemplated the subject at sufficient length through his work, we must surely be in agreement about it? Isn't my special love of that particular book evidence of the congruence of my mind and the author's?

And yet, in spite of my old fear and my perennial wishes on this subject, I find myself having to disavow my most famous and admired novel, *A Thousand* Acres. All this spring, at lectures and on my book tour, I have had questions about *A Thousand Acres* that I have had a hard time answering, and, worse, I have had reader after reader thrust the novel at me with the remark that this is their favorite novel of mine, one of their favorite novels of all, and I have had to say that my interpretation of *King Lear*, the very source of the novel, has changed in significant ways and that *A Thousand Acres* is not a novel I could write today in the same way I wrote it 10 years ago. I suppose it should not come as a surprise to me that I have changed over the years—better that I have, for me as a woman and a citizen—but it does come as a shock. I was so sure of my interpretation, and I wrote with such conviction!

Two years ago, I was invited to give a talk on my novel at the International Shakespeare Congress and then sit in on a seminar on 20th-century women's rewritings of Shakespeare plays. At the very end of the seminar session, an older English scholar, whose name I do not know, said, "I don't think you can understand *King Lear* until you have seen your parents go into decline. Shakespeare's father was in decline for a long time, possibly with Alzheimer's or something like it."

At that very moment, I felt my interpretation, which had just been accorded all kinds of attention and respect, shift. Whereas I had interpreted *King Lear* as a brief for the patriarchy, with the author identifying with Lear himself, and allowing him all sorts of leeway as a father in comparison to the daughters, who were narrowly defined as either brutes when they didn't give him his way or angels if they sacrificed themselves for him, with no intermediate choices, I now felt that perhaps, in looking at his father's troubles and his responsibilities as a son, Shakespeare was identifying with the daughters and doing what we often do when we are required to ameliorate pain that can't be ameliorated—that is, to propose a solution that isn't humanly possible. Goneril and Regan, who seem in the beginning of the play to be rather normal women, are found to be inhumanly vicious, and Cordelia's self-sacrifice is the only daughterly response that is moral, that is, the only one that expresses sufficient love for the father. My interpretation shifted from a political one to a psychological one that I felt was truer and more subtle, in the process answering the question of why Cordelia is an impossible character to play sympathetically—she is a projection of ideal virtue that even the author didn't understand. Well, I kept this new interpretation to myself, though I quite liked it.

And then, this spring, my interpretation shifted again, from psychological to philosophical. This time, I wasn't thinking of the characters at all, but of the definition of love that Lear proposes in the first act—a quid pro quo exchange of goods for love, based on a sense of obligation on both sides that quickly transforms into resentment when the love proves insufficient to satisfy Lear's unsatisfiable neediness and the goods prove insufficient to satisfy everyone else. In the airless, animal, physical world of the play, this definition of love cannot be escaped, and must result in death. The tragedy results from a failure of imagination or spiritual vision—no one in the play, even Cordelia, ever knows what love is or where it comes from, and so the final remarks of the surviving characters are peculiarly meaningless.

How would I write *A Thousand Acres* now? The fact is, I probably wouldn't. The inevitability of the characters' downfall, the almost mechanical working out of their fates, doesn't appeal to me anymore. I just don't believe it. I am more drawn to Shakespeare's *Winter's Tale* and, in fact, would love to see a rep company do *The Winter's Tale* and *King Lear* together, same actors, same sets, same costumes, because I think Shakespeare wrote *The Winter's Tale* to answer King Lear's tragedy with hope. The crucial difference between Leontes and Lear is that Leontes lives to regret and rethink his early selfish definition of love (of course he has the help in this of the delicious nag, Paulina, who says, "It is required / You do awake your faith . . .") and to accept the miracle of Hermione's revival. The play redefines love as a miracle and a gift, which, once accepted, allows all things, not only reappearances and resurrections, but even total forgiveness.

But whatever I think of *A Thousand Acres*, and however I go on with my own work, the book has legs, as they say, and it is ever more with me.

Perhaps political, psychological and philosophical interpretations of the play are not mutually exclusive but mutually enlightening. That would let me off the hook, wouldn't it? But I don't really believe it and don't have the Yeatsian energy to bring the novel in line with my current thinking. Like Shakespeare, I only have the energy to go on to new things and to hope that some future reader might see the evolution in what seems to me a revolution, the *même chose* in the change. I am not sorry I am no longer attracted to the dire mechanism of tragedy, but I see that one's life and one's literature perhaps inevitably must part. To those readers who adore *A Thousand Acres*, I have to say, it is more your book now than mine, I have run out of things to say on the subject, and, more important, I have run out of the desire to say them. I have made way in my mind for something else that may not have the same legs or the same impact. The paradox of literature is that everything must be written with total commitment, or the work reads falsely and insincerely, and yet all total commitment is to partial knowledge. As writers age and learn, they can't help rethinking and perhaps regretting earlier commitments. Perhaps readers forgive them more readily than they forgive themselves for taking on the mantle of "authority." At any rate, I know a little better why Chaucer disavowed his writings. The wholesale nature of his choice still scares me, but now it seems courageous rather than frightening, the last literary act of a mind that never stopped working over the largest questions life has to offer.

June 21, 1998

Michael Chabon

The Chinese have a saying, "Court glory, win disaster," the point being that it's best to keep one's head down, plod along, not strike the gods as being too lucky, too beautiful, too soon. Mediocrity has a way of keeping demons from the door.

Surely by now the gods have noticed the decidedly unmediocre Michael Chabon, who launched his writing career at age 26 with a rousingly successful novel—*Mysteries of Pittsburgh*—and whose 3 books since display a talent that seems as unlikely to fade as his remarkable good looks. He may not have courted it, but glory is all about him. Little wonder he's worried about golems. Little wonder he's modest as can be.

Chabon was raised in Columbia, Md. "Columbia affected me in ways I'm only beginning to understand," he says. The city was conceived by utoplans, designed to be economically, racially and religiously integrated. His high school had no interior walls. His neighbors were more black than white. The faith center had no denominations. "I was a willing participant in all of it," he says. But just as he began to see that Columbia's realities were "skewed and mistaken," his parents divorced, sending his pediatrician father to Pittsburgh and fragmenting his childhood world.

"My two paradises, family and town, were shattered at the same time. It's an experience common to writers—take Kipling or Nabokov." And indeed he started to write.

He produced stories at first, made a firm decision to become a writer. The plot from there spins like a dream. He majored in English at the University of Pittsburgh, wrote *Mysteries of Pittsburgh* for a graduate course at the University of California at Irvine. When his professor sent it to an agent, it was happily accepted and sold in auction, and his career has done nothing but hum: *A Model World and Other Stories* (1992); *Wonder Boys* (1996; film, 1999); *Werewolves in Their Youth* (stories, 1999). The autumn following the appearance of this essay in *Book World* brought *The Adventures of Kavalier & Clay* (2000), a novel that was to win Chabon the Pulitzer Prize. It had been inspired by the true story of two 16-year-olds who dreamed up the comic strip Superman, sold the rights for a mere $100, and then sat back and watched their phenomenon rise. That is to say, they were the most unsuccessful successes in America—the unluckiest lucky-boys on earth. Now you tell me: Were the gods smiling or scowling? Or perhaps it was neither glory nor disaster. And perhaps that would be the point.

M. A.

Writer, Be Afraid

BY MICHAEL CHABON

"Golem: Jewish legend: a man artificially created by cabalistic rites: a robot."
WEBSTER'S NEW WORLD DICTIONARY

The best-known—shaped from the clay of the River Moldau to be a servant or protector of the Prague ghetto—is the most dubious, having largely been devised and popularized by a series of novelists and film makers over the past 100 or so years. The most ancient is Adam, the original lump of earth into which, on the sixth day of creation, the inspiration of the Divine Name was breathed. But the story of the golem has a hundred variants, from the clay calf that was summoned to life and promptly eaten by 2 hungry rabbis, Hanina and Oshaya, in Babylonia 2,000 years ago, to such refinements as von Frankenstein's golem of quilted corpses, and Gepetto's wooden son. As I worked on my novel, *The Amazing Adventures of Kavalier & Clay*, I discovered that its plot would require the famous Golem of Prague to play a small but crucial role. Once this surprising fact had become apparent to me, I went looking for information on golems. What I found was an insight into the nature of novel-writing itself. All golem hunters inevitably end up at the feet of the brilliant Gershom Scholem, whose essay "The Idea of the Golem" probes dauntingly deep into the remote, at times abstruse, sources of the enduring motif of the man of clay brought to life by enchantment. Enchantment, of course, is the work of language; of spell and spiel. A golem is brought to life by means of magic formulae, one word at a time. In some accounts, the animating Name of God is inscribed on the golem's forehead; in others, the Name is written on a tablet, and tucked under the blank gray tongue of the golem. Sometimes the magical word is the Hebrew word for truth, *emet*; to kill the golem, in this case—to inactivate him—you must erase the initial letter *aleph* from his brow, leaving only *met*: dead.

There is good reason, in Scholem's view, to believe that some accounts of the making of golems are factual. Certain rabbis and adepts during the medieval heyday of kabbalah—those who long pondered the Sefer Yetsirah or Book of Creation—culminated their studies and proved their aptitude at enchantment by actually making a golem. There were specific guidelines and rituals—recipes, as it were, for golem-making. The rabbis did not expect to get a tireless servant, or even a square meal, out of these trials. The ritual itself was the point of the exercise; performing it—reciting long series of complicated alphabetic permutations while walking in circles around the slumbering lump of clay—would induce a kind of ecstatic state, as the adept assumed a privilege ordinarily reserved for God alone: the making of a world. It was analogical magic. As the kabbalist is to God, so is a golem to all creation: a model, a miniature replica, a mirror—like the novel—of the world.

Much of the enduring power of the golem story stems from its ready, if romantic, analogy to the artist's relation to his or her work. And over the years it has attracted many writers who have seen the metaphorical possibilities in it. On the surface, the analogy may seem facile. The idea of the novelist as the little God of his creation—*présent partout et visible nulle part* (present everywhere but visible nowhere)—is a key tenet of the traditional novelist, one that Robert Coover explored and exploded, once and for all, it might have been thought, in his *The Universal Baseball Association, J. Henry Waugh, Prop*. But what gripped me, as I read and re-read Scholem's essay, was not the metaphor or allegory of the nature of making golems and novels but that of the consequences thereof.

"Golem-making is dangerous," Scholem writes; "like all major creation it endangers the life of the creator—the source of danger, however, is not the golem . . . but the man himself." From the golem that grew so large that it collapsed, killing a certain Rabbi Elijah in Poland, to Frankenstein's monster, the creatures frequently end by threatening or even taking the lives of their creators.

When I read these words, I saw at once a connection to my own work. Anything good that I have written has, at some point during its composition, left me feeling uneasy and afraid. It has seemed, for a moment at least, to put me at risk.

Of course, there have been and remain writers for whom the act of writing a novel or poem is fatal, whose words are used to condemn and to crush them. I just returned from a tour of parts of the former Soviet Union, where I met writers who once had to weigh every word they wrote for its inherent power to destroy them; during my stay I was reading the stories of Isaac Babel, imprisoned and executed not only for his words but also, according to Lionel Trilling, for his silence, too. Compared to the fate of a Babel, the danger I have courted in my own writing hardly seems worthy of the name.

For me—a lucky man living in a lucky time in the luckiest country in the world—it always seems to come down to a question of exposure. As Scholem writes, "The danger is not that the golem . . . will develop overwhelming powers; it lies in the tension which the creative process arouses in the creator himself." Sometimes I fear to write, even in fictional form, about things that really happened to me, about things that I really did, or about the numerous unattractive, cruel or embarrassing thoughts that I have at one time or another entertained. Just as often, I find myself writing about disturbing or socially questionable acts and states of mind that have no real basis in my life at all but which, I am afraid, people will, quite naturally, attribute to me when they read what I have written. Even if I assume that readers will be charitable enough to absolve me from personally having done or thought such things—itself a dubious assumption, given my own reprehensible tendency as a reader to see autobiography in the purest of fictions—the mere fact that I could even imagine someone's having done or thought them, whispers my fear, is damning in itself.

When I wrote *The Mysteries of Pittsburgh*, I feared—correctly as it turned out—that people would think, reading the novel, that its author was gay. In part it was a fear of being misunderstood, misjudged, but in my apprehension there was a fairly healthy component of plain old homophobia and the fear of homophobia. Submitting to the Irvine writers' workshop (where I was working on my MFA) the portion of the novel containing a brief but vivid love scene between two men remains one of the scariest moments of my life as a writer. In *Wonder Boys*, I presented a character whose feelings of envy, failure and corroded romanticism, not to mention heavy reliance on marijuana to get the words flowing, seemed likely to amount, in the view of readers, to a less than appealing self-portrait. Again, my fears proved well-founded: On my recent northern European tour, the first question out of one interviewer's mouth was, "Your Grady Tripp is full of drugs and having sex with many women. Mr. Chabon, how about you?" And there was the writing of "Green's Book." This story, of a man whose relations with his young daughter have been gravely damaged by his lingering guilt and shame over a childhood incident of babysitting gone awry, took me years to finish, so troubled was I by the conclusions I felt it might lead readers to come to about my own past and my behavior as a father.

Since reading "The Idea of the Golem," I have come to see this fear, this sense of my own imperilment by my creations, as not only an inevitable, necessary part of writing fiction but as virtual guarantor, insofar as such a thing is possible, of the power of my work: as a sign that I am on the right track, that I am following the recipe correctly, speaking the proper spells. Literature, like magic, has always been about the handling of secrets, about the pain, the destruction and the marvelous liberation that can result when they are revealed. Telling the truth, when the truth matters most, is almost always a frightening prospect. If a writer doesn't give away secrets, his own or those of the people he loves; if she doesn't court disapproval, reproach and general wrath, whether of friends, family, or party apparatchiks; if the writer submits his work to an internal censor long before anyone else can get their hands on it, the result is pallid, inanimate, a lump of earth.

The adept handles the rich material, the rank river clay, and diligently intones his alphabetical spells, knowing full well the history of golems: how they break free of their creators, grow to unmanageable size and power, refuse to be controlled. In the same way, the writer shapes his story, flecked like river clay with the grit of experience and rank with the smell of human life, heedless of the danger to himself, eager to show his powers, to celebrate his mastery, to bring into being a little world that, like God's, is at once terribly imperfect and filled with astonishing life.

July 16, 2000

Ward Just

"The house of fiction has not one window, but a million . . . but they are, singly or together, as nothing without the posted presence of the watcher." So wrote Henry James in the preface to *The Portrait of a Lady*. Little wonder, then, that a man who has been called the Henry James of our time would find himself in Paris, nursing his coffee, glancing up at the fenestration, waiting for shutters to fly.

Ward Just is the author of 19 books, among them *Jack Gance* (1988), *The Translator* (1991), *Echo House* (1997) and *A Dangerous Friend* (1999). He is known primarily for tales that play out in Washington corridors: dry, ironic novels perched in high places that watch a character's machinations with a merciless eye. His most recent, *The Weather in Berlin* (2002), is the story of a failed American film director who returns to the scene of his last good movie to mourn his squandered art, only to have the past rush back in another form.

Ward Just began his career as a 13-year-old reporter for the *Waukegan News-Sun*, an Illinois newspaper owned by 3 generations of his family. "Our dinner conversations were endless discussions about politics. Halfway into the main course the telephone would ring and my old man would be called to hear someone begging to keep a friend of a friend's name out of the paper—the kid who was a reckless driver, the daughter who had eloped. I learned at a very early age what tremendous power a newspaper could wield."

When he was a high school senior, the managing editor fired him for wearing shorts to work. His father supported the editor completely: "Lack of respect," he barked. "Kid oughta stay fired." But he didn't stay fired for long. He went off to Trinity College, dropped out and returned to become a full-time reporter. In 1959, *Newsweek* hired him to write features. By 1965, Ben Bradlee had brought him to *The Washington Post*.

He ended up covering the war in Vietnam, taking a bellyfull of shrapnel from a stray grenade. When he returned to *The Post*'s newsroom, it was to the editorial department.

In 1968, at the age of 32, he published *To What End*, a book that questioned the wisdom of the Vietnam War. By 1969 he decided to quit journalism altogether. He retreated to Vermont to pore over the work of Henry James, William Faulkner, Edith Wharton, and to write books—nonfiction at first and then a long string of novels.

"I'd always wanted to write fiction," he says. "It was just a matter of time." His ideas seem to come quite literally from windows. "I see something. It hits me, then suddenly I'm looking at 20 pages of copy. And I'm thinking, By God, this is absolutely unique! How to explain something that is so magical?"

M. A.

In Search of the Next Idea

BY WARD JUST

A few months ago I was living again in Paris and beginning a novel, the usual formless tappa-tappa, gestures struggling to become acts. Over the years my wife and I have rented 6 apartments in Paris, but this was the first owned and occupied by a painter, an English friend who had temporarily decamped to Savannah, Ga. So I began my book surrounded by his portraits, and when my own work flagged I took thoughtful turns around the studio looking at his work, and wondering how he had made the choices that he had—the leggy nude girl lying beside a swimming pool reading, hills towering above her, rising in various shades of green and brown, pressed by a lid of pale blue sky; the middle-aged man in a T-shirt, arms crossed, staring at a paint box, crumped tubes of oil paint spilling from it; the dapper gent in a fedora, lunchtime at a brasserie, Lipp perhaps, or one of the Montparnasse hangouts.

I felt I was surrounded by the painter's repertory company (there were self-portraits also), faces that were in motion but speechless, all unmistakably drawn by the same hand. They did not speak for themselves, the artist spoke for them. I recognized only one—the writer Graham Greene, looking heartbroken, though perhaps that was owing to my own particular angle of vision. I wondered if these characters were there for the taking, the leggy girl reading in the blazing sun, the middle-aged man in the T-shirt, the gent in the fedora, his expression so belligerent you would believe his wife had just left or someone had stuck him with the check. And what book was the girl reading? A sentimental novel? Purgatorio? From the cant of her sun tanned jaw propped on her closed fist, I had the idea that whatever it was, she was bored by it. This girl had something else on her mind, and only the artist knew for sure what it was.

I had this idea, too. If I appropriated these characters for my own, gave them names and fresh identities and relationships each to each, I would have an answer at last to the impertinent question that so irritates writers of fiction that they answer falsely as a matter of course. Stupid question, misleading answer. Who is this character in your nuvvel based on? Close friend, close enemy, wife, former wife, mom, dad? In complete candor I could reply, They are all based on Anthony Palliser. Every damned one, even the leggy girl, especially the leggy girl. Wanna know more? Ask the painter Palliser. I'll give you his number in Savannah.

The portrait belongs to the artist. Picasso's Madame de Canals or Max Beckmann's Quappi surely did not see themselves as the artist saw them, whether or not they found the likeness true or flattering or a masterpiece or all 3. Picasso and Beckmann capture a soul all right; no telling whose, because the specific is unknowable. The portrait is a perverse enterprise (I use the Washington writer John Newhouse's definition of perverse, as he applied it to the long-ago SALT talks: something that enlists your curiosity while discouraging your understanding). As in biography, there are conventions to be followed, some minimal regard for the physical facts of the matter. No one would mistake Madame de Canals for Quappi or vice versa, and neither resembles del Sarto's Madonna of the Harpies. The fidelity of portrait to subject is problematical, and the greatest of portraits can bear only a superficial resemblance to the human being who posed for it (and sometimes with Francis Bacon, not that), with the soul or spirit left to the restless eye of the beholder.

No such conjecture with a novel's people. The character lives on the page or doesn't, and no one with any sense would think to say—Whatever could Robert Penn Warren have been thinking? Willie Stark isn't anything like Huey Long! Or, the ludicrous reverse: Warren's got Huey down to his socks. The great characters in fiction are utterly original, cut from whole cloth, from Faust to Flem Snopes, and that is not to say they are entirely knowable, either. They aren't, composed as they are from letters of the alphabet, like a melody from the notes on the score.

There were bookshelves in the studio, laden with art books as heavy as anvils—Goya, Caravaggio, Raphael, Kitaj, Bacon—and in the tiny loo off the dining room a score or more postcards from the Louvre—Rembrandt's self-portraits from stormy youth to shipwrecked old age, arranged on historical principles. I wondered if these paintings weighed like an anvil on my friend's spirit, the way great books sometimes weighed on mine. Not too greatly, I decided. Great artists, painters or writers or musicians, were not censors; they were provocateurs. Antony was a painter who got up in the morning and drew, as I got up in the morning and wrote, playing the hand we dealt ourselves or was dealt to us.

I see Paris as a painter's city, somehow more Degas than Balzac, so painters are always lurking in my mind when I am there, presenting themselves at unexpected moments. One day a decade or so ago, at loose ends and my typewriter cold, Paris failing to work the magic she promised, I left my apartment for lunch at the Petit St. Benoit, a tiny restaurant around the corner from the ominous Café Flore. The day was warm, and they had set up tables on the sidewalk. I was late and therefore got a table at once, ordered the special and a carafe, and sat back and waited for something to happen. Nothing did, so I read the newspaper, ate slowly, ordered a coffee, and thought about my cold typewriter. By then it was mid-afternoon. There was a grade school up the street, and I idly watched women and a few men arrive, waiting for their children to be released. The French call this time *l'heure de maman,* mother's hour. The street is narrow, and as I watched the adults mill about, smoking cigarettes and glancing at their wristwatches while they waited for their children, something on the top floor of the apartment building opposite caught my eye.

A window flew open, and a woman's head emerged, a disheveled blonde-haired head, middle-aged, sleepy from the look of it. She remained only a moment or two, long enough to fling her arms wide greeting the afternoon, give a puzzled look to the gathering in the street below, and duck back inside, closing the window with a snap that could be heard by anyone sitting at a table in the Petit St. Benoit. I waited for her to re-emerge, staring at the window as if it were a stage and she an actress preparing for an encore. My coffee was forgotten, and when the waiter handed me the check, I ignored him. In my mind's eye, I saw her at her tiny stove, preparing coffee and something to go in it, cognac or calvados, something refreshing; and she had obviously just woken up. There were easels in the room, and canvasses in various stages of becoming. Is that not the existential life? A life in a steady state of becoming? Of course her bed was unmade, and the room itself in a condition of cheerful disorder.

I had an idea she was one of those painters who worked at night and slept during the day. She believed in darkness, hospitable darkness when the ghosts could gather safely around her. She was a landscape painter from Los Angeles via Chicago. She had been manhandled in Los Angeles, a disgusting business, and hastened to Paris to achieve—equilibrium. She had no friends save for the musician who lived down the hall, an emigré jazz pianist with a bad left hand. He brought her stories from the cabaret he worked in, charming stories of Pigalle nightlife. His name was Alfred. She was painting wonderfully in Paris and at the same time working on a philosophical problem. She was trying to get straight in her head the connection between ambition and love. She meant ambition for herself and love of her work. They were often in opposition, ambition degrading love. The reverse was also true, but much less harmful.

With that in mind, she picked up a brush and began to complete the landscape she had begun the night before, a grassland she saw in her mind only, a low rise ending in stubble with the roof of a house just beyond the horizon. And when she touched brush to canvas, she vanished, suddenly lost to view. I was back at the Café St. Benoit, the last man on the street, the coffee cold, the lunch check tucked under the saucer. The street was empty, the parents having collected their children and gone about their business. I remained a few minutes more, glancing now and then at the window, waiting for the encore that I knew was never going to happen. I wanted to see again the woman's embrace of the day, though I had the picture fixed in my mind. It is there now, an unforgettable gesture, abrupt as a fish breaking water, at most 2 or 3 seconds in duration. But from it, I knew I had a character and, from the character, a novel.

May 5, 2002

PUBLICAFFAIRS is a publishing house founded in 1997. It is a tribute to the standards, values, and flair of three persons who have served as mentors to countless reporters, writers, editors, and book people of all kinds, including me.

I. F. STONE, proprietor of *I. F. Stone's Weekly*, combined a commitment to the First Amendment with entrepreneurial zeal and reporting skill and became one of the great independent journalists in American history. At the age of eighty, Izzy published *The Trial of Socrates,* which was a national bestseller. He wrote the book after he taught himself ancient Greek.

BENJAMIN C. BRADLEE was for nearly thirty years the charismatic editorial leader of *The Washington Post*. It was Ben who gave the *Post* the range and courage to pursue such historic issues as Watergate. He supported his reporters with a tenacity that made them fearless, and it is no accident that so many became authors of influential, best-selling books.

ROBERT L. BERNSTEIN, the chief executive of Random House for more than a quarter century, guided one of the nation's premier publishing houses. Bob was personally responsible for many books of political dissent and argument that challenged tyranny around the globe. He is also the founder and was the longtime chair of Human Rights Watch, one of the most respected human rights organizations in the world.

. . .

For fifty years, the banner of Public Affairs Press was carried by its owner Morris B. Schnapper, who published Gandhi, Nasser, Toynbee, Truman, and about 1,500 other authors. In 1983 Schnapper was described by *The Washington Post* as "a redoubtable gadfly." His legacy will endure in the books to come.

Peter Osnos, *Publisher*